THE
UNEXPECTED
PRESIDENT

THE
UNEXPECTED
PRESIDENT

THE LIFE AND TIMES OF
CHESTER A. ARTHUR

SCOTT S. GREENBERGER

Da Capo

Da Capo Press
Hachette Book Group
1290 Avenue of the Americas
New York, NY 10104
www.dacapopress.com

Printed in the United States of America

First Edition: September 2017

Published by Da Capo Press, an imprint of Perseus Books, LLC, a subsidiary of Hachette Book Group, Inc.

The publisher is not responsible for websites (or their content) that are not owned by the publisher.

Print book interior design by Amy Quinn

Library of Congress Cataloging-in-Publication Data

Names: Greenberger, Scott S., author.
Title: The unexpected president : The life and times of Chester A. Arthur/ Scott S. Greenberger.
Description: Boston, MA : Da Capo Press, 2017. | Includes bibliographical references and index.
Identifiers: LCCN 2017014581| ISBN 9780306823893 (hardback) | ISBN 9780306823909 (ebook)
Subjects: LCSH: Arthur, Chester Alan, 1829–1886. | Arthur, Chester Alan, 1829–1886—Political and social views. | Presidents—United States—Biography. | United States—Politics and government—1881–1885. | BISAC: BIOGRAPHY & AUTOBIOGRAPHY / Political. | HISTORY / United States / 19th Century.
Classification: LCC E692 .G74 2017 | DDC 973.84092 [B]—dc23
LC record available at https://lccn.loc.gov/2017014581

ISBNs: 978-0-306-82389-3 (hardcover), 978-0-306-82390-9 (ebook)

LSC-C

10 9 8 7 6 5 4 3 2 1

For Michele

Contents

Author's Note

CHESTER ARTHUR, OUR nation's 21st president, frequently lands on lists of the country's most obscure chief executives. Few Americans know anything about him, and even history buffs mostly recall him for his distinctive facial hair. People who flock to Arthur's former home in Manhattan, a brownstone that still stands, typically come to shop at a store that sells Indian and Middle Eastern spices and foods, not to see the only site in New York City where a president took the oath of office. Arthur's statue in Madison Square Park, erected by his friends in 1899, is ignored. Arthur's fascinating and surprising story had a lasting impact on the country—so why have we forgotten it?

The first reason is that Arthur rose to power and served in the White House during an era that is a bit foggy in the minds of most Americans. We frequently dissect and rehash the events of the Civil War (and rightly so), but we often ignore the crucial decades immediately following the war. We shouldn't. The social, political, and economic changes that shook America during the 1870s and 1880s were the birth pangs of the society we have today. Arthur became president 136 years ago, but the era Mark Twain dubbed the "Gilded Age" doesn't feel distant at a time when political corruption, economic inequality, and corporate malfeasance are once again shaking people's faith in the American experiment.

The second reason is that Arthur had a deep distrust of the press and paid little attention to cultivating his public image, either for his contemporaries or for posterity. Newspapers treated him harshly before he assumed the presidency, and he remained wary of reporters even after attitudes shifted in his favor.

But the main reason Arthur's story is unknown is that he left little behind, creating a challenge for historians. Shortly before he died, he ordered most of his letters, journals, and private papers to be destroyed, for reasons that will be revealed in the pages ahead. For many years, Arthur was represented in the Library of Congress by a single document, a letter he had written during the Civil War and that the library purchased in 1902. Pains-taking work by chief librarians over many years gradually added to the hold-ings, but the collection is meager compared to what is available for most presidents.

In writing this book, I have relied on the letters and papers that do sur-vive, together with the memories—published and unpublished—of the men and women who knew Arthur and the wonderfully vivid descriptions that filled the newspapers of the time. Anything between quotation marks comes from a letter, memoir, or other written document, and when I ascribe feel-ings to Arthur I do so based on his own statements or those of the people around him.

Despite the relative scarcity of writings by Arthur himself, I hope I have done justice to his story. It is the tale of a good man who veered off the right path, but rediscovered his better self with the help of an ordinary young woman who believed in him.

Garfield, Arthur, Harrison, and Hayes . . . were the lost Americans: their gravely vacant and be-whiskered faces mixed, melted, swam together in the sea-depths of a past intangible, immeasurable, and unknowable.

●◆●

THOMAS WOLFE, "The Four Lost Men"

Prologue

THE *ST. JOHN* sliced through the last wisps of haze and steamed south toward the Canal Street pier, where a messenger stood with a telegram clutched in his damp fingers. It was the morning of July 2, 1881, a Saturday, and the ship was running late. In the fog the pilot had steered her cautiously, straining his eyes and ears to avoid a collision with another steamer. Now he was trying to make up for lost time. Picking up speed, the *St. John* churned past the mammoth ice-harvesting warehouses, and then the sheer cliffs of the Palisades, where an advertisement for Drake's Plantation Bitters was painted on the rock face in letters 20 feet high.

Finally, the island came into view. On the shore, the great trans-Atlantic steamships, their smokestacks blackened with soot, slumbered under towering wooden sheds. Ferries crisscrossed the Hudson, carrying passengers to and from the railroad depots that connected the great metropolis to points south and west. The bells of the ferries clanged fiercely, challenging the *St. John* to stay out of their way.

The engine thrumming in the belly of the 418-foot *St. John* had been salvaged from the steamer *New World*, which had been converted into a hospital for Union soldiers during the Civil War. Propelled by a pair of paddle wheels, one on each side, the *St. John* was the largest inland steamship in the world when she was built in 1864. She had since relinquished that title, but she still belonged among the floating palaces that operated the overnight service between Albany and New York City. She had gracefully curved deck lines, and her grand staircase was carved of St. Domingo mahogany, inlaid with white holly. Passengers could walk out of their lushly decorated staterooms onto a gallery overlooking the two-story saloon, which extended from stem to stern. A line of Corinthian columns ran down the saloon's center,

1

concealing masts that extended through the *St. John's* superstructure to its wooden hull. The steamer catered to passengers' every whim, from tables piled high with all of the delicacies of the season to the company of young women who took up residence on board and never wanted for customers.

On this steamy morning, the *St. John* carried two New York machine politicians accustomed to such opulence.

The boss of New York's vaunted Republican machine stood six foot three, with broad shoulders and reddish-blond hair. He wore a manicured beard, and a curl he combed onto the middle of his broad forehead. His polka-dot tie was fastened with a gold pin, and he had tucked a checked handkerchief into the upper pocket of his cutaway coat. He wore English gaiters and pointy shoes, freshly polished, and held a sun umbrella.

His loyal lieutenant was an inch shorter, and a thousand late nights of eating and drinking had swelled him to a hearty 225 pounds. His face was florid and puffy, framed by mutton-chop sideburns trimmed to perfection. Unlike most politicians, who tended to wear dreary long-tailed frock coats and slouch hats, he wore a derby over his wavy hair, and a stylish sack coat. Like the boss, he was fastidious about his clothes—sometimes he had his Prince Albert coats, light trousers, and high hats imported from London, and he bought dozens of vests and pairs of trousers every year. The son of a rigid abolitionist preacher, he had left the discipline and deprivation of his Vermont youth far behind. Now he had a five-story brownstone on Lexington Avenue, a taste for expensive Havana cigars, and, his friends noted, extraordinary powers of digestion.

The two New Yorkers were protagonists in a national debate. Leaders of the "Stalwart" faction of the Republican Party, they were vociferous supporters of the spoils system, under which victorious candidates rewarded their cronies—and perpetuated their power—by handing out government jobs. Once in office, "spoilsmen" like the men on the *St. John* collected "voluntary" campaign donations from government employees, who knew they would be fired if they declined to contribute.

To Republican reformers, the spoils system was a mortal threat to American democracy. Driven by an almost religious fervor, they had become a powerful political force. At large gatherings held in all the nation's major cities, they sang songs praising reform and condemning the spoils system as an unadulterated evil. Without reform of the civil service, they argued, it would be impossible to curb the trusts that were beginning to dominate the nation's economy, since there would be nothing to prevent them from buying influential posts for their allies. "At present there is no organization save that of corruption; no system save that of chaos; no test of integrity save that of partisanship; no test of qualification save that of intrigue," one leading reformer proclaimed. "We have to deal with a widespread evil, which defrauds the country in the collection of taxes on a scale so gigantic that the commissioners of revenue, collectors, assessors, and Treasury officers—at least those of them who are honest—bow their heads in shame and despair."

• ◆ •

Near the Canal Street pier were barrels and boxes of kitchen offal on the sidewalks and heaps of manure in the streets, all mellowing in the midsummer heat. The gutters were clogged with straw, eggshells, orange peels, potato skins, and cigar stumps. The overall effect, even when combined with the savory smells of cooking that emanated from some of the tenements, was nauseating. Wagons and trucks clustered around the wharf as sweltering stevedores loaded and unloaded the vessels docked there. At about 10:30, the *St. John* finally came within hailing distance. Standing on the shore, Baggage Master Turner cupped his hands around his mouth and bellowed to Steward Burdett on the deck of the *St. John*. Burdett froze for a moment, stunned. Then he rushed into the saloon to deliver the news to the two machine politicians lounging inside.

At first, they didn't believe him. "It can't be true," sputtered the lieutenant. "This must be some stock speculation." Then the *St. John* kissed the pier, and the messenger came on board with his telegram. He handed over his dispatch and stood by silently. As the words sunk in, the lieutenant blanched and collapsed into a chair. The boss took the telegram from his protégé and read the news for himself: President James A. Garfield had been shot and seriously wounded at a railroad station in downtown Washington. If he died, the corrupt politicians on board the *St. John* would become the most powerful men in the United States.

CHAPTER ONE

Elder Arthur

THE MOB BAYED just outside the church doors, bellowing for the blood of the abolitionists huddled inside, but Elder Arthur wasn't frightened. The dark-haired minister, known for his ringing sermons and his crippled leg, had an iron belief in his own rectitude. That belief brooked no doubt, and an ungodly rabble could not shake it. Utica's grocers and taverns had started selling liquor when the first rays of autumn sunlight were still creeping over the foothills of the Adirondacks, and they had extended credit freely. "Open the way! Break down the doors! Damn the fanatics!" cried the members of the mob, with rage reinforced by their early-morning purchases.

The steeple of the Second Presbyterian Church was painted white, the shutters were green, and the cupola was covered with tin. It was a cheerful-looking building, bright and sparkling. But the mob's ugly threats slithered through the walls and under the church doors, which remained, for the moment, shut tight. The date was October 21, 1835, and nearly three decades before the Civil War tore the Union apart, most Utica residents were no more interested in abolishing slavery than the residents of Charleston or Richmond.

Set in New York's Mohawk River Valley, Utica was a prosperous city with nearly nine thousand residents and more than a hundred banks, inns, stables, dry goods stores, and taverns. It had its share of abolitionists—citizens of Oneida County sent a steady flow of money to antislavery groups. But the dominant sentiment, expressed in a motion at a Republican gathering days before, was clear: the abolitionists were "wicked or deluded men, who, whatever may be their pretensions, are riveting the fetters of the bondman, and enkindling the flames of civil strife."

The leader of the anti-abolitionist mob banging on the church doors was none other than Congressman Samuel Beardsley, a former state senator and county judge serving his third term in Washington. "The disgrace of having an abolition convention held in the city would be deeper than that of 20 mobs, and it would be better to have Utica razed to its foundations, or to have it destroyed like Sodom and Gomorrah, than to have the convention meet here," Beardsley had roared at a meeting of concerned citizens several days before. A fierce-looking man with a furrowed brow and wings of white hair on either side of his rectangular head, the 45-year-old Beardsley had served as a lieutenant in the War of 1812. As usual, his views prevailed.

By 9 o'clock on Wednesday morning, Beardsley and his followers were mobilizing at the Oneida County Courthouse. An hour later, six hundred abolitionists gathered inside the Second Presbyterian Church, just two blocks away on Bleecker Street. The shutters softened the sunlight that streamed in through the church's windows, brightening the white walls and ceiling, but they could not muffle the sounds of the mob. New York had already banned slavery, in 1827, but the abolitionists inside the church wanted to form a New York State Anti-Slavery Society to advocate for freedom nationwide. They began with a short prayer. Then the man who had called the meeting, 45-year-old Alvan Stewart, a prominent local attorney, rose to speak. "You, for this moment, are the representatives of American liberty," he began. The menacing shouts from the street grew louder, but the handsome lawyer with the high forehead and the aquiline nose seemed to draw strength from them. "If you are driven from this sacred temple dedicated to God, by an infuriated mob, then my brethren, wherever you go, liberty will go, where you abide, liberty will abide, when you are speechless, liberty is dead!" Elder Arthur and the other abolitionists nodded their heads in assent. Then the mob burst through the church doors.

• ◆ •

William Arthur was born in 1796 in Antrim, Ireland, to a respectable family that could provide him with an education, but little more. From an early age William walked with a pronounced limp, the result of a "fever sore" on his knee that had become infected. A talented and determined student, he mastered Latin and Greek and earned a college degree in Belfast, but he knew his family's lack of money and connections would limit his prospects in Ireland. In 1819 he sailed for Canada, bent on pursuing a legal career in the New World. He lived for a time in Stanstead, Quebec, then moved to nearby Dunham to work as a teacher while he studied the law. There he met

Malvina Stone, a 19-year-old girl from Berkshire, Vermont, a short distance across the border. Malvina was from old New England stock—her grandfather Uriah Stone had served as a corporal in the Continental Army during the American Revolution. In 1821 William and Malvina were married, and three years later the young couple moved to Burlington, Vermont, where William thought he could make more money as a teacher while he studied law in the office of a prominent attorney.

In Burlington, the life of the aspiring lawyer abruptly changed course. New England was in the throes of the Second Great Awakening, a religious reaction to the rationalism and deism that had challenged Calvinist piety throughout the eighteenth century. In the 1770s and 1780s, the conflict with Great Britain focused Americans' attention on political upheaval, rather than on religious salvation, and membership in New England churches plummeted. In the 1790s, New England pastors feared the French Revolution would spread godlessness to America's shores, and some of them embarked on a campaign of vigorous preaching to strengthen Americans' spirituality. In the early decades of the nineteenth century, their efforts bore fruit. "Sects and creeds, doctrines and disquisitions, preachers and people, sermons and societies, plans and projects; excitements and conversions, you may hear talked of wherever you go—in stage-coaches and steam-boats, in shops and bar-rooms, nay in ball-rooms and parties of pleasure, and in short, every where," Orville Dewey, an Englishman traveling in New England, wrote to a friend back home in 1827. It was a revival meeting in Burlington that ignited the religious fire in William. Convinced he had been "called," William left behind the law and his Anglican upbringing to become a Free Baptist preacher. He was ordained in Waterville, Vermont, in 1828.

A short time later, William accepted an offer to lead a congregation in Fairfield, Vermont, in the northwest corner of the state. It was a bucolic setting: Fairfield was nestled in the Green Mountains, and in the surrounding valleys brooks flowed lazily toward the Missisquoi River and Lake Champlain. The parish was in the process of building a parsonage, so William, Malvina, and their four daughters—Regina, Jane, Almeda, and Ann Eliza—were housed in a large log cabin. At first, William preached in a nearby schoolhouse. The new minister moved haltingly around his pulpit, dragging his injured leg behind him, but he did not waver in preaching the gospel. Speaking in a strong Irish accent, he admonished his parishioners that the words in the Bible were without error and were to be taken literally. He told them that all of Adam's descendants had inherited his fallen nature, and thus had a natural inclination to sin. Man could only be pardoned and forgiven for his sins when he admitted to God that he was a sinner, and when in godly sorrow he turned from those sins and trusted in the work of Christ as redemption for them. Salvation came by grace alone, not by works. God was wise and benevolent, but the preacher, now known as Elder Arthur, left his listeners with a stark warning: if they refused to repent and believe, if they drank or fornicated, they would forfeit their chance to be saved, condemning themselves to eternal damnation.

It was a harsh message, but many were eager to hear it. Before long, the crowds that came to hear Elder Arthur preach had grown too large for the schoolhouse, forcing him to move to a neighboring barn. Women and girls sat on planks and blocks of wood on the bare floor, while the men sat in the hayloft and on the scaffolds and the boys perched on the high roof beams, their skinny legs dangling in the musty air.

On one memorable occasion Elder Arthur preached for four straight hours, and some of his listeners "became so weary and excited that they got up their teams, put whips to their horses, and were never seen there again." The preacher was witty and passionate, and in small gatherings his penetrating eyes and erudite conversation held listeners spellbound. But he also could be bitingly sarcastic, and his lack of tact alienated many potential friends. At one Baptist convention, a fellow minister, recently returned from the West, delivered a lengthy address describing conditions on the frontier. "I can tell the brethren," the minister boasted, "that if they think any kind of ministers will do for the West, they are mistaken." Elder Arthur jumped to his feet. "Mr. Moderator," he said, "I never knew before why the brother came back."

Sometimes Elder Arthur was brought low by the privations of his life as a young preacher, especially during the long winter months, when it was difficult for him to hobble outside for bread or firewood. To earn extra money, he took in students. "Instead of my attending school I recited to Elder Arthur, as he was called. He maintained the most rigid government in his family," one former student remembered. "He was a hard-shell Baptist in the strictest sense of the word, and was earnest and enthusiastic in preaching his doctrines." A half century later, when a newspaperman came to town to ask people what they remembered about Elder Arthur, Old John Baker claimed the preacher often joked about his injured leg. "He was a bit lame, and used to say in fun that he'd had a stone wall fall on his feet," the old man recalled—adding that Elder Arthur said he was sorry he could not chase down his students to punish them.

On October 5, 1829, a momentous event prompted uncharacteristic joy in the mostly joyless preacher: Malvina gave birth to a son. The boy was named Chester, after the doctor who had delivered him, Dr. Chester Abell, who also happened to be Malvina's cousin. Unable to contain his happiness, Elder Arthur momentarily succumbed to the devil's wiles and danced a celebratory jig.

Elder Arthur's dedication to the abolitionist cause did not endear him to church deacons, trustees, or parishioners. A man "who formed his opinions without much reference to the views of others," he would not smooth the rough edges of his beliefs or soften his pronouncements in deference to prevailing opinion. After two years, Elder Arthur was no longer welcome in Fairfield. Fortunately, the outspoken minister was offered another Baptist congregation in Williston, Vermont, a flourishing town of about 1,600 on the stagecoach route between Burlington and Montpelier. It had an academy taught by the Baptist pastor, and Elder Arthur succeeded in this dual role—but only temporarily. A year later, the family was on the move again, this time to a nearby congregation in Hinesburgh. That position only lasted two years, and the Arthurs joined a steady flow of migrants to western New York, settling first near the Erie Canal in Perry, and then moving 14 miles north, to York. By this time the Arthurs had two more children, a son named William and a daughter named Malvina.

●◆●

When the church doors banged open, the first protesters who rushed inside charged immediately for the bell rope. Spencer Kellogg, an abolitionist who owned a nearby dry goods store, had been standing in front of the church, trying to pacify the surging crowd. He had failed in that mission, but he was determined to prevent the mob from disrupting the abolitionists' meeting by ringing the bell. Kellogg grabbed the rope, but as he did a half-dozen men tackled him, ripping the coat from his back. "Kill him! Kill the damn fanatic!" somebody cried. When Kellogg's son rushed to his aid, the mob left the merchant sprawled on the floor and turned its attention to what was going on inside the church. "Stop that reading! We won't hear it!" the men shouted as they swarmed into the aisles. "Knock him down! Hustle out old Stewart! Beardsley, say the word and we will tear old Stewart to pieces in an instant!"

Lewis Tappan, an abolitionist leader who later would become known for his efforts to free the Africans on the Spanish slave ship *Amistad*, hurriedly read a declaration of principles and called for a vote to adjourn. But the mob was not pacified. It surrounded Oliver Wetmore, the elderly minister who had been recording the proceedings, and ordered him to hand over the minutes. Rutger Miller, a court clerk, took the lead. "I will be damned if I don't have the papers if I have to knock you down to get them!" In a final humiliation, Reverend Wetmore had to relinquish the minutes to his own son, who was among those who had stormed the church.

Later the mob would display the minutes, along with other captured abolitionist documents and the key to the church, as trophies at the Oneida County Courthouse. The mob harangued and shoved Elder Arthur and the rest of the departing abolitionists, many of whom headed for Clark's Hotel, where Gerrit Smith, a well-known attorney and philanthropist, was staying. An active campaigner for temperance, Smith had established one of the nation's first "temperance hotels" in his hometown of Peterboro, some 25 miles away. Smith wasn't an abolitionist, but he was appalled by Utica's persecution of them, and he offered to host their convention at his Peterboro estate. The abolitionists gratefully accepted Smith's invitation, perhaps swayed by the continuing taunts of their enemies, who had now assembled outside the hotel. As the abolitionists left town, the remnants of the Utica mob pelted them with mud, eggs, clubs, and stones, knocking one abolitionist unconscious.

During the 1830s anti-abolitionist riots were a common occurrence, even in the North. On the same day the mob broke up the abolitionists' convention in Utica, William Lloyd Garrison narrowly escaped a public lynching by a mob determined to break up a meeting of the Boston Female Anti-Slavery Society. Men wielding knives cut Garrison's clothes and hat to tatters and were prepared to do worse when "two burly Irishmen" seized him and turned him over to constables. They shoved the abolitionist into a carriage and bolted to the Leverett Street jail, where he was locked up overnight for his own protection. In July 1834, anti-abolitionist rioters rampaged for four nights in New York City. In July 1836, a Cincinnati mob destroyed the presses of the *Philanthropist*, an abolitionist newspaper; the next year, editor Elijah P. Lovejoy of Alton, Illinois, was shot and killed in a similar melee. In 1838, a mob in Philadelphia torched Pennsylvania Hall just three days after it opened because abolitionists had been allowed to hold a meeting there.

• ◆ •

In the autumn of 1839 the Arthurs moved yet again, this time to Union Village, near Saratoga. Chester was nine years old, and up to that point he had received his schooling at home, from his father. In Union Village, Chester enrolled in a local academy to begin his formal education. "Frank and open in manners and genial in disposition," Chester impressed his teachers and was popular with his classmates. When the children in the neighborhood built a mud dam after a downpour, Chester was the kind of boy who took charge of the project. He ordered this boy to bring stones, that one sticks, and another scoops of mud to finish the dam. He enjoyed giving orders and his friends followed them—but he didn't like to get his own hands dirty.

Even before Elder Arthur arrived, the church at Union Village had been roiled by disagreements over slavery and temperance, and the new minister churned the waters. He forged a close friendship with Gerrit Smith, who had converted to the abolitionist cause after the Utica riot and was now an organizer of the antislavery Liberty Party, and with Erastus D. Culver, an abolitionist lawyer and state assemblyman. Again, Elder Arthur's friendships and radical views alienated many of his parishioners. In the summer of 1844, the Arthurs moved to Schenectady, where Elder Arthur became pastor of the First Baptist Church.

Schenectady was struggling economically, but it had two well-respected educational institutions: the Lyceum and Academy, and Union College. Now a teenager, Chester continued his formal education at the Lyceum, which was housed in a three-story octagonal building at the corner of Union and Yates Streets. After a year, he enrolled as a sophomore at Union College.

The president of the college was Eliphalet Nott, who was in his fifth decade at the helm. Seventy-two years old when Arthur arrived, "Old Prex" was a beloved figure who rode around campus in his custom-made three-wheeled carriage. Raised "pious and poor" on a hardscrabble farm in Ashford, Connecticut, Nott spent much of his childhood living and working in the home of his brother Samuel, a Congregationalist minister who was 19 years older. Samuel beat his little brother regularly. When Eliphalet grew up to become a teacher and principal, he made up his mind to "substitute moral motives in the place of the rod" in his own dealings with young people.

From the time he became president of Union in 1804, Nott welcomed the admission of many young men (the college did not admit women) who had been expelled from other institutions, earning Union College the nickname of "Botany Bay," a reference to the first planned penal colony in Australia. Union College was a prestigious institution—at the time it was considered on par with Harvard, Yale, and Princeton—but Nott believed in instilling self-discipline in young men, rather than subjecting them to strict external control. "Disgraceful punishments are not inflicted," the course catalogue assured Arthur and his fellow students, a group that included a future governor of Pennsylvania, a future Tammany mayor of New York City, and James Roosevelt, whose son Franklin would lead the country through depression and war. "But no young man who indulges in gaming, intemperance, or other vice, who is absent from his room at night, or who habitually neglects his studies, can be allowed to remain."

Union College was non-denominational, but it was firmly Christian. Monday through Saturday, the three hundred students were required to attend morning prayers (about 10 minutes) and late afternoon prayers (about 20 minutes) in the college chapel, and on Sundays they had to attend services in a local church designated by their parents. Each day started at 6:30 a.m., when bells rang across the heavily wooded campus to awaken students for early morning prayers, which began at 7 a.m. After that students attended the first recitation, then breakfast, study at 9 a.m., another recitation at 11 a.m., study at 1 p.m., another recitation at 4 p.m., and study at 7 p.m.

The unpopular bells were a frequent target of student mischief. In one incident, students "offended with the bell-ringer" tried to blow up the South Colonnade bell in the middle of the night. Another time, students stole the clapper and left it on President Nott's doorstep. Chester, known to his classmates as Chet, was an eager participant in such pranks. He once threw the West College bell into the Erie Canal, and he carved his name at least twice into college buildings. He was fined for breaking a pane of glass, and for skipping out on chapel. During his senior year, he had to pay a hefty fifty-cent fine for writing in ink in a book.

In addition to being an educator, Nott was a well-known inventor who had patented 30 different kinds of stoves and designed an innovative steamship boiler. Under his leadership, Union became one of the first colleges in the United States to offer courses of study in natural science and engineering. But Chet opted for the traditional classical curriculum, which meant three years poring over Livy, Horace, Herodotus, Thucydides, Cicero, and Homer in the original Greek and Latin. Elder Arthur, who spoke Latin, Greek, and Hebrew, might have pushed his son in that direction.

Like all Union students, in his senior year Chet took a class taught by Nott, which was nominally based on the 1762 book *Elements of Criticism* by the Scottish jurist Henry Home, or Lord Kames. In fact, it was a lesson in independent thinking, and it became so famous that students transferred to Union just to take it. Nott wanted students to "believe nothing merely because it is asserted by any author." William James Sullivan, who took Nott's course the same year Arthur did, remembered it as "a perpetual contest of our wits against his; he showed us the shallowness of our acquisitions, and dissected mercilessly both textbook and the responses to the questions he had drawn from it, admitting nothing and pushing the pupil perpetually into the deeper water as soon as he began to think his foot had touched firm land."

Slender and sociable, with fashionably long hair and a cheerful disposition, Chet was popular among his classmates. He was elected to one of the social fraternities, Psi Upsilon, and was president of the Delphian Institute, a debating society. Though not a particularly diligent student, he still ranked high in his class: He was elected to Phi Beta Kappa—though a third of his 78 classmates were, too. Ten of the graduating seniors had a perfect record of 500 and seven, including Arthur, got 499. Arthur's graduation ceremony in July 1848 featured 44 student orations, in addition to prayers, Greek and Latin salutatories, four musical interludes, and the awarding of the degrees. Chet, the eleventh speaker, spoke on "The Destiny of Genius."

After graduation Chet followed his father's first career path, setting out to become a lawyer. He had spent his college vacations teaching school in nearby Schaghticoke to help cover his college tuition and expenses. After a few months at the State and National Law School in Ballston Spa, he studied law on his own while teaching in Schaghticoke to make money.

Arthur was doggedly practical in pursuing his legal career, but there was another aspect to his personality. Even as he waded through cases and instructed his young charges, he forged passionate friendships with two other young men, relationships suffused with the romanticism of the middle of the nineteenth century. Chester referred to Campbell Allen as "John," and Campbell called him "Zack." Together with a third young man, James Masten, who would marry Chester's sister Almeda, the three were devoted companions. In a letter to John, Chester describes "sitting up like owls till two or three in the morning with our pipes, over the warm fire—quite satisfied with our little world within and philosophically discussing the world without—laying bare to each other our mutual plans, hopes & fears, adventures and experiences & so cozily chatting and smoking—& then tumbling into bed in the 'wee sma hours' & falling soundly asleep in each other's arms."

In 1851, Elder Arthur helped secure a position for his son as the principal of a school in a church basement in North Pownal, Vermont. In November 1852, Chester moved on to the High Department of the District School in Cohoes, New York. He was appointed principal and assigned to teach a rowdy group of boys who had chased out four of his predecessors. His sisters Almeda, 26, and Malvina, 20, also were teachers there. Arthur was determined to "conquer the school or forfeit his reputation."

On his first morning in class, he told the students he was aware of their dismal record but that he saw no reason why teachers and students could not live together in harmony—provided they respected each other's rights. He would not threaten them, he promised, but he would insist that they obey him. The class ringleaders smirked, and then one 13-year-old sent a marble shooting across the floor. Arthur strode over to the perpetrator. "Get up, sir." The boy remained in his seat. "Get up, sir," Arthur repeated, this time seizing the transgressor by his collar, as if to drag him to his feet. At this the boy stood up, trembling. Arthur commanded him to follow him into the hall. Then, unbeknownst to the boy's classmates, he marched him into the classroom where the primary grades were meeting. "I have a pupil for you," Arthur said, presenting the troublemaker to the teacher there. Arthur's face was blank when he returned to the other students, and he did not reveal what he had done.

During the course of the morning, he gave the same treatment to two other boys—again, without disclosing to the remaining students what had happened to them. The three remained in the primary room through recess. At the end of the day, Arthur confronted them. Instead of berating them, however, he spoke kindly to them, merely urging them to do better before sending them home. Somehow, the strategy worked. Within two weeks, Arthur had tamed the unruly students and earned their admiration.

There were lectures, church meetings, and reading societies to stimulate and entertain the residents of Cohoes after working hours, but on many frigid nights people preferred passing the time in each other's homes. Almeda and Malvina were living with their eldest sister, Regina, and her husband, William Caw, and Chester and his friends often stopped by to visit. On January 19, 1853, Malvina described a typical night's entertainment in her diary. Early in the evening, Regina and Almeda attended a sewing society meeting, while Malvina visited her close friend Josephine. Malvina returned to the Caw residence shortly after 9 p.m., "and found here Chester, Campbell, and Mr. Masten, and just now they are having considerable fun trying to make the table tip by magnetizing it." On February 1, Malvina, Chester, and Josephine went to hear Mrs. C. Oakes Smith lecture on "The Dignity of Labor," then "had a dull time" at Mrs. Brown's before returning home at around midnight. And a few weeks after that, Malvina concluded "another rainy, gloomy day" with an evening party at Mary Clarke's. "Had a miserable time, had worked myself into a miserable frame of mind, before I went. To my shame be it confessed. I should be the last one to complain of the thoughts and actions of those around me, I who make myself so miserable, with my jealous, selfish feelings."

Cohoes depressed Malvina—she called it a "little dirty <u>cubby hole</u>"—but it was heaven compared to living with her parents. Chester's appointment at the Cohoes District School ended on March 1, 1853, and Malvina and Almeda lost their teaching jobs there at the end of the same month. Now, to Malvina's horror, she would have to return to her parents' home. The young woman worshipped her mother, who sang in the church choir and dutifully accompanied her husband on visits to parishioners' homes. "Ma came up to take a look at me before she went to bed. I do believe if ever there was an angel on the face of the earth it is her. I wish I could be more careful about grieving her," she wrote.

The problem was Elder Arthur. His staunch self-righteousness and unwavering faith oppressed Malvina, who confided to her diary that she was not even a Christian. "I do wonder that I can sit unmoved Sabbath after Sabbath, and be so little affected by the sermons I hear. Nothing on the subject appears to affect me." She acknowledged she felt happy every time her father left the house, and admitted, guiltily, that she wished "I could be let entirely alone. It disturbs me to have him distress himself so much about me. I could keep out of his way if it were not for coming to the table."

As an unmarried woman, Malvina had little choice but to remain with her parents until she found a husband. But Chester had no such restriction. He was ready to work in an attorney's office and make his final preparations for passing the New York bar. He had soaring ambitions, and he knew he could not fulfill them in tiny Cohoes. The great and growing metropolis to the south was the natural place for the aspiring lawyer to chase his fortune. Elder Arthur's abolitionist friend Erastus D. Culver, who had moved to Brooklyn in 1850, had a thriving law practice at 289 Broadway in Manhattan, and he agreed to take on his friend's son. Chester left upstate New York and his father's rigid rule for a new life in the big city.

CHAPTER TWO

"This Is the Place"

ARTHUR DIDN'T DOUBT his decision to move to New York, but during his first months there he longed for his family and his friends James and John, the other two members of what the three affectionately dubbed "the Triangle." His separation from John, who was bedridden with what was probably tuberculosis, was especially painful. "I feel often sad and lonely, and unusually so this morning because my thoughts are with you," Chester wrote to his ailing friend in December 1853. "I sometimes get very weary and tired of city life and think I would not like to pass my days here after all. Yet if one is ambitious and makes it the great object of life to succeed there is no doubt but this is the place."

The past was tugging at Arthur again when he sat down to write John a month later. "How innumerable are the thoughts that come thronging up, the remembrances, painful and pleasant, as I write 1854 and in reviewing the past year, its joys and sorrows, hopes and fears, successes and disappointments, the associations of the Triangle stand out like golden threads in all the tangled web."

The letters Arthur wrote to his friends and family were affectionate, but they also were filled with apologies—for not writing more often, for not coming home to visit. He wanted to be a loyal son, brother, and friend, but despite his bouts of nostalgia he was focused on his future, and that future lay in New York City.

The metropolis itself was hurtling forward, as was evident from the piles of timber, iron, and stone heaped on the sidewalks outside Erastus Culver's law office. Not long before, English writers had belittled Broadway's flimsy wood-frame houses and stubby brick stores, but now the modest buildings crouching between Bowling Green and Canal Street were being swept aside by five- and six-story structures of marble and granite. By the time Arthur arrived in New York in March 1853, English visitors marveled that Broadway's stores and hotels were "more like the palaces of kings than places for the transaction of business." Scarlet and yellow omnibuses thundered up and down Broadway, the biggest fish in a river pulsing with private carriages, hotel stagecoaches, two-horse hackneys, and carts and wagons piled high with merchandise. The sound of iron wheels on granite pavement was like "the sound of Niagara . . . but sharper and harsher—a great corroding roar, that seems to gnaw the earth like corroding fire." Omnibus passengers paid their fares—six cents for any distance—through an opening in the roof, and pulled a strap attached to the driver's ankle when they wished to stop. Gentlemen gallantly jumped out to help ladies alight from the vehicles and held umbrellas over them if it was raining. But pedestrians crossing Broadway risked sinking into a sea of mud. To reach the safety of the sidewalk, they had to run a gauntlet of wheels and hooves.

Even among the palaces, Alexander T. Stewart's department store, at the corner of Broadway and Chambers Street, stood out. At Stewart's, where cashmere shawls could be had for a stunning $2,000, shoppers were drawn into an oval-shaped rotunda, illuminated by a dome and ringed by a gallery designed as a place for ladies to promenade. The frescoed floor and ceilings portrayed symbols of commerce, and three hundred salesmen and clerks serviced its two acres of floor space. In Broadway's luxurious hotels, many people experienced gas lighting, interior plumbing, and steam heat for the first time. In an early experiment in climate control, the Astor House courtyard featured an iron and glass enclosure in which warm air was blown in from below during the winter months and jets of cool air, moistened by fountains, were blown in during the summer. At the St. Nicholas, 322 servants catered to a thousand guests. In the hotel's mirrored dining room, diners could choose from 2 soups, 2 kinds of fish, 10 boiled dishes, 9 roast dishes, 6 relishes, 17 entrees, 3 cold dishes, 5 varieties of game, 13 vegetables, 7 pastries, and 7 types of fruit. "Groups of extraordinary-looking human beings" lounged on the doorsteps of the leading Broadway hotels at all hours, smoking, whittling, and reading newspapers. "There are southerners sighing for their sunny homes, smoking Havana cigars; western men, with that dashing free-and-easy air which renders them unmistakable; (and) Englishmen, shrouded in exclusiveness, who look on all their neighbours as so many barbarian intruders on their privacy," wrote Isabella Bird, the 23-year-old daughter of an English missionary.

There were hundreds of oyster cellars, coffee houses, ice cream saloons, and restaurants on Broadway, but "the most superb of these," Bird and many others believed, was on the corner of Broadway and Franklin Street. At a time when most eateries were reserved for men, Taylor's Saloon was known as a mecca for lady shoppers, who made the rounds of Broadway's fashionable stores wearing costly silks and rich brocades that swept the sidewalks like so many dustmen. Taylor's had a marble floor, marble walls, and a marble ceiling decorated with intricate scrollwork carved into gilded cornices that soared 22 feet above the diners' heads. The white marble walls were covered with mirrors in gilded frames, and a row of fluted marble pillars ran down either side of the room. An alcove at one end of the restaurant was filled with orange trees, and a 17-foot crystal fountain cooled the diners, who lounged on chairs and sofas covered with crimson and gold cloth. The air was "redolent with the perfume of orange blossoms, the sound of trickling water and the melody of musical snuff boxes." Many came to Taylor's just to see it, and instead of sitting down for a meal they ordered ice cream from large reservoirs that shined like polished silver, sparkling in a hundred burning gas lamps. Even at midnight, passersby who peered through the windows could watch waiters flitting up and down noiselessly, pirouetting between marble tables. "'Tis here that mothers suffer young daughters to come at this untimely midnight hour to drink 'light wines,' or eat ice cream, drugged with passion-exciting vanilla," one disapproving observer wrote.

Clustered around Mercer Street, just west of Broadway, were gambling houses and brothels so "open, free, and undisguised," the *Tribune* noted sarcastically, that surely they could not be what they seemed. They had to be respectable, the paper declared, because "they are frequently visited by gentlemen of the best standing . . . such as aldermen, judges, lawyers, assemblymen, state officers, country merchants and others." Barnum's American Museum, housed in four conjoined buildings at the corner of Broadway and Ann Street, offered different delights. The showman Phineas T. Barnum presented, by his own count, 850,000 exotic animals, paintings, wax figures, and historical artifacts, not to mention sideshow curiosities such as the Feejee Mermaid—billed as a mummified maiden, but actually the desiccated head of a monkey and the body of an orangutan, attached to the back of a fish—and the famous midget Tom Thumb. When Barnum discovered the four-year-old Charles Sherwood Stratton, who stood 25 inches high and weighed only 15 pounds, he "at once determined to secure his services from his parents and to exhibit him in public." Barnum hired the boy for three dollars a week, plus room and board, and billed him as 11-year-old "General Tom Thumb, Man in Miniature," recently arrived from England.

The everyday people on Broadway were as exotic as Barnum's attractions. Arthur admired the businessmen who swaggered down Broadway in their conservative suits, the bearded dandies who strutted by wearing slim trousers, and the women who floated above the pavement in their fluttering ribbons and rainbow silks. But while New York's upper classes shopped, dined, and entertained themselves on Broadway, the city's richest residents lived on Fifth Avenue. Hulking brownstone mansions with massive staircases lorded over what a contemporary guidebook described as "the most magnificent street on this continent." Silver door handles and bell pulls granted entry to interiors "gorgeously fitted up with satin and velvet draperies, rich Axminster carpets, marble and inlaid tables, and large looking-glasses."

To an immigrant preacher's son from upstate, all this seemed otherworldly—and yet not unattainable. This was not Europe, where the wealthiest class was composed of aristocrats who had inherited their money and didn't work. The wealthiest New Yorkers were businessmen, most of them still actively engaged in commerce. The upper echelons of New York society were "in a state of constant fluctuation, in accordance with the fluctuating fortunes of commercial life," wrote Alexander Mackay, an English lawyer and journalist, in 1846. "Its doors are guarded, but they seem never to be closed, and you have a constant stream flowing in and out." Americans heard the term "millionaire" for the first time during the 1840s, and many of the men who earned the title had come from nothing. Men such as John Jacob Astor, a poor German immigrant boy who amassed $20 million trading furs and buying and selling New York real estate. Or George Law, who left his father's upstate farm, walked to Troy, studied masonry, found work on the Delaware and Hudson Canal, and went on to make millions in construction. And then there was Cornelius Vanderbilt, the richest of them all, who launched a ferry service between Staten Island and Manhattan when he was only 16 and transformed it into a steamship and rail empire. When "the Commodore" died in 1877, he was worth a staggering $100 million, about $2.3 billion in 2017 dollars.

And yet there was another side of New York, one that could be glimpsed by peering down Broadway's side streets, where pigs picked over rotten vegetables and the detritus of modern life—old hats without crowns, worn-out shoes, lidless flour barrels, and toppled earthenware jars full of coal ashes—made it difficult for pedestrians to pass. On those streets, ragged women carried bundles of broken boards and old timbers from demolished buildings, trailed by children loaded down with only slightly lighter burdens. Hobbled old men and shoeless scrawny girls in filthy cotton frocks carried cedar pails filled with ears of corn, trying to tempt well-dressed New Yorkers with their plaintive cries of "Hot corn! Here's your nice hot corn—smoking hot, smoking hot, just from the pot!" Many of the vagrant children who wandered lower Manhattan—an estimated three thousand of them in 1850—survived by scavenging or selling fruits, nuts, or petty merchandise. Others stole from stores or the docks, or became pickpockets or junior members of adult gangs. In 1851, a fourth of the 16,000 criminals sent to City Prison were younger than 21—eight hundred were younger than 15 and 175 were younger than 10. To many New Yorkers, the specter of young girls living on the streets was especially horrifying. "No one can walk the length of Broadway," George Templeton Strong wrote in 1851, "without meeting some hideous troop of ragged girls, from 12 years old down, brutalized beyond redemption by premature vice, clad in the filthy refuse of the rag picker's collections, obscene of speech, the stamp of childhood gone from their faces, hurrying along with harsh laughter and foulness on their lips . . . with thief written in their cunning eyes and whore on their depraved faces."

Many of the poorest New Yorkers were recent immigrants—by 1850, nearly half of the city's residents had been born overseas. The newcomers, most of them Irish and German, were packed into squalid, suffocating tenements in slums such as Five Points, where cholera, typhus, and tuberculosis were rampant and the murder rate was the highest in the Western world. "Debauchery has made the very houses prematurely old," Charles Dickens wrote after visiting Five Points in 1842. "See how the rotten beams are tumbling down, and how the patched and broken windows seem to scowl dimly, like eyes that have been hurt in drunken forays." Vicious gangs—the Plug Uglies, the Dead Rabbits, the Bowery B'hoys, and others—terrorized Five Points and similarly dismal districts, stealing, brawling, and killing without interference from the overmatched police.

Then there was the smell. The horses of New York—some 22,500 pulled the city's omnibuses and streetcars, and individual households owned many more—left steaming tons of manure in the streets. The stench from milk factories, cattle yards, and pigpens; the rotting corpses of horses, cows, pigs, dogs, and cats, which might lie in the street for days; overflowing cesspools and faulty sewers; the bones, blood, and offal left over from the slaughtering process—all of it combined to create "atmospheric poison" and "gaseous filth" that filled one's lungs with "vaporized decomposing gutter mud and rottenness," Strong wrote in his diary in 1854. Poor sanitation contributed to periodic cholera outbreaks; during an epidemic in 1849, one out of every hundred New Yorkers perished. But even in years without cholera, the mortality rate was extraordinarily high: fewer than half of the children born in the city in the 1850s survived to the age of six.

•—◆—•

In this city of stark contrasts and multiple nationalities, black New Yorkers occupied peculiar ground. Freed from slavery in 1827, they were native-born Americans who were treated as second-class citizens—at best. Like immigrants, they were forced to live in neighborhoods shunned by the middle and upper classes. They were barred from many restaurants and workplaces, and attended segregated schools and churches. Some of the omnibuses and horse-drawn streetcars barred all black riders, while others restricted them to specially designated cars that ran at infrequent intervals. Even P. T. Barnum, loath to turn away any paying customer, permitted African Americans to visit his American Museum only at certain advertised times. Once admitted they had to sit in special sections set aside for "colored persons."

A young schoolteacher who refused to tolerate the indignity she suffered on a streetcar gave Chester Arthur his first chance to shine as an attorney.

Elizabeth Jennings, 27, taught at the private African Free School and was the organist at the First Colored Congregational Church. Her grandfather, Jacob Cartwright, had been a soldier in the Revolutionary War, and her father, Thomas L. Jennings, was a founder of the New York African Society for Mutual Relief and a leader in the black community. Born to a free black family in New York, Thomas was a successful tailor who invented a process called "dry scouring" for cleaning clothes, for which he received a patent from the state of New York in 1821. He used his initial earnings to purchase his wife out of indentured servitude (under New York's gradual abolition law of 1799, children born to slave mothers after July 4, 1799, were considered born free, but had to serve apprenticeships to their masters until they were young adults).

On Sunday, July 16, 1854, Elizabeth and her friend Sarah Adams walked to the corner of Pearl and Chatham Streets to catch the Third Avenue streetcar, which was pulled by horses on an embedded steel track. After a few minutes the Number 6 appeared, and Jennings raised her hand to signal the driver to stop. The car did not have a "Colored Persons Allowed" placard in its rear window, but the women were running late for church, and they didn't have time to wait for a car that did. Holding her bonnet in place with one hand and clutching her organ music in the other, Elizabeth stepped forward to board the car. Even though the driver had pulled over to allow Jennings and Adams to board, the conductor blocked her way, informing her in a thick Irish brogue that the car was full. Jennings explained that they could not wait for another car, because they were in a hurry to get to church. The conductor held firm. "He then told me that the other car had my people in it, that it was appropriate for 'my people.' I told him I had no 'people.' I wished to go to church and did not wish to be detained. He still kept driving me off the car; said he had as much time as I had and could wait just as long. I replied, 'Very well, we'll see.'" A few tense minutes passed. The streetcar driver shifted uncomfortably in his seat. Finally, the conductor relented.

"Well, you may go in," he said. "But remember if the passengers raise any objections you shall go out, whether or no, or I'll put you out."

This pricked the pride of the young teacher. "I am a respectable person, born and raised in New York," Jennings declared, her voice rising in anger. "I don't know where you were born, but you are a good-for-nothing impudent fellow for insulting decent persons while on their way to church!"

The conductor, enraged, grabbed Jennings to eject her from the car, but she got hold of the window sash and refused to budge. "Do not lay hands on me!" she cried. When the conductor managed to wrench her hand from the window, Jennings transferred her grip to his coat. The woman's strength surprised the conductor, who shouted at the driver to secure the horses and help him subdue her. Together they seized the teacher's arms and began dragging her from the car, her feet in the air and her head brushing against the platform. "Murder!" screamed Jennings, her dress soiled and her bonnet smashed. "You'll kill her! Don't kill her!" Adams cried. The driver released his grip and returned to his reins. The struggle was over—but only temporarily. "You shall sweat for this," the conductor snarled, ordering the driver to keep going until he saw a police officer or station house. When they spied a policeman on the corner of Walker and Bower, the driver halted the horses so the officer could climb aboard. After listening to the conductor's account, the policeman ordered Jennings out of the car, taunting her to "get redress if I could . . . after dragging me off the car he drove me away like a dog, saying not to be talking there and raising a mob or fight."

The next day, Jennings admitted being "sore and stiff from the treatment I received from those monsters in human form," but she was unbowed. She wrote up an account of the incident, which was read aloud at a meeting of prominent black citizens at the First Colored Congregational Church. It was then forwarded to the *Tribune*, edited by the abolitionist Horace Greeley, and to *Frederick Douglass' Paper*. Both reprinted it in full. With the financial backing of her family and the outraged black community, Jennings filed a lawsuit against the conductor, the driver, and the Third Avenue Railroad

Company, seeking $500 in damages. Thomas Jennings hired the firm of Culver, Parker and Arthur to represent his daughter.

Jennings v. Third Avenue Railroad Company was assigned to 24-year-old Arthur, the firm's junior partner. The case came to trial on February 22, 1855, in the New York Supreme Court, Brooklyn Circuit. In arguing the case, Arthur called Judge William Rockwell's attention to a recently enacted state law holding common carriers liable for the acts of their agents and employees, whether those acts were committed negligently or maliciously. The lawyers for the Third Avenue Railroad Company knew their defense had crumbled when Rockwell instructed the jury that common carriers were bound to transport any respectable person, "even colored persons, if sober, well-behaved, and free from disease." The jury awarded Jennings $225, to which the court added $25 plus costs. "Railroads, steamboats, omnibuses, and ferry boats will be admonished from this, as to the rights of respectable colored people," Greeley's *Tribune* wrote. "It is high time the rights of this class of citizens were ascertained, and that it should be known whether they are to be thrust from our public conveyances, while German or Irish women, with a quarter of mutton or a load of codfish, can be admitted."

The Jennings decision did not immediately desegregate all of New York's streetcar lines, which were owned by several different companies, but it set the process in motion. For years after, the Colored People's Legal Rights Association celebrated the anniversary of the verdict.

•◆•

Arthur told his family and friends that he was working hard; Culver had been elected city judge of Brooklyn and had handed over many of the day-to-day legal duties to his junior partner. But there is no evidence that the young lawyer boasted of his role in the momentous Jennings case. "I have been quite well all winter and have worked pretty hard, but aside from business, no event of unusual interest has occurred to change the 'even tenor of my way,'" Chester wrote to his sister Annie less than three weeks after his historic triumph. "Mr. Culver, our 'senior,' as you may have learned has been elected City Judge of Brooklyn for a term of six years, and though he has not left the firm still he can not devote much of his time to our business and consequently much more devolves on me than before, as I have to fill his place as well as I can in the trial of causes in the courts. It will be much better for me in the end but it comes rather hard at first."

On many evenings Arthur left the office at 6:30, too exhausted for after-hours entertainment. Sometimes he visited the Culver residence for a home-cooked meal, and occasionally he ventured out to the theater, but on most nights he returned to his boarding house, changed into his dressing gown and slippers, and lounged in a plush armchair pulled close to the warm grate of the fireplace. He often stayed up chatting with his roommate, Henry Gardiner, another fledgling lawyer in the Culver firm. "I have not been to a place of amusement three times during the winter. I do not care much for it," he wrote his mother.

Now almost 26, Arthur was strikingly handsome. He had a powerful build, a wispy beard, and stylishly long hair, which he carefully arranged to reveal just the lobes of his ears. But at an age when many of his peers were starting families, Chester had never been in love. "I am yet heart-whole and bid fair, I fear, to become an old bachelor," Chester wrote his sister Annie in March 1855:

> I feel the want of near and dear friends—more near and dear than any I have here—who can sympathize with and cheer me when I am dispirited and harassed with the cares and vexations of business—of sisters and brother, father and mother who I know love and care for me, and who I assure you dear sister are becoming nearer and dearer to me every day, for I feel every day how hard it is to fill their place—I have been as lonesome at times this winter as a little homesick schoolboy.

To an inexperienced young man from upstate, the fashionable ladies of New York, who conformed strictly to the *Journal des Modes* that arrived from Paris every fortnight, must have been an intimidating lot. They wore the finest and costliest embroidered muslin, and carried extravagantly expensive fans with ruby or emerald pins. "Surely Solomon in all his glory or the Queen of Sheba when she came to visit him in state was not arrayed so magnificently as these New York damsels," William Makepeace Thackeray wrote in 1852.

Arthur's romantic fortunes changed in 1856, when the 19-year-old cousin of a second roommate, a young medical student named Dabney Herndon, came to visit New York. Ellen Herndon's dark brown hair and eyes contrasted sharply with her ghostly white skin, giving her an ethereal quality. She was thin, and stood with her elbows tucked in at her waist. But her dignified carriage belied a sunny personality, and she took great pride in her rich contralto singing voice. She was the daughter of US Navy captain William Lewis Herndon, an explorer who had become famous a few years before for leading an expedition that explored the Amazon River from its headwaters to its mouth. Nell, as everybody called her, was born in Culpeper House, Virginia, and her family's roots in the Old Dominion reached back to the seventeenth century. But she had spent most of her life in Washington, where her mother, the former Elizabeth Frances Hansbrough, hobnobbed with the capital's elite. As a young girl, Nell sang in the youth choir of St. John's Church on Lafayette Square, across from the White House. There she met and befriended another member of the church, former First Lady Dolley Madison, nearly 70 years her senior. As a teenager, Nell helped her mother entertain Washington's leading political and military figures, and during summers the two women (Captain Herndon was often absent) moved between the upper-class resorts of Newport and Saratoga Springs, where they mixed with the elite of other cities. One contemporary described her as "one of the best specimens of the Southern woman."

Smitten, Chester courted Nell in Saratoga and Lake George in the spring and summer of 1856. In the "soft moonlight nights of June," the lovers cuddled "in our old place in the window-seat at Saratoga," and together they relished "the golden fleeting hours at Lake George." Chester had never been happier. "I know you are thinking of me now. I feel the pulses of your love answering to mine," he wrote. "If I were with you now, you would go & sing for me 'Robin Adair' then you would come & sit by me—you would put your arms around my neck and press your soft sweet lips over my eyes. I can feel them now."

But Arthur wrote that love letter to Nell, now his fiancée, from St. Joseph, Missouri, where he and Gardiner were waiting for a steamer to take them down the Missouri River to Kansas Territory. The nation's long struggle over slavery was starting to boil in "Bleeding Kansas," but new towns were springing up there like golden asters from the prairie. For ambitious young men like Arthur and Gardiner, there were fortunes to be made.

CHAPTER THREE

Bleeding Kansas

HEAVY SNOW WAS so rare in Kansas that farmers ploughed the prairies in January. The air was dry and pure, and cool western breezes blew steadily during the summer. There was no better land in the country for growing crops or raising livestock, and it was "safe to predict that, before another year rolls round, stores, mills, and manufactures will be in full operation . . . and all of the necessaries, as well as most of the luxuries of life will be found there." To reach the Promised Land, all an enterprising emigrant had to do was cross the Missouri River, procure a horse or mule (assuming he already had a rifle and saddle bags), select a plot of land, record the boundaries, build a log house, and start working.

The New York "Kanzas" League promoted the wonders of Kansas Territory in a 58-page booklet it published in 1855. Chester Arthur may or may not have visited the league headquarters at 110 Broadway—just a short walk from Erastus Culver's law office—or read the booklet, but he and his roommate Henry Gardiner certainly swallowed its claims. In the summer of 1857, the two lawyers joined thousands of farmers, land speculators, and railroad promoters flocking to Kansas after the Kansas-Nebraska Act opened the land for settlement in 1854.

Under the law, white male settlers in Kansas and Nebraska would be allowed to vote on whether to allow slavery, effectively repealing the Missouri Compromise of 1820, which had outlawed slavery in the former Louisiana Territory north of the 36°30' latitude. Nebraska was so far north it was virtually guaranteed to become a free state, but Kansas was next to the slave state of Missouri, casting its fate into doubt. Thousands of proslavery and antislavery settlers flooded into Kansas to tip the scales, aware that the outcome of the election would alter the balance of power between North and South.

The New York Kanzas League and groups like it wanted to ensure that Kansas became a free state by encouraging the migration of like-minded settlers. They secured reduced railway and steamboat fares, organized emigrants into settlement groups, and raised capital to construct mills, hotels, and other local improvements that might attract settlers from the North.

New Englanders and New Yorkers were only a small fraction of the Kansas settlers, but rumors spread throughout the South that hordes of Northerners were flooding into the disputed territory. To counter them, armed Missourians known as "Border Ruffians" poured over the Missouri-Kansas line to vote, illegally, for proslavery candidates for Congress and the territorial legislature. Their ballots brought to power a proslavery legislature that recreated the Missouri slave code, which made it illegal to even write or speak against slaveholding. The penalty for assisting a fugitive slave was 10 years of hard labor—or death. Outraged slavery opponents set up their own legislature in Topeka. Though congressional investigators concluded that the election that produced the proslavery legislature was fraudulent, Washington recognized the proslavery government as legitimate.

Emboldened by that stance, a judge ordered a grand jury to indict the leaders of the free-state legislature for treason. On May 11, 1856, a federal marshal claimed residents of Lawrence had interfered with the execution of the indictments and called for "law-abiding citizens of the territory" to gather for an incursion into the town. Ten days later, a force of about 750 Border Ruffians and recently arrived Southerners, led by proslavery sheriff Samuel J. Jones, swarmed into Lawrence. Marching under a South Carolina flag and carrying banners with inscriptions such as "THE SUPREMACY OF THE WHITE RACE," they pillaged homes and stores and destroyed the offices of two abolitionist newspapers. "This is the happiest moment of my life," Sheriff Jones said as he surveyed the smoldering ruins of the Free State Hotel, which had been built by the New England Emigrant Aid Company. "I determined to make the fanatics bow before me in the dust, and kiss the territorial law, and I have done it—by God, I have done it."

The fiery abolitionist John Brown, who had recently joined several of his adult sons in Kansas, was enraged by the sacking of Lawrence, and by the townspeople's failure to put up a fight. He would lead the forces of light on a mission to avenge that disgrace. On the night of May 24, Brown, three of his sons, and four other followers crept out of their encampment south of Lawrence and marched six miles north, toward the intersection of Mosquito Creek and Pottawatomie Creek. They were armed with revolvers, rifles, knives, and army surplus broadswords Brown had procured a few months earlier on his way to Kansas. The broadswords were hollow and loaded with quicksilver, which slid from the hilt to the point when the upraised weapon was swung, increasing the force of the blow. Broadswords were designed to slash and bludgeon, to mutilate and maim. Emblazoned with ornamental eagles, they were perfect for Brown's purpose: to strike terror into the hearts of his enemies.

Brown and his followers didn't find anybody in the first cabin they approached. The next cabin was the home of proslavery man James P. Doyle and his sons, William and Drury. When the elder Doyle answered the door, they ordered the old man to summon his sons and come outside. Instead, Doyle rushed inside to get his gun, but the abolitionists were prepared for a siege: they had balls of hay soaked in wet gunpowder, which they lit on fire and rolled into the cabin. Within minutes, the coughing and gasping Doyles staggered outside. After marching the family a quarter of a mile down the road, John Brown drew his revolver and shot James Doyle in the forehead, killing him instantly. Brown's two younger sons immediately attacked the Doyle boys with their broadswords. They killed one of the sons quickly; the other managed to flee down the road a short distance before the Browns cut him down. Before the night was over, John Brown and his avengers had killed two other men at two other cabins. They left one of the corpses floating in Pottawatomie Creek.

Arthur knew all about the Border Ruffians and John Brown from reading the New York newspapers, but the groups encouraging settlement downplayed the dangers. "In traveling through slave States, the emigrant should avoid all unnecessary allusion to slavery; as on this topic, the slaveholder is peculiarly sensitive," the New York Kanzas League noted drily. Its booklet reassured would-be settlers that, "by a courteous demeanor in his intercourse with the slaveholder, and proper reserve on the subject of slavery, the emigrant, without sacrifice of principle, will not only secure for himself kind treatment, but will also aid in removing the unjust prejudice now existing in the minds of slaveholders against Kanzas emigrants from free States."

•◆•

Whatever the risks, Arthur was determined to seek his fortune in Kansas. He and Gardiner left New York early in the summer of 1857, traveling first to Michigan, then west to Wisconsin, where they visited Madison, Beloit, and Janesville. They spent some time in the Iowa towns of Burlington and

Keokuk, and in St. Louis. On August 30, Arthur wrote Nell from St. Joseph, Missouri, a bustling town on the Missouri River where many pioneers
gathered supplies before heading out in wagon trains to the Far West. Arthur and Gardiner were there for about a month, waiting for a steamer to
take them 80 miles down the river to Leavenworth, Kansas. "It is a great
waste of time to travel on the river. It is so low that the boats can make but
slow progress, but even then it is much preferable to [traveling by stagecoach]
in this new country," Arthur reported. "I am desirous to learn as much as I
can about the affairs and condition of Kansas." He quickly shifted to more
personal matters. "This is your birthday, my own precious darling, my own
Nell. The remembrance came with my first awaking in the early morning—
as the thought of you always does—and as I kissed your dear image, darling,
my heart was full to overflowing with love and prayer for you!"

Leavenworth was a world away from New York: men tucked their pants
into their boots and swaggered through swirls of dust with their revolvers
holstered in plain sight. The town was a magnet for trappers, wagon train
men, and people from the surrounding plains who came to participate in
elections that were held on the slightest pretext, merely for entertainment.
The next political event was a debate at the Planters' House, a hotel in the
center of town, and Arthur and Gardiner decided to attend. In a region
where some hotels posted signs reminding male guests to remove their
boots before getting into bed, the four-story, brick Planters' House was a cut
above: its light and airy bedrooms were elaborately furnished, and the tables
in the hotel dining room were laid with silverware and dishes made by New
York's master craftsmen. The original owner, a proslavery man, ran it under
"exclusive Southern principles"—that is, he turned away guests who openly
opposed slavery. But soon two men from Michigan took over, announcing
they would accept anybody.

The new policy managed to offend both sides: slavery opponents were
upset that two Northerners accepted proslavery men as guests, while Southern sympathizers bristled at the ownership of two confirmed abolitionists.
To keep the business of both camps, the owners came up with an ingenious
system: in the bar and billiard room, they always had two bartenders on
duty, one an abolitionist, the other proslavery. When a proslavery man came
in, sunk his knife into the top of the bar and shouted, "I can lick any man
born north of Mason and Dixon's line!" the proslavery bartender encouraged him. At the same time, an abolitionist who claimed he could whip any
man south of the dividing line received encouragement from the barman
representing his camp. Any kind of talk was acceptable, but when angry

words turned into action, the offender, no matter his politics, was sent to the basement to cool off.

On the day of the meeting, Arthur, Gardiner, and several other Eastern gentlemen were escorted to places of honor on a temporary platform erected outside the windows of the hotel office. John Calhoun, the surveyor general of the territory and a prominent proslavery figure, was scheduled to debate Marcus Parrott, the free-state legislature's nominee for delegate to Congress. A parade of partisans from each side, "including earnest young lawyers from the South, who affected broadcloth and high-heeled boots," took turns addressing the crowd. Parrott's fiery speech aroused both camps. "You're a liar!" a heckler shouted, prompting a retort from somebody sitting on the platform. Suddenly a shot rang out—and then another. Bullets ricocheted off the walls of the hotel as Arthur, Gardiner, and the other men on the platform scrambled for cover. As many as 30 shots were fired, but only one man was hit—and his injury was minor.

Later a stagecoach trip to Lawrence gave Arthur another lesson in the harshness of the new land. The solid-oak coach was braced with iron bands and suspended on heavy leather straps for shock absorption, but the driver couldn't avoid all of the rocks or the ruts the heavier wagons of the settlers had cut into the tough prairie sod. The coach tipped over repeatedly, and when it did Arthur and Gardiner had to jump down and help pry the vehicle out of mudholes and sloughs with a fence rail the driver had brought along for that purpose. In some places the mud, greasy and thick as dough, was waist deep. For long stretches of the journey the young lawyers walked beside the coach to give the exhausted horses a rest.

When they finally arrived in Lawrence, Arthur and Gardiner sought out two prominent free-state leaders to brief them on the situation in the territory. James Henry Lane, 43, was a charismatic veteran of the Mexican-American War and a former lieutenant governor of Indiana who had voted for the Kansas-Nebraska Act as a member of Congress. Though not an abolitionist, the "Grim Chieftain" was a magnetic speaker widely known for his withering denunciations of the slave power. Samuel Walker, 34, was a cabinetmaker from Pennsylvania who was a founding member of the Bloomington Guards, an antislavery militia, and who had served in the free-state legislature. Arthur spoke to Lane and Walker several times over the next few days, and listened carefully to what they had to say.

One sunny morning a few days later, Arthur and Gardiner set out on horseback for Lecompton, the proslavery capital. As they traveled along the Kansas River, Lane and Walker rode up beside them. The two antislavery leaders were heading to Lecompton to attend to business in the territory's land office, despite threats by residents of the town that they would hang Lane if they ever saw him there. Suddenly, several horsemen approached from the direction of Lecompton. When they spied Lane and Walker, they huddled for a moment, then put spurs to their horses and galloped back toward the capital. A few minutes before, Lane had told Arthur and Gardiner he didn't believe he would be in danger in Lecompton; now he was nervous. He asked Arthur whether he was armed. When Arthur told him he was not, Lane handed him his extra revolver, which the New Yorker promptly stuck into his belt.

Lecompton consisted of a few scattered houses along a straggling street. The land office was at the end of it, and as Arthur and his companions made their way toward it, a large crowd of teenage boys ran behind them. "There goes Jim Lane! Let's hang him!" they cried. Arthur shifted nervously in his saddle, suddenly conscious of the pistol rubbing against his leg. Several dozen men stood outside the land office, coldly eyeing the four visitors as they approached. Somebody had stabbed an antislavery man to death the night before; the suspect was still at large, and nobody knew whether the crime had been personal or political. The air crackled with menace, and Lane decided he'd better turn back. But the crowd allowed Arthur and the other two men to dismount and enter the land office without molesting them.

Shaken but no longer fearing for their safety, Arthur and Gardiner left the land office to visit Robert J. Walker, a former Mississippi senator and treasury secretary appointed territorial governor just a few months before. Walker supported slavery but opposed the constitution approved by the proslavery legislature—a tenuous political position. He lived and worked in a narrow house with two rooms on the ground floor and a tiny bedroom and anteroom on the upper half floor. The stairway was on the outside of the building. Upon entering Walker's office, the New Yorkers noticed there was no carpet or furniture, save a round table covered with green baize and a plain wooden chair. An old saddle and a battered trunk were lying on the floor, and in one corner was a tottering pile of law books "thrown down in the promiscuous manner of corn sacks." Walker, his shoulders slumped under the heavy mantle of his office, was buried deep in a pile of papers, but for more than an hour he described the political situation to his young visitors. The governor's grim view was that the fate of the Union depended on whether Kansans would be allowed to vote on the slavery question in a free and fair election—a standard that would be hard to reach as the violence mounted. "If this principle should be defeated here, the slavery agitation must be renewed in all elections throughout the country, with increasing bitterness, until it shall eventually overthrow the government."

• ◆ •

As Arthur mulled his options in Kansas, a steamship far away began the final leg of its voyage from Panama to New York. One of a new generation of side-wheel steamers, the *Central America* was sleek and black, with three majestic masts and a red stripe running nearly three hundred feet along her lower wale from stem to stern. She was powered by two monstrous steam engines, which together weighed 750 tons and sat on oak timbers as thick as a half-dozen railroad ties.

Most of the nearly six hundred passengers aboard the *Central America* were miners returning to the East from the California Gold Rush. The ship carried 30,000 pounds of consigned gold in her hold. Squirreled away in their trunks, pockets, money belts, and carpetbags, most of the passengers carried their own stashes, and they looked forward to their triumphant arrival in New York five days hence. "We were jubilant and made the old ship ring with our voices," one passenger recalled.

The *Central America* left Havana harbor on Tuesday, September 8, 1857. As she traveled northeast across the Straits of Florida, many passengers sought relief from the tropical heat under a large awning on the weather deck. When the sun finally kissed the ocean off the port side, most of the first- and second-class passengers went below decks to the dining saloon, where they ate supper sitting at long tables. After the meal, some returned topside to entertain themselves with impromptu skits and poetry readings, sometimes accompanied by fellow passengers playing banjo, guitar, or fiddle.

Those lucky few who had been invited to sit at the captain's table remained rooted in their seats. Long after the nightly card games had begun at the other tables, the captain's guests smoked Cuban cigars, drank fine claret, and reveled in the stories and self-deprecating humor of their famous host.

Captain William Lewis Herndon, Chester Arthur's future father-in-law, had a slender build, and his hairline was receding. His red beard ran along the fringe of his jaw from temple to temple, and he wore thin gold spectacles. If not for his gold epaulets, the 43-year-old captain might have been mistaken for a banker or a professor. He had spent 29 years at sea, and rarely saw his wife or his daughter, Nell, now engaged to a promising young lawyer from New York. In 1857, Captain Herndon was well known for his exploration of the Valley of the Amazon six years earlier. Following the navy's orders, Herndon had recorded the weather, studied the flora, and measured and skinned small animals and birds. But he wrote his report as a narrative, and his descriptions of natives, animals, plants, and geological features were so vivid Congress published 10,000 copies as a book.

The table laughed uproariously when Captain Herndon recalled a troublesome meal of monkey meat and monkey soup during his Amazon adventure. "Jocko, however, had his revenge, because I nearly perished of nightmare," the captain remembered. "Some devil, with arms as nervous as the monkey's had me by the throat, and starting on me with his cold, cruel eye, expressed his determination to hold on to the death. . . . Upon making a desperate effort and shaking him off, I found that I had forgotten to take off my cravat, which was choking me within an inch of my life." At one point, the conversation turned to shipwrecks. In a notorious incident three years before, the captain and crew of a sinking ship had commandeered the lifeboats, leaving 259 of the 282 passengers—including all of the women and children—to drown. "Well, I'll never survive my ship. If she goes down, I go under her keel," Herndon declared. "But let us talk of something more cheerful."

Passengers who arose early on Wednesday morning noticed that the wind had picked up during the night. At first the change was refreshing, but as the day wore on the sudden shift in the weather "changed our feelings and drove the waves into mountains and valleys and made the old ship stagger." The heaving of the ship made many of the passengers seasick, and few of them ventured into the dining saloon for lunch. By twilight, "there was a raging storm such as we had never before seen," a passenger recalled. "The waves and sky were crashing together."

That evening, Captain Herndon calmly led a game of whist at his table, but most passengers were too sick and scared to visit the dining saloon. From his narrow berth in steerage, one passenger heard only "the crying of children and the moans of those suffering seasickness, and rising above all the sounds that proceeded from the inside of the vessel was the continued dashing and splashing of the waves against the sides of the ship, and the howling of the storm as the wind surged through the steamer's rigging."

The weather worsened. At noon the next day, sideways rain was pelting the *Central America* like bullets and the steamer was laboring against headwinds that topped 50 knots. At nightfall, the waves breaking over the steamer began sloshing into staterooms, forcing some first- and second-class passengers to abandon them. Through it all, Captain Herndon kept the ship on course. "Let it blow," chief engineer George Ashby shouted to an experienced seaman who was traveling on the *Central America* as a passenger. "We're ready for it."

But Ashby was less confident than he let on. When he encountered the passenger he had been on his way to deliver a report to the captain, and the news was not good: The ship had sprung a leak. Water was rising in the bilge, and Ashby could not determine where it was coming from. By noon on Friday, the rising water had popped out the floor plates in the fire room. The firemen, whose job was to shovel coal into the furnaces, had to hold on to iron bars lashed into place to keep their balance in the waist-deep water. That night, frightened passengers huddled in the dining saloon, seeking solace amid the flickering oil lamps.

Their numbers had grown into the hundreds by the following afternoon. Amid the gloom, two little girls giggled at the dishes smashing and crashing around them. The adults indulged them, but their laughter was a weak antidote to the suffocating sense of dread filling the room. Suddenly the captain's boy burst into the saloon. "All hands down below to pass buckets!" Now the female passengers "burst into lamentations, knowing then that the vessel was in peril." Captain Herndon appeared at the door of the saloon a few moments after the boy dashed away. He knew the water in the hold was nearly 10 feet deep, but his face betrayed nothing and his voice was even. "All men prepare for bailing the ship. The engines have stopped, but we hope to reduce the water and start them again. She's a sturdy vessel and if we can keep up steam we shall weather the gale." Several men in the saloon immediately stood up and took off their coats to obey the captain's command. Herndon approached another male passenger and smiled. "You must take off your broadcloth and go to work now."

Using wash buckets and water pitchers, three bailing brigades scooped water from the hold and passed it up to the weather deck where the last man dumped it into the sea. Captain Herndon seemed to be everywhere at once. "Work on, m'boys!" he cried. "We have hope yet!" Energized by the captain's enthusiasm, the men sang songs as they worked, trying to forget the knotting muscles in their shoulders, backs, and forearms. But they were losing the race; every hour, the water rose about six inches higher in the hold.

On Saturday morning, Captain Herndon pointed to the thinning clouds and predicted that the storm was nearing its end. He told the men that if they could continue passing the buckets for several more hours, the *Central America* might be saved. He repeated the message to the passengers in the main hold. But Captain Herndon was only trying to prevent panic;

he knew the only way to save the lives of his passengers was to transfer them to a passing ship. The *Central America* was doomed.

Hope arrived at 2 p.m. on Saturday, when one of the lookouts who was watching the horizon cried out, "Sail ho!" The news quickly spread throughout the ship, prompting "shrieking, crying, weeping; agonies of joy, where late was nothing but agonies of death." Captain Herndon ordered the signal guns fired and hoisted a flag of distress. An hour later, when the brig *Marine* passed within hailing distance, Captain Herndon shouted into the storm "with all the calmness of an ordinary occasion" that his ship was in sinking condition, and asked the *Marine* to stand by until morning.

Captain Herndon knew his ship could not be saved, but he was determined to preserve as many lives as he could. The *Central America* left Havana with six lifeboats, but one had been smashed to pieces by the storm the night before. Under normal conditions, each of the boats could carry four oarsmen, a helmsman, and 40 to 50 passengers. But the sea was so rough the captain didn't think the oarsmen could transport more than 20 people at a time.

As soon as the *Marine* came close enough, Captain Herndon ordered his crew to lower two of the lifeboats, one on the port and one on the starboard. But when they tried to lower a third boat, the sea immediately seized it and dashed it against the hull of the *Central America*, shattering it. Another boat also was destroyed, leaving only three to ferry passengers to the *Marine*. Captain Herndon didn't know how many people he could save, but one thing was certain: under his command, no man would get into a lifeboat until every woman and child did. To reduce weight, the women had been instructed to remove their undergarments and layers of skirts, and they were given life preservers, some made of cork but most of tin. Older children also got preservers, while babies were wrapped in blankets.

The women, their dresses long and sagging without hoops and petticoats, were quickly drenched as they waited for their turn to be tied into a rope sling and lowered into the lifeboats. "The captain tied a rope around me, and I think he was one of the men that had hold of it when I was lowered down," one woman remembered. "As soon as I got into the boat, I looked up and saw the captain was fixing a cape around my child, and a few moments afterward he lowered her down to me." The roiling seas and blasting winds made it impossible for the *Marine* to hold its position, and by the time the lifeboats were off the brig had drifted two miles away. As the oarsmen pulled towards her, she drifted another mile. It took an hour and a half for the lifeboats to reach her. Meanwhile, the *Central America* settled ever lower in the water.

As he waited for the lifeboats to return from the *Marine*, Captain Herndon asked a passenger named Theodore Payne to go into his office and fetch his gold watch and chain. "If you are saved, deliver them to my wife. Tell her to . . . " The captain choked up, standing silently for a few moments. When he gathered himself, he asked Payne to meet with the president of the steamship company to tell him what had happened. Then he sat down on a nearby bench and put his head in his hands.

When the first of the lifeboats returned from the *Marine*, Herndon stood up again and took control. Now that the women and children were safe, he ordered his crew to dispense with the rope sling. If they wanted to board a lifeboat, the passengers, firemen, and stewards clustered on deck would have to jump. Once they had all the men they could safely carry, the lifeboats set off again for the *Marine*. But with their oarsmen exhausted and the distance between the two ships now grown to five miles, the three lifeboats would never return to the *Central America*.

At nightfall, there were approximately four hundred men standing on the deck of the steamer, while the remaining hundred or so sought refuge in the corridors and cabins of the sinking ship. "The prayers of the pious and the penitent, the curses of the maddened, and the groans and shrieks of the affrighted, were all comingled together, added to which were numerous angry contests between man and man, in many instances amounting to outright fight, for the possession of articles on which to keep themselves afloat in the water." Many men took their hard-won gold dust and sprayed it upon the floor, or tossed their coins into the wind. Now it was nothing more than dead weight.

Captain Herndon retired to his quarters and emerged in full dress uniform, with the oil silk covering removed from the gold band on his cap. Then, accompanied by one of his officers, he stood stoically on a deck above the wheelhouse, gripping the iron railing with his left hand as the timbers cracking and splintering below decks heralded the beginning of the *Central America's* final act. Within minutes, her stern pierced the surface and her bow rose up, like an outstretched arm protesting her fate, before she spun into a vortex and vanished.

Captain Herndon was roundly hailed as a hero, an exemplar of chivalry and a model of American manliness. Two towns, in Virginia and Pennsylvania, and two navy ships would be named for him. A monument was erected in his memory at the US Naval Academy in Annapolis. "Devotion to duty, Christian conduct and genuine heroism respected and revered" were the words inscribed on a gold medal the Virginia General Assembly presented to his widow.

Nell sent Chester a telegram informing him of the disaster, and asking him to return to New York to help her and her mother settle the great man's affairs. He immediately agreed to do so, cutting his Kansas adventure short. What's more, the amount of gold lost on the *Central America* was so substantial it helped precipitate a financial panic and an economic slump, darkening the prospects of making a fortune in Kansas—or anywhere else.

The sinking of the *Central America* off Cape Hatteras on September 12, 1857, changed the course of Chester Arthur's life. He left Kansas and returned to New York, and to whatever the great metropolis had in store for him. Captain Herndon's character and conduct during the doomed ship's last hours were an inspiration to millions of Americans. As Arthur embarked on a life with Herndon's daughter, he hoped to live up to that sterling example.

CHAPTER FOUR

Playing the Game

ARTHUR RETURNED FROM Kansas to a city wracked by the financial crisis. Spooked by the failure of the Ohio Life Insurance and Trust Company, New York bankers tightened credit and demanded immediate payment on all mature loans. Depositors rushed to withdraw their gold from banks, draining reserves by $20 million. Now the gold aboard the *Central America*, which was supposed to help replenish that supply, was at the bottom of the Atlantic Ocean. Banks suspended gold payments and brokers pummeled each other on the floor of the New York Stock Exchange as the market sank. "In Wall Street every man carries Pressure, Anxiety, Loss written on his forehead," George Templeton Strong wrote in his diary. Shipbuilding ceased and foundries fired hundreds of mechanics. The printers' union lost two-thirds of its members, and many young women who had worked as milliners, servants, or peddlers resorted to prostitution to survive. Hundreds of small merchants failed, and those who held on posted placards with scribbled announcements of drastic price cuts. Construction on Fifth Avenue mansions halted, and Broadway buildings begun during the spring and summer stalled at two stories, looking like hedges with their tops lopped off.

As many as 100,000 New Yorkers were out of work, and throngs of the jobless gathered to listen to "seditious speeches." Some threatened to seize food, clothing, and other necessities by force if they were denied honest labor. In early November, four thousand radicals, unionists, and land reformers marched from Tompkins Square to City Hall Park to present a "Mass Petition for the Unemployed" to Mayor Fernando Wood. "Every human being has a RIGHT to live, not as a mere charity, but as RIGHT, and governments, monarchical or republican, MUST FIND work for the people if individual exertion proves not sufficient," it read. Perched on a fountain basin, one speaker heaped scorn on New York's wealthier citizens. "Ladies throng Broadway every day buying silk robes, while the wives and children of honest laborers are starving."

Even under the best economic conditions, building a law practice in New York was a challenge. In 1857 Arthur was still a relatively recent arrival in the city, with little money and few family connections. He had attracted some favorable attention with his victory in the Jennings case, but now he was engaged and he had a long way to go before he could support Nell, and the children they hoped to have, in the style they craved. Arthur needed connections to prominent men. One avenue promised to provide them.

The turmoil in Kansas had helped draw New York's disparate antislavery elements together, and in 1854 a "Free Soil" convention in Saratoga—which Chester Arthur and Erastus Culver attended—had led to the creation of the Republican Party in the state. Gradually Arthur had stepped up his involvement in political activities. On election days, he worked as an inspector at a polling place in a carpenter's shop on Broadway and 23rd Street. In 1856, the military officer and explorer John C. Frémont had been the Republican Party's first presidential nominee, and Arthur had contributed to the cause by joining the "Eighteenth Ward Young Men's Fremont Vigilance Committee." Frémont lost the election to Democrat James Buchanan.

Arthur's growing involvement in Republican politics allowed him to observe and learn from a master of the game. Thurlow Weed was the publisher of the Albany *Evening Journal*. He also was the undisputed boss of New York's Whig Party and then, when it faded away, the Republicans. Weed's newspaper background gave him a deep knowledge of current affairs and the ability to write clear, incisive English. He never spoke in public, but he was a natural politician who liked to work secretly with his opponents. At a series of dinners he hosted annually, Weed entertained legislators of both parties, and he boasted that he was personally acquainted with every member of the legislature over the course of 30 years. Railroad magnate Dean Richmond, chairman of the New York Democratic Party, was a close personal friend.

When Arthur returned from Kansas in 1857, Weed was a vigorous 59 years old. He was tall and powerfully built, with eyes set deeply beneath his shaggy brows and receding gray hair that added to his air of authority. The man known as "The Wizard of the Lobby" did not like to be crossed, but his character was a complicated mix of cynicism and generosity. He often came to the rescue of new immigrants who had been duped by the unscrupulous "runners" who lurked near the Castle Garden depot, offering to transport the newcomers' belongings to decrepit boardinghouses where they charged exorbitant rates and held people's possessions as "security" if they could not pay. Women in particular were drawn to Weed, who was a captivating conversationalist and a thoughtful friend who shared financial advice and brought them books and flowers when they were ill.

Born into a family of farmers in tiny Cairo, New York, Weed had little formal schooling and spent much of his youth working on boats on the Hudson River. He grew up in an America that was poor and sparsely populated, a country of handicrafts, fledgling factories, and primitive roads. By the 1850s, that nation no longer existed. Now the country's manufacturing exceeded its agricultural output, and it had 17,000 miles of operating railroads and five million tons of shipping. The Empire State was at the forefront of these changes. It was the most populous state in the Union, with more than three million inhabitants—nine times as many as when Weed was born. It had 2,345 miles of railroad in operation within its borders, and nearly 1.3 million tons of shipping were registered at New York City's port—nearly five times the amount registered in 1815.

In New York, business and politics were being braided together, and Weed derived his power from those thickening ties. He hobnobbed with bank presidents and railroad tycoons, merchants and ship owners, lobbyists and speculators. The businessmen provided a steady source of money for campaigns, and Weed repaid them by soliciting their views on legislation relating to railroads, steamboats, wharfs, or anything else that could affect their fortunes. More delicate men, less versed in the ways of Albany, denigrated this as a perversion of the democratic process. "The Dictator" saw it differently. "Obnoxious as the admission is to a just sense of right and to a better condition of political ethics, we stand so far 'impeached,'" Weed confessed in the *Evening Journal* when he was accused of pushing railroad-backed bills in exchange for donations to the party. "We would have preferred not to disclose to public view the financial history of political life. . . . Public men know much of what 'the rest of mankind' are ignorant. We suppose it is generally understood that party organizations cost money and that presidential elections especially are expensive."

To this practical motivation Weed added a patriotic one: he believed that industrial growth was good for the country. Therefore, advancing the interests of businessmen was in the public interest. "There have been legislative measures, right in themselves, and promotive of the general welfare, in which we have had, in common with other citizens, ultimate or prospective interests. In this category belong New York city railroads."

One of Weed's main responsibilities as political boss was to distribute government jobs to the party faithful, and the New York of the 1850s offered a dizzying array of patronage opportunities. At the bottom of the patronage pyramid were jobs such as laborer, street sweeper, and bell ringer. Moving up, there were positions for policemen, health wardens, tax assessors, judges, and commissioners of deeds. Weed could help a loyal Republican get elected as a local alderman, mayor, or state assemblyman. At the top of the heap were the coveted federal jobs, about seven hundred of them at the New York Custom House, located in a "Grecian temple" on Wall Street. New York City was the main port of entry for goods entering the United States, and the Custom House collected about 75 percent of the nation's import duties. The chief collector made an astronomical $6,400 per year, and even the night watchmen made $1.50 per night at a time when workingmen were fortunate to make $500 a year.

In the mansions on Fifth Avenue, government jobs, especially local ones, were considered to be undignified. Upper-class reformers believed public offices were a public trust that should be divorced from individual interests. But people on society's lower rungs saw things differently. They sought government jobs because they craved a steady salary and a sense of identity—a way up. They believed that if you worked hard on behalf of a victorious political party or faction, a patronage job was your just reward.

Weed was an unabashed defender of the spoils system. He argued that the regular rotation of public jobs was fair and democratic, and if that resulted in an unstable and inefficient civil service, so be it. Patronage was the oil that lubricated the Republican machine, perpetuating Weed's power. It also provided a steady flow of campaign contributions, through "voluntary assessments" levied on officeholders' salaries. For Weed, there was no more important task than finding jobs for loyal Republicans—even it could be taxing at times. "I am shakey [sic], but it is, I think, from the pressure of those who need places or assistance," Weed wrote to a friend. "From two till five A.M. I am beset by numbers, some worthy, others shiftless, but all needy. Last week my head gave out and I was compelled to give up and go to Saratoga. I came Home better, but the same exposure to importunity produced the same consequences. Out of a dozen or more that apply every day I can generally help three or four."

Weed's personal code of honor prevented him from securing appointments for his relatives. There is no evidence that he ever supported a bill he believed to be harmful to the public welfare, or that he ever accepted a bribe from an office seeker. His dealings in Albany offered him ample opportunity to enrich himself, and he became a wealthy man. But he bristled at the suggestion that money clouded his perception of what was in the public interest. There has "scarcely been a session of the Legislature for more than a quarter of a century out of which, if we had chosen to do so, a large amount of money could not have been made," Weed acknowledged. But "during the more than thirty years that we have been connected with this Journal . . . no pecuniary consideration—no hope of favor or reward—has tempted us to support a measure which did not commend itself to our judgment and conscience, or to oppose a meritorious one."

And yet, Weed was the prototype for the machine politician, the model for a long line of bosses and lobbyists who gradually corroded Americans' faith in their government. Less than a century before, the country's founding fathers conceived a political system engineered to produce good laws. Weed and his ilk twisted it into a game of place and power, a contest in which the ultimate prize was getting and maintaining party control—even if that meant handing out government jobs to inexperienced men, or using brass-knuckled tactics to win elections. However he might justify it, Weed eagerly did the bidding of railroad tycoons, Wall Street financiers, and titans of industry, even as those businesses grew, and combined, and wielded ever-increasing power over Americans' lives. It would be up to future Republicans—most notably the eldest son, Theodore Jr., of a prominent New York City businessman and philanthropist named Theodore Roosevelt—to restore the balance.

At times, even Weed himself seemed to question the morality of what he did. He wanted obedience but also respect, and it cut him deeply when prominent men denied him the latter. "I do not dislike Mr. Barnard, personally though we differ so widely in political sentiment and sympathy," Weed wrote to Hamilton Fish, who served as New York's governor, a US senator, and later President Ulysses S. Grant's secretary of state. "My difficulty is that he puts me so low down in his scale of political morality (rightly enough, perhaps, for we are compelled to do things that will not bear a blaze of light to elect to office even as good men as he is) that I do not feel fit for his society. But I wish him nothing but happiness and I would not cross his path with a straw." When a rift opened between Weed and Fish, the boss lamented that sometimes he mistook political allegiance for actual friendship. "There is no course left but school myself into the belief that I have never understood the motives that governed me; and henceforth 'to see myself as others see me.' And yet it would have been more agreeable, in one's old age, to feel that life had not been wholly wasted."

For his part, Chester Arthur embraced Weed's approach to politics. He marveled at the Wizard's organizational genius, noting that his plans extended to the smallest details and were carried out to the letter. On election days, Arthur watched in awe as "heelers" broke up lines of opposing voters—sometimes poking them with awls to disperse them—and flagrantly stuffed ballot boxes. The tactics were simple, effective, and wholly acceptable; this was simply how the game was played.

• ◆ •

The Herndons of Fredericksburg, Virginia, were still mourning their brother William's death aboard the *Central America* when the captain's widow and daughter came to visit in February 1858. "There is but one subject of thought and conversation among us. Visions of the dreadful scene present themselves day & night," William's brother, Brodie Herndon, a physician and father of eight, recorded in his diary. The grieving family found consolation in the public recognition of Captain Herndon's heroism—and in their religious faith. "The NY Herald said, 'The loss of such an officer was itself a national calamity,'" Brodie wrote. "Oh, we shall surely meet again dear sweet brother! The memory of thee shall ever be very precious."

Dr. Herndon noted that his sister-in-law and niece were "overwhelmed with grief," but that "their friends in NY are very kind." One of those "friends," Nell's fiancé, Chester, accompanied the two women on the journey to their ancestral home in Virginia. Steam travel, whether by water or by land, had made such visits commonplace, and Southern families such as the Herndons maintained close ties with faraway cousins, uncles, and aunts. The increasing ease of travel made it possible for Dr. Herndon to send his son Dabney to New York to study, while his daughters often went to Savannah to visit relatives there.

When Arthur passed the row of silver maples in front of 623 Caroline Street and walked through the front gate with its sturdy locust posts, he crossed into foreign territory. The Herndon household owned seven slaves, ranging in age from 12 to 53. There was a "slave house" in the back, and when one of the slave women became pregnant, the younger Herndon girls argued about whose maid the baby would be. The son of the abolitionist preacher had never been to the South, and it was jarring to see Nell and her mother being served by slaves. Chester shared his father's opposition to slavery, but those feelings were overshadowed by his love for Nell, and by his determination to impress her blueblood relatives. During his two weeks in Fredericksburg, Arthur either kept his antislavery sentiments to himself or expressed them tactfully enough that he avoided offending his hosts. "He is a fine looking man and we all like him very much," Dr. Herndon wrote in his diary.

Less than a year later, in October 1859, the Virginians came north for Nell and Chester's wedding at the Calvary Episcopal Church on Park Avenue in Manhattan. The newlyweds began their life together in a home owned by the bride's mother, at 34 West 21st Street. In December 1860, Chester sent a jubilant message to his own relatives in upstate New York: he and Nell were parents. "Lewis Herndon Arthur aged 4 ½ hours sends his compliments to his cousin Arthur and other kin folks in Cohoes & has only time to say further that his mother is doing better than could be expected and his father will send further advice tomorrow."

• ◆ •

In his quest for connections Arthur also joined the New York state militia, and was commissioned judge advocate of the 2nd Brigade. This experience, together with his Republican labors and the influence of friends, led to Arthur's first real break in politics—and a valuable, lifelong alliance with another leading Republican, Edwin D. Morgan.

Morgan was born in 1811 into modest circumstances in Connecticut, and he began his career as a Hartford grocer. But Morgan was ambitious, and when he was in his mid-20s he moved to New York City. In the metropolis he rapidly transformed himself into a prosperous wholesaler, banker, and broker with interests that extended throughout North America to Brazil and China. Morgan owned ships and invested in real estate, railroads, public utilities, banks, and insurance companies.

Morgan began his political career as a Whig, serving first as a New York City alderman and then as a state senator. In 1856, a year after switching to the Republicans, he became chairman of the Republican National Committee. He was a handsome man, with an aquiline nose and a narrow head covered with stiff brown hair. His morose expression masked an energetic personality, a firm sense of duty, and an ability to quickly grasp the essence of a problem. As a politician he was a poor orator but a natural organizer, and he skillfully melded local interests and factions into a unified national party during the Republicans' first decade.

When New York Republicans convened in 1858 to choose a nominee for governor, Weed had no doubt who would be the strongest choice. Morgan had limited experience in elected office, but he brought other advantages that more than compensated for that deficiency. "One of Mr. Weed's arguments was that the Democrats were in power everywhere and could assess their office holders, while the Republicans would have to rely for campaign funds upon voluntary contributions, which would come nowhere so freely as from Mr. Morgan and his friends," one delegate remembered. "When the convention met Mr. Weed had won over a large majority of the delegates for his candidate. It was a triumph not only of his skill but of his magnetism, which were always successfully exerted upon a doubtful member."

Morgan won the nomination and the election, and in 1860 he was reelected to a second two-year term. Soon afterward, he formed a new "general staff," a corps of young men outfitted in uniforms and gold braid whose job was to appear martial at public ceremonies. In fact the corps had no military function; it was purely decorative. Weed told Morgan he had a perfect candidate for the corps: a young Republican attorney, uncommonly handsome, who stood taller than six feet and exuded a confidence and dignity unusual in a man his age. On the first day of 1861, Morgan invited Chester Arthur to join the group.

At first, Arthur's job was purely ornamental. Soon it turned deadly serious.

CHAPTER FIVE

Barracks and Blankets

N O SOLDIERS SNAPPED to attention and no musicians struck up a patriotic tune as the brightly decorated locomotive arrived in a gush of steam and clanging bells. The throngs of ordinary New Yorkers at the Hudson River Railroad depot in Manhattan surged forward to catch a glimpse of the president-elect, but New York City had not prepared an official welcome. There were no drums, uniforms, or speeches to detain Abraham Lincoln.

After a hurried walk through the depot and "a five-minute delay for an inscrutable something about the baggage," Lincoln's cortege was ready to depart. The roughly six thousand people who had been waiting for hours on 30th Street and Tenth Avenue let out a cheer and those watching from the windows waved white handkerchiefs. Climbing into a barouche, Lincoln gracefully raised his stovepipe hat to acknowledge them. Whips cracked beside the horses and the double line of carriages headed downtown. The procession turned left at 23rd Street, then right onto Fifth Avenue. At Union Square, the columns slanted onto Broadway. The avenue had been cleared of vehicles, and the formation traveled toward the Astor House in perfect order. The people crowded the side streets, doors, balconies, and windows and lined the roofs of the buildings on either side of Broadway to gain a clear view of the man who had pledged to save the Union. They, too, were waving white handkerchiefs—so many the *New York Illustrated News* claimed Lincoln "moved forward on the white bosom of a huge linen billow of colossal dimensions."

It was February 19, 1861, and the president-elect had stopped in New York on his way to Washington for his March 4 inauguration. The previous December, South Carolina had seceded. By February 1, Mississippi, Florida,

Alabama, Georgia, Louisiana, and Texas had left, too, but the conflict had not yet turned violent. Many, perhaps most, New Yorkers were hoping Lincoln would reach a deal with the South to avoid bloodshed.

Diarist George Templeton Strong saw the procession as it passed St. Thomas Church, with an "escort of mounted policemen and a torrent of ragtag and bobtail rushing and hooraying behind." Strong glimpsed the face of "the great rail-splitter" and thought it keen, clear, honest, and not nearly as ugly as it appeared in portraits. Without the omnibuses and other vehicles that usually roared up and down Broadway, there was an unusual hush as several of the barouches drew up to the Astor House entrance. Lincoln unfurled himself from one of them. He paused on the sidewalk, gazed up at the looming granite walls of the old hotel, and stretched his arms and legs. He was dressed entirely in black, and his hat was pushed back on his head, revealing a thatch of dark, bushy hair. Holding his hands behind him, he turned around and scanned the crowd for a minute with a bemused look on his wrinkled brown face.

Walt Whitman was on top of an omnibus that had been pulled over to the side of the street to let Lincoln's procession pass. From that vantage point, the poet had "a capital view of it all, and especially of Mr. Lincoln, his look and gait—his perfect composure and coolness—his unusual and uncouth height." Whitman had been on Broadway when New York welcomed Lafayette, Andrew Jackson, and the Prince of Wales. On those occasions, the great avenue had reverberated with "the glad exulting thunder-shouts of countless unloos'd throats of men." This time, it was cloaked in an eerie silence. "The crowd that hemm'd around consisted I should think of thirty to forty thousand men, not a single one his friend—while I have no doubt (so frenzied were the ferments of the time), many an assassin's knife and pistol lurk'd in hip or breast pocket there, ready, soon as break and riot came," Whitman recalled. "But no break or riot came. The tall figure gave another relieving stretch or two of arms and legs; then with moderate pace, and accompanied by a few unknown looking persons, ascended the portico-steps of the Astor House, disappear'd through its broad entrance—and the dumb-show ended."

Early the next morning, Thurlow Weed took Lincoln to the Fifth Avenue home of the daughter of a prominent New York shipping magnate named Moses Grinnell. There the president-elect had breakfast with about a hundred of the city's most prosperous merchants, some of them leading Republican proponents of compromise with the secessionists. Many members of New York's business community were in no hurry to sever their lucrative ties with the South. One breakfast attendee pointed out to Lincoln that there were numerous millionaires in the group, a less than subtle reference to New York's financial clout. But the president-elect would not be intimidated. "Oh, indeed, is that so?" he replied. "Well, that's quite right. I'm a millionaire myself. I got a minority of a million in the votes last November." (Lincoln actually got nearly 1.9 million votes—less than a majority but enough to defeat the three other candidates.)

Later in the day, Lincoln delivered brief remarks to Democratic Mayor Fernando Wood and the City Council before a huge crowd at City Hall, while Mary Lincoln visited Barnum's museum and received ladies at the Astor House. That night, after an elaborate dinner and reception, Lincoln attended a performance of Giuseppe Verdi's new *A Masked Ball* at the Academy of Music. Lincoln arrived shortly after the curtain rose, causing a stir in the house as "one thousand opera glasses turned in one direction." When the lights went up for intermission, the president-elect acknowledged the shouted cries of "Lincoln!" by rising from his seat and bowing. A reporter in attendance described the initial expression on Lincoln's face as "stern, rugged and uncompromising." But then Lincoln smiled, and the reporter felt confident that "justice would be tempered with mercy and stern principle would be leavened with that wisdom which springs from a knowledge of the human heart."

Several months later, Whitman also went to see Verdi's *A Masked Ball*. The performance ended around midnight, and the poet was walking down Broadway on his way back home to Brooklyn when he heard the loud cries of the newsboys, who were "rushing from side to side even more furiously than usual." Whitman bought a paper and strode across Broadway so he could read it under the gaslights of the Metropolitan Hotel: Confederate batteries had opened fire on Fort Sumter at dawn that morning. The Civil War had begun.

•◆•

On Monday, April 15, 1861, President Lincoln proclaimed that there was an insurrection in the South and called for 75,000 loyal Union men to crush it. Recruiting and equipping those troops would be up to individual states. Each governor oversaw his own war department, and the federal government took control of the regiments formed by each state only when they had reached full strength and had a proper complement of officers. On April 16, the New York Legislature approved $3 million to recruit, arm, and equip 30,000 troops for two years of service. Before the end of the month,

Governor Morgan ordered the creation of 38 New York regiments, each with 780 men, to be mustered in New York City, Albany, and Elmira.

New York's business community, cool to the cause before Fort Sumter, now rallied behind Lincoln and the Union. In the weeks immediately following the attack on Fort Sumter, the city's leading merchants helped launch a Union Defense Committee charged with organizing volunteer regiments, providing local relief to the wives and children of soldiers, and supplying the army with equipment. Impressed by the New Yorkers' efforts, Lincoln transferred $2 million in federal money to the committee. New York was designated as the headquarters of the army's Department of the East, and four military depots were established to process recruits.

The business community's change of heart corresponded with an outpouring of popular enthusiasm. Hundreds of thousands of shouting and singing people attended rallies in Union Square. Still in their civilian clothes, recruits paraded up and down Broadway in front of cheering multitudes. It seemed that the Stars and Stripes hung from every window in the city, and every vehicle—from omnibuses to common horse carts—was decked out in red, white, and blue. "The battle cry was sounded from almost every pulpit—flag-raisings took place in every square . . . and the oath was taken to trample Secession under foot, and to quench the fire of the Southern heart forever," wrote William Howard Russell, a correspondent for the *London Times*.

The challenge for Governor Morgan was to channel that popular enthusiasm into the recruitment of real soldiers, trained and equipped for battle. For that, he turned to Arthur. Morgan made the young lawyer a brigadier general and assigned him to be the state quartermaster general's New York City representative. Arthur would be responsible for feeding, housing, clothing, and equipping thousands of enlisted men, not only from the city but thousands from New England, too, since regiments from that region were streaming into New York on their way south. From his second-floor office in a large military storehouse at 51 Walker Street, Arthur awarded contracts, audited expenditures, and quickly became an expert in rations, blankets, ammunition, and underwear.

State regulations prescribed the uniform of the New York militiaman: he was to wear a dark blue jacket, cut to flow from the waist and to fall four inches below the belt; sky blue trousers; a sky blue overcoat; and a dark blue cap with a waterproof cover with a cape attached. Each soldier was issued two flannel shirts, two pairs of flannel underwear, two pairs of woolen socks, one pair of pegged-sole cowhide shoes, and one double Mackinaw blanket. But the sudden demand for military uniforms and other supplies soon exhausted the existing stocks, and the private firms that were supposed to manufacture more struggled to fulfill their contracts. Inevitably, this led to corner cutting. Brooks Brothers had a contract to furnish 12,000 New York uniforms—jacket, trousers, and overcoat—at a cost of $19.50 per uniform. But army-grade wool was scarce, so the firm made 7,300 of the uniforms using an imitation satin that not only failed to protect the soldiers from the elements, but literally disintegrated in the first rain. The New York Assembly ended up hauling the Brooks brothers—Daniel, John, Elisha, and Edward—before an investigative committee. Procuring high-quality blankets was similarly difficult, as some contractors saved money by using hemp and cotton instead of pure wool.

Finding enough housing for the growing number of troops in the city was another vexing problem that Arthur had to solve. At the beginning of the war, military authorities relied on local citizens to volunteer their buildings. When that quickly proved to be inadequate, Arthur supervised the construction of temporary barracks in Central Park and on Staten Island, Riker's Island, and Long Island.

Then there were the soldiers themselves. After New York's initial 38 regiments were recruited, all sorts of adventurers managed to procure commissions to raise troops. One of the most colorful was former boxer and Democratic alderman Billy Wilson.

Many members of Wilson's 6th New York Regiment were Irish immigrants he had wrangled at a dog-fighting and rat-baiting house on White Street in the Five Points. Some of Wilson's recruits wanted to risk their lives for the Union to undercut the nativist argument that Irish Catholics were unworthy of American citizenship, while others sought escape from the city's dismal slums. Many of "Billy Wilson's Boys," unable to foresee the years of slaughter to come, viewed the war as a lark, a glorified street brawl that would be over in a matter of weeks. Before departing for their encampment on Staten Island, Colonel Wilson formally mustered his men at Tammany Hall. As uniforms, he had given them gray shirts and pants, brown felt hats, brogans, and leather belts, and each man was armed with a seven-inch knife, a slungshot, a Minnie rifle, and either one or two revolvers. Holding a saber in one hand and the American flag in the other, Wilson knelt on the floor and led his men in a pledge to support the flag, and "never flinch from its path through blood or death." When Wilson said he would lead the regiment to secessionist Baltimore and march through the city or die trying, the men sprang to their feet and flung their hats in the air, shouting "Death to the secessionists! Death to the traitors!" They also swore to vanquish the "Plug Uglies," a notorious Baltimore street gang. Slashing the air with his sword, Wilson vowed that the regiment would "leave a monument of their bones in the streets of Baltimore."

Encamped on Staten Island, Billy Wilson's Boys scrapped with other regiments, plundered local restaurants, and drank prodigiously. When restaurant owners appealed to Morgan for relief, the governor ordered Arthur to rein in Wilson and his rowdy regiment. A short time later, Wilson strutted into Arthur's Walker Street office wearing his colonel's uniform. When Arthur delivered Morgan's message, Wilson was irate. "Neither you nor the governor has anything to do with me," he shouted. "I am a colonel in the United States service, and you've got no right to order me."

"You are not a colonel," Arthur replied calmly, "and you will not be until you have raised your quota of men and received your commission."

"Well, I've got my shoulder-straps, anyway, and as long as I wear them, I don't want any orders from any of you fellows."

At this, General Arthur bolted from his chair, ripped the straps from Wilson's shoulders, and had the insubordinate colonel placed under arrest.

Arthur also had to bring the "Fire Zouaves" to heel. Led by Colonel Elmer Ellsworth, a personal friend of President Lincoln's, the 11th New York Regiment drew its men from the ranks of the city's many volunteer fire companies. The regiment got its nickname from its uniforms, which were inspired by the Franco-Algerian Zouaves. Like their North African counterparts, the Fire Zouaves wore red billowing trousers, loose tunics, sashes, and turbans. Unlike the Algerians, the New Yorkers were fond of breaking into taverns and charging restaurant meals to Jefferson Davis. One day the men refused to obey Ellsworth's order to unpack their muskets, and the colonel appealed to Arthur for help. The general, accompanied by several policemen, visited the regiment's headquarters on Canal Street and had the ringleaders arrested.

Arthur performed his job so well that in February of 1862, Morgan made him inspector general. In July 1862 Morgan promoted Arthur again, this time to quartermaster general for the state of New York. Arthur's responsibilities broadened: he inspected forts and defenses throughout New York, and helped come up with a plan to block New York harbor in the event of an attack by the British navy, which seemed likely for a time after a Union warship removed two Confederate emissaries from a British vessel. He assigned a quartermaster to each New York regiment and brought the men to Manhattan to learn the intricacies of that vital position. To save state money, he used enlisted men to construct more than two hundred temporary barracks and forged special contracts with the railroads to transport troops to the front. Between August and December, Arthur's office clothed, equipped, and transported to the front 68 infantry regiments, two cavalry battalions, and four battalions and ten batteries of artillery. Morgan called Arthur "my chief reliance in the duties of equipping and transporting troops and munitions of war." During a time when many used their positions of influence to reap personal profits, Morgan praised Arthur for displaying "not only great executive ability and unbending integrity, but great knowledge of Army Regulations. He can say No (which is important) without giving offence."

Arthur's service for the Union did not sit well with everybody. His mother-in-law was openly sympathetic to the South—fortunately, she spent much of the war in Europe. Several of Nell's Southern relatives, including Dr. Brodie Herndon and two of his sons, Chester's close friend Dabney and Brodie Jr., enlisted in the Confederate army. It was difficult for the Herndons of Fredericksburg to reconcile their warm memories of the polite young man they had welcomed into their home with their burning hatred of the Union soldiers who had invaded their homeland. "Mr. Arthur is an officer in Lincoln's army. How the people here do abuse him," Dr. Herndon wrote in his diary in 1861.

In the spring of 1862, Union troops occupied Fredericksburg, forcing residents to endure the humiliation of blue-coated Yankees walking their streets. "We can hear nothing from our army or our friends, nothing which might tend in some measure to alleviate the affliction under which we are sorrowing," one of the Herndons' neighbors wrote in her diary in the middle of May. "We are shut in by the enemy on all sides and even the comforts of life are many of them cut off, no one is allowed even to bring wood to town and we know not how we are to be supplied with the means of cooking the small amount of food we can procure."

Around the same time, Arthur traveled to Fredericksburg to review the Union troops stationed there. Though it must have been uncomfortable, he paid a visit to his wife's relatives to see how they were holding up. Arthur "was very affectionate & kind. He thought we might be suffering and delicately proffered aid. We told him we forgot the General in the man," Dr. Herndon wrote in his diary. But a cousin by marriage whose house had been ransacked by the Yankees wasn't so forgiving. Upon seeing Arthur she "tossed her head, and with nose in air turned away from him . . . and walked away."

Arthur's sister Malvina also lived in Virginia while Arthur was serving in the New York militia. Malvina met her husband, Henry Haynesworth, a South Carolinian, when she took a teaching job in the South in 1854. Now Henry was a Confederate civil servant stationed in Petersburg.

Relations with Malvina and the Herndons were challenging enough; Arthur also had to navigate perilous shoals at home, where his own wife was a quiet but steadfast Confederate sympathizer.

The Arthurs and their infant son were living in a plush two-story family hotel near 22nd and Broadway, and they often entertained guests after Arthur returned from his work on Walker Street. Nell was a graceful and charming hostess, and Chester tried to lighten the mood by joking about his "little rebel wife," but there was a chill in the household the couple could not conceal from their visitors. Silas Burt, a frequent guest during this period, thought that Nell almost surely shared her mother's sympathies "but she certainly suppressed them at most times and was loyal to her husband's position and views." He remembered, however, "one or two passages between them that indicated much friction and probably heat in their respective relations to the war. Mrs. Arthur was in a cruel position during those dreadful four years—her husband prominent in the effort to subdue her kindred while she herself was the only child of a widow whose feelings were strongly enlisted for the rebels."

When Nell's beloved cousin "Dab" Herndon was captured, she asked Chester's permission to visit him at the Union prison camp on Davids' Island in Long Island Sound. Another Herndon cousin was wounded, while a third went missing in battle and was never found.

• ◆ •

The war was not going well for the Union in the fall of 1862. Tens of thousands had been killed or maimed at Shiloh, Seven Days, Second Bull Run, and Antietam. A series of defeats in the East overshadowed some scattered victories in the West, and the eruption of public enthusiasm that followed the attack on Fort Sumter dissipated. Strong confided to his diary that in New York "traitors" were "now beginning cautiously to tamper with the great torrent of national feeling that burst out in April 1861."

In November, voters in New York and other key Northern states registered their discontent with the ruling Republicans at the ballot box. Morgan, who had his eye on a US Senate seat, declined to run again for governor, and Democrat Horatio Seymour narrowly defeated the GOP candidate chosen to succeed him. The Democrats won every statewide position on the New

York ballot and half the seats in the State Assembly. When Seymour took office on January 1, 1863, Morgan and his staff, including Arthur, lost their military commissions.

Though Arthur could have volunteered to fight, he didn't. One reason was that Seymour was unlikely to give him a commission as high-ranking as the one he was being forced to give up. Family tension was another deterrent, and like many conservative Republicans, Arthur seems to have been disenchanted with the Lincoln administration's shifting justifications for the war. Conservative Republicans like Arthur took their cue from the *New York Times*. "Slavery has nothing whatever to do with the tremendous issues now awaiting decision," the paper argued. "The issue is between anarchy and order,—between Government and lawlessness,—between the authority of the Constitution and the reckless will of those who seek its destruction." But Lincoln was gravitating toward the Radical Republican view that the primary aim of the war should be to end slavery. Military defeats, increasing debts, and the threat of a draft led many New Yorkers to question whether that goal was worth fighting for.

But there was another factor dissuading Arthur from reenlisting: he wanted to get rich. Nell was socially ambitious, and to play a role in high society, like her mother, she had to live in a fine home with servants. Arthur shared his wife's aspirations, and as a high-ranking officer in the militia, he had begun to cultivate some expensive tastes. An old college friend noted that Arthur took "great interest in matters of dress and [was] always neat and tasteful in his attire. . . . He loved the pleasures of the table and had an extraordinary power of digestion and could carry a great deal of wine and liquor without any manifest effect other than greater vivacity of speech." Arthur's military service had given him an array of useful contacts, and he had become an expert in supplies, contracts, and military law. Many people with similar skills and experience were making fortunes. Arthur set out to do the same.

CHAPTER SIX

The Shoddy Aristocracy

ARLY IN THE evenings, they put on velvet coats and convened around the curved mahogany bar at the Astor House. Beneath a blanket of cigar smoke, they haggled over boots and bullets, caps and carriages, with lips slickened by beer foam and roasted meat. They dined at Delmonico's, where partridge stuffed with truffles—a house specialty—cost a sum that could support a soldier and his family for a year. Afterward they headed to the theater, or to one of the city's six hundred brothels, which operated so openly the madams of the finest houses were featured prominently in the penny press and New York guidebooks.

Their wives, cocooned in mink and sable, passed the days at the milliner's or at department stores. As the ladies promenaded down Fifth Avenue or Broadway, many protected their silk gowns from the slush and mud with Mme. Demorest's Imperial "dress-elevator," a popular contraption with weighted strings that allowed the women to raise or lower their skirts. On Sundays the prosperous couples circled Central Park in gleaming carriages, sporting thousand-dollar camel's hair shawls purchased at Stewart's.

The demand for such shawls was "monstrous," and why not? Nearly every city industry was being stoked by war contracts, and while young men were being slaughtered on the battlefield, contractors and speculators in New York were getting rich. The need for soldiers' uniforms and a steep tariff on imported clothing boosted the garment industry. The city's ironworks flourished by filling the navy's orders for vertical and horizontal engines, boilers, furnaces, plates, and anchors. Cooper, Hewitt & Co. turned out gun carriages and gun-barrel iron. The Enterprise Rubber Works prospered on orders for hard rubber flasks, cups, and buttons. The city's carriage makers were producing hundreds of ambulances and baggage wagons. Before the war there had been a few dozen millionaires in New York. By the end of it, there were several hundred. "Things here at the North are in a great state of prosperity. You can have no idea of it," the successful New York merchant William Dodge wrote to a friend in England in 1863. "The large amount expended by the government has given activity to everything and but for the daily news from the War in the papers and the crowds of soldiers you see about the streets you would have no idea of any war. Our streets are crowded, hotels full, the railroads, manufacturers of all kind except cotton were never doing so well and business generally is active."

Dodge might have been proud of his city's resourcefulness, but many others were appalled by the "shoddy aristocracy" created by the provision of substandard supplies to Union troops. In July 1864, *Harper's Monthly* denounced the contractors and speculators who were profiting from the carnage. "It is in our large cities especially where this boasted insensibility to the havoc of war is found. It is there in the marketplace and exchange, where fortunes are being made with such marvelous rapidity, and in the haunts of pleasure, where they are being spent with such wanton extravagance, that *they don't feel this war*," the author lamented. "They are at a banquet of abundance and delight, from which they are not to be unseated, though the ghosts of the hundreds of thousands of their slaughtered countrymen shake their gory locks at them."

Chester Arthur wanted to claim a seat at that banquet. His time as quartermaster had made him an expert on military supplies and government contracts, and in 1863 his political patron Edwin Morgan became a US senator. Arthur cashed in on his knowledge and connections by lobbying for clients seeking government contracts in Washington and Albany. He reunited with his friend Henry Gardiner, and their firm "became celebrated for the speed with which it could draft and put through legislative bills." Arthur also collected lobbying fees from R. G. Dun, the owner of the Mercantile Agency, the nation's first credit reporting firm. With his ballooning income Arthur purchased a brownstone row house at 123 Lexington Avenue, between East 28th and 29th Streets. It was five stories high, with cast iron railings that rose along the wide brownstone stoop before turning to form balconies at the parlor windows. Nell filled the house with the finest furniture and accessories, and Chester hired a staff of Irish immigrant servants. The young couple finally had a home suitable for lavish entertaining.

Elder Arthur, the Irish immigrant preacher, might have made a biting remark or two about his son's servants, had the two men communicated more often. But their relationship turned chilly during the war. Chester's parents were pressed for money, but their lawyer son didn't volunteer to help them, and he rarely visited. Religion played a role in their estrangement. Unlike several of their older sisters, Chester and his younger brother William, a major in the 4th New York Volunteer Artillery, rejected the fervid faith of their parents. Sometimes Chester attended a local Episcopal church with Nell—that is what proper people did. But his life in Manhattan—the lavish parties, the extravagant meals, and the mad scramble for wealth and status—mocked Elder Arthur's backwoods fundamentalism. "Dear Son, how long will you live in rebellion against God and refuse to obey his commandments?" Malvina Arthur wrote to William in January 1863. "O that God would answer this my prayer, that before I am taken from life, you and Chester may come out publickly [sic], confess Christ, and be willing to be fools, for his sake. I know that he will lead you to everlasting life and glory if you are willing."

◆

On the muggy morning of July 8, 1863, Northern newspapers triumphantly detailed the Union's bloody victory at Gettysburg the week before. "The enemy, by a partially secret and ignominious retreat, has awarded to this gallant army the acknowledgment of victory. His forces are now on their way back to Virginia, beaten, weakened and demoralized by a terrible defeat; he is hotly pursued, a victorious army on his rear, a strong local force on his flank, and a swollen river in his front, are the obstacles to his successful retreat," a *New York Times* correspondent wrote. The same day, the papers confirmed that after an 11-day siege, Union troops under the command of General Ulysses S. Grant had taken the Confederate stronghold of Vicksburg. This second triumph handed control of the Mississippi River to the Union, a vital strategic advantage. The fall of Vicksburg, according to the *Times*, was "the crowning sheaf in the full harvest of Independence Day Victories."

But the piercing rays of those triumphs—signs that the war might finally be turning in the Union's favor—could not penetrate the black night that had enveloped Chester and Nell. At 6 a.m. that morning, as early risers in the North read the encouraging news from Pennsylvania and Mississippi, William Lewis Herndon Arthur died from a mysterious illness. He was only two and a half years old. "We have lost our darling boy," Chester wrote to his brother William. "He died yesterday at Englewood, N.J., where we were staying for a few weeks—from convulsions, brought on by some affection of the brain. It came upon us so unexpectedly and suddenly. Nell is broken hearted. I fear much for her health. You know how her heart was wrapped up in her dear boy."* Arthur, a sensitive and emotional man, was crushed by his son's death. His consuming grief was compounded by guilt, since he and Nell were convinced the boy had fallen ill because they had overtaxed his brain with intellectual demands. When they had a second son, Chester II (who would be known as "Alan") in July 1864, the Arthurs indulged him lavishly to prevent a recurrence of the tragedy.

A month after they became parents for the second time, the Arthurs' happiness was dampened by frightening news from Virginia: Chester's brother, William, had been shot and seriously wounded at Ream's Station while commanding a battalion of artillery. The young major was transported to Seminary Hospital in Washington, and Chester rushed there to visit him.

The red-brick hospital, one of more than 50 that treated wounded soldiers in the capital, was a converted women's seminary at the rear of the Union Hotel in Georgetown. Sitting at the bedside of his ailing brother, Chester could hear long trains of army wagons rumbling by on N Street. Glancing out the window, he could see surgeons in passing ambulances attending to the wounded. Other vehicles were crammed with amputees on their way to be fitted for artificial limbs, or were stacked with rough coffins. Barouches with wounded officers rolled by, followed by carriages "loaded with pretty children with black coachmen, footmen, and maids." "[William] is hit in the face, the ball entering the right side of the cheek just above the upper lip—passing straight through and coming out at the back of the head. I cannot see why it did not kill him outright but think it must have been a ball from a hunting rifle—the hole it made being very small," Chester reported in a letter to his sister Mary. "He suffers greatly from the matter running from the wound internally which chokes him and makes him constantly uncomfortable."

The bullet damaged William's hearing—he was left almost totally deaf—and dug a jagged scar across his face, but he survived. When William was well enough to leave the hospital, Chester accompanied him to New York to help him settle into a new life. Chester reached out to Edwin Morgan for help, and the senator helped secure a commission in the regular army for his protégé's brother.

---

*It was typical for a man of Arthur's time to focus on his wife's feelings and to downplay his own—strong emotions were the province of women, not gentlemen. Arthur and his contemporaries had a more intimate relationship with death than twenty-first-century Americans do. People died at home, not in hospitals, and often at young ages.

By this time, Arthur had become so disenchanted with the Lincoln administration he was "almost a copperhead" and "would not vote at all rather than vote for Lincoln for next President," according to one of his sisters. During the summer of 1864 the Confederates showed they had plenty of fight left in them, despite their crushing defeats at Gettysburg and Vicksburg. In July, Confederate troops under the command of Lieutenant General Jubal Early came within five miles of the White House, firing on Fort Stevens in Northwest Washington as Lincoln watched from the parapet. The Confederates killed, wounded, or captured more than 65,000 Union soldiers during that bloody summer, compared to 108,000 Union casualties during the first three years of the war. The horrifying losses resulted in a new nickname for General Grant, who was now the commander of all Union forces: "The Butcher." The depressing developments on the battlefield convinced many in the North that it was time to elect a president who would make peace with the South.

Arthur's own doubts about the war eased his conscience as he hustled to profit from it. As Lincoln fretted over his dimming reelection prospects, Arthur took on a new lobbying client: a New York hatter named Thomas Murphy, who hired Arthur to represent him in Washington. Murphy had been accused of delivering inferior hats and caps to Union troops, and Arthur's patron Edwin Morgan happened to sit on the special Senate committee investigating the matter. Arthur's work on behalf of his unscrupulous client blossomed into a personal friendship, and the two men became partners in several real estate speculations.

In November 1864 Lincoln won a second term, his fortunes boosted by Northern elation over the fall of Atlanta two months before. His defeated Democratic opponent was George McClellan, a former Union general running on a "peace platform" that promised a truce with the Confederacy (though McClellan earlier had repudiated that position). This time Lincoln won 55 percent of the popular vote and 212 of 233 electoral votes—a landslide.

In New York, the Union ticket swept the Democrats in the contests for governor and other statewide offices, but the results were much tighter: a razor-thin margin of just 8,000 votes out of 730,000. The state election was notable for an important innovation in campaign finance: it was the first in which Republicans relied heavily on financial contributions from government employees and contractors to bolster their candidates. Morgan played an important role as head of the Republicans' Union Executive Committee, charged with collecting assessments from postmasters and other appointees who owed a political debt to the party. Morgan tapped Arthur and Murphy to collect the assessments and to gather donations from their wealthy contractor friends.

•—◆—•

Six months after the elections, on April 3, 1865, George Templeton Strong was walking down Wall Street when he caught sight of a brief announcement on the bulletin board of the *Commercial Advertiser*: "Petersburg is taken." Desperate for details, Strong rushed inside the newspaper office to find a man behind the counter, slowly painting an update on a large sheet of brown paper. "Richmond is . . . " the man had written. "What's that about Richmond?" Strong demanded. Without answering, the man continued to write. Slowly, a capital "C" appeared on the paper, then a capital "A." Suddenly Strong saw what the man was writing: "Captured!"

As word spread that the Confederate capital had fallen, throngs of people descended on Wall Street, cheering and singing patriotic songs. They belted out "Old Hundred" and "John Brown" and "The Star-Spangled Banner," repeating the last two lines of Francis Scott Key's song (which had not yet become the national anthem) again and again. Each time they finished it, they let loose a massive roar and waved their hats in unison. Men embraced, kissed each other, and then retreated into doorways to dry their eyes before returning to the celebration. On April 9, Lee surrendered the Army of Northern Virginia to Grant in the McLean House in the village of Appomattox Court House. The Civil War was over.

Less than a week later, the jubilation turned to shock, grief, and rage. "O, fatal day. O, noble Victim. Treason has done its worst," Horatio Nelson Taft, a US Patent Office examiner, wrote in his diary late on the night of April 14, 1865. "The President has been Assassinated. It has just been announced at my door that he was shot a half hour ago at Fords Theatre. Is it possible? I have just come from near the scene, it is too True." In the 10 days following Lincoln's death, New York stopped: shops closed and residents and business owners draped black and white muslin around every column and façade, "so that hardly a building on Wall Street, Broadway, Chambers Street, Bowery, Fourth Avenue [was] without its symbol of the profound public sorrow." People pinned rosettes to their windows, and even the poorest households displayed tiny twenty-five-cent flags with scraps of crape attached. "Never, I think, has sorrow for a leader been displayed on so great a scale and so profoundly felt," Strong wrote in his diary. "It is very noteworthy that the number of arrests for drunkenness and disorder during the week that followed Lincoln's murder was less than in any week for very many years!" The mood was somber, but fury bubbled underneath the placid surface: many New Yorkers who had expressed pity for their defeated Southern brethren when Lee surrendered—some had even called for a general amnesty—now demanded to see leading rebels dangling from the hangman's noose.

With the approach of summer, returning Union veterans began streaming into the city. Some came by sea, but most rode trains to Jersey City and then took the ferry to Manhattan. They landed near the open space by the Battery and marched uptown with yapping dogs—company mascots—trailing behind them. Some of the men wore "wide-awake" military caps, while others donned simple straw hats. But even those who had changed into civilian clothes were immediately recognizable by their knapsacks, bronzed faces, and loud talk. Raucous crowds cheered the return of famous units such as the 90th Illinois Volunteer Infantry, better known as the Irish Legion. The homecoming of the 52nd New York Infantry Regiment, made up almost entirely of German immigrants, was more sobering: of the 2,600 men who had been on its muster rolls, only 300 returned.

Lucrative military contracts vanished with the war's end, but the friendship between Arthur and the hatter Thomas Murphy deepened. In November of 1865, Arthur helped Murphy win election to the New York Senate from a predominantly Democratic district. Murphy's 39th Street home became the de facto headquarters of New York's conservative Republicans. To Nell's consternation, Chester was there almost every night, smoking cigars, drinking whiskey, and talking politics into the early morning hours. He was stimulating company, always ready with a humorous story or apt limerick. "Sooner or later, but always unfailing, was the well-known ring and footstep of General Arthur, as we used to call him," recalled another frequent visitor to Murphy's house. "Always smiling and affectionate in manner toward his friends, and apparently attached to Mr. Murphy's family as though they were his nearest and dearest relatives." After long nights at Murphy's house Arthur typically slept in, arriving late or not at all to his law office. He set up an office in his home so at odd hours he could make up the legal work he was missing.

Arthur made valuable connections at Murphy's house. Charles Folger was a moody state senator from Geneva who chaired the powerful judiciary committee and often spent the entire weekend at the Murphy residence. Another regular was Richard Crowley, a state senator from Lockport and one of Folger's closest friends. General George Sharpe, the head of the Bureau of Military Information during the war, became a special agent of the US State Department, which sent him to Europe in 1867 in search of Americans who might have been involved in the Lincoln assassination. Alonzo B. Cornell, son of the university founder, was a member of the Republican state committee who helped oversee the construction of the new state capitol at Albany and ran unsuccessfully for lieutenant governor in 1868.

The late nights of eating and drinking added pounds to Arthur's large frame, and gave his cheeks a ruddy color. But those changes were less profound than the effects the long nights had on his political outlook—and on his character. The country faced great questions in the aftermath of the Civil War—the reunification of North and South; race relations and civil rights for the freed slaves; rapid industrialization and the growing economic and political power of large corporations. Arthur and the other men who convened nightly at the Murphy house were intensely interested in politics, but it was the pursuit and maintenance of political power that animated their discussions, not the ways in which it might be used to solve the pressing questions of the day. Silas Burt, a fellow Union College graduate with a reformist bent, observed that Arthur "expressed less interest in the principles then agitating parties than in the machinery and maneuvers of the managers."

With Senator Morgan's assistance, Arthur's standing in the party rose steadily. In 1867, he joined the executive committee charged with setting party policy and supervising assembly districts in New York City, and the next year he assumed a similar position at the state level. Arthur's political prospects took a hit in 1869 when New York Republicans declined to nominate Morgan for a second Senate term, choosing former governor Reuben E. Fenton instead. But Arthur soon found an even more powerful patron.

CHAPTER SEVEN

The Lordly Roscoe

Roscoe Conkling and Chester Arthur both were born in October 1829. Like Arthur, Conkling grew up in upstate New York under the stern gaze of a formidable father. Both men were careful dressers. But while Arthur's backslapping bonhomie greased his rise through the Republican ranks, Conkling was a politician who didn't care much for people. Unlike Arthur, always ready with a joke or an amusing anecdote, Conkling had no sense of humor, and was easily offended. He cringed when somebody laid a hand on his shoulder or grasped his arm. He always folded a bill into quarters, lengthwise first, before pocketing it. He did not borrow or lend books, and loathed tobacco smoke, cigar ashes, and men who spat.

Conkling's political education began early. His father, Alfred Conkling, served a term in the US Congress in the early 1820s, and when his youngest son was born he was a federal judge and a leader of New York's Whigs. Former presidents John Quincy Adams and Martin Van Buren, US Supreme Court Justice Smith Thompson, and political boss Thurlow Weed were frequent visitors to the judge's home in Auburn, New York, at the edge of Owasco Lake.

Roscoe was handsome, confident, and athletic. When he was 10, a horse kicked him and broke his jaw, but the incident didn't diminish his love of horses or his good looks. On the afternoon of the incident, he sneaked out of his bedroom to make and fly a kite. He loved to box, and was "very athletic, vigorous in his movements, and easily superior to all others in the games and sports of childhood," according to a classmate. He was "as large and massive in his mind as he was in his frame, and accomplished in his studies precisely what he did in his social life—a mastery and command which his companions yielded to him as his due."

When he was 13, Roscoe's father sent him to the Mount Washington Collegiate Institute in New York City, where he studied under the guardianship of his oldest brother Frederick, a 30-year-old wholesale dry goods salesman who was also a talented political speaker. The brothers took oratory lessons together. They pored over a textbook called *The Art of Speaking* and honed their skills by delivering speeches to each other. After a year, Roscoe returned home to attend Auburn Academy. Judge Conkling was a graduate of Union College—Arthur's alma mater—and he expected his son to follow in his footsteps. But after three years at the academy, Roscoe decided to skip college and become a lawyer. In 1846, he joined the Utica law offices of Joshua Spencer and Francis Kernan. Striding through the courthouse, he looked "like a tall, blond young lady" with a "tall, silk hat, a frock coat with a velvet collar; his cheek was as fresh as a rose, and he had long red ringlets clustered about his neck."

At 20, Conkling was admitted to the bar. He tried his first case in Utica before a familiar judge—his own father. He won it. The fledgling lawyer liked to bully witnesses, and to make jurors weep. He was fastidious—he always wrapped his legal books in paper before he set them on the lawyer's table, to prevent other attorneys from knowing which authorities he planned to cite—and carried himself with an air of superiority that did not endear him to his colleagues. Once he had finished arguing a case, he flipped open a newspaper to signal his confidence in a favorable verdict. When his opponent rose to address the jury, he remarked, "Are you going to sum up *this* case?" Even against more experienced or erudite opponents, "his arrows were never entangled in the quiver, but were quickly drawn, and driven to the mark."

The young lawyer was a voracious reader. He was fond of poetry, especially Byron, and he loved Shakespeare and Milton, Hobbes and Locke. He had a prodigious memory, and could recall much of what he had read verbatim. Spencer, one of the two partners in the firm, was an active Whig, and one day a fellow party member came to his office to request a speaker. "Send us someone who can assert himself, for there's a big bully among the Democrats who breaks up our meetings," the man told Spencer. "I shall send Mr. Conkling," the attorney replied. "I think he will make himself heard." It was Conkling's first political speech.

Conkling's seemingly effortless oratory required extensive preparation. First, he gathered all the pertinent facts. Then he wrote or dictated the speech, tapping his vast store of quotations. Then he rewrote it—and rewrote it again. He rehearsed by walking through the countryside, reciting the speech at the top of his lungs, or by spending hours delivering it in front of a mirror. On the morning of the speech, he recited it to members of his household while he dressed for breakfast.

In his earliest speeches, Conkling paced nervously as he spoke. But he soon trained himself to stand straight and still, with one foot thrust forward and his head thrown back. He let his carefully pronounced vowels do the work, never shouting or stamping his foot, bending down or pounding his fist. During a speech he tended to concentrate his gaze on two or three listeners, but sometimes he turned to different parts of the house so he could bow to a friend—or scowl at an enemy. Occasionally he referred to notes he had jotted down on the back of an envelope, but this was a ruse to give the audience the impression that he was speaking extemporaneously. In fact, he always had his speech memorized—even when it was two or three hours long.

In 1852, Conkling stumped for Whig presidential candidate Winfield Scott. But three years later, he married into one of the most prominent Democratic families in the state. Julie Catherine Seymour of Utica was two years older than Roscoe, and her brother Horatio had just completed a term as New York's governor. Horatio, 19 years older than Roscoe, strongly opposed the marriage. Dignified and gracious, he clashed repeatedly with his cocksure brother-in-law.

When the Whigs split over slavery, Conkling joined the new Republican Party, and after a brief stint as mayor of Utica, he was elected to Congress in 1858. He immediately made an impression in Washington. At six foot three, with broad shoulders and "an erect carriage," he was physically imposing. He wore a Van Dyke beard and had a prominent nose and bluish-gray eyes. But the physical feature that everybody remembered—and that caught the eye of cartoonists—was the little reddish-blond curl he twirled into the center of his pale forehead. Conkling welcomed the attention, and puffed up the hair on either side of his head to make the curl even more noticeable. Unlike most politicians, who wore Prince Albert frock coats, Conkling wore a more formal black cutaway coat. He usually complemented it with a light-colored vest and trousers, a vivid red or blue bow tie, and English gaiters buttoned over his freshly polished, pointed shoes. Conkling was an excellent poker player, and he always carried a pistol. Washington wags tittered that he wrote his personal letters in mauve ink, and had the handwriting of "an ultra-fashionable schoolgirl."

Conkling attracted some loyal followers, but his imperious manner alienated many others. When he strutted to the House floor and prepared to speak, his chin lifted and his deep nostrils quivering and stretching into an expression of scorn, he could whip his opponents into a fury before he had uttered a single word. "He did not dress, or talk, or walk, or play, as other men did, and do," one journalist observed. "There was something in his manner, there was something in his style, different from that of other men. He knew it and gloried in the fact."

As an orator, Conkling had only one peer in the House: James Gillespie Blaine, a Republican representative from Maine. Conkling and Blaine were the same age, and they both aspired to be the leader of their party. But while Conkling was supercilious and aloof, the breezy and buoyant Blaine was known as the "Magnetic Man." In conversations, Blaine came across as totally frank, even as he carefully weighed and filtered every word. "He is irresistible," an admirer once said. "I defy anyone, Republican or Democrat, to be in his company half an hour and go away from him anything else than a personal friend." Conkling and Blaine were "as jealous of each other as two women rivals in love." A clash was inevitable.

It came in April 1866, during a debate over an army reorganization bill. After several days of rising tensions, Blaine accused Conkling of improperly receiving extra government pay for his work as a prosecutor in the court martial of an army major. After a lengthy defense of his actions, Conkling concluded caustically that "if the member from Maine had the least idea how profoundly indifferent I am to his opinion upon the subject which he has been discussing, or upon any other subject personal to me, I think he would hardly take the trouble to rise here and express his opinion."

Blaine responded with a diatribe that cemented the eternal enmity between the two men—and that reverberated for decades to come. "As to the gentleman's cruel sarcasm, I hope he will not be too severe," Blaine sneered. "The contempt of that large-minded gentleman is so wilting, his haughty disdain, his grandiloquent swell, his majestic, super-eminent, overpowering, turkey-gobbler strut has been so crushing to myself and to all the men of the House, that I know it was an act of the greatest temerity for me to venture upon a controversy with him."

The House hissed, but Blaine's insults hit home. Conkling did have a "turkey-gobbler strut," and he never spoke to Blaine again—in fact, he never again acknowledged his presence. "That attack was without any provocation by me as against Mr. Blaine," he told a fellow Republican member. "I shall never overlook it."

Conkling's feud with the more popular Blaine did not dim his star in Washington. On the contrary, he beat his rival to the US Senate, taking a seat in the upper chamber in 1867. As he had in the House, Conkling quickly attracted notice. "Tall, well proportioned, with his vest opening down to the waist and displaying his full chest and broad shoulders to the best advantage, his hair tossed back from his massive brow with studied carelessness, his white and slender hands set off by spotless linen, he looked every inch a Senator." To summon a page in the Senate Chamber, Conkling clapped his hands above his head as if he were a Roman emperor, and transmitted his message to the terrified boy "as if he were conferring knighthood upon him; but woe to the boy who made a mistake in the delivery of the message."

Then as now, there were perquisites to being a senior senator, and newcomers were expected to defer to longer-serving colleagues. But deference was not in Conkling's nature and he refused to take orders from party leaders. Even in an institution in which the thirst for power was endemic, Conkling's ambition stood out. He had only been in the Senate for several months when the Washington *Chronicle* observed "no new senator has ever made in so short a time such rapid strides to a commanding position in that body."

Journalists weren't the only ones to take note of New York's dashing new senator: the ladies' gallery was always packed when Conkling was scheduled to speak. While her husband was in Washington, Julia Conkling preferred to remain in Utica, devoting herself to gardening and charity work. Julia's absence fueled widespread rumors of Roscoe's relationships with other women. According to one story, the editor of a weekly paper in Washington was poised to publish a long article about Conkling's romantic exploits. The senator heard about it, confronted the editor, and demanded to see the proofs. After he had read them, Conkling turned to the editor and calmly asked, "Do you intend to print this article?"

"I do," the editor replied.

"Then I will kill you," Conkling said.

The editor's assistant "saw the fear of imminent death seizing the soul of my chief. There was in Mr. Conkling's voice something so unspeakably fierce and cruel and in his savage gaze something so appalling that few men, I think, could have withstood him." The editor ordered the proofs destroyed, and the story never appeared in print.

Conkling had many paramours, but his affair with the Washington belle Kate Chase Sprague confirmed his lofty status in the capital—and gained him a canny political adviser. The relationship came to light in the spring of 1870, when 29-year-old Kate plucked a spray of flowers from her conservatory and sent them to Conkling's desk on the Senate floor. An Ohio native, Kate was the daughter of US Supreme Court Chief Justice Salmon Chase—and the wife of one of Conkling's colleagues, Republican senator William Sprague of Rhode Island. She sat in the front row of the ladies' gallery, wearing a royal purple velvet suit and a hat that looked like a daisy with the leaves bent into a bonnet shape.

Salmon Chase, a former governor of Ohio, had come to Washington in 1861 to join President Lincoln's cabinet as treasury secretary. Seven years later, people still talked about Kate's debut at the Lincolns' first White House party. The March levee was Mary Lincoln's introduction to Washington society, and the First Lady was determined to make an impression: She wore a bright rose-colored moiré antique dress, a garland of red flowers on her dark hair, and earrings and bracelets that rattled when she tossed her head or shook hands. But as Mary stood in the receiving line next to her husband, she was horrified to see that her guests kept turning to watch the stately Kate float across the Blue Room. The younger woman didn't wear any jewelry or flowers in her hair, so there was nothing to distract admirers from the perfect line and fit of her dress and its rustling white silk crinoline sprayed with jasmine. Next to Kate, Mary appeared almost vulgar—and Mary never forgave her for it.

Undoubtedly, Kate was pretty: she had a slightly upturned nose and wavy golden brown hair, and her hazel eyes, flecked with green, were shaded by long lashes and arched over by proud eyebrows. But it was the way she carried herself, as much as her beauty, that drew eyes in her direction. Uncommonly tall, she sat in a chair "with the graceful lightness of a bird that, folding her wings, perches upon the branch of a tree," and there was something imperial in the pose of her head.

She also radiated a fierce intelligence, and could converse on equal terms with the capital's most powerful men. In part, this was because she had been involved in politics since she was a teenager: At 16, she had returned home from her New York boarding school to be mistress of the household of her widower father, who was then governor. She worshipped him, and her burning ambition was to make him president.

When Kate married William Sprague in November 1863, it was the social event of the season and a welcome distraction from the mounting horrors of the war. The 33-year-old groom, the handsome heir to a textile fortune, had just been elected to the Senate, but he had already served as Rhode Island's governor and was a Union general. The wedding ceremony was held in Secretary Chase's Washington home, and was followed by a lavish reception for five hundred guests, including President Lincoln (Mary did not attend). "The reputation of Ex-Gov. SPRAGUE, not alone as Executive Officer of the State of 'Little Rhody,' and as a statesman, but as a brave and gallant soldier, is world-wide," read an account of the wedding published by the *New York Times*. As for Kate, she was as "modest and retiring in her manners, yet blending withal a dignity and ease that singles her out to the least observant eye as a woman endowed with a nobility of heart, fitting her for any position in life, no matter how exalted."

But Kate soon discovered that her husband was a drunkard, and the marriage was miserable. It was said that Kate was courted as much after her marriage as before, but the only man to capture her heart was Roscoe Conkling. She was captivated by his ambition and iron will, which matched her own. For his part, Conkling began to rely on Kate's wise political counsel. "I know your bright mind will solve this quicker than mine," he was in the habit of saying to her. Her advice was invaluable as he jockeyed for his biggest political prize yet: Republican boss of New York.

In the summer of 1870 Thurlow Weed was 72 years old and his political power was waning. Two main contenders vied for the crown slipping from his grasp: Conkling, and New York's second US senator, former two-term governor Reuben Fenton. The key to the kingdom was the New York Custom House.

The Custom House, located in a Greek Revival building at 55 Wall Street, had jurisdiction over the waters and shores of New York state and most of Hudson and Bergen Counties in New Jersey. New York was the primary port of entry for goods coming into the United States, and the New York Custom House was the single largest federal office in the nation, with hundreds of patronage jobs that could be doled out to loyal supporters, who could then be tapped for campaign cash. There were four chief offices: collector, surveyor, naval officer, and appraiser. Each was in charge of an important department and was appointed for a four-year term, but the collector employed the most clerks—nearly eight hundred—and was the largest dispenser of spoils, and thus was the most powerful of the four. Nominally, the collector was responsible for recording the arrival of cargo-laden ships and collecting the duties owed—a job requiring commercial and administrative experience. In fact, he was a political operative whose primary task was satisfying all of the party leaders clamoring for jobs for their supporters. That wasn't easy, and he rarely lasted a full four years.

In July 1870, President Grant nominated Arthur's good friend Tom Murphy, the unscrupulous New York hatter, to be collector. Grant had met the genial Irishman the previous summer at his vacation home in Long Branch, New Jersey, and the two had forged a friendship over their mutual love of horses. The nomination was widely understood to be a direct attack on Fenton's aspirations to be New York boss. As a congressman during the war, Fenton had spent much of his time investigating fraud in military contracts, and he was a persistent defender of the welfare of the American soldier. He knew all about Tom Murphy and his shoddy caps, and recoiled at the idea of his heading the Custom House.

Fenton, a lawyer and former lumber merchant with a thatch of dark hair and a bushy beard, was a practical man who "had about as much sentiment over political relations as a farmer over his barnyard." For Conkling, political disagreements were always personal. Fenton "can go around in his stockings during a heavy shower and dodge among the drops without wetting his feet," he muttered to a friend. Conkling had not asked Grant to appoint Murphy, though the press credited him for the choice. He quickly realized, however, that he could use the appointment to destroy Fenton. If Fenton insisted on trying to thwart the president's will, Conkling would solidify his alliance with the Grant administration and win Murphy's loyalty—and the patronage power of the Custom House—by championing Murphy's confirmation.

At around 2 p.m. on July 11, Fenton took the Senate floor to speak against Murphy. For more than three hours, he read excerpts from 37 different Republican papers and presented affidavits and records proving, he said, that Murphy was not a loyal Republican, and that he had cheated the government during the war. Fenton alleged that Murphy had colluded with Tammany Hall Democrats in New York City, and produced a certified copy of a deed showing that Murphy co-owned real estate with leaders of the Tweed Ring, the corrupt Democratic machine that ruled the city.

As Fenton droned on, Conkling confided in his friend and ally Republican senator William Stewart of Nevada, another upstate New York native who had moved to the West during the California Gold Rush: "It's just as I feared! Fenton will read newspaper clippings until he wears out the patience of the Senate, and they will lay aside the consideration of the nomination." Stewart reassured him—he had a plan. When Fenton finally sat down, the Nevada senator stood up to suggest that the Senate adjourn until 8 p.m. At that time, Stewart proposed, Conkling would be given an hour to respond to Fenton's charges. Stewart recommended that Fenton be allowed a final half hour for concluding remarks, and then the Senate would vote. Stewart knew there would be a quorum following the recess, because there were other pending nominations and "everybody had a desire to have some friend confirmed." His proposal prevailed.

Conkling was afraid that one hour would not be enough, but he used the recess well. When the Senate reconvened, Conkling took the floor and launched a withering attack on Fenton, "every sentence of which was replete with logic, sarcasm, reason, and invective." Conkling's slashing oratory held the senators spellbound and prompted several standing ovations, but he saved his best for last. Like many others in New York politics, but few in Washington, Conkling had heard of an embarrassing episode from Fenton's youth. Fenton had been entrusted with $12,000 to carry from western New York to Albany, but when the future senator reached his destination the money was missing, and he reported it stolen. Investigators soon found it—in Fenton's bedclothes. They arrested the young courier and launched an inquiry. Fenton maintained his innocence, and eventually the authorities released him, but the story was a black mark on his otherwise spotless record. As he neared the end of his speech, Conkling stalked down the aisle and halted directly across from Fenton's seat.

"It is true that Thomas Murphy is a mechanic, a hatter by trade; that he worked his trade in Albany supporting an aged father and mother and a crippled brother," Conkling said, employing the melodrama he had used to such great effect in the courtroom. "And while he was thus engaged there was another who visited Albany and played a very different role"—Conkling drew a court record of the Fenton case from his breast pocket and aimed it at his hapless adversary—"the particulars of which I will not relate except at the special request of my colleague." Fenton dropped his head onto his desk "as if he had been hit by a club." He declined to take his final half hour, and Murphy was confirmed with only three dissenting votes. "If you had spoken of me in that way I should have killed you," a friendly Southern senator remarked to Conkling. The triumphant New Yorker just smiled.

That night at Willard's Hotel, parlors 34 and 36 were filled with New York politicians and lobbyists "holding high carnival over their victory," and they drank numerous toasts to Fenton's political demise. "It is astonishing to see how many Murphy men there are since 9 o'clock this evening," a reporter for the *New York Tribune* observed. "It would seem, to hear them talk, that there never existed an anti-Murphy man, excepting Senator Fenton himself.

Senator Conkling is the hero of the occasion." Roscoe Conkling was now New York's undisputed Republican boss, with a seemingly limitless future. Many believed he would end up in the White House.

One of the men celebrating at Willard's was Chester Arthur, who had come to Washington to lobby for his friend Tom Murphy. Arthur and Conkling had been on the same side in the unsuccessful fight to save Edwin Morgan's Senate seat from Fenton, but the battle over Murphy's nomination cemented their friendship. Arthur became Conkling's loyal lieutenant, and for the next decade they advanced together, accumulating power and influence until they stood at the threshold of the highest office in the land.

CHAPTER EIGHT

The Collector

NOT LONG BEFORE Conkling humiliated Fenton on the floor of the Senate, Arthur's Union College friend Silas Burt visited him at his law office on shadowed Nassau Street in Lower Manhattan. Burt was a year younger than Arthur, and after college the two had lost touch until the summer of 1861, when they ran into each other at the state capitol in Albany. Burt remembered that at Union, Arthur was slender and affable and liked to wear a green frock coat to signify his support for Irish independence. The Arthur he met at the capitol "had grown stout" but "exhibited the same genial countenance and pleasing manners as when a collegian." When Arthur became quartermaster general he had added Burt to his staff.

But after the war Burt noticed a change in his friend. The collegiate Arthur was earnest and idealistic, and as quartermaster he had been a conscientious steward of the state's money. This new Arthur was different. Republicans and Democrats were clashing over Reconstruction, taxes, and trade. New industries were transforming the American economy, and giant trusts were beginning to dominate it. But Arthur no longer viewed politics as a struggle over issues or ideals. It was a partisan game, and to the victor went the spoils: jobs, power, and money.

Burt also was troubled by Arthur's deepening involvement with Tom Murphy, and by both men's connections to the Tweed Ring. New York City's population was exploding, from 300,000 in 1840 to nearly 943,000 in 1870, and honest municipal officials were unable to provide housing, sanitation, health care, and employment for the growing multitudes. Between 1866 and 1871, William Tweed and his henchmen stepped into the breach—while plundering the city coffers of millions of dollars. Public works contracts and franchises for horse car lines and ferry companies offered ample opportunities for graft. Boss Tweed and his accomplices also made fortunes in printing and advertising by creating their own companies and then handing them lucrative city contracts. Members of the Tweed Ring were the main shareholders in the Manufacturing Stationers' Company, which sold $3 million worth of stationery supplies to city offices and schools in 1870. For six reams of notepaper, two dozen penholders, four bottles of ink, a dozen sponges, and three dozen boxes of rubber bands, the firm charged the city $10,000 (about $185,000 in today's dollars).

The Tweed Ring seized power and held onto it by mobilizing an army of thugs and corrupt election officials to stuff ballot boxes, intimidate voters, and miscount votes. But Boss Tweed also won the genuine support of many immigrants and downtrodden New Yorkers by doling out city jobs, bowls of soup, and beds in cheap boarding houses, while good-government types prattled on about civic responsibility, government efficiency, and lower taxes. Though not quite six feet tall, Tweed weighed nearly three hundred pounds, and he had an outsized personality that matched his appearance. He was a jolly rogue who collected friends from every stratum of society.

It was true, as Fenton alleged on the Senate floor, that Murphy was close to Tweed. The erstwhile hatter and the New York City boss were friends of more than a decade, and they owned real estate together. (As Murphy's attorney, Arthur played a part in these deals.) Murphy also sat on a three-member commission overseeing a project to widen Broadway between 34th and 59th Streets. He used that position to help members of the ring buy some of the affected properties and to secure generous assessments and damages when the city had to buy them to complete the project.

In 1869, Murphy asked Boss Tweed for a favor: would he create a job for Chester Arthur? The new post was "counsel to the New York City tax commission," and it paid Arthur $10,000 a year. It isn't clear exactly what Arthur did to earn that money, but Tweed and his accomplices regularly raided tax collections to pad their personal treasuries, and Tweed would not have fulfilled Murphy's request without asking for something in return. As counsel for the tax commission, Arthur certainly was in a position to provide favors to the boss.

To reformers, Tweed and Murphy were both "greedy adventurers" who pursued politics not for the public good, but "for the same reason that other men pick locks and forge bills—to avoid honest labor, fill their bellies with rich food, and adorn their bodies with rich clothing." As Murphy's attorney and close friend, Arthur had more than a whiff of the Tweed taint.

As for the Custom House, Arthur and Murphy agreed that Republicans should use it to keep their stranglehold on state politics. On the spring day in 1870 that Burt called on Arthur at his law office, he nearly collided with a departing Murphy, who was "jubilantly sarcastic concerning the fate of Fenton and his followers." As Burt shifted uncomfortably in his seat, Arthur proceeded to explain what *he* would do if he were collector of the Custom House. His scheme was to give each county in the state a certain number of Custom House jobs, based on the rate of its Republican vote. The party committee for each county would choose the men to fill the allotted slots, and would be responsible for ensuring that they remained loyal—and contributed a portion of their salaries—to the Republican machine. In this way, Arthur boasted, "the whole party machinery could be consolidated, unified and concentrated for any purpose; this would prevent all the scandalous and injurious contests in primaries and conventions and make the party so compact and disciplined as to be practically invincible." In other words, any independent-minded Republican who dared to challenge the machine would be crushed. Burt was appalled but not surprised by Arthur's plan, judging it "a fair exposition of Arthur's political creed which favored the substitution of management and discipline for principles and convictions."

As collector Murphy devoted almost all of his time to politics, while leaving the day-to-day operation of the Custom House to his underlings. He collected "voluntary" campaign contributions from Custom House employees; organized pro-Conkling delegations to the Republican state convention of 1870; and offered Custom House positions to Tammany politicians, who were urged to distribute the jobs to like-minded Republicans who could be counted on to follow Conkling's lead as delegates to the state convention. Murphy also paid a ward politician to defeat Greeley in his district, denying the crusading *Tribune* editor a voice at the convention.

To their delight, Murphy and his associates soon "found more profit in running the Custom-House than in feeding on the crumbs which fell from the Tammany table." Their swindle was simple. When a vessel arrived in the harbor, it unloaded its goods on the pier, where Custom House authorities weighed or gauged them. Sometimes the importer paid the appropriate duties and took immediate possession of his property. But often, the importer presented a bond for payment, and the Custom House workers moved the goods to a warehouse. This was where casks of wine mysteriously sprung leaks and bottles of gin vanished from cases, replaced by wood shavings. Importers complained that they frequently lost between 5 and 25 percent of their property while it was under the supervision of Custom House officials. Murphy shared the wealth with his good friend Arthur: together they sold $10,000 worth of whiskey—apparently tax free—during Murphy's time as collector.

Sometimes the thieves did their work while the goods were still sitting on the pier. Even "taking the extra precaution of delegating a person to follow and watch the goods in transit and on the pier, we have not been able to stop thieving," complained Charles Schultz of Clarke & Schultz, importers of ales, wines, and condiments. "In one case where our watcher left the pier only 20 minutes in order to apprise us of the arrival of the Custom-House carman, he discovered on his return that two casks were missing, and no person could give any information in regard to them, yet during the entire time they were in the charge of the Government officials."

Murphy ingratiated himself with the Grant administration by spooning out some of the Custom House drippings to two of the president's corrupt cronies, George Leet and Wilbur Stocking. If a merchant failed to take possession of his goods and pay taxes on them within 48 hours of a ship's entry into port, the collector could issue a "general order" to unload the cargo and transfer it to a warehouse. The importer had to pay for the transfer and a minimum of a month's storage rate to retrieve his property. Murphy gave Leet and Stocking exclusive control over the general-order warehouses along the Manhattan shore of the Hudson, and they used their monopoly to hike cartage and storage fees and block merchants from retrieving their goods, thereby costing them even more money. When a hundred importing firms signed a letter of complaint, Grant ordered Murphy to cut ties with Leet. But the president backed off when Murphy insisted that Leet and Stocking were being unfairly maligned.

In the fall of 1871, Horace Greeley's *Tribune*, the source of many of Fenton's charges against Murphy during the nomination fight in the Senate, went on the attack again. Murphy had "a record as rotten as his hats" and had been "proved guilty of the worst practices of the worst shoddy contractors, to say nothing of party treason, official relation to Tammany, and personal affiliation with its leaders," Greeley thundered.

Robert Murray, who had served as US marshal for New York during the war, sparked the *Tribune's* renewed crusade against Murphy. In a letter published in the newspaper, Murray claimed that Murphy, facing an investigation into his military contracting practices, came into the marshal's office and "began to cry and sob like a child" as he offered Murray a $10,000 bribe to make the charges go away. Murray said he declined the money, but he admitted that out of sympathy for Murphy's plight, he arranged for the hatter to meet with the investigating detectives. Murray hinted in his letter that Murphy had bribed the detectives to escape justice. "We mean to make his standing so plain that our skirts at least shall be clear of the guilt of his retention in power," Greeley wrote. "He is an enemy whose power for harm must be destroyed." Newspapers from around the country hailed the *Tribune*'s coverage and echoed its call for Murphy's removal.

Finally Grant gave in to the political pressure, and in November of 1871, he accepted Murphy's resignation. But Murphy's departure was a hollow victory for reformers, because Grant allowed the disgraced collector to name his successor: Chester Arthur. The *Tribune* reported that according to people close to Murphy, "he intended only nominally to relinquish the Collectorship of the Port for the sake of appearances, and that his successor was to hold office through him and by him, and was to obey his dictates." One disgusted citizen grumbled to a *Tribune* reporter that Arthur was merely "Tom Murphy under another name." Grant chose Arthur over more qualified merchants and jurists because "he can 'run the machine' of party politics better than any of them," the *Tribune* groused.

On the night he got the job, Murphy led a group to the new collector's Lexington Avenue brownstone to offer personal congratulations to Arthur, who feigned surprise at his selection. Now Arthur could implement his political schemes and prove his loyalty to Conkling—and get rich doing it.

•◆•

The ground was frozen and the wind whipped through Lower Manhattan on December 1, 1871, Arthur's first day as collector. He reported for work in a building befitting his enhanced stature: the solid granite Custom House was "one of the handsomest structures in the city." It occupied an entire block, with a colonnaded main entrance on Wall Street and a central dome that rose 124 feet above the sidewalk. Inside, a four-faced clock stood at the center of a majestic rotunda crowded with merchants, brokers, and ships' captains. Deputy collectors and clerks scribbled and stamped at desks arranged in rows around the clock. Arthur's grand office was at the end of a long corridor, past a secretary in an anteroom, beyond an assistant collector sitting in a reception room, at the far end of an anteroom thronged with office seekers.

Arthur took the helm the day after New Yorkers celebrated Thanksgiving. He had much to be thankful for: his loyalty and striving had landed him the most lucrative job in the entire federal government. In addition to his regular salary, Arthur received a cut of the fines and forfeitures levied by frequently overzealous customs inspectors. In total, he grossed more than $50,000 a year (about $1 million in today's dollars)—more than cabinet members, Supreme Court justices, the vice president, or Grant himself. Arthur also took advantage of his position to diversify his investment portfolio. In 1872, the state legislature chartered the Gilbert Elevated Railroad Company to help meet New York City's growing need for rapid transit. Arthur secured a seat on the five-member commission charged with mapping out the route, then bought heavily discounted stock in the Gilbert. He bought more discounted railroad stock through the Wall Street brokerage Morton, Bliss & Company, headed by two Conkling loyalists.

Arthur had to hand over some of his growing fortune to the Republican Party, but he had plenty left over to support a luxurious life. He and Nell employed five household servants, and paid for private schooling for their children. (A daughter named Ellen but called Nell, like her mother, was born on the day Arthur was named collector.) They hired a French tutor for Alan, and made sure he became an accomplished horseman and sailor. Arthur was a dandy: during one eight-month period as collector, he spent $125 just on hats—about $2,600 in today's dollars.

In the New York City of the early 1870s, a contemporary guidebook archly observed, society "stands not as it should upon the personal merits of those who compose it, but upon a pile of bank-books." The Arthurs' newfound wealth launched them into the upper echelons of New York society, and they eagerly embraced the privileges and obligations of their elevated status. The names in Nell's address book were organized by street, and included most of the prominent Republicans of the period, from William Vanderbilt to Theodore Roosevelt, father of the future president. Hosting such distinguished company in the appropriate style was expensive, and the Arthurs did so regularly. At many such events, the hosts rolled out a carpet from the front door to the curb and covered the walkway with a temporary awning, so that guests alighting from their carriages would not have to tread on the sidewalk or be exposed to the elements. Once inside, French servants wearing black swallowtail coats and pants, with immaculate white vests, cravats, and gloves were "as active as a set of monkeys" in fetching food and drink. To Nell, a social climber like her mother, all this was a dream come true. "Mrs. Arthur was a very ambitious woman," a friend recalled. "There was no happier woman in the country than she when her husband was made collector of the port of New York."

But Nell soon saw the dark side of her husband's new role. Arthur liked to linger late into the night—or into the early morning—with "the Mikes, Jakes and Barneys of politics," eating, drinking, smoking Havana cigars, and dreaming up ways to strengthen the machine. On most days, the collector didn't show up at the Custom House until 1 p.m., three hours after it opened. One of the machine boys who participated in the festivities later recalled that "Arthur was always the last man to go to bed in any company and was fond of sitting down on his front steps at 3 a.m. and talking until anyone dared to stay."

According to Burt, Arthur "could drink a great deal without any visible symptoms of intoxication," though he and his companions often drank so much Bordeaux wine and whiskey that "all but one or two absolutely succumbed and fell prone from their seats." The collector also "was much addicted to the game of 'poker' which strangely has strong allurements for professional politicians."

Often Arthur and his machine buddies ventured beyond the front stoop for more stimulating entertainment at what Burt discreetly called "very questionable resorts." One of the agents later assigned to investigate the Custom House alluded to "the many nefarious places visited at night time, by Arthur, in company with 'Clint' Wheeler & others." Those "nefarious places" almost certainly included concert saloons, where patrons drank and sang surrounded by fluttering "waiter-girls" wearing low bodices, short skirts, and high-tasseled red boots. Many of the girls had been camp followers during the war, and were available for assignations in an upstairs room or nearby brothel. New York had about 80 such saloons in the early 1870s, but gentlemen like Arthur and his friends tended to favor the higher-class establishments such as the Gaiety, on Broadway near Houston, which attracted a crowd that was "respectable, though by no means stilted in manner," or the marble-columned Louvre, on Broadway and 23rd.

A favorite haunt for New Yorkers of all types and classes was Harry Hill's, "known the world over in sporting circles." A gigantic blue-and-red glass lantern hung outside the two-story brick building at 25 Houston Street, along with a sign promising "Punches and juleps, cobblers and smashes, to make the tongue waggle with wit's merry flashes." Harry was an English immigrant and former boxer who won a medal of valor for helping the police in the draft riots of 1863. He proudly welcomed members of Congress, judges, lawyers, merchants, doctors, and other well-to-do professionals along with dockworkers and the racetrack crowd. Harry graciously provided a private sobering-up room for his more respectable customers, to reduce their chances of being waylaid by his rougher patrons once they ventured outdoors.

Harry's had a bar downstairs, but the real action was the dance hall on the second floor, which male customers could reach by slipping through a narrow opening between the counters and paying twenty-five cents. (Women, who entered through a separate entrance, were admitted free.) Here, in a dingy, low-ceilinged room, shop girls frolicked with state legislators and the wives of prominent lawyers twirled through the sawdust with gangsters from the Bloody Sixth Ward. There were runaway teenagers and wives who had fled their husbands, bar maids and bankers, politicians and prostitutes, and prizefighters and pickpockets, all jumbled together in a maelstrom of gaudy crimson silks and sparkling jewels and stifling cigar smoke. The well-dressed crowd at Harry's contrasted with the shabby surroundings, "as if upper New York, in their best outfit, had taken possession of a low dwelling in Five Points." Some of the men and women were dressed as if going to the opera; others would not have looked out of place sitting in a church pew.

One scold had to admit that the women at Harry's were far more attractive than those at lesser concert saloons, since "most of them have just begun their life of shame. The crimson hue has not left their cheeks." Nevertheless, he warned, "out of one hundred girls and women present, not one can be found who has not started on the road to ruin." A gentleman's guide to the city's erotic pleasures, published in 1870, put a more positive spin on Harry's offerings: "An hour cannot be spent more pleasantly than at this celebrated establishment."

Nell resented Chester's frequent absences, and his nighttime activities put a strain on their marriage. But she mostly suffered in silence, taking solace in family vacations and visits to the opera on the arm of an elderly friend. Meanwhile, all the late-night eating and drinking swelled the already hearty collector, and he started wearing a corset.

●◆●

Arthur's limited hours at the Custom House were fruitful ones. His charm and elegance played well with the wealthy merchants and importers who had business at the Custom House, even though many continued to grumble about the money they lost there. Arthur's college education and membership in the prestigious Union League Club distinguished him from Murphy and other less-sophisticated party hacks. Arthur was no expert on mercantile issues, but he knew the law and held business-friendly views on tariffs and trade.

Arthur also was popular with his Custom House employees. He demanded personal and party loyalty from them, but he fiercely resisted efforts to reduce their salaries. Because his predecessors had removed nearly 1,700 employees during the previous five years, and because Murphy had filled the ranks with Conkling loyalists during his short tenure, Arthur could concentrate on keeping employees and adding new ones, rather than thinning the ranks.

Unlike the outgoing Tweed, Conkling succeeded as boss despite his personality. The supercilious senator happily left the day-to-day management of the state machine to his loyal collector. It was Arthur who had the social skills, and Conkling leaned heavily on him to lubricate the relationships that kept the machine humming. Arthur exerted his influence in the nominations and campaigns of hundreds of office-seekers, and he took an interest in even the smallest public jobs. When New York City aldermen were considering nominations for police justices, for example, Arthur wrote them letters instructing them how to vote. He forged alliances with both Tammany and anti-Tammany Democrats to build Republican strength in the city. Whenever possible, he performed small favors for leading Republicans, such as personally shepherding through customs 205 cases of champagne for Grant, cabinet members, and Murphy.

In the fall of 1872, Arthur faced an unexpected challenge: the application of new civil service rules to the Custom House. The regulations barred mandatory campaign contributions by government workers and required the use of civil service exams in hiring them. But in Arthur's Custom House, the new rules were "treated with a jocular indulgence," according to Burt, who witnessed Arthur's attitude as deputy naval officer at the Custom House. Arthur "gave outward respect to the law but never concealed his contempt for the principle the law was intended to enforce."

The collector certainly had no intention of halting campaign assessments—especially not when Grant was running for reelection. In a mendacious letter to the chairman of the new, largely toothless civil service commission, Arthur claimed that some of his subordinates, "wholly without my knowledge or communication with any other than their own members, voluntarily raised a sum of money to be devoted towards paying the legitimate expenses" of Republican campaigns. However, he said, "until after the receipt of your letter none of these facts were known to me. Since they became known, I have not thought it either my duty or my right to interfere with such contributions or solicitations, or the use which my subordinates voluntarily make of their own money."

In the past, Burt had dutifully paid his campaign assessments, but now he believed in civil service reform. When, along with other Custom House employees, he received the circular asking him to contribute a portion of his salary to support Republican candidates in 1872, he ignored it. Word of Burt's defiance soon reached Arthur, and he called his old friend into his office. The collector calmly explained that by accepting a government job, Burt had entered into a contract, albeit an unwritten one, to donate a portion of his salary to help keep his party in power. Refusing to do so was ungrateful and selfish. Burt listened politely to his friend and boss, but he didn't back down. He pointed out that while he had contributed in the past, the new civil service rules now made it illegal to do so. At this, Arthur lost his patience, accusing Burt of "treachery against the very politicians to whom he owed his job." Burt left, but Arthur didn't give up. A few days after the argument, the chief clerk of the naval office approached Burt with a proposition. If Burt was reluctant to compromise his reform principles by publicly pledging a certain portion of his salary, the Custom House could quietly deduct 4 percent from his paycheck and leave it at that. Burt angrily refused. "I learned later that it had been considered important to break down the influence of my example which might be followed by others and materially reduce the amount of 'contributions.'"

As for the required civil service exams, Arthur made sure they were a farce. Under the rules, he was supposed to create a three-member board to formulate questions for the exams, administer the tests, grade them, and issue certificates of appointment. To fill the spots he tapped three good friends, all of them party workers loyal to Conkling. One soon became post-master of New York and did not have time to participate in the proceedings; Arthur kept him on the panel anyway. Arthur's second selection was so adamantly opposed to reform he refused to show up for meetings—he, too, was retained. The remaining board member, assisted by a drunken clerk and a messenger, was left to run the examination process himself.

It wasn't a very difficult job. The only applicants who were allowed to take the test were ones Arthur had already decided to hire. The exam questions never changed, and were widely circulated. Even so, many of the candidates who became Custom House employees did not ace the test. Asked to name the three branches of the US government, candidate Charles F. Meserole answered, "the army and the navy." What were the executive departments of the federal government? Candidate George M. Logan wrote,

"Publick stores, Navy Yard." Logan apparently misread the question, "By what process is a statute of the United States enacted?" Thinking he was being asked about *statues*, he answered frankly, "never saw one erected and don't know the Process."

When the board began meeting, Burt attended out of curiosity—until Arthur sent word that he should stay away. Despite mounting evidence to the contrary, Burt believed he could steer Arthur back to a righteous path. So when he learned Arthur's chief deputy was corrupt, he went to his old friend to share the information. Receptive at first, Arthur soon grew exasperated with the hectoring Burt. "You are one of these goody-goody fellows who set up a high standard of morality that other people cannot reach," he snarled.

Burt was amazed at Arthur's "double life." Publicly, he was "bland and accommodating to merchants who were deferential or did not worry him; courteous and agreeable to all strangers, genial and 'cultured' at the clubs and in other social relations; a fastidious connoisseur in art and taste." But as Conkling's chief lieutenant, Arthur was "the leader of a corps of partisan mercenaries; intimate and jovial with Mike, Steve, Jake and their fellows; cajoling and trading with the vulgar gang of aldermen; arranging those moves at the primaries or trades at the polls that would best suit the purposes of his own clique." The Republican Party, Burt lamented, had become "a mere stalking horse for as corrupt a band of varlets as ever robbed a public treasury."

• ◆ •

Conkling ruled the most populous state in the Union, but he wasn't the only Republican boss. With Grant's approval, Senators Simon Cameron of Pennsylvania, John A. Logan of Illinois, Zachariah Chandler of Michigan, Oliver P. Morton of Indiana, and Matthew Carpenter of Wisconsin all wielded similar patronage power. Like Conkling, they controlled nearly all of the elected and appointed offices within their states, and those who filled the jobs were expected to contribute time and money to sustain the machine. In 1872, they were ordered to work for the reelection of President Grant. "The whole civil service of the country from the Cabinet minister down to the meanest postmaster, is converted into a vast political agency to secure the president's re-election," Missouri Senator Carl Schurz, a leading reformer, declared several months before the election. Arthur made sure that Custom House employees did their part.

Reformers backed *Tribune* editor Horace Greeley as a Republican alternative, but Grant easily won the party's nomination. Desperate Democrats adopted Greeley as their standard-bearer, but Grant swamped him in November, winning 286 out of 352 electoral votes. Republican machines around the country looked forward to another four years of solidifying their rule.

Grant was inaugurated for the second time on March 4, 1873. That evening, revelers gathered in a temporary wooden structure in Judiciary Square. An enormous American eagle suspended from the center of the 25-foot ceiling gripped a US shield in its talons. Red, white, and blue streamers a hundred feet long stretched to 37 state seals mounted on the walls. The room was draped in white muslin, and dozens of birdcages dangled in the air, filled with hundreds of canaries expected to sing joyously in the glare of thousands of gas jets. Architects feared the vibrations of thousands of dancing feet might shake the building, so the floor was not connected to the walls. The organizers had thought of everything—except heating. That night the temperature plunged to 4 degrees, a record low for Washington, and a wet, biting wind added to the misery. The champagne and wine froze solid, the coffee turned to slush, and the canaries did not sing—because many of them were dead. The room emptied quickly when the stiffened birds began toppling off their perches and landing on the heads of the dancers below.

It was a fitting beginning to Grant's second term. For the next four years, politicians from Washington to New York to the Pacific Ocean engaged in an orgy of venality and corruption unmatched before or since.

CHAPTER NINE

From Grant to Hayes

COLONEL WILLIAM H. Crook would be a presidential bodyguard and clerk for close to 50 years, starting with Abraham Lincoln and ending with Woodrow Wilson. He knew presidents in their private moments, behind the public speeches and posturing, so his insight into the character of Ulysses S. Grant carries weight. "At the beginning of his administration, I believe that the President did not consider it possible that a great soldier could fail to be otherwise a great man," Crook observed. "This fact explains much that follows."

What followed was "the all-time low point in statesmanship and political morality in our history," according to historian C. Vann Woodward. Grant's countrymen hoped he would be another George Washington, who led in the political arena as assuredly as he did on the battlefield. But Grant was no Washington. Many of the qualities that helped Grant lead the Union to victory were crippling liabilities in the White House. He was unswervingly loyal, especially to men who had served with him in the war, and never adjusted his military attitude toward discipline and insubordination. He was accustomed to issuing commands, not seeking advice.

Unlike Washington, whose dominating physical presence burnished his mystique, Grant in the flesh didn't quite live up to Grant the legend. He was shy and stood barely five feet eight inches tall, with a brown beard and mustache and graying hair. A devoted family man, he was so attached to his wife Julia that in the White House he rarely sat down for a meal without her. In the mornings, he waited impatiently in the library for her to finish dressing, take his arm, and join him for a hearty meal of broiled Spanish mackerel, steak, and bacon and fried apples, washed down with a pot of strong coffee. When young Nellie and Jesse Grant dined with their parents, the president liked to toss rolled-up balls of bread at them, kissing them on their faces when his missiles hit the mark.

If the Grants were especially joyful in the White House, it was because they could remember much leaner times: less than a decade before moving into the Executive Mansion, Grant was working as a clerk in his father's leather goods store, scrabbling to survive.

Grant was born in Point Pleasant, Ohio, in 1822. His father, Jesse Grant, was a successful tanner, but he knew his eldest son had no love or talent for the business, and he arranged for him to attend West Point. Grant graduated in 1843, ranked 21st in a class of 39. He was glad to leave the academy, and planned to resign his commission as soon as he had completed four years of mandatory military service. But the Mexican-American War broke out in 1846, and Grant ended up serving for eight more years before retiring.

After leaving the military, Grant launched several unsuccessful business ventures and failed as a farmer. Things grew so desperate during the winter of 1857 that he was reduced to selling firewood on St. Louis street corners, bundled up against the cold in his faded blue army overcoat. When the Civil War began, the future savior of the Union was selling saddles and harnesses in his father's store, poverty nipping at his heels. The war changed Grant's fortunes, and he rose quickly from commander of a company of Illinois volunteers to commanding general of the Union Army. "One of my superstitions had always been when I started to go any where, or to do anything, not to turn back, or stop until the thing intended was accomplished," Grant wrote in his memoirs. He was referring to his courtship of Julia, but Lincoln put his faith in Grant because the general demonstrated the same steely determination on the battlefield.

Lincoln also transcended a humble background to reach the White House, but he traveled a steady upward trajectory, from lawyer to congressman to president. Grant's sudden rise from clerk to national icon left him with feelings of inferiority and a deep suspicion of men who were more educated or talented. As president he was vulnerable to the wiles of men on the make, politicians and businessmen who were newly arrived, as he was. "Selfish men and ambitious men got the ear of that simple and confiding president," wrote George Hoar, a Massachusetts congressman of the period. "They studied Grant, some of them, as the shoemaker measures the foot of his customer."

The times demanded a president of sterner stuff. The moral deterioration of the post–Civil War period permeated politics and many other aspects of

American life. The South was fiercely resisting Reconstruction, and corruption flourished as the carpetbag governments teetered. Federal troops were used to intimidate Democrats, and the Ku Klux Klan employed violence and murder to cow newly freed blacks. The rot in Southern legislatures received the most attention, but state lawmakers in other regions of the country were similarly unscrupulous. Political rings similar to Tweed's ruled many of the largest American cities. Railroad and mining titans boasted of the legislatures and judges they bought as they carved out empires from the public domain. The Civil War had been a boon to speculators, subsidy-seekers, and dishonest government contractors, and many of them—Tom Murphy was one—rode it from obscurity to wealth and power. Meanwhile, civil service reform sputtered. In 1874, Congress refused to budget any more money for the Civil Service Commission, and competitive examinations were discontinued in March 1875.

From the beginning, Grant's administration was tainted by scandal. In the summer of 1869, Jay Gould, Jim Fisk Jr., and Abel Rathbone Corbin, a corrupt lobbyist who was the president's brother-in-law, tried to corner the New York gold market. Grant was warned of the conspiracy but failed to act before hundreds were financially ruined. Crédit Mobilier, a construction company for the Union Pacific Railroad that received loans and land grants from the government, bribed members of Congress before Grant took office, but by 1873 it had been revealed that Schuyler Colfax, Grant's first vice president, and Henry Wilson, his second, were among the lawmakers who had accepted the money. Robert C. Schenck, Grant's minister to Great Britain, sold his name to the shady operators of the Emma Silver-Mining Company of Utah, who used it to market company shares in Britain. English investors howled when the mine went under—just after Schenck sold his shares at a high price.

The putrid carcasses kept bobbing to the surface: a congressional investigation found James F. Casey, another Grant brother-in-law, guilty of gross misconduct as collector of customs in New Orleans; Secretary of the Treasury William A. Richardson turned a contract for the collection of delinquent taxes into an extortion racket; Attorney General George H. Williams, who bungled the Crédit Mobilier investigation, spent Department of Justice money to buy an expensive carriage for his wife; and Secretary of the Navy George M. Robeson grew rich from naval contracts.

Grant had learned in the army never to desert a man under fire, so rather than dismissing these rogues, he defended them. As the mayhem swirled around him, he went on smoking his black cigars, driving his four-in-hands, and relaxing at his summer cottage in Long Branch, New Jersey, from June to October.

If the swindles and scandals had a common element, it was Grant's private secretary and close friend General Orville Babcock, who had been on his staff since Vicksburg and was at Appomattox for Lee's surrender. "Bab" was handsome, with a ruddy complexion, dark hair, and a reddish mustache and goatee. Grant had complete trust in his old comrade, unable or unwilling to see that he was a scoundrel who "fished for gold in every stinking cesspool." Babcock and Tom Murphy became friends, and together they convinced the president to appoint Murphy's bankrupt brother-in-law minister to Peru at a salary of $10,000 per year.

Babcock soiled his hands in many schemes, but the one that nearly landed him in jail—until Grant intervened—was a far-ranging conspiracy to steal millions in federal excise taxes on whiskey. The so-called Whiskey Ring sold liquor under the table, and then instead of paying the taxes due, they used forged federal revenue stamps to siphon the money into their own pockets. Led by Internal Revenue collector John A. McDonald of St. Louis, a close associate and friend of Babcock's, the ring grew to include an assortment of treasury officials, numerous revenue collectors and politicians, and a St. Louis newspaper publisher. For his aid, Babcock received cigar boxes filled with thousand dollar bills, as well as diamonds, rare liquors, and the services of a prostitute.

The conspirators also shoveled money into Republican campaign coffers. Arthur, one of the party's leading fundraisers, often wrote letters to Babcock asking for favors and discussing patronage, and it is possible, if not likely, that he knew of the ring before it was publicly exposed. In 1872, when members of the ring contributed to the campaign of Senator Oliver P. Morton of Indiana, they channeled the money through Arthur. When Babcock was acquitted, thanks to Grant, a number of administration loyalists started a fund to cover his legal expenses. George Bliss, Clint Wheeler, and William E. Chandler—all Arthur associates—contributed. Conkling, who vociferously defended the obviously guilty Babcock, gave his blessing to the collection effort.

It was only a matter of time before the tide of corruption sloshed onto the Custom House steps. In early 1874, it came to light that customs officials had strong-armed the respected importing firm of Phelps, Dodge, and Company into paying a $217,017 fine. Tipped off by a disgruntled former employee of the firm, Special Agent B. G. Jayne of the Custom House searched the company's books and determined that it had underpaid duties on a shipment valued at $1.75 million. Technically, that was the total amount the government could collect. Jayne summoned William E. Dodge to his office and convinced him to settle the case for $217,017, the portion of the shipment that, supposedly, had been undervalued. Under the Custom House rules, Collector Arthur, Naval Officer A. H. Laflin, and Surveyor Alonzo Cornell each received $21,906; Jayne got $61,718, out of which he paid a share to the informer.

But Phelps, Dodge officials soon discovered that they had been deceived. In fact, only $6,658 worth of goods had been undervalued, for which they owed $1,664.68 in duties. Company leaders demanded, and got, a congressional investigation.

Arthur claimed to know nothing about the fraud. But Judge Noah Davis told members of the House Ways and Means Committee about a meeting in the Custom House during which Arthur, Laflin, Jayne, and Conkling discussed the Phelps, Dodge case. The men invited Davis, the outgoing US attorney for the Southern District of New York, so he could give them advice on how much money they might extract from the businessmen.

In response to the scandal, Congress quickly approved the Anti-Moiety Act in June 1874. The vote in the House was unanimous, and in the Senate there were only three dissenting votes. Tom Murphy and other machine politicians urged Grant to block the bill, but public outrage over the Phelps, Dodge case made a veto politically impossible. Overnight, Arthur's annual income dropped from approximately $56,000 to a fixed salary of $12,000.

Arthur still stood on his Custom House perch, but the ground beneath him was beginning to tremble.

•◆•

As Collector Arthur reveled in the trappings of his success, heedless of the ethical boundaries he trampled in his quest for power and prestige, his austere father was fading.

After Malvina died in 1869, the widowed Elder Arthur remained in tiny Newtonville in upstate New York, pursuing various literary projects. The family was shocked when he married for a second time, to a woman named Mary who soon locked her new husband in a barn and refused to live with him. By October 1875 Elder Arthur was nearly 80, living under the care of his daughters and fatally ill with what might have been stomach cancer.

Chester was summoned to his father's deathbed. When he arrived, his sister Regina took him into Elder Arthur's bedroom. "Chester is here," she announced. At first the dying man didn't understand, but when Regina repeated the news his face lit up and he tried to untangle his hand from the sheets so he could grasp his son.

"You know me, don't you Pa?"

"Oh yes," Elder Arthur cried, finally freeing his arms and wrapping them around Chester's neck.

Regina assured her father that Chester was going to stay "all night and tomorrow and a long time." At this Elder Arthur displayed "such a satisfied look"—but it wasn't true. The collector had pressing business in New York, and couldn't stay long. When the old firebrand finally slipped away on October 27, his son was gone.

• ◆ •

For the first time since the Civil War, it seemed possible that Democrats might win the White House in 1876. Democratic reformer Samuel Tilden, who had helped depose Boss Tweed in 1871, had been elected governor of New York in 1874. Tilden used the governorship to take on another corrupt gang, the Canal Ring, which stole taxpayer money by overcharging for construction and maintenance of the state's canal system. Tilden's exploits had made him a leading contender for the Democratic presidential nomination. Undoubtedly, he would be an attractive candidate to the many voters disgusted by the scandals of the Grant administration.

Reformers were rising on the Republican side, too. At the New York Republican convention in Saratoga, delegates elected George William Curtis, the editor of *Harper's Weekly* and a leader in the civil service reform movement, as chairman. In his youth, the now "silver-haired and priestly" Curtis had helped build Thoreau's cabin on Walden Pond. He was a moralist who constantly exhorted the "educated class" to fulfill its public duty by engaging in politics. "The time has come when the people of this country must grapple with the trading politicians, the men who trade in politics for their own advantage, the vampires who suck the moral life-blood of the nation," Curtis proclaimed to a meeting of the American Social Science Association. "They will scornfully and desperately resist. . . . Let them cry; our business is to rout them." In May 1876, Curtis and Missouri senator Carl Schurz convened the inaugural meeting of the Republican Reform Club at the Fifth Avenue Hotel. Among the intellectuals, educators, and business leaders in attendance was Theodore Roosevelt, father of the future president.

But even as the reform movement gained momentum, Conkling remained the most powerful man in the Senate. He still had control of the Custom House and close ties to the sitting president—and he was determined to take Grant's place in the White House.

Unlike the Democrats, who were widely expected to (and eventually did) nominate Tilden, the race on the Republican side was more unsettled. In addition to Conkling, the other top contenders heading into the Cincinnati convention included one of Grant's few sterling cabinet appointments, Secretary of the Treasury Benjamin Bristow, a Kentuckian who had broken up the Whiskey Ring; Senator Oliver P. Morton, the Republican boss of Indiana; Governor Rutherford B. Hayes of Ohio; and Conkling's old nemesis, James G. Blaine of Maine.

At about 9 p.m. on June 9, five days before the official beginning of the proceedings, a train packed with about 150 Conkling supporters steamed into Cincinnati. Conkling had decided to stay away from the convention, but Chester Arthur and a handful of the senator's top lieutenants, who had arrived in the city the day before, were at the station to greet the Conkling troops. They had come with their own band and a huge banner with a portrait of their hero, and despite the relatively late hour, they formed ranks and marched noisily to the Grand Hotel, shouting and singing in the silvery rays of a limelight they had brought with them.

Reinforcements arrived over the next few days, until there were nearly 1,500 Conkling supporters in Cincinnati, all of them wearing blue badges emblazoned with the candidate's name. At one point a crowd of them marched to the Gibson House, where members of the Republican Reform Club were staying, and hung a "For President, Roscoe Conkling" banner right beneath the reformers' own banner. There were so many New Yorkers in Cincinnati—the vast majority of them Conkling supporters—that it was "almost as if they had captured the city and were occupying it to the exclusion of the delegates of other States." Correspondents for the *New York Times* noted their brash confidence. "During the day they have their band and shouters at the Grand, Gibson, Burnet, St. James and other hotels. In each, and on the route from one to the other, there are music from the bands, and many hurrahs for Conkling. They astonished the staid residents by their vigor in shouting and their prolixity in music."

The *Times* also noted that the Conkling machine seemed to have barred its more unsavory ward heelers from making the trip. "The machine is in the very best working order, and represented only by its smooth-spoken, well-dressed, and presentable adherents. No others have been allowed to come to Cincinnati."

The strains of music and oratory spilled out of hotel lobbies decorated with colored lights and banners. In this competition for the man on the street, the enthusiastic Conkling backers were unsurpassed. Meaningful party primaries were nearly a century in the future, and the opinions of the Republican rank and file didn't matter much. The real decision-making wasn't happening in the hotel lobbies; it was taking place in the stifling rooms upstairs, where favors were traded and loyalties bought. "All these things are designed to affect the outside crowd," the *Times* said of the speeches and banners and colored lights. "But meanwhile the real work of President-making goes on in private corners and places where the clamors of music are not heeded except when it interrupts conversation, and then it is heartily cursed."

On June 12, two days before the convention was scheduled to begin in cavernous Exposition Hall, the 70 official New York delegates met in caucus and voted 68–2 to support Conkling. The New Yorkers dismissed a motion to endorse a tepid civil service reform measure. But as big as it was, the Empire State delegation represented only a fifth of the votes needed for the nomination. Conkling would need support from other states, and it was unclear where it would come from. Behind the scenes, the senator's enemies were working hard to make sure he never got it.

Temperatures climbed into the 90s and the air was filled with dirt and grime, but members of the Republican Reform Club dashed from one steamy hotel room to another to rally opposition to Conkling. Roosevelt, who probably covered a large part of the club's expenses in Cincinnati, was inexhaustible. That night, he made an anti-Conkling speech from the balcony of the Gibson House. A band hired by the club "tendered a sere-nade" from the street below as a large crowd, bathed in torch light, cheered Roosevelt's biting attacks on the New York boss. It was "altogether like a scene from one of those electioneering rows," Roosevelt proudly wrote to his daughter Bamie, "but all perfectly good [and] natural." At one point a pro-Conkling band tried to drown out Roosevelt. He paused until the music died down, and then remarked that the forces of political corruption were always trying to suppress the honest expression of public opinion. "The crowd cheered violently," he reported to Bamie. "We were all in perfect har-mony." No text of Roosevelt's speech survives, but word of his withering attack reached Conkling. He hated Roosevelt from that day forward.

Edwin Morgan, Arthur's former patron and the chairman of the Republican National Committee, called the convention to order at noon on June 14, 1876. Arthur and other Republican dignitaries who were not official dele-gates sat on the stage, along with about 130 reporters for the leading daily newspapers. The 756 Republican delegates were seated immediately in front of the stage, filling about a third of the wooden building. About as many alternates, separated from the delegates by a railing, were seated directly behind them. In the remaining space on the floor and in the galleries, about 1,500 people who had managed to obtain tickets waited for the drama to unfold. It didn't take long for Conkling's opponents to give it to them.

Two hours after the opening prayer, George William Curtis took the stage to read a message from the New York Republican Reform Club regarding the political conditions in the Empire State. "Federal office-holders have here usurped the organization of the Republican Party, and abuse it to exclude large classes of its members from any voice in its councils," Curtis asserted. "They treat the tenure of their offices as depending on the caprice of the Republican senator from this state, because he is the patron who dictated their appointment, and not on the will of the President or the people." At this, some of the New York delegates exchanged sickly smiles. "They have banded themselves into an odious and intolerable oligarchy which menaces the very system of our government," Curtis declared.

Curtis's speech was stirring, but the nomination wouldn't be decided by soaring oratory in sweltering Exposition Hall. Tilden was looming on the horizon, and the mass of Republican delegates knew they couldn't beat him with a candidate closely tied to the scandal-ridden Grant administration. Conkling's weakness was revealed on the first ballot, when he received only 99 votes, far behind his competitors. On the sixth and final ballot, the delegates reached a decision: the Republican nominee would be Rutherford B. Hayes, the Ohio governor. In deference to the Empire State and its electoral importance, the party chose as Hayes's running mate New Yorker William A. Wheeler—an avowed enemy of Conkling.

Arthur was disappointed, but he was a pragmatic politician, and knew he had to move on. Stepping off the stage at the conclusion of the proceedings, the chairman of the Hayes campaign buttonholed him. "How is New York?" the chairman asked. "All right," Arthur replied. "All the time for Hayes." The chairman handed Arthur a white Hayes badge, and the collector took off his blue Conkling badge and put it on.

Trim and compact, with auburn hair and a beard just starting to turn gray, the 53-year-old Hayes was viewed by most reformers as a satisfactory, if not thrilling, choice. The city solicitor of Cincinnati at the beginning of the Civil War, Hayes joined the Union Army as a major. He had three horses shot from under him and was wounded four times, most seriously at the Battle of South Mountain in 1862. By the end of the war, he had been promoted to major general and elected to the US House of Representatives. In

Congress he supported civil service reform legislation, and as governor he pushed for a civil service amendment to the Ohio constitution. Hayes had no obvious ties to the Grant administration and no known enemies, and had compiled a political career "never for a moment sullied by association with ring thieves."

The Republican platform referred only indirectly to civil service reform. After the convention, leading reformers urged the new nominee to make an explicit promise to dismantle the spoils system. In his July 8 acceptance letter Hayes did just that. "This system destroys the independence of the separate Departments of the Government; it tends directly to extravagance and official incapacity; it is a temptation to dishonesty," Hayes wrote. "It ought to be abolished. The reform should be thorough, radical and complete." To increase his chances of success, Hayes pledged to serve a single term.

But Hayes's proclamation couldn't mask the Republicans' fundamental weaknesses. No Republican could completely escape the shadow of "Grantism," while Tilden, now officially the Democratic standard-bearer, had built his entire political career on rooting out corruption. As the party in power, the Republicans got most of the blame for the economic depression that gripped the country in 1873, and Reconstruction had only added to their unpopularity in the South.

The Republicans desperately needed campaign cash. They turned to a familiar source: the New York Custom House. Arthur did his duty, collecting campaign assessments in a manner "more severe and ruthless than I ever known it," according to Burt. Arthur tapped Colonel Joseph J. Pinckney, a Republican alderman and a personal friend, to lead the effort. Pinckney established a headquarters right across the street from the Custom House, and employees were ordered to make their payments there. The office was located on Hanover Street, but Custom House workers had another name for it: "Hand-Over Street." Custom House weighers were ordered to contribute 5 percent of their salaries, deputies 4 percent. "No place of want or distress could induce Col. Pinckney or his assistants to make any abatement from the sum opposite any one's name," Burt recalled. "From the utter banality and insulting conduct of these political tax-gatherers I am certain that it was thought necessary by intimidation to crush out any spark of revolt."

While Arthur, a loyal Republican, did what he could to elect a man he didn't particularly like, Conkling found it impossible to set aside his personal animus toward Hayes, and especially Wheeler. In August, Hayes wrote Conkling a personal letter praising a speech he had made for Grant during the 1872 campaign and asking him to deliver a series of speeches for the Hayes-Wheeler ticket in Ohio and Indiana. "The more meetings you can address the better," Hayes wrote. However, claiming he was ill, the great orator gave only a single speech on behalf of the ticket, in October at the Utica Opera House.

In early September, Conkling did deliver brief remarks to a Republican crowd that unfurled a Hayes-Wheeler banner in town and then marched to the senator's house to serenade him. But Conkling's speech wasn't exactly what Hayes had in mind. In fact, Conkling didn't once mention the name of the Republican nominee or his running mate.

"It seems, in some quarters, to be regarded as rather disreputable to belong to the Republican Party and to have battled for its maintenance," Conkling huffed. "We are told the Republican Party is a machine. Yes. A government is a machine; a church is a machine; an army is a machine; an order of Masons is a machine; the common-school system of the State of New York is a machine; a political party is a machine.

"Every organization which binds men together for a common purpose is a machine," he continued. If its purposes are not honest, it should be hewn down and cast into the fire. But if its purposes are loyal and patriotic; if its aims are justice, civilization, progress, then it is a useful machine, and it ought to be preserved for the good that is in it."

• ◆ •

Hayes surely knew about the methods employed by Arthur and others on his behalf, but he raised no objections. Instead, he assured reformers that once in the White House, "this whole assessment business will go up, 'hook, line and sinker.'"

As it turned out, Hayes needed every vote and campaign dollar he could get—however they were procured. The initial returns showed Tilden with 4,284,020 votes to Hayes's 4,036,572. But the Democrat's 184 electoral votes were one short of the majority he needed to win the White House. Hayes, with 165 electoral votes, was 20 electoral votes away. Louisiana, South Carolina, Florida, and Oregon, where the count was still being disputed, held the missing electoral votes. Fortunately for Hayes, Republicans still controlled the electoral boards in the three Southern states, and they threw out enough Tilden votes to hand the White House to Hayes. Republican operative William E. Chandler, who organized his party's efforts during the dispute, later praised Arthur for his contribution, which probably consisted of fundraising. "Gen. Arthur's activity in connection with the contested countings in the southern states was of vital importance," Chandler wrote.

The day of Hayes's inauguration, March 5, 1877, was cold and cloudy with occasional snow flurries, but the weather was balmy compared to the frigid start to Grant's second term. Despite the disputed election and Hayes's loss of the popular vote, the crowd massed on Pennsylvania Avenue was "one grand ovation" as the carriage with the old and new presidents passed by on its way from the White House to the Capitol. Many people tossed their hats into the air in celebration, and at various points cheering spectators blocked the carriage.

The first order of business at the Capitol was Vice President Wheeler's inauguration in the Senate Chamber, which was observed by Arthur, Murphy, and dozens of other American and foreign dignitaries. After the ceremony, Grant and Hayes walked arm-in-arm onto the east portico, trailing the chief clerk of the Supreme Court, who was carrying a bible. The US flags and red, white, and blue bunting that hung from every corner and circled every pillar of the Capitol rippled in the gentle breeze.

Cheers erupted for several minutes when the crowd recognized that Hayes had descended to the front of the platform. When the shouting and clapping finally faded away, Hayes began to speak. It didn't take long for him to turn to the topic most interesting to Arthur, Conkling, and the New York machine.

"I ask the attention of the public to the paramount necessity of reform in our civil service—a reform not merely as to certain abuses and practices of so-called official patronage . . . but a change in the system of appointment itself—a reform that shall be thorough, radical and complete," Hayes proclaimed.

"The fact that both the great political parties of this country in declaring their principles prior to the election, gave a prominent place to the subject of reform of our civil service . . . must be regarded as the expression of the united voice and will of the whole country upon this subject, and both political parties are virtually pledged to give it their unreserved support.

"The President of the United States of necessity owes his election to office to the suffrage and zealous labors of a political party," Hayes declared, "but he should strive to be always mindful of the fact that he serves his party best who serves the country best."

Hayes climbed into his carriage amid the pealing of bells and the firing of cannon. As he set off for the White House, Arthur and his friends had to conclude that a new day had dawned in Washington—and that shadows were falling on their New York fiefdom.

CHAPTER TEN

His Fraudulency the President

ROSCOE CONKLING MAY or may not have been too ill to campaign for Rutherford B. Hayes in 1876—years later, Dr. William Watson claimed Conkling "was under my professional care during September, October and November of that year, and was suffering from malaria to such an extent that he was unable actively to engage in the political campaign"— but there is no doubt the New York boss detested the new president. Still smarting from his Cincinnati defeat, Conkling "never spoke of [Hayes] in public or private without a sneer." He questioned the legitimacy of Hayes's victory over Tilden, referring to him privately as "Ruther-fraud B. Hayes" or "His Fraudulency the President." Hayes's cabinet choices only deepened Conkling's distaste. In December 1876, Hayes confided to his diary that a Conkling ally had urged him "forcibly and with much feeling" to make the senator the secretary of state, assuring Hayes that Conkling would have participated in the campaign if he had been healthy. But Hayes appointed William Maxwell Evarts, a New York reformer, to that position. He selected the reformer Carl Schurz as secretary of the interior, and as postmaster general he tapped lifelong Democrat and former Confederate officer David Key, ignoring Conkling's pleas on behalf of his friend Tom Platt. Meanwhile, the president continued to rely on *Harper's* editor George William Curtis for advice on what Conkling called "snivel service reform."

The strutting New Yorker in the English gaiters and the dour Ohioan in the plain frock coat had little in common. Conkling spent his free hours cavorting with his glamorous mistress, Kate Sprague, or gambling at the poker table. Hayes and his teetotaler wife Lucy—reporters dubbed her "Lemonade Lucy"—were strict Methodists who observed the Sabbath. They entertained their Sunday guests by handing them hymnbooks and herding them around the harmonium, which Lucy played. Lucy usually wore black velvet trimmed with white lace, and she brushed her dark hair straight down from a broad part in the middle of her head. Fashionable ladies of the time favored huge bustles, décolleté necks, long trains, and lap dogs, but Lucy disdained all of that. She had a college degree—a first for First Ladies—and a forceful personality that outshone her colorless husband's, fueling speculation that she was the one running the country. She certainly ran the White House, and upon moving in she decreed there would be no alcohol served there. It was not a popular policy, and the chef in charge of state dinners often took pity on the guests by serving a rum-soaked sherbet concealed in a box made from the frozen skin of an orange. It became known as "the life-saving station." Somebody who met Secretary of State Evarts after one White House dinner asked him how it had gone. "Excellently," he replied. "The water flowed like champagne."

In April 1877, Hayes solidified his status as an enemy of Conkling—and of machine politicians around the country—when he ordered Treasury Secretary John Sherman to investigate charges of political influence and corruption in the nation's customs houses. Sherman urged Hayes to spare New York in the interest of Republican unity. But Hayes knew any reform effort that didn't include the nation's biggest source of patronage would be hollow. What's more, he was bitter about Conkling's failure to help his campaign, and had heard of his disparaging remarks about his legitimacy.

The investigation was well under way on May 14 when Hayes attended a Chamber of Commerce dinner at Delmonico's in Manhattan. When the president entered the restaurant under an arch constructed of Hartford fern and lilies of the valley, the band in the balcony struck up "Hail to the Chief" and the three hundred guests gave him a standing ovation. Conkling was conspicuously absent, but the crowd included other leading characters in the unfolding drama. Arthur and George Sharpe, the surveyor of the port, represented the New York Custom House. From Hayes's cabinet came Evarts and Schurz. There was William Dodge, the businessman whose complaints had launched the last New York Custom House investigation, and John Jay, who was leading the current probe. The men dined amicably under chandeliers festooned with smilax, amid tall stands of tropical plants and flowers. But after the coffee had been served and the cigars lit, Schurz punctured the blue haze with a searing indictment of Conkling and his henchmen.

"The public service ought not to be a soup-house to feed the indigent, a hospital and asylum for decayed politicians," Schurz declared, prompting cheers from the prosperous men at the tables—and almost certainly a few

furtive glances at Arthur. "It ought not to be a nursery for political mercenaries and a mere machine for carrying out selfish partisan ends. The offices
of the Government ought to be regarded as places of duty, trust, and responsibility, and nothing else.

"Officers ought to be selected with consideration of their fitness—their
ascertained fitness—for the places they are to fill, and not . . . their ability to
pack a caucus or to run primaries, or to be a good hand at draw-poker, in the
political sense," Schurz continued. The audience laughed, and he waited for
the last guffaws to peter out before continuing.

"Now, gentlemen, when such a reform is introduced, you will not only
have improved the machinery of the civil service itself, but you will have
lifted up the whole tone and character, intellectual as well as moral, of our
public life. You will have withdrawn their sustenance from that class of politicians whose power does not rest upon real ability and sound information,
but upon a shrewd management and manipulation of the public plunder."

Ten days later, the Jay Commission issued its first report on the New
York Custom House, and it was scathing. Custom House positions were
doled out "generally at the request of politicians and political associations
in this and other States, with little or no examination into the fitness of the
appointees beyond the recommendations of their friends," it stated. This
system was "unsound in principle, dangerous in practice, demoralizing in
its influence on all connected with the customs service, and calculated to
encourage and perpetuate the official ignorance, inefficiency, and corruption
which, perverting the powers of Government to personal and party ends,
have burdened the country with debt and taxes."

The panel called for a 20 percent cut in the Custom House's 1,038-man
workforce, the elimination of certain positions, and longer business hours.
(Among the 1,038: novelist Herman Melville, toiling in anonymity on a
Hudson River wharf for four dollars a day.) But these were only first steps.
It emphasized that stamping out "the evils wrought by mismanagement and
corruption, can be accomplished only by the emancipation of the service
from partisan control." In other words, Arthur and the rest of Conkling's
gang had to go.

This was the result that Hayes had hoped for. "Party leaders should have
no more influence in appointments than other equally respectable citizens,"
he wrote to Sherman. "No assessments for political purposes on officers
should be allowed."

Conkling quietly watched the Jay Commission do its work, hopeful that
Arthur—a far less divisive figure than he was—could weather the storm.

Arthur knew how to charm people, and he had managed to perform his political dirty work while doing a serviceable job for the city's mercantile and commercial interests. So on June 16, 1877, Conkling boarded the German Lloyd line steamer *Mosel* for a long-planned trip to Europe, while his wife remained behind in Utica. He was making the journey, he said, to recover his health, though gossips noted that he and Kate Sprague would have overlapping stays in Paris.

Less than a week after Conkling's departure, Hayes issued an executive order. No federal employee "should be required or permitted to take part in the management of political organizations, caucuses, conventions, or election campaigns," it stated, and "no assessment for political purposes on officers or subordinates should be allowed." Rumors that Hayes was ready to fire Arthur wheeled between Washington and New York.

The pressure intensified when the Jay Commission issued follow-up reports on July 4 and July 21. The July 4 report found "ignorance and incapacity on the part of the employees in all the branches of the service, creating delays and mistakes, imperiling the safety of the revenue, and the interests of the importers, and bringing the service into reproach." Department chiefs told investigators that "men were sent to them without brains enough to do the work, and that some of those appointed to perform the delicate duties of the appraiser's office, requiring the special qualities of an expert, were better fitted to hoe and plow."

●—◆—●

On August 10, 1877, a foggy Friday morning, somebody spotted the German steamer *Neckar* off Fire Island. A short time later, the *Thomas Collyer*, "gaily decked with bunting and well-loaded with enthusiastic Republicans," set out from Hoboken to meet her. As the *Collyer* rounded Sandy Hook, a southwest wind routed the fog, revealing numerous yachts and pleasure boats also decorated with bright bunting. Steamboats and tugs whistled, and schooners, riding idly at anchor, raised flags and streamers in tribute.

As the *Collyer* drew near to the *Neckar*, the cannon it had borrowed for the occasion belched forth a welcome and the Republicans crowded on the upper deck rent the air with cheers. On the bridge of the *Neckar*, a regal figure waved his hat in greeting. Roscoe Conkling was coming home.

When the *Neckar* reached the wharf at Hoboken, the senator glided down a gangplank draped with red, white, and blue bunting as the band played "Hail to the Chief" and passengers waved white handkerchiefs and small American flags. "Mr. Conkling seems the picture of health," the anti-Conkling *Tribune* reported. "His appearance is in marked contrast with his haggard look when he departed for Europe." The *Sun* ran the story of Conkling's return on its front page, proclaiming that "no statesman returning to his native land after a brief sojourn abroad was ever gratified with a warmer and more enthusiastic reception."

After the mayor of Jersey City delivered brief welcoming remarks, Conkling marched behind a line of musicians to the *Collyer*, which was docked nearby, for the short trip to Manhattan. When he arrived he climbed into a waiting carriage and was whisked across town to the Fifth Avenue Hotel.

That evening, a crowd of nearly 1,500 gathered outside the hotel, eager to hear Conkling rail against Hayes and his "snivel service reform." But the senator kept them waiting for hours while he socialized with friends and associates inside (Arthur was absent). Meanwhile, "a number of fashionably attired ladies" sent bouquets of flowers to Conkling's rooms. When one of the senator's visitors asked him about Hayes's executive order, he "listened rather impatiently," then tore up a note he held in his hand, tossed the fragments into the fireplace, and withdrew to a distant corner of the room.

Conkling finally emerged at 11 p.m., squinting in the glare of two calcium lights secured to streetlamps on either side of the hotel's front portico. A 60-piece band played "Swanee River" as the crowd pushed forward to hear a rousing defense of the machine. Instead, the senator spooned out commentary on the "rapid and cheap transit" in London, and—in a sop to the many New Yorkers of German extraction—the "magnanimity of Germany" in sparing the parks and palaces of Versailles during the Franco-Prussian War. "What about Hayes?" one man called out. "Give us your views on civil service reform!" cried another. Conkling either didn't hear their pleas or he ignored them.

Four days later, Conkling quietly boarded the 10:30 a.m. train to Utica. He spoke briefly from his car to crowds that met him at stations along the way, but he didn't discuss politics. In his hometown he received a royal welcome and made his longest speech yet, but still he refused to mention Hayes or the Custom House.

Meanwhile, Hayes turned the screws tighter. On September 6, Sherman wrote in a confidential letter to Arthur that the president wanted him, along with the Custom House surveyor and naval officer, to resign. He invited the collector to Washington to discuss the matter. But before the letter reached Arthur, Sherman inexplicably leaked the news to the press. Arthur's pique was evident in his written reply, which confirmed receipt of Sherman's letter "informing me officially of facts which had already come to my knowledge through newspapers of this morning." Arthur agreed to come to Washington, but claimed that pressing business in New York would detain him for another week. When Sherman and Arthur finally met on September 17, the secretary offered the collector the consulship to Paris in exchange for his resignation. Arthur said he would consider it. Sherman was relieved; perhaps a bloody intraparty battle could be averted.

A week later the New York Republicans gathered for their annual convention in Rochester. Arthur, obeying Hayes's June 22 executive order, stayed home. But Conkling, who rarely attended state conventions, came with a large group of machine delegates. He had remained silent on the Custom House controversy for more than a month. That was about to change.

George William Curtis fired the first salvo by offering a resolution that "the lawful title of Rutherford B. Hayes to the Presidency is as clear and perfect as that of George Washington." The *Harper's* editor delicately criticized Conkling and other New York Republicans who were defying the president, then tweaked the senator personally by suggesting he won so many federal court cases because the judges and opposing attorneys owed their appointments to him.

The Conkling delegates buzzed as their champion, nostrils wide, eyes blazing, mounted the rostrum like a man about to run a race. Conkling began by questioning whether it was appropriate for a state political convention to tackle national issues. Then he wheeled his cannon toward Curtis and the other reformers.

"Who are these men who, in newspapers or elsewhere, are cracking their whips over me and playing schoolmaster to the party?" Conkling roared. "They are of various sorts and conditions. Some of them are man-milliners, the dilettanti and carpet knights of politics, whose efforts have been expended in denouncing and ridiculing and accusing honest men." The Conkling delegates exploded with laughter at the mention of "man-milliners"—a reference to the fact that *Harper's* had recently begun to publish articles about ladies' fashion.

"Some of them are men who, when they could work themselves into conventions, have attempted to belittle and befoul Republican administrations and to parade their own thin veneering of superior purity." If it was corrupt for officeholders to participate in politics, Conkling said, then "the Republican Party has been unclean and vicious all its life." In his seat, Curtis was staggered by Conkling's vitriol—made harder to endure by the knowledge that under convention rules, he would not have a chance to respond.

"Remarkable!" he muttered to those sitting near him. "What an exhibition! Bad temper—very bad temper!"

Conkling pressed on, stalking up and down the aisle between the seated delegates. "Some of these worthies masquerade as reformers," the senator said, bowing in mock reverence, his face twisted in a sneer. "Their vocation and ministry is to lament the sins of other people. Their stock in trade is rancid, canting self-righteousness." These political amateurs "forget that parties are not built up by deportment, or by ladies' magazines, or gush," Conkling growled. He leaned forward and tilted to one side so he could point his index finger at Curtis, and hurled his words at the hapless editor like a boy flinging stones.

For two hours, Conkling poured "every resource of sarcasm" upon his victim. His followers were thrilled, but more neutral observers viewed the speech as a political disaster: the Republican boss in the largest and most important state in the Union had just declared war on the newly elected Republican president.

A *Herald* reporter acknowledged Conkling's speech was "bristling with good points," but added, "there will not be a shadow of a chance to elect a State ticket this fall." Conkling "has not only drawn the sword and thrown away the scabbard; he has dipped his weapon in venom," the *Herald* wrote. "He used his personal triumph for flinging a firebrand of discord into the Republican Party. . . . The Senator has acted the part of a blind and infuriate Samson who crushed himself beneath the edifice against whose pillars he leaned his mighty shoulders."

Even Greeley's *Tribune* had to admit the speech was magnificent. "The Great Senator of New-York, as his friends are fond of calling him, had his innings yesterday and last night," it reported. "As an exhibition of oratorical power, of brilliant sarcasm, well rounded, graceful periods, eloquent invective, great personal force, and individual momentum, it is conceded to be a masterly effort." However, it went on, "no one of his most partial friends pretends to-day to deny that the speech was exceedingly injudicious and unwise, and that the effect upon both himself and the party must be damaging."

Curtis was stunned by the barrage. "It was the saddest sight I ever knew, that man glaring at me in a fury of hate, and storming out his foolish blackguardism," he wrote to his friend Charles Eliot Norton, a Harvard art professor, author, and social critic. "I was all pity. I had not thought him great, but I had not suspected how small he was." Curtis said the text of Conkling's speech, which was published in the newspapers, did not reflect what it was like to sit through it. "You do not get all the venom, and no one can imagine the Mephisophelean leer and spite."

A few days later, Arthur notified the Hayes administration that he was not interested in going to Paris, and that he would not resign as collector. "The treatment of the whole matter has been so unfortunate that I feel I cannot now resign," Arthur wrote to Sherman. "Before your letter of September sixth or any suggestion to me of a resignation, official and public announcement was made that I was to be removed. The general understanding that it is a removal cannot now be changed."

President Hayes didn't smoke, didn't drink, and didn't swear. He indulged in one cup of coffee at breakfast and single cup of tea at lunch, and at dinner he drank only water. He walked laps through the halls of the White House after every meal, and never missed his morning exercises or his afternoon nap. But those who dismissed the president as a milquetoast underestimated the steel in his spine. Hayes knew members of his own party objected to some of his policies, including civil service reform. But he did not consider backing down. "How to meet and overcome this opposition is the question," he wrote in his diary. "I am clear that I am right. I believe that a large majority of the best people are in full accord with me. Now, my purpose is to keep cool; to treat all adversaries considerately, respectfully, and kindly, but at the same time in a way to satisfy them of my sincerity and firmness."

Hayes had offered Arthur and the other Conkling cronies the opportunity to step aside gracefully, and they had rebuffed him. Now he would mount a frontal assault. With Congress about to reconvene, Hayes decided to nominate new men—better men—to replace the rogues who had defied him.

CHAPTER ELEVEN

"The One I Loved Dearest"

T HEODORE ROOSEVELT SR. was a dutiful husband, the father of four children, and a faithful communicant at the Madison Square Presbyterian Church, where on many Sundays he attended not one service but two. He belonged to the Union League Club and the Century Association. In 1877 he was 46 years old with an athletic build and a square Dutch jaw. His eyes were grayish-blue, and his hair and beard were chestnut brown. He wore suits of the finest fabric, beautifully tailored. He lavished attention on his stunning wife, Mittie, and when the couple attended dinners and balls together they left an indelible impression. "To see him put on her wraps and escort her from room to room was beautiful," one man recalled. "It seemed to me that I never knew till then what the word 'gentleman' meant."

Roosevelt had no great love for music and art, as Mittie did. He did not write, and could not charm his companions with sparkling after-dinner conversation. His passion was children—his own and others. He taught his two sons and two daughters to ride horses and climb trees, and often joined in their games. "My personal impression," a nephew remembered, "is that he was a large, broad, bright, cheerful man with an intense sympathy with everything you brought to him. He loved children especially." But even as his children bathed in "the sunshine of his affection," they respected their father as the ultimate moral authority. He did not tolerate deceit or cowardice, selfishness or idleness.

Roosevelt was a junior partner in the prosperous family business— Roosevelt and Son, importers of plate glass—but he had little interest in the work. His true calling was providing aid to the needy and building up the city that he loved. Soon after the war, he helped launch the New York

Orthopedic Dispensary and Hospital, for the treatment of children with spinal diseases. He also helped found the Metropolitan Museum of Art and the American Museum of Natural History. "Whatever he had to do, he did all out," the philanthropist and social worker Charles Loring Brace recalled. Roosevelt's friend John Hay referred to his "maniacal benevolence." In a letter to his wife, Theodore explained that, "as much as I enjoy loafing, there is something higher for which to live."

One of Roosevelt's favorite causes was the Children's Aid Society, founded by Brace in 1853. There were more than 20,000 homeless children in New York. They sold newspapers and day-old flowers, indentured themselves to oyster peddlers, carried sloshing pails of beer for barkeeps, and begged outside the theaters and opera houses. The society tried to coax them off the streets with religious classes, reading rooms, industrial schools, and workshops. The ultimate goal was to return them to their families, if they had them, but more often to transport them on "orphan trains" to foster families in the Midwest. One of the society's projects was the Newsboys' Lodging House on West 18th Street, where every night several hundred boys, most of them newsboys, gladly paid five cents for a clean bed in a warm room. When Brace asked Theodore whether he'd be willing to visit the boys at the Lodging House every other Sunday evening, Theodore said his "troublesome conscience" would not allow it—he pledged to be there *every* Sunday.

In October 1877, President Hayes offered Roosevelt his first political post: collector of the New York Custom House. The year before, Grant's scandals and Conkling's presidential bid had persuaded Roosevelt to dip his toe into party politics for the first time in Cincinnati. Now this public-spirited man—Curtis called him "the image and figure of the citizen which every American should hope to be"—was being called upon to purify the nation's most notorious patronage den. "I will take the office not to administer it for the benefit of a party," he told the papers, "but for the benefit of the whole people."

A week after Hayes submitted Roosevelt's name to the Senate for its approval, the nominee appeared at City Hall on behalf of the State Board of Charities to report on conditions in New York's hospitals, orphanages, asylums, and prisons. Roosevelt had seen criminals and patients confined together in overcrowded, filthy, and airless facilities at Bellevue Hospital and on Blackwell's Island, Hart's Island, and Randall's Island. The food was rancid, and the hospital wards lacked linens, towels, and soap. The conditions were scandalous, but to Roosevelt they were merely symptoms of "the great fundamental evil of the system by which they are governed." Like the clerks in the Custom House, the wardens and attendants in these institutions were hired based on their political connections, not on their fitness for the job. The result, predictably, was an absence of accountability and a workforce riddled with incompetence and "graver moral deficiencies." Spending more money would not solve the problems he had found, Roosevelt said, because "there is no responsible head to any one of these hospitals or asylums; no Superintendent who has authority to issue orders and to punish his subordinates if they are disregarded." He warned city leaders that, "so long as political pressure is allowed to have weight with you in the choice of employees, so long will the charitable institutions of the City be badly managed."

So here was the connection between Roosevelt's humanitarian work and Conkling's machine. How could government improve the lives of citizens, or be trusted to try, if it was a repository for unqualified political hacks?

Before Roosevelt could replace Arthur and clean up the Custom House, he had to be confirmed by the Senate. The first step in that process was consideration by the Senate commerce committee—chaired by none other than Roscoe Conkling.

Hayes sent his nominations for the top Custom House posts to the Senate on October 24, 1877, less than two weeks after the 45th Congress convened in a special session. Conkling sat on the nomination for nearly a month. He expressed confidence that New Yorkers stood behind him, disparaging the reformers as a tiny minority. "There are about 300 persons here [in New York City] who believe themselves to occupy the solar walk and milky way, and even up there they lift their skirts very carefully for fear even the heavens might stain them," he quipped to a *Herald* reporter. "Some of these people would vote against a man because he had been nominated. . . . They would have people fill their offices by nothing less than divine selection." Almost sadly, he added that his enemies "were after the unattainable in human government."

In the middle of November 1877, Conkling sent President Hayes a detailed request for all evidence related to "the question of removing Chester A. Arthur," including all communications asking for Arthur's removal or retention; any charges of personal or official misconduct; any communication from Hayes or Sherman censuring Arthur or disapproving of any of his actions; and Roosevelt's recommendations for the job. Hayes, who was not legally obligated to explain why he was removing the collector or any other federal official, simply ignored the request. Meanwhile, behind the scenes, Arthur and his allies were lobbying Democrats on the committee to ensure they voted with the chairman.

A week after Conkling made his request, Arthur wrote a letter to Secretary Sherman, protesting that the Jay Commission had "sought out all that could be said against the officers of the customs, and, of course, took a partial and one-sided view." He accused the panel of relying heavily on hearsay, and complained that he and other Custom House officers were given "no opportunity for cross-examinations and little for rebuttal or explanation."

On November 30, Conkling's committee unanimously rejected Hayes's Custom House nominations. (The three Democrats on the panel abstained.) Congress had been meeting in a special session, and it expired on December 3, 1877. But Conkling successfully lobbied his Senate colleagues to reconvene immediately, a maneuver that prevented Hayes from suspending Arthur and replacing him with Roosevelt during the recess, which he had the power to do.

Many Republicans were eager to make peace between Conkling and Hayes. In early December, two congressmen presented Hayes with a petition, signed by 15 of New York's 17 representatives, urging the president not to resubmit the same names for the New York Custom House. Hayes refused. "I am now in a contest on the question of the right of Senators to dictate or control nominations," Hayes wrote in his diary. "Mr. Conkling insists that no officer shall be appointed in New York without his consent, obtained previously to the nomination. This is the first and most important step in the effort to reform the civil service."

Hayes resubmitted his Custom House nominations. This time Conkling's committee confirmed Edwin A. Merritt as surveyor, but it again rejected Roosevelt and LeBaron Bradford Prince, Hayes's choice for naval officer. Before the full Senate voted, Conkling spoke for nearly an hour and a half, defending Arthur, railing against Hayes and Roosevelt, and suggesting the nomination had been made with the express purpose of humiliating him. After a six-hour debate, senators voted 31–25 to reject Roosevelt and Prince. "The triumph of Senator Conkling is as complete as the defeat of Evarts, Hayes, and the fraudulent Administration is crushing," the pro-Conkling *Sun* crowed. The newspaper saw the roots of Conkling's victory in his now-famous speech at the Rochester convention. "When all the other would-be leaders of the Republican Party hesitated to assert their manhood and give voice to the sentiment of the millions of voters they were too faint-hearted to represent, he uttered the clarion notes that rallied a disheartened and disgusted following."

Arthur was elated. "I cannot tell you how gratified I am at the splendid victory you have won, apart from & way beyond any personal considerations of my own," he wrote to Conkling. "The whole town is excited by the event & the current of popular feeling is all with you."

Despite the papers' portrayal of the vote, Hayes believed it was just a temporary setback. "In the language of the press, 'Senator Conkling has won a great victory over the Administration,'" Hayes wrote in his diary. "But the end is not yet. I am right, and shall not give up the contest."

In a letter to his son Theodore, a Harvard sophomore, Roosevelt downplayed his personal disappointment. "The machine politicians have shown their colors and not one person has been able to make an accusation of any kind against me. Indeed, they have all done me more than justice," he wrote. "I never told your mother but it would have practically kept me in the city almost all the time in summer and that would be no joke."

But Roosevelt, who had suffered from severe intestinal pains during the final weeks of the nomination battle, dreaded what machine politicians might do to American democracy. "I feel sorry for the country, however, as it shows the power of the partisan politicians who think of nothing higher than their own interests," he wrote his son. "I fear for your future. We cannot stand so corrupt a government for any great length of time."

Dejected reformers blamed Hayes for being outmaneuvered twice by the cagey Conkling. As 1877 turned into 1878, Arthur seemed secure in his Custom House redoubt, and the prospects for meaningful civil service reform were bleak. "The friends of reform are alternately disheartened and disgusted by performances that render the President's pretensions ridiculous, while its enemies chuckle over his inconsistencies, and point mockingly to his tortuous, hesitating course," the *Times* editorialized.

As the winter wore on, Roosevelt's stomach pains grew worse. He was diagnosed with inflammation of the bowels, but in fact he had stomach cancer, and it was malignant and inoperable. On February 7, 1878, he was well enough—or sufficiently sedated—to take a sleigh ride with one of his daughters, and that afternoon he was cheered by a letter from his son Theodore. But the next day, after another sleigh ride, his excruciating pain returned and the family sent for a doctor. By now the newspapers had learned of his condition, and on February 9, a Saturday, a crowd gathered outside the Roosevelt home on West 57th Street, with many newsboys and ragged street children participating in the vigil. An urgent telegram was dispatched to young Theodore in Cambridge, instructing him to return home immediately.

At 11:15 p.m., the patient opened his eyes and his son Elliott motioned to the doctor, who tried to administer brandy through a tube. A few moments late, the suffering man groaned, threw up his arms and turned over with one hand under his head and the other hanging over the edge of the sofa. His wife and daughter were kneeling by his side, next to Elliott, when Theodore fluttered his eyelids, breathed deeply three times, and died.

Young Theodore, who idolized his father, was crushed by the death of "the one I loved dearest on earth." He vowed to keep his father's letters forever as "talismans against evil." Perhaps the family believed Theodore's crushing political defeat contributed to his demise, though nobody said so explicitly. But young Theodore almost certainly carried the memory of his father's Custom House fight with him in his own bid to make government a force for good. "How I wish I could ever do something to keep up his name," Theodore wrote in his diary shortly after his father's death.

• ◆ •

True to his word, Hayes refused to capitulate to Conkling. In the summer of 1878, with Congress in recess, he seized the opportunity to fire Arthur and put Merritt in his place. Without Senate approval the move was only temporary, but Democrats had gained a majority in the 1878 election. A few months later, their support proved decisive: Conkling could not muster the votes to reverse Hayes's gambit, and Arthur was out for good.

It was a stunning turn of events, but Arthur landed on his feet. He returned to practicing law, and now he had so many friends and connections in New York he had no trouble making a comfortable living. He also owned real estate purchased during his lucrative Custom House years, and when Nell's mother died in 1878 the couple inherited a modest sum. Arthur's main focus, however, continued to be politics. In February 1879, he became the permanent president of the Republican Central Committee, which headed the New York City party and was the most important cog in the statewide machine.

Arthur's immediate concern was preparing Republicans for the statewide election of 1879, the first in which all of the state's chief officers, including the governor, would be elected at the same time. But he and Conkling also had a bigger prize in mind: the White House. Since Hayes had pledged to serve a single term, the 1880 presidential election would be an opportunity to erase the reforms implemented by "His Fraudulency."

The man Arthur and Conkling envisioned as Hayes's successor was on a worldwide tour with his wife and son, being feted by heads of state and hailed by cheering throngs from England to Egypt to Japan: Ulysses S. Grant. The Grants were traveling with a reporter from the *Herald*, who sent home glowing descriptions of the adulation that met the man who had saved the Union. Other newspapers published the reports, and before long, memories of Grant's scandal-plagued administration began to fade. By the summer of 1878, a year into the Grants' triumphant tour, many in the North were calling for the ex-president to run for an unprecedented third term. The calls grew louder in the fall, when the election left Democrats in control of both houses of Congress. Only Grant, many Republicans believed, could save their party.

In August 1879, Grant and his family were in Japan, staying at the summer palace of Emperor Mutsuhito and Empress Haruko. In New York, the state campaigns were beginning to heat up. But many New Yorkers were more interested in a story out of Rhode Island, one that was receiving front-page coverage in the *Sun* and the *Times*.

On August 10, Roscoe Conkling's long affair with Kate Sprague finally came to a head when her husband, Senator William Sprague, returned home early from a business trip to discover that Kate had been hosting Conkling at their house in Narragansett Pier. Sprague ordered Conkling to leave immediately, but Conkling refused. "A few high words ensued," and then Sprague went upstairs to retrieve his shotgun. When he realized he had no percussion caps for his weapon, he dashed into town to get some. He returned home to find Conkling still there. Again Sprague ordered him to leave, but Conkling demurred, pointing out that his baggage wasn't packed and he had no carriage. Sprague pulled out his pocket watch and warned Conkling that if he didn't leave in 30 seconds, he would blow his brains out.

At this point, a carriage pulled up outside the Sprague home—apparently somebody had summoned it while Sprague was in town searching for percussion caps. In some versions of the story, Conkling escaped through a bedroom window, clutching his trousers. However he exited the Sprague residence, Conkling scampered into the waiting carriage and rode off. His baggage followed sometime later.

Sprague, still boiling, decided to follow Conkling into town to reiterate his threat. He found the New York senator pacing on the sidewalk outside a café. "I want you," Sprague said. Conkling approached cautiously, speaking softly to Sprague in an effort to calm him. This only fueled the rage of the Rhode Islander, who "denounced Conkling violently and told him plainly that he had had enough of his intimacy with Mrs. Sprague, and did not propose to have any more of it." Sprague asked Conkling whether he was armed; Conkling said he was not. "Then go and arm yourself, and hereafter go armed. I don't intend to shoot an unarmed man; but I tell you now that if you ever cross my path again, I will shoot you at sight." With that, Sprague returned to his carriage and drove off.

Conkling refused to comment on the incident, but his enemies were overjoyed. "The Conkling scandal is the newspaper sensation of the time," Hayes wrote in his diary. "This exposure of C's rottenness will do good in one direction. It will weaken his political power, which is bad and only bad."

•—◆—•

Despite the scandal, Republicans triumphed in the 1879 New York elections. Conkling's lieutenant, Alonzo Cornell, became governor, and Republicans won all but one of the other statewide offices and control of the state Senate and the Assembly. In early January 1880, Arthur left for Albany to help shape the structure of the legislature. Republicans had selected George Sharpe, another Conkling crony, to be Assembly speaker, and Arthur was helping Sharpe dole out committee assignments when he received an urgent telegram from home: a bad cold Nell caught while waiting outside for a carriage after a concert had turned into pneumonia.

The only way Arthur could get back to Manhattan on January 11, a Sunday, was to travel on a milk train, which had to stop at a succession of milk stands and creameries as it crawled downstate. Through the window, Arthur could see ice floes floating down the Hudson, broken up by two weeks of temperatures in the 40s. In Albany, his mind had been consumed by the cold math of committee assignments, but now it was suffused with warm images of Nell, the girl who tenderly kissed his eyelids on the Saratoga window seat, the lover whose photo he had kissed every morning in Kansas. As a young man, he had considered her happiness to be "a precious sacred trust, dearer than life itself." Over time, other priorities had taken precedence. The social and financial benefits of his political career had thrilled both of them, but it had taken a heavy toll on their marriage. While Chester ate and drank and frolicked with waiter-girls in low-cut bodices, Nell had to find companionship on the arms of elderly friends. When Nell's mother died in France in April 1878, she crossed the Atlantic alone to retrieve the body, because Chester was not willing to leave in the middle of the Custom House crisis. According to friends, "the shock and nervous tension caused by her bereavement and her long, sad journey" had been a serious blow to her health.

By the time Arthur finally reached his Lexington Avenue brownstone it was late at night and his ailing wife was asleep, sedated by morphine administered by her physician. For 24 hours he sat at her bedside, stroking her hair, holding her hand. But the "pulses of love" he had felt as far away as St. Joseph, Missouri, were growing fainter. Late on the night of January 12, Nell died. She was only 42.

At Nell's funeral at the Church of the Heavenly Rest on Fifth Avenue, Arthur was surrounded by nearly every important member of the New York Republican machine. Their presence, a reminder of his neglect, must have provided little comfort as he stared at the silver-handled casket, draped in a black cloth with a crown of immortelles, which held the woman he loved "fondly, truly, devotedly, always." The Mendelssohn Glee Club sang the hymn, "There Is a Blessed Home," and then Arthur departed for a train to Albany, where his wife would be buried in the Rural Cemetery, just north of the city. Arriving there in the early afternoon, Arthur was met by Governor Cornell and a delegation of state lawmakers.

Arthur was "completely unnerved and prostrated" by Nell's death, according to a friend. When he returned to Manhattan, he tried to find comfort in yet another late night with Tom Murphy. But the two men did not visit a saloon or theater. Instead, Arthur kept Murphy walking back and forth on 29th Street between Third and Fifth Avenues until 2 a.m., spilling out his sorrow.

CHAPTER TWELVE

Dark Horse

THE SUN ROSE in a cloudless sky and an easterly breeze rippled the banners bobbing toward Michigan Avenue. Most of the men carrying the signs wore colorful badges, some with portraits of Grant, others of Blaine, and a few featuring the rugged face of John Sherman, stamped in black on green satin.

"Here's your Blaine lemonade!"

The vendor hawking large glasses of water with floating slices of soggy lemon—"ice cold," he claimed, and only a dime—found few takers among the singing, cheering throngs that were spilling out of Adams and Monroe Streets. Many were distracted by the newspapermen waiting outside the ticket office, grumbling and cursing in a long line that snaked toward the swamp where P. T. Barnum's circus had pitched its tents. Chicagoans had been enjoying the exploits of Emma Lake, "Queen of the Side Saddle," and marveling at "The Leopard Boy" since Sunday. Now the eyes of the nation were focused on the city's Interstate Exposition Building, ready to be riveted by a production with far greater import: the 1880 Republican National Convention.

President Hayes's decision not to seek a second term opened the door to a slew of Republicans eager to succeed him. When the delegates and newspapermen converged on Chicago at the beginning of June, Grant was viewed as the strong favorite. Conkling's old enemy James G. Blaine, now a US senator from Maine, was the leading "anti-Grant" candidate. Secretary of the Treasury John Sherman of Ohio, a former congressman and senator, and Senator George Edmunds of Vermont also had significant support.

Conkling was the leader of the Grant forces and the undisputed star of the convention. He didn't have to share the spotlight with Grant or any of the other declared candidates because they weren't there; at the time, it was considered unseemly to compete in person for the nomination. Whenever Conkling appeared in a hotel lobby or on the street, men and women stopped to point and stare at the lordly senator from the Empire State. More than a few remarked that Conkling in the flesh was even more impressive than the newspapers had described him. In trying to rally support for Grant, Conkling had softened his usual imperiousness. He mingled freely with the crowds in the lobbies of the Grand Pacific Hotel and the Palmer House, shaking hands and bantering with delegates and admirers.

The official proceedings began at noon on Wednesday, June 2, 1880. Striding arm-in-arm, Conkling and Arthur led the large New York delegation to the Exposition Building, where half a dozen flags flew from the corner towers and central dome. The doors and gateways of the glass-and-metal colossus, some reserved for delegates, others designated for alternates or telegraph operators, were guarded by stern policemen wearing special red-and-gold badges. Inside, more American flags draped the front of the long galleries and hung from the braces supporting the arched roof. A huge portrait of Washington was suspended over the delegates. Lincoln's likeness was stretched across the rear of the auditorium, flanked by the concluding words of the Gettysburg Address: "And that government of the people, by the people and for the people shall not perish from the earth."

For several days, the delegates debated committees, credentials, and rules. On one occasion, the squabbling ceased as soon as Conkling entered the hall. As the Lordly Roscoe passed down the aisle, the crowd erupted in cheers. He remained stone-faced, but his cheeks colored as the waves of applause washed over him. He bowed to a few friends and sat down, but a few more minutes passed before it was quiet enough for normal business to resume. Queen Victoria's youngest son, Prince Leopold, who happened to be traveling through Chicago, watched some of the proceedings from a place of honor on the platform. The prince wore a gray summer suit, carried a cane and a fan, and had "a chin less suggestive of weakness than that of some other members of the family." He must have wondered about this American senator who carried himself, and was treated, like royalty.

On Thursday night at the Grand Pacific Hotel, Conkling gave a speech expressing confidence in Grant's eventual triumph. The voting had not begun, but Conkling assured his audience that Grant had three hundred delegates who would stand by him, no matter what, from the first ballot until the last. That was far less than the 379 needed to secure the nomination, but Conkling said the necessary converts would rush to Grant once they realized that no other candidate could possibly muster a majority.

On Saturday, Conkling arrived in the hall shortly after 11 a.m. wearing a light blue tie and clutching a soft felt hat. He offered words of encouragement to his hard-pressed troops and bowed, with knit brows and compressed lips, as his brigade commanders gave him the latest news. It was sweltering, and he fanned himself vigorously. The delegates spent the day voting on more rules and resolutions before breaking for dinner. They returned just after 7 p.m., ready to hear the nomination speeches.

The clerk called the roll of the states. The first state to speak up was Michigan. James Frederick Joy, a railroad magnate and former member of the Michigan House who had been a close confidant of Lincoln's, nominated Blaine. Next, a delegate from Minnesota rose to nominate William Windom, the state's senior US senator. Neither speech electrified the delegates.

"New York!" the clerk shouted.

Conkling paused, allowing the excitement to mount, before he unfolded his athletic frame and strode to the reporters' platform in the middle of the hall. He climbed atop the center table, bowed in each direction, and saluted a friend in the gallery. When the crowd's roar subsided, the convention chairman invited Conkling to take the main stage. The senator said he preferred to remain where he was. Then for a few moments he stood stock-still, with his head and shoulders thrown back and his left thumb hooked in a waistcoat pocket. His gray eyes were flashing, and his Hyperion curl was perfectly arranged on his forehead. The multitude waited, silent and breathless. Finally Conkling's baritone reverberated around the hall:

> *When asked what state he hails from,*
> *Our sole reply shall be,*
> *He comes from Appomattox*
> *And its famous apple tree!*

The recitation of these well-known lines, a Union soldier-poet's paean to General Grant, ignited an explosion of cheers and applause. For 10 minutes Conkling waited, perfectly poised, until the last echoes died out. Grant, he went on, was the only candidate who could "carry New York against any opponent, and can carry not only the North, but several states of the South." But Grant's claim went beyond electoral politics, Conkling emphasized. "Never defeated—in peace or in war—his name is the most illustrious borne by living man," the senator declared. "His services attest his greatness and the country—nay, the world—knows them by heart."

What about the scandals that marred Grant's previous administration? These were nothing more than "assaults upon him [that] have seasoned and strengthened his hold on the public heart." Conkling took a gulp from a glass of water and sucked a lemon to restore his voice. "Calumny's ammunition has all been exploded. The powder has all been burned once, its force is spent, and the name of 'Grant' will glitter a bright and imperishable star in the diadem of the republic when those who have tried to tarnish that name have moldered in forgotten graves." Conkling blew right through the five-minute barrier set for nomination speeches. "Time! Time!" Blaine's supporters shouted from the galleries. But Conkling silenced them with the palm of his ivory hand.

The speech was a triumph. After it was over, one spectator asked Conkling how he had managed to make himself heard over the clamor. "By speaking very deliberately, and carefully pronouncing the vowels," he replied.

The clerk continued the roll call of the states. When he called, "Ohio!" a muscular, bearded man with a prominent forehead and a Roman nose stood up. Congressman James A. Garfield had come to the convention to nominate fellow Ohioan John Sherman, but he had not written a speech, and was nervous about addressing such a large crowd. Like Conkling, Garfield decided to forgo the main platform and instead mounted the wooden reporters' table. He cautioned the delegates not to get carried away by the emotional power of Conkling's address. "As I sat in my seat and witnessed this demonstration, this assemblage seemed to me a human ocean in tempest," he said. "I have seen the sea lashed into fury and tossed into spray, and its grandeur moves the soul of the dullest man; but I remember that it is not the billows, but the calm level of the sea from which all heights and depths are measured." Garfield pointed to Sherman's long experience in public life, and his stainless reputation in an era of scandal. "For 25 years he has trodden the perilous heights of public duty, and against all the shafts of malice has borne his breast unharmed."

The crowd applauded Garfield's speech, but some Sherman partisans groused that Garfield had neglected to mention Sherman's name until the final sentence. A few accused him of promoting himself, not Sherman. "The sickly manner in which Garfield presented your name has disgusted your friends here," a close confidant wrote to Sherman, who had remained in Washington. "He has been of no service to you . . . he was extremely lukewarm in your support. He is a Garfield man." Garfield, worried that he would be branded as disloyal, recoiled at the charges. He was in Chicago to boost Sherman, he insisted, not himself.

The next day, a stiff gale from the north and sheets of rain swept through Chicago, whipping the flags and bunting to tatters. Because it was Sunday, the convention remained in recess. The pious Massachusetts delegates attended church, but many of the New Yorkers spent the day playing poker in one of the hotels, joined by a few delegates from the South and West. Corks popped and the halls were redolent of tobacco. Some delegates, exhausted by the previous four days, awoke late to find the barbershops already closed, and wandered through the hallways with frowsy beards and unoiled hair. In the conservatory of the Palmer House, the roses arranged around a painting of Grant were beginning to wilt. That night, Conkling and Grant backers visited the Southern delegations to "stiffen the spinal column" of those who might be wavering in their support of the former president.

On Monday morning, the band played selections from Offenbach's "Orpheus in Hell"—can-can music—as the delegates filled the hall, eager to begin the balloting. Garfield's entrance prompted polite applause, but when Conkling walked down the aisle, ladies fluttered their handkerchiefs and the Grant men stamped their feet. The convention chairman, Senator George F. Hoar of Massachusetts, banged his gavel and a Chicago clergyman led the delegates in prayer, though only the Massachusetts men bowed their heads. Finally, it was time to vote. The results on the first ballot illuminated the delegates' challenge: Grant came in first with 304 votes, followed by Blaine (284) and Sherman (93). Edmunds (34), former diplomat Elihu Washburne of Illinois (30), and Windom (10) trailed far behind the three leaders. Grant was 75 votes short of a majority, and he performed surprisingly poorly in three key states. Despite Conkling's oratorical efforts, only 51 of the 70 New Yorkers voted for Grant on the first ballot. The former president got only 24 of Illinois's 42 delegates, and only 32 of Pennsylvania's 58 delegates. When the results were shared with Grant, who was home in Galena, Illinois, he remained silent, serenely smoking his cigar. His wife Julia, fearing a deadlock, urged her husband to make a surprise appearance in Chicago, but he demurred, saying it would be bad manners.

The delegates cast 18 more ballots before taking a recess for dinner, and when they returned they cast 10 more. The numbers hardly budged: on the 28th and final ballot of the night, Grant got 307 votes, Blaine got 279, and Sherman got 91.

The delegates reconvened at 10 a.m. Tuesday morning to try again. On the 29th through 33rd ballots, the vote totals of the three leaders waxed and waned, but Grant placed first each time without topping 309 delegates. The Republicans were deadlocked.

Then, on the 34th ballot, 16 of the 20 Wisconsin delegates switched their votes to a man who hadn't received more than two votes on any previous ballot: James A. Garfield. Garfield shot out of his seat. "I challenge the correctness of the announcement," he protested. "No man has a right, without the consent of the person voted for, to announce that person's name, and vote for him, in this convention. Such consent I have not given." But Hoar rejected Garfield's plea. "The gentleman from Ohio is not stating a question of order. He will resume his seat. No person having received a majority of the votes cast, another ballot will be taken." It was the first crack in the ice.

On the next ballot, 27 of the 30 Indiana delegates—most had been Blaine and Sherman supporters—moved into Garfield's column. Four Maryland delegates and one delegate each from Mississippi and North Carolina followed, giving Garfield a total of 50 votes. Grant's supporters remained solidly behind him—he received 313 votes—but his opponents' followers were uniting behind Garfield. Anchored to his seat, Conkling watched the convention slipping away.

On the 36th ballot, the Garfield wave swelled with each state called. By the time the clerk reached Wisconsin, Garfield had 361 votes. Wisconsin's 20 delegates held the nomination in their hands. The crowd rose to its feet but Conkling remained seated with his back to the aisle, cupping his hand to his ear so he could hear Wisconsin's tally. "Eighteen votes for James A. Garfield and two votes for Ulysses S. Grant," a Wisconsin delegate announced, seemingly giving Garfield exactly 379 votes—but then he wavered.

"Is it in order to correct the vote of Wisconsin?" the delegate asked Hoar.

"You can correct a numerical error, but cannot change a vote," the chairman replied.

"It is a numerical error," the delegate said. "The vote should stand 20 for James A. Garfield."

A tornado of cheering and singing swept through the hall. Hats were tossed into the air "like popping corn," and delegates rushed up the aisles with their state banners to cluster around the nominee. Men tied their handkerchiefs to their canes and waved them aloft as artillery boomed outside. Garfield's friends swarmed around him, shaking his hand so vigorously it appeared his shoulder might be yanked from its socket. The band struck up "Hail to the Chief," then "Yankee Doodle." When the musicians played the "Battle Cry of Freedom," 15,000 voices joined in the chorus:

Freedom forever, hurrah, boys! Hurrah!
Down with the traitors, up with the stars;
And we'll rally round the flag, boys, rally once again,
Shouting the battle cry of freedom!

Conkling swallowed his bitterness—or seemed to. When the celebration died down, he was the first to stand up and propose that Garfield's nomination be made unanimous. "I trust the zeal, the fervor and now the unanimity seen in this great assemblage will be transplanted to the field of the final conflict, and that all of us who have borne a part against each other will be found with equal zeal bearing the banner—with equal zeal carrying the lance of the Republican Party into the ranks of the enemy," he said. After the delegates approved Conkling's motion, Hoar banged his gavel and announced a recess until 5 p.m., at which time the convention would choose Garfield's running mate.

Republican leaders knew hot anger smoldered behind Conkling's magnanimous façade. The reform-minded "Half-Breeds" had put their candidate at the top of the ticket. But it would be a hollow victory if the man from Mentor, Ohio, never made it to the White House. Without New York, the most populous state in the Union, Garfield had little hope of winning the election. And without Conkling and his Stalwart faction of the party—on the final ballot, 50 of 70 New Yorkers had voted for Grant—Garfield had little chance of winning New York. Clearly, the Republicans had to placate the Lordly Roscoe.

Moments after the convention adjourned, William Dennison, a former Ohio governor, waded through the New York delegation until he reached Conkling. Dennison asked the senator to select a New Yorker to be the vice-presidential candidate, pledging Ohio's support for whomever he chose. But Conkling, still seething, declined to offer up a name. Steve French and Clint Wheeler, two machine politicians from New York City, overheard the conversation and rushed to their friend Arthur to gauge his interest in the prize. Just months after being battered by the loss of his wife and his Custom House perch, Arthur was inclined to accept this shot at redemption—but first he wanted to consult with the boss.

Arthur found Conkling in a room adjoining the main platform of the convention hall. The space had been set aside for newspapermen, but as the balloting dragged on, delegates had retreated there for private discussions. Conkling wasn't consulting with anybody. Instead, he was marching up and down the long aisle between the press tables, muttering and gesticulating with a dark expression on his face. The two men met in the middle of the room.

"I have been hunting everywhere for you, Senator," Arthur said.

"Well, sir."

Taken aback by Conkling's harsh tone, Arthur's face grew flushed. He cleared his throat and paused for several uncomfortable beats before continuing. "The Ohio men have offered me the vice presidency," he said.

"Well, sir, you should drop it as you would a red hot shoe from the forge!" Conkling snarled. There was a flash of resentment in Arthur's eyes. "I sought you to consult, not—"

"What is there to consult about? This trickster of Mentor will be defeated before the country."

"There is something else to be said."

"What, sir, you think of accepting?" Conkling shouted.

Arthur hesitated before answering in a determined tone. "The office of the vice president is a greater honor than I ever dreamed of attaining. A barren nomination would be a great honor. In a calmer moment you will look at this differently."

"If you wish for my favor and my respect you will contemptuously decline it."

Arthur looked Conkling in the eye. "Senator Conkling, I shall accept the nomination and I shall carry with me the majority of the delegation."

Conkling glared and then stormed out of the room. Arthur, his face shadowed by regret, watched him leave.

When the delegates reconvened that evening to conclude their business, Conkling was nowhere to be found. It fell to Stewart Woodford, the US district attorney for the Southern District of New York, to nominate Arthur for the second-highest office in the land. "In behalf of a large number of the New York delegation, I desire to present the name of one of our most distinguished citizens, upon whose private character there is no stain of reproach, and who, I am sure, will add strength to the ticket in the state of New York; and that is the name of my valued friend, a true man, a true gentleman, Chester A. Arthur of New York." Arthur won on the first ballot with 468 of the 661 votes cast, far ahead of his nearest competitor. At 7:25 p.m., Hoar banged his gavel and the bedraggled delegates filed out of the hall, their work finally done.

Arthur joined Garfield in a large parlor at the Grand Pacific Hotel, where the candidates formally accepted their nominations and shook hands for two hours, a frenzy of gripping and squeezing that swelled Arthur's right hand and tore the skin off his fingers. The space between his third and fourth fingers was so inflamed he had to have a ring he had worn for years filed off to relieve his agony.

Some in the parlor were perplexed, and a bit uneasy, when they saw that Arthur still had a Grant badge pinned to his lapel. Publicly, Republicans expressed support for their ticket, but privately many of them doubted the wisdom of including Arthur on it. "The nomination of Arthur is a ridiculous burlesque, and I am afraid was inspired by a desire to defeat the ticket," Sherman wrote to a friend. "He never held an office except the one he was removed from. His nomination attaches to the ticket all the odium of machine politics, and will greatly endanger the success of Garfield. I cannot but wonder why a convention, even in the heat and hurry of closing scenes, could make such a blunder."

The *Nation* consoled its reform-minded readers with a reminder that "there is no place in which [Arthur's] powers of mischief will be so small as in the Vice Presidency, and it will remove him during a great part of the year from his own field of activity.

"It is true General Garfield, if elected, may die during his term of office, but this is too unlikely a contingency to be worth making extraordinary provision for."

•◆•

Dust motes and cigar smoke swirled in soft rays of sunlight under the arched glass ceiling of the Grand Central Depot. All of New York City's leading Republicans were clustered on the platform swapping convention stories and campaign predictions. The first shouts rang out at 7 p.m. "Here he comes!" "Here's the train!" Suddenly there was a series of explosions in quick succession—"track torpedoes," small charges placed on the track to herald the arrival of a New Yorker who had suddenly become a national figure. When the train pulled in, the passengers in the forward cars gazed out the windows in wonderment, not realizing who was traveling with them. The crowd, now numbering roughly 1,500, rushed toward the back of the train. Chester Arthur stepped out of the last car carrying his linen duster, an umbrella, a cane, and a satchel. Arthur grinned at the sight of his friends and associates, but a look of dismay crossed his face when he realized his belongings would prevent him from grasping the many hands reaching for him. Then somebody grabbed the items, and he plunged into the thicket with tears in his eyes. "Three cheers for General Arthur! Three cheers for the next Vice President! Welcome back, General!" Arthur removed his hat. "My friends, I am glad to be home and with you again, and am surprised and gratified at the warmth of this reception, but I am pleased—" A cheer cut him off and then he had to contend with fresh battalions rushing up to shake his hand. After five minutes, police officers escorted him outside to a waiting carriage that whisked him home.

During dinner, eight-year-old Nell presented her father with a bouquet of flowers to congratulate him. The little girl's kiss caused all the emotions of the past week to spill out of Arthur. "There is nothing worth having now," he sobbed. He had climbed higher than he ever thought possible, but he had reached the summit alone. His happiness was tempered by regret—and guilt—over the fact that his wife, who had suffered the most from his strivings, had not lived to see this triumph.

•—◆—•

After dinner, Arthur entertained a group of his political chums who had come to congratulate him. As the boys rehashed the Chicago drama in a haze of cigar smoke on Lexington Avenue, a Connecticut-bound steamship was groping through a soupy fog in Long Island Sound. The *Narragansett* was traveling from Manhattan to Stonington, where most of its three hundred passengers planned to transfer to trains bound for Boston and Providence. Those who had booked berths or staterooms had retired to them. The rest of the passengers settled in for a less restful sleep on the sofas and easy chairs scattered around the richly furnished saloon. Only the splashing of the paddle wheels, the groaning of the engine, and the occasional, piercing cry of the ship's fog whistle disturbed the stillness of the tar-black night.

Suddenly, just before midnight, the ship lurched violently and there was a sickening crash. The lights went out, and plumes of scalding steam shot through the cabin. Terrified passengers screamed as the ship's officers began shouting orders and calling for aid. The *Stonington*, a Manhattan-bound ship from the same line, had crushed through the port side of the *Narragansett*, just forward of the wheelhouse. The *Stonington* destroyed three of the *Narragansett's* staterooms on impact, and when it backed out, it left its bowsprit and three feet of its stem in its sister ship.

On the *Narragansett*, panic reigned. Partially dressed men, women, and children rushed shrieking out of their staterooms. Many ended up in the darkened saloon, where they shoved and elbowed each other in a mad scramble to reach the deck. Passengers could feel the *Narragansett* settling lower in the water. They fought over life preservers, and competed for chairs, mattresses, and anything else that might keep them afloat. In the chaos, husbands were separated from wives, and parents from their children.

The crisis quickly worsened. The bow of the *Stonington* had penetrated the boiler of the *Narragansett*, scattering burning coals on the oiled woodwork of the second steamer. The coals ignited a fire, and the passengers' terror spread with the rioting flames. Some people rushed for the lifeboats, and without officers to oversee the escape they cut the boats adrift and "piled into them like sheep." The first vessel to reach the water quickly swamped.

Stonington passengers massed on deck in their life preservers, expecting their vessel to sink, too. They watched, horrified, as flames devoured the *Narragansett* and men, women, and children fled the searing heat by plunging into the sound, clutching chairs, mattresses, planks, and whatever else they could lay their hands on. One mother jumped into the water with an infant, only to have it wrenched from her grasp and sucked into the blackness. People flailing in the waves cried out for divine help. Many who ended up in the lifeboats were men who had forgone chivalry in favor of self-preservation. Passengers in half-empty lifeboats plucked women out of the water by their hair, while those in overcrowded boats beat them back with wooden oars. One *Narragansett* passenger who survived the disaster described the hellish scene to a reporter. "I drifted alongside of a mattress. There was a man clinging to it, and the mattress was borne slowly in toward the burning boat," she said. "The flames made the man wild, and as we got nearer he let go his hold and was sucked in by the current, shrieking, right into the blazing fire and smoke. It was horrible. I thought my face would roast with the heat, it was so intense." Dozens of people burned or drowned to death.

A scrawny 38-year-old man with a closely cropped beard was among the *Stonington* passengers who witnessed the destruction of the *Narragansett*. "I saw and heard the wailing of the poor people who were in her, but we were utterly powerless to do anything. Our boat was badly damaged, and for two or three hours we had our life preservers on. We thought we were going down, too," he later remembered. An itinerant preacher, he beseeched God to spare him—and his prayer was answered. The *Stonington* had sustained only minor damage. It did not sink, and everybody on board survived.

Many of the passengers on the *Stonington* must have thanked God for their safety, but the preacher believed God had spared him for a special purpose. Before long, that purpose became plain to him. When he fulfilled it, he changed the course of American history.

CHAPTER THIRTEEN

"A Great Deal of Soap"

R EPUBLICANS DREW INSPIRATION from their nominee's life story. James Abram Garfield was an impoverished farm boy who grew up to become a scholar, a school president, a Civil War general, and a congressman—proof, it was said, that in America courage and resolve could overcome any disadvantage.

Born in 1831 in a log cabin in the backwoods of Ohio, James was a toddler when his father Abram died, leaving his mother Eliza to manage the family farm and raise James and his two older siblings alone. It was a harsh life, and James was desperate to escape it. His formal schooling was limited, but he devoured piles of books, and he was inspired by a series of nautical novels to become a sailor. At 16, he left home to work on Cleveland's Lake Erie waterfront.

Garfield didn't find high seas romance on the Ohio and Erie Canal. Moving barges loaded with iron and copper ore from Western mines to Eastern factories required teams of horses and mules to tow the vessels. Garfield worked as a bowman, deckhand, and steersman, grueling labor made more miserable by swarms of mosquitoes and frequent tumbles into the muddy water. In October 1848, he gave up his seafaring dreams and returned home.

Garfield heeded his mother's pleas to pursue an education. He began at Geauga Academy in nearby Chester, where for a year and a half he studied grammar, mathematics, philosophy, ancient and modern languages, and elocution. He excelled as a member of the debate society, finding "glory in defending unpopular truth against popular error." In the fall of 1851, Garfield continued his studies at Western Reserve Eclectic Institute in Hiram, which was poorly staffed and funded but which allowed motivated students to study the classical curriculum at an accelerated pace. Garfield read Homer, Livy, and Demosthenes in the original Greek and Latin and mastered geometry on his own—all while earning a living as a janitor. When he wasn't studying or sweeping, Garfield relaxed by hunting, fishing, playing billiards, and socializing with his female classmates. (One of the young women, a shy, dark-eyed brunette named Lucretia "Crete" Randolph, eventually became his wife.)

The Eclectic Institute did not award bachelor's degrees, so in September 1854 Garfield enrolled at Williams College in Massachusetts. Between his first two terms, Garfield taught penmanship at a small school in North Pownal, Vermont. (The year before, the position had been filled by a young man from upstate New York—Chester Arthur.)

Studying at Williams awakened Garfield's interest in politics. He attended the antislavery lectures of Henry Ward Beecher, and was exposed to the great issues of the day, from the Kansas conflict to the Crimean War. He gave his first political stump speech in the spring of his senior year, at a meeting in support of Republican presidential candidate John C. Frémont. After graduating from Williams with honors in 1856 (he had been admitted as a junior), Garfield returned to the Eclectic Institute as an instructor in classical languages, though he also taught English, history, geology, and mathematics. In 1857, he became president of the school.

By this time Garfield was a sought-after Republican spokesman, and in 1859 he was elected to the Ohio Senate. The chamber's youngest member earned the respect of his elders with his oratory, his grasp of complicated issues, and his facility in forming friendships. During the 1860 presidential campaign, Garfield traveled the state speaking in support of Republican nominee Abraham Lincoln.

An ardent abolitionist, Garfield preferred war to the extension of slavery to new territories. "I do not see any way, outside a miracle of God, which can avoid civil war with all its attendant horrors," he wrote a friend in January 1861. "I am inclined to believe that the sin of slavery is one of which it may be said that without the shedding of blood there is no remission." In April he welcomed the fall of Fort Sumter, believing it would rouse the North to crush the Confederacy. By the fall, he was a colonel in command of the 42nd Ohio Infantry.

Garfield shined as an officer. In January 1862 at the Battle of Middle Creek, his outnumbered troops seized control of eastern Kentucky from the rebels, earning him a promotion to brigadier general and a mention in the *New York Times*. In September 1863, he was chief of staff to General William S. Rosecrans at the disastrous Battle of Chickamauga. After accompanying Rosecrans to a relatively safe position, Garfield rode to the front under enemy fire to survey the situation for his commander, helping to save the Army of the Cumberland. Rosecrans was discredited by the defeat, but Garfield was promoted to major general.

Garfield had national political ambitions, and throughout the war he tried to publicize his exploits. In November 1862 he had been elected to the US House of Representatives—though he had not campaigned for the position—and in December 1863 he resigned from the military to take his seat in Congress. As a radical Republican in Washington, Garfield supported the vigorous prosecution of the war, the seizure of rebel property in the North, and the execution or exile of Confederate leaders.

During Reconstruction, Garfield grew more moderate. To assuage angry Democrats after the disputed 1876 election, he backed the end of military occupation of the South, effectively ending Reconstruction. He was a skilled parliamentarian, and as Republican minority leader during the Hayes administration, he brokered compromises between his party's warring factions and with the Democrats. "He was a man who gained friends on both sides of the aisle, and was noted as having a great fondness for peering and jumping over the garden wall of politics to play with those on the other side," one journalist recalled.

At a time when Capitol Hill was rife with corruption, Garfield could not escape the taint of scandal. He was one of several congressmen to accept stock in Crédit Mobilier, allegedly in exchange for using their influence to weaken oversight of the company. He also was linked to a corrupt paving contract, and was criticized for backing a retroactive salary increase for members of Congress.

While some saw in Garfield an admirable instinct for compromise, others perceived an absence of firm conviction. "He was a large, well developed, handsome man, with a pleasing address and a natural gift for oratory," John Sherman observed. "But his will power was not equal to his personal magnetism. He easily changed his mind, and honestly veered from one impulse to another. This, I think, will be admitted by his warmest friends."

Whether positive or negative, Garfield's political dexterity would figure prominently in the 1880 campaign. To beat Democratic nominee Winfield Scott Hancock—another Civil War hero—the Republican nominee would have to unite Conkling's Stalwarts with Blaine's Half-Breeds, at least temporarily. And to do that, Garfield had to convince both factions he would advance their interests as president.

Garfield's first challenge was to craft an official letter of acceptance that would appeal to everyone. In writing it, he solicited the opinions of a wide array of Republicans, including Arthur. In the final version, published on July 12, Garfield declined to endorse Hayes's civil service measures and renounced his order barring federal officeholders from participating in politics. He also pledged to consult with Congress in filling federal posts. Garfield's careful language was intended to get Conkling and the Stalwarts to work hard for the ticket. Reformers noticed. In a letter to Garfield, Carl Schurz lamented the candidate's "positive abandonment of ground taken, and to a great extent maintained, by the present Administration with regard to the civil service." Schurz said Garfield's letter had been "universally interpreted as opening a prospect of the reestablishment of the party machine in the civil service." Garfield could only hope that Conkling had drawn the same conclusion.

Given his history at the Custom House, Arthur's own letter of acceptance was less surprising. Like Garfield, he thought federal officeholders should be free to engage in politics, and he questioned the wisdom of using civil service exams in hiring them. He emphasized, however, that "appointments should be based upon ascertained fitness" and that "positions of responsibility should, so far as practicable, be filled by the promotion of worthy and efficient officers. The investigation of all complaints, and the punishment of all official misconduct, should be prompt and thorough. These views, which I have long held, repeatedly declared, and uniformly applied when called upon to act, I find embodied in the [platform] resolution, which, of course, I approve." Arthur's civil service pronouncements prompted a chuckle from George William Curtis. "Arthur's letter is very amusing to one who knows of some of his performances, as I do," he wrote to Silas Burt.

Conkling quickly got over his anger at Arthur for accepting the vice-presidential nomination. In mid-July, he and his protégé traveled to Canada for several days of salmon fishing. "Every day and everything was enjoyable," Conkling wrote a friend upon his return. "Arthur's constant effort was to make everybody else happy. No wonder we all like him." But Garfield's acceptance letter and the rapprochement with Arthur were not enough to get Conkling to work for the Republican ticket. Conkling wanted concrete assurances that a Garfield administration would respect him and his New York machine—a personal pledge, delivered by the candidate himself.

Garfield left his farm in Mentor to meet with Conkling in New York on August 3, 1880. Arthur and Governor Alonzo Cornell greeted Garfield in Albany and traveled with him to Manhattan. At 7:25 p.m. on August 4, a booming artillery salute at Harlem heralded the approach of Garfield's train, and 15 minutes later it steamed into the Grand Central Depot, welcomed by an enthusiastic crowd of three thousand. Outside the station, under a leaden sky, Garfield climbed into a waiting carriage and rode through muddy streets to the Fifth Avenue Hotel. There he found the lobby, the corridors, the hotel entrance, and the street overflowing with more supporters.

The candidate must have been pleased—until he realized that Conkling, who had checked into the Fifth Avenue Hotel two days earlier, was nowhere to be found.

Arthur and his associates were left the unenviable task of explaining Conkling's absence. They told Garfield that Conkling had empowered them to negotiate on his behalf, but the nominee expressed his "chagrin, mortification and indignation" at the senator's insult. "Telegrams were sent to various points where it was thought Mr. Conkling might be, explaining the great embarrassment and begging him to return," recalled Thomas Collier Platt, one of the Conkling men left to meet with Garfield. "[But] he went where he knew no importunities could follow."

Early the next morning, Garfield met privately with Arthur, Platt, and two New York congressmen who were Conkling lieutenants, Levi P. Morton and Richard Crowley, in Morton's hotel suite. The men exchanged greetings, took their seats, and then sat for several minutes in an awkward silence. The fuming Garfield spoke first, demanding to know why Conkling was not there. The Conkling men tried to calm the nominee by arguing that Conkling's absence was a good thing, because it would make it more difficult for people to accuse the two of them of cutting a deal. Garfield wanted assurances that Conkling would deliver at least two or three speeches for him in Ohio, and when Conkling's men agreed, he reluctantly accepted them as the boss's representatives. With that settled, Platt got right to the point.

"Mr. Garfield, there seems to be some hesitation on the part of the other gentlemen present to speak; but I might as well say that we are here to speak frankly and talk business," he began. "The question we would like to have decided before the work of this campaign commences is whether, if you are elected, we are to have four years more of an administration similar to that of Rutherford B. Hayes [or] whether you are going to recognize and reward the men who must do the work in this State." In other words, if Conkling's Stalwarts helped deliver New York, they expected to be rewarded with control of New York patronage. If Garfield could not make such a promise, the Stalwarts would "retire from the active work of the canvass."

According to Platt, Garfield responded by harshly criticizing the Hayes administration and its civil service reforms. He recognized Conkling's control of the New York party machinery, acknowledged he could not win the election without Conkling's help, and promised that the Stalwarts' wishes "should be paramount with him, touching all questions of patronage." Garfield said he would have to reward the New Yorkers who had sided with him in Chicago, but that he would "consult with [Conkling's] friends and do only what was approved by them. These assurances were oft repeated, and solemnly emphasized, and were accepted and agreed to by all those present," Platt recalled.

Afterward, Garfield and Morton retired to another room to discuss fundraising. Morton said he could collect a large amount of money from New York businessmen, but only if Garfield promised to make him treasury secretary or minister to England, or put him in charge of funding the federal government's bonded debt. Garfield gave his word that he would. After the meetings, Arthur and the other participants told reporters they were perfectly aligned with Garfield, and "no obstacles stood in the way of the prosecution of a zealous and vigorous contest." Several days later, Conkling met with Arthur at the Fifth Avenue Hotel so Arthur could brief him on what Garfield had said. Apparently Conkling was satisfied, because he subsequently announced he would personally campaign for the Republican ticket.

But what the Stalwarts understood as an ironclad promise to protect their patronage power meant something different to Garfield, who believed he had held firm against Conkling's demands. "No trades, no shackles, and as well fitted for defeat or victory as ever," he wrote in his diary after he returned to Mentor. The gap in their perceptions would loom large in the cataclysmic events of the next year.

Arthur, whose responsibilities as Garfield's running mate were minimal, managed the day-to-day operations of the New York campaign. From his headquarters at the Fifth Avenue Hotel, Arthur recruited speakers and coordinated campaign rallies and meetings in New York. He also organized a Midwest speaking tour by Conkling and Grant. Political operatives and eager volunteers, including the strange preacher who had survived the collision of the *Stonington* and the *Narragansett*, buzzed around the parlors of the hotel, looking for assignments.

Arthur's most important task was fundraising. He oversaw the distribution of letters requesting "voluntary" contributions from Custom House employees, judges, police officers, postmasters, and lighthouse keepers— anybody who drew a public paycheck. Even construction workers building the new capitol in Albany were not spared. Arthur also helped Morton collect contributions from wealthy businessmen, with much of the money earmarked for Indiana, one of two states (along with Ohio) that would vote in October. The Democrats had won Indiana in 1876 and 1878, and Republicans were determined to return it to their column in 1880.

Democratic newspapers and party operatives portrayed the vice-presidential nominee as a political hack, a crook who would stop at nothing to secure votes for his side. The Democrats hired a New York attorney to explore rumors that Arthur was born in a foreign country and thus ineligible for the vice presidency. At first the lawyer claimed Arthur was born in Ireland, then in Canada. But the charges gained little traction.

In the end, Garfield and Arthur triumphed by fewer than 10,000 votes, out of nearly nine million ballots cast. Arthur's impact was most evident in the Electoral College, where New York's 35 votes gave Garfield a total of 214. If Hancock, who won 155 electoral votes, had captured New York, he would have won the election.

Hancock went to his grave convinced that he, like Tilden in 1876, had been cheated of the presidency. The chairman of the Democratic National Committee claimed there were at least 20,000 illegal votes cast in New York—roughly the Republicans' margin of victory in the state. Democrats groused that Republicans had imported voters from Vermont, Massachusetts, Pennsylvania, and even Canada to ensure victory in the Empire State.

At the Fifth Avenue Hotel, Arthur basked in the victory. He, as much as anybody else, was responsible for the Republican triumph—and everybody knew it. As vice president he would have to learn how to preside over the US Senate, but that was a minor matter. His main job would remain the same: doing whatever he could to strengthen the Conkling machine. As for the vice presidency, he didn't expect it to be very taxing. "Thank you for your congratulations and good wishes," he wrote to Mary Dun, the wife of his friend R. G. Dun, owner of the credit reporting company that would become Dun & Bradstreet. "I hope that you and your husband appreciate the fact that it is considered a part of the Vice President's duty to 'go-a-fishing' and I hope we shall go together always."

Garfield's hard work began at once. His first task as president-elect was to select a cabinet both Half-Breeds and Stalwarts could accept. Reformers, meanwhile, were urging him to disregard politics in making his selections. It was an impossible task, and Garfield hit the first hurdle at the end of November, when he met with Levi Morton. In return for his fundraising services, Morton expected to be offered one of the jobs Garfield had promised him during their summer meeting at the Fifth Avenue Hotel.

Morton's preference, he told Garfield, was to be treasury secretary. But the president-elect either had a different memory of his summer pledge or, with the White House won, no longer felt bound to honor it. He told Morton he could not head the treasury because of his ties to Wall Street. When they met again the next day, Garfield proclaimed, "I will not tolerate nor act upon any understanding that anything has been pledged to any party, state, or person."

The Stalwarts were angry, and they rejected the consolation prize, secretary of the navy, that Garfield subsequently offered to Morton. But this slight paled in comparison to the news that Garfield had tapped James G. Blaine to be secretary of state. Conkling and his men considered Blaine to be their archenemy and feared he would dominate the pliable Garfield. They had good reason to be wary: in a December letter to Garfield, Blaine referred to the Stalwarts as "all the desperate bad men of the party" and advised the president-elect, "they must have their throats cut with a feather"—that is, the deed must be done silently, without calling attention to itself.

As the political storm clouds darkened over Conkling's realm, Kate Sprague appealed to the one person who might be able to press her lover's case with Garfield: Chester Arthur. She told Arthur that Conkling had given her a lithograph of the vice president–elect. "The Senator, your friend, never passes the table where the likeness stands, that he does not apostrophize it with some hearty expression of real affection, such is rare in man to man & a tribute from this self-contained but noble & true nature that any man may feel fond to possess," she wrote him on January 18. "Garfield & Sherman & Blaine (as it looks to private forecast) are to combine forces to overthrow & crush the power that saved them, but which they recognize only to fear & hate. . . . Surely, the Senator's friends, his tried friends & true will not cripple or soon embarrass the man to whom they owe so much?"

Kate need not have doubted Arthur's loyalty to the boss—the two men soon were living together in Washington in a house on 14th and F Streets. But she overestimated Arthur's influence with Garfield. Arthur's standing in the incoming administration was not enhanced by an ill-considered—and perhaps drunken—speech he gave at Delmonico's just three weeks before the inauguration. The dinner was in honor of Stephen Dorsey, the head of the National Republican Committee during the campaign, and focused in large part on the Republicans' surprising victory in Indiana. The elaborate floral decorations included an Indiana state seal with the prairie, rising sun, and buffalo in the design made of flowers, grass, and moss. Two hundred prominent Republicans from New York and around the country attended, including Grant, John Jacob Astor, J. Pierpont Morgan, Jay Gould, Thurlow Weed, and Henry Ward Beecher.

By the time Arthur rose to speak, the men had been eating and drinking for three hours, and they had lit their cigars. It was a friendly crowd, largely made up of experienced campaigners and Republican financiers. But reporters were there, too, and even though Arthur acknowledged their presence he went ahead with remarks that reinforced the widely held view that he was a machine politician unfit for high office. "I don't think we had better go into the minute secrets of the campaign, so far as I know them, because I see the reporters are present, who are taking it all down; and, while there is no harm in talking about some things after the election is over you cannot tell what they may make of it, because the inauguration has not yet taken place," he began. "If I should get going about the secrets of the campaign, there is no saying what I might say to make trouble between now and the 4th of March.

"Indiana was really, I suppose, a Democratic state," he continued. "[But] it had always been put down in the book as a state that might be carried by close and careful and perfect organization and a great deal of—" Arthur paused, and several audience members called out "soap!"—slang for purchased votes. The crowd laughed. "I see the reporters are here, and therefore I will simply say that everybody showed a great deal of interest in the occasion, and distributed tracts and political documents all through the country." The audience loved it. When the laughter and cheering finally subsided, he went on. "If it were not for the reporters I would tell you the truth, because I know you are intimate friends and devoted adherents to the Republican Party."

Arthur's amusing performance was a big hit at Delmonico's, but it played differently outside the restaurant. "The cynicism of this, coming from such a veteran Machinist as Mr. Arthur, was not surprising, but people were rather shocked—though we do not see why they should have been—when they remembered that it came from the lips not of Mr. Conkling's 'lieutenant' in this city, but of the Vice-President-elect of the United States," E. L. Godkin wrote in the *Nation*. "We say we 'do not know why they should have been,' because nobody but the extraordinarily simpleminded can have supposed that making Mr. Arthur Vice-President would, at this time of his life, raise him above the arts which he has practiced for so many years."

● ◆ ●

The weather on Inauguration Day was raw and slushy, forcing ladies on the spectators' stand to wrap themselves in carriage rugs and boys to crawl underneath their mothers' shawls in search of warmth. Sodden flags clung to

their staffs, and banners and bunting hung limply on houses, trees, and telegraph poles. Out-of-town visitors had taken every room in town, forcing
hundreds to sleep on cots set up in hotel parlors. Now thousands of spectators were arrayed along Pennsylvania Avenue, shivering and stamping their
feet in more than an inch of snow, many wondering why they had come at
all. Their spirits lifted when they saw a glittering forest of bayonets approaching. The Cleveland Mounted Troop, which had accompanied Garfield from
Ohio, surrounded the pair of four-horse carriages carrying Garfield and Arthur from the White House to the Capitol. From the sidewalks, windows,
and temporary balconies, spectators cheered as the procession passed by.

In the Senate Chamber, where Arthur and incoming senators would be
sworn in, the colorful dresses and fluttering fans of the mostly female crowd
were like butterflies that had alighted on the wooden chairs. Several dozen
diplomats had come to witness the ceremonies, some wearing ordinary evening dress, others in uniforms heavy with gold lace and the jeweled badges
of ancient orders. The Turkish minister wore a red fez, and the elderly Chinese representative wore a silk petticoat with a fur-lined cloak. Frederick
Douglass, with his nimbus of white hair, and the defeated Hancock in full
military regalia stood out in the crowd. At 11:55 a.m., onlookers filled all the
seats and nearly all the standing room, but word reached the elderly Senate
doorkeeper that Garfield and Arthur were still more than five minutes away.
To prevent them from being late, he seized a staff and turned back the minute hand of the Senate clock by five minutes.

When Garfield arrived, he walked into the chamber arm-in-arm with
President Hayes. The two men took chairs in front of the Senate secretary's
desk, a vantage point that allowed them to see their wives, who were sitting
together. Lucy Hayes, wearing a sealskin dolman over a black brocaded silk
dress and a white bonnet with ostrich feathers, held a large bouquet of lilies
of the valley. At her right sat Lucretia Garfield, who wore a dark green velvet
dress and matching bonnet. The nation's new First Lady held a bouquet of
red roses, flowers that failed to brighten her plain, careworn face. To Arthur,
the wives' presence must have been a wrenching reminder that Nell was
not there to share his achievement. After outgoing Vice President William
Wheeler introduced Arthur to the chamber, the widower bowed low and
gracefully before asking the assembled senators for forbearance as he learned
the rules of their institution. Then he turned to Wheeler, raised his right
hand, and took the oath of office.

After Vice President Arthur swore in the new senators, everybody adjourned to the east front of the Capitol to watch the presidency change

hands. Many in the crowd of 50,000 couldn't help but focus on Arthur: the stylish New Yorker, dressed in light trousers, a blue Prince Albert coat, a colored necktie, and light gloves, was "strong, keen-eyed, and handsome as ever, and because of his commanding form and military bearing, a central attraction."

On his second day in office, President Garfield sent his list of cabinet appointees to the Senate, and it included none of Conkling's Stalwarts. Without an ally in the cabinet besides Arthur, the Stalwarts' last hope was that Garfield would give them control of key federal posts in New York, especially the collectorship of the Custom House. Their situation seemed to brighten on March 22, when Garfield nominated five Conkling men to fill two US attorney posts, two marshal posts, and the collectorship of Buffalo. Earlier Garfield had appointed Levi Morton as minister to France—not one of the jobs he had promised the financier at the Fifth Avenue Hotel, but close. Perhaps Garfield wasn't determined to destroy the New York machine after all.

The next day, Arthur was presiding over the Senate when an emissary from the White House handed him a list of additional nominations. When Arthur saw the name at the top of the list, he immediately folded the paper, leaving the name exposed, and summoned a page to deliver it to Conkling. Conkling, stone-faced, read the note and then rose from his seat to show it to Platt, now the junior senator from New York. The news it contained was grim: without consulting Conkling or Platt, Garfield had nominated a new Custom House collector. His choice was William Robertson, who was a powerful New York state senator, a member of the Republican state committee, and an avowed enemy of Conkling and the Stalwarts. "The nomination of Senator Robertson was a complete surprise," a *Sun* reporter wrote. "There seems to be but one opinion to-night, and that is, that by this nomination Garfield and Blaine invite immediate attack from Conkling, and no one seems to doubt that they will be gratified." For Garfield, as for Hayes, there was a broader principle at stake. "This brings on the contest at once and will settle the question whether the President is registering clerk of the Senate or the Executive of the United States," he wrote to a friend.

Hoping to change Garfield's mind, Stalwarts visited the White House and organized New York import merchants in opposition to Robertson, but the president would not budge. Arthur was intimately involved in these efforts—proof, critics said, that he was Conkling's flunkey and a traitor to the administration he served. Arthur's contributions were "reprehensible and disgusting in the second officer of the Government," the Chicago *Evening Journal* proclaimed. Republicans "did not elevate him to the high position he now holds in order that he might condescend to foment jealousies and to grease the New York machine, nor to play the boss at the back of Lord Roscoe, but to deport himself in a gentlemanly and respectable manner."

Arthur didn't hide his loyalties in a conversation he had with *Herald* editor J. L. Connery in early May. Hoping to recruit Connery as an ally, Conkling had invited Connery to a private meeting in the Washington boarding house where he and Arthur were renting rooms. Conkling was not there when the editor arrived, so Arthur sat down with him to smoke and chat until the senator showed up.

Connery wasn't sure why Conkling had summoned him. "What is all the mystery about?" he asked Arthur.

"Garfield has not been square, nor honorable, nor truthful with Conkling," Arthur replied. "It is a hard thing to say of a president of the United States, but it is, unfortunately, only the truth. Garfield—spurred by Blaine, by whom he is too easily led—has broken every pledge made to us. Not only that, but he seems to have wished to do it in a most offensive way."

"How so?"

"It is a long story, and I would rather you received it from Conkling himself."

Conkling soon joined the men, "quite serene and unconcerned, like one who had well breakfasted." But a shadow crossed his face when Arthur told him Connery wanted to hear the case against Garfield. Forcing a smile, the senator reminded Connery of an earlier meeting, during which the editor had pledged the *Herald*'s general support for the Stalwarts. That was true, Connery acknowledged, but he needed to know more before he would consider launching a direct attack on the president.

Conkling had been leaning against the mantelpiece, but now he started pacing the floor silently, occasionally glancing at Connery in an "extremely disagreeable" manner. In calm, measured tones, he rehashed the Chicago convention and Garfield's surprising—and to his mind, suspicious—nomination. His hands were clasped behind his back as he stalked back and forth, and with each trip, the springs of his rage wound tighter and tighter. His voice grew louder as he railed against Robertson's "base perfidy" in abandoning Grant for Garfield at the convention. But he saved his sharpest scorn for Blaine. It was Blaine who pestered the president night and day about the need to crush the New York machine; Blaine who "infused backbone into the president whenever the slightest sign of limpness appeared"; and Blaine who had convinced Garfield that Robertson and the other Chicago traitors should be rewarded.

Conkling paused for a moment to rifle through his papers, pulling out a January article from the *Tribune* detailing Garfield's intention to reward the New Yorkers who had sided with him in Chicago. "The administration's idea of the best way to foment no quarrels is to make war—war, sir!—war upon the larger branch of the Republican Party of the Empire State!" Conkling, trembling with rage, threw down the clipping and pointed his finger menacingly at Connery. "What was the meaning of that article? What was the meaning of it, if not to give me timely warning that the men who had voted faithfully for Grant—the men who clung to their pledges and honor—need expect no quarter from the administration, while the men who had basely violated their pledges by abandoning Grant for Garfield, and thereby turned the tide of voting in favor of Garfield, were to be rewarded for their treachery?"

Now Conkling turned his attention to the promises Garfield made at the Fifth Avenue Hotel. "How willing Garfield then was," he sneered, "when everything looked blue and defeat seemed to stare him in the face; how willing he was to concede anything and everything to the Stalwarts if they would only rush to the rescue and save the day!"

●◆●

On May 9, 1881, Republican senators discussed the Robertson nomination for five hours. Conkling spoke for two and a half of them, repeating the arguments he had made to Connery and accusing Garfield of acting in bad faith. Many of the senators were sympathetic, and wished Garfield had not flouted senatorial courtesy in making the appointment. Even so, some grumbled that it was impolitic to defy a GOP president still trying to find his footing. The reservations had spread by the time the Republicans reconvened a few days later, and it quickly became apparent that most of the senators were not willing to stand with Conkling. Enraged, the New York boss stormed out of the room, vowing never again to attend another party caucus.

Conkling and the Stalwarts seemed to be out of options. Shut out of the cabinet and denied the patronage of the Custom House, they would be hard-pressed to maintain their hold on New York. But Senator Platt had an idea. He persuaded his boss that a bold play was required, one that would dramatize their stand and demonstrate that New Yorkers stood squarely behind them. Arthur opposed Platt's plan, but Conkling decided it was the only chance he had.

On May 16, Arthur entered the Senate Chamber a few minutes late, and during the opening prayers he seemed flushed and nervous. He soon regained his composure, and when the prayers and the official recounting of the previous day's proceedings were finished, he coolly handed a note to the clerk, who read it aloud:

> *Sir:*
>
> *Will you please announce to the Senate that my resignation as Senator of the United States from the State of New-York has been forwarded to the Governor of the State? I have the honor to be, with great respect, your obedient servant.*
>
> *Roscoë Conkling*

Many of the senators, engrossed in private conversations or reading papers at their desks, didn't hear the announcement, but those who did gasped in disbelief. Senator Conkling what? Surely there had to be some mistake. Somebody asked the clerk to repeat the message. He did, and then Arthur handed him another one. This was Platt's resignation, and by the time the clerk finished reading it, the Senate was in an uproar. The *Times* grasped for words to describe the scene. "The sensation created to-day by the announcement of the resignations of Messrs. Conkling and Platt was not exceeded by any event that occurred in the most exciting days of the rebellion."

Conkling and Platt resigned to demonstrate just how deeply the Robertson nomination had offended them—but they had no intention of leaving the Senate permanently. The New York legislature was in Republican hands, and they assumed their allies in Albany would quickly reelect them to their posts (American voters did not directly elect senators until 1913), thereby sending a powerful signal to Garfield that Empire State Stalwarts were not to be trifled with.

But cracks in the scheme appeared almost immediately. The dual retirement produced the intended drama—but not the hoped-for sympathy and support. Conkling and Platt expected GOP senators to delay the Robertson nomination until they were restored to their positions. But even supportive senators decided that since Conkling and Platt had deserted them, they were no longer bound by senatorial courtesy to oppose Robertson. Two days after Conkling and Platt stepped down, the Senate confirmed him as collector with only a handful of dissenting votes.

A few newspapers praised Conkling and Platt for taking a principled stand. "There are two men in the country at least to whom self-respect is more than office; two men who will not sit silently and see their state antagonized," the Chicago *Inter Ocean* editorialized. "Senators Conkling and Platt have not resigned out of pique nor for nothing," the *Indianapolis Journal* agreed. The Robertson nomination, it said, "was solely, purely, an attack on Mr. Conkling—so conceived, so understood, so expressed by every one." But according to the *Times*, most New Yorkers felt "impatience and disgust that the State should have been made the laughing-stock of the country by the childish display of temper on the part of its Senators."

Still, the *Times* hoped some good might come from the episode—though it would not be an outcome Conkling would like very much. "It is to be hoped that the risk and humiliation now so needlessly brought upon the party may open the eyes of reasonable Republicans to the absolute necessity, from a party point of view, of a reform that shall take the public service out of politics," the *Times* opined. "When the management of patronage ceases to be the chief occupation of our Senators, such mortifying situations as that in which we are now involved will become impossible."

Several days later, Arthur sneaked into the side entrance of the Fifth Avenue Hotel for a meeting with Conkling that went past midnight. After a few hours of rest, Arthur hosted Conkling and a larger group of loyalists at his Lexington Avenue brownstone. The latest intelligence from Albany was that resistance to reelecting Conkling and Platt was stronger than expected; the Stalwarts decided that Conkling, Platt, and other top machine men should go to the state capital to ensure the game was won. Vice President Arthur would join them there, even though the ultimate point of their mission was to humiliate President Garfield.

Conkling was ebullient on May 24, 1881, when he and Arthur checked into the Delavan House in Albany, cheered by a crowd that filled the hotel corridors "almost to suffocation." Usually, the senator ignored the hotel clerk and went straight to his room. This time, he signed the register boldly, flashed a "winning smile" for the crowd, and shook dozens of hands on his way upstairs.

Setting up headquarters in a Delavan House parlor, Conkling began lobbying state lawmakers that same day. He was uncharacteristically cordial, and "put up with even the most tiresome men without shrinking." Arthur stood by his side, cooling his flushed face with a large fan. He was playing the same role he'd played for a decade: Conkling's loyal lieutenant. But now he was Vice President Arthur, and many thought it was unseemly for him to use the weight of his office to serve the boss. The *Tribune* contrasted Arthur's behavior with that of previous vice presidents from New York. "It is

not enough to say that no one of them was ever guilty of such an impropri-
ety as this; it would never have been possible for one of them to conceive of
such a gross lapse of dignity," it charged. "If General Arthur does not desire
four years of public contempt he would do well to desist from the business
in which he is now engaged before his inexcusable indiscretion becomes a
National scandal."

The legislature's first vote, on May 31, indicated serious trouble for
Conkling and Platt. The minority Democrats, who had sworn to support
one of their own, coalesced behind two candidates, one for each of the open
Senate seats. But there were 18 Republican nominees for Platt's seat, and 20
for Conkling's. With 105 Republican lawmakers present, Conkling could
muster only 35 votes, while Platt got 29. Each man was the leading GOP
vote getter in his race, but their totals were far short of the majority needed
to win. The result was a deadlock.

Under state law, if the legislature was unable to fill the Senate vacancies
on its first day of balloting, it had to meet every day and vote at least once
each day until a choice was made. Conkling and his loyalists girded for a
protracted fight; they were ready to keep the legislature in Albany for the
entire summer if they had to. If they could hold on that long, perhaps New
York voters would break the logjam by changing the composition of the legislature in that fall's regular elections.

The daily balloting, which continued for the next month, was front-page
news in the *Times* and other newspapers. On the seventh ballot, Republican
Chauncey Depew passed Platt. On the 16th, former vice president Wheeler
passed Conkling. But because no man had won a majority, the balloting
went on. After the 22nd ballot, one exasperated legislator suggested keeping
the legislature in session on bread and water until two senators were elected.
At the end of June, Democrats challenged Stalwarts to a baseball game, to
relieve the monotony and to raise money for the widow of a laborer who had
been killed constructing the new capitol building.

On July 1, after the 31st ballot, Platt suddenly quit the race. The New
York papers were coy about the reason. The *Sun* referred to "an alleged escapade last night on the part of a prominent Senatorial candidate (not Roscoe Conkling), involving family honor," while the *Times* mentioned talk "of
social rather than political character," adding that "there is no occasion to
repeat the stories which are told and retold here in explanation of his disap-
pearance as a candidate, nor to distress anybody with the scandal."

The *Chicago Tribune* had no such compunctions, and gleefully recounted the tale for its readers on July 1. Two nights before, it reported,

an aide to one of the state senators opposed to the Stalwarts' reelection saw Platt sneaking a woman down an isolated corridor of the Delavan House and entering room 113. The woman was not Mrs. Platt, and "thinking that something was in the wind," the aide reported what he had seen to a number of his allies. After a brief discussion, 17 of them went to room 113 to investigate. Somebody found a stepladder, and one of the men used it to peek through the window above the door. A bright light was burning inside the room, so the first man—and the others who subsequently took their turns—had a clear view. "The details of the scene are unfit for publication," the *Tribune* reported. "It will suffice to say that the couple were scantily attired and were caught in flagrante delictu [*sic*]."

The Stalwarts' grim situation had just gotten decidedly worse. Reporters were eager to buttonhole Conkling and Arthur to ask them about their strategy in light of Platt's withdrawal. But the boss and his lieutenant had left town on board the steamship *St. John*. They planned to spend the weekend in Manhattan, plotting their next moves.

CHAPTER FOURTEEN

"An Ugly Wound"

A S THE WIND and the current pushed the *St. John* toward Manhattan, the preacher who had been a passenger on the *Stonington* lay on his bed at the Riggs House, a downtown Washington hotel where President Garfield liked to play billiards. As the preacher stared at the ceiling, the events of the past year flashed through his feverish mind.

Originally a Grant man, he had accepted Garfield's nomination as the will of God. "Nothing but an Act of God can prevent Grant's nomination," Conkling had proclaimed in Chicago. That meant that God must have selected Garfield as the GOP nominee, so the preacher did what he could to help the Republican ticket.

After Garfield won, the preacher revised a campaign speech he had written for Grant and sent it to GOP headquarters at the Fifth Avenue Hotel. He met Arthur and other party leaders at the hotel, and they were friendly to him, but they assigned him to deliver the speech only once, to a black audience. He didn't like the crowd, and it was a sultry night made hotter by torches and gaslights, so he cut short his remarks. For the rest of the summer and fall, the preacher was a frequent presence at the Fifth Avenue Hotel.

In October he wrote to Garfield at Mentor and sent him the speech. His letter also called attention to the fact that he was about to marry a wealthy lady in New York, and that the two of them could represent the United States at Vienna with dignity and grace. But after Blaine was appointed secretary of state he knew he had no chance of getting the Austrian mission, because it would go to a Blaine man, and the preacher was a Stalwart.

In March, the week after the inauguration, he called on Garfield again. The president recognized him immediately and was cordial. This time, since the Austrian mission was out of the question, he requested Paris. Garfield was noncommittal.

In the following weeks, he called on Blaine at the State Department a half dozen times and sent him as many notes regarding the Paris post. The last time, Blaine lost his patience. "Never speak to me again on the subject of the Paris consulship," he said. Stung by Blaine's rejection, the preacher turned his attention to the president. He called frequently at the White House but would find 50 or 100 people already there, petitioning the president for jobs. He wrote a note to Garfield asking, "Can I have the Paris Consulship?" The doorkeeper brought back an answer from Garfield's private secretary saying it would be impossible for the president to see him that day. He understood that response to mean that as soon as Garfield got the current consul out of the way gracefully, he would give him the office.

The preacher was worried about the dangerous split in the Republican Party. He wrote several more times to Garfield, warning him that if he did not do something, if he did not hurry, the Republican Party would go to wreck and ruin and there would be trouble in the country. But Garfield's decision to appoint Robertson as New York collector, over the objections of Conkling and Platt, signaled the president's intent: he didn't care about party unity, and wanted to crush the Stalwarts and clear the way for his renomination in 1884.

When the preacher read in the newspaper that Senators Conkling and Platt had resigned in protest, he was perplexed and depressed. But before he fell asleep that night, the solution came to him in a flash: if only President Garfield were out of the way, the difficulty would all be solved. For the next two weeks, the idea kept grinding and oppressing him. At first he was horrified, and tried to throw off the idea. But it kept growing on him, until at the end of the two weeks he had made up his mind.

By now, the divinity of his inspiration was no longer in doubt. The preacher prayed that if the Lord objected to the removal of the president, He should in some way interrupt it. He didn't.

The preacher had no ill will toward President Garfield—on the contrary, he considered him a political and personal friend. But he was determined to execute the divine will for the good of the American people, to unite the two factions of the Republican Party and thus prevent a Democratic takeover and another civil war.

It was "the Deity" who furnished the money with which he bought the revolver, on June 8, from John O'Meara's sporting goods store in Washington. The preacher was not familiar with firearms, and so frightened by the sight of the gun he had the storekeeper load it for him. He asked how to

THE REVEREND WILLIAM ARTHUR: "Elder Arthur," known for his ringing sermons and his crippled leg, had an iron belief in his own rectitude.

CHESTER A. ARTHUR AT AGE TWENTY-ONE: After graduating from Union College, Arthur set out to become a lawyer.

MALVINA ARTHUR, CIRCA 1860: Arthur's sister kept a diary that painted a harsh portrait of Elder Arthur.

ARTHUR IN 1859, THE YEAR OF HIS MAR- RIAGE: "[Arthur] is a fine looking man and we all like him very much," one of Nell's relatives wrote in his diary.

ELLEN HERNDON ARTHUR: The Civil War strained Arthur's relationship with Nell, his "little rebel wife."

WILLIAM LEWIS HERNDON: Arthur's father-in-law was roundly hailed as a hero for his actions aboard the doomed ship *Central America*.

ARTHUR WITH HIS BROTHERS-IN-LAW: James Masten married Arthur's sister Almeda. Henry Haynesworth, who married sister Malvina, was a South Carolinian who became a Confederate civil servant.

ARTHUR IN THE CIVIL WAR: During the war many used positions of influence to reap personal profits, but Arthur served with integrity.

THE SEVENTH NEW YORK VOLUNTEER INFANTRY REGIMENT MARCHING DOWN BROADWAY: As a Union quartermaster, Arthur was responsible for feeding, housing, clothing, and equipping thousands of enlisted men. *New York Public Library*

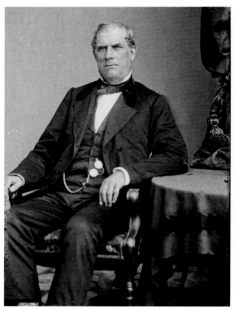

THURLOW WEED: For Weed, the ultimate prize was getting and maintaining party control. Arthur embraced his approach.

ROSCOE CONKLING: Conkling was a politician who didn't care much for people, but he rose to become the undisputed boss of the New York Republican Party.

KATE CHASE SPRAGUE: Her affair with Roscoe Conkling was the worst-kept secret in Washington.

EDWIN MORGAN: The New York governor was Arthur's first political patron.

THE NEW YORK CUSTOM HOUSE: New York's Merchant Custom House had hundreds of patronage jobs that could be doled out to loyal supporters, who could then be tapped for campaign cash.

THE ARTHURS AND FRIENDS IN COOPERSTOWN, NEW YORK, CIRCA 1876: Arthur had his Prince Albert coats, light trousers, and high hats imported from London.

ARTHUR WITH FAMILY: In this undated photo, Arthur poses on a porch with a group of people believed to be family members.

ULYSSES S. GRANT: The legendary general saved the Union, but his second term in the White House was plagued by corruption.

RUTHERFORD B. HAYES: As president, Hayes took on Conkling and the New York machine.

REPUBLICAN NATIONAL CONVENTION IN CHICAGO, JUNE 2, 1880: After being dead-locked for days, the Republicans picked a surprising nominee for president—and for vice president.

JAMES A.GARFIELD
REPUBLICAN CANDIDATE FOR PRESIDENT

CHESTER A.ARTHUR
REPUBLICAN CANDIDATE FOR VICE PRESIDENT

JAMES A. GARFIELD AND CHESTER A. ARTHUR, THE REPUBLICAN NOMINEES FOR PRESIDENT AND VICE PRESIDENT IN 1880: Arthur was placed on the ticket to placate Conkling, who could deliver New York for the Republicans. Nobody dreamed that Garfield would fail to serve out his term.

VICE PRESIDENT CHESTER A. ARTHUR: Many were appalled when Vice President Arthur went to Albany to help Conkling in his bid to return to the Senate.

PRESIDENT JAMES A. GARFIELD: The New York Stalwarts thought candidate Garfield had promised to defer to them on patronage. President Garfield had a different view.

JAMES G. BLAINE: When Garfield tapped Conkling's main rival as secretary of state, Stalwarts feared the worst.

JAMES A. GARFIELD: On the morning he was shot, Garfield was so giddy at the prospect of leaving the capital he turned handsprings over the bed of his son.

CHARLES J. GUITEAU: His attack on Garfield was the violent climax of a tortured life. When he was arrested, the would-be assassin expressed a motive that cast suspicion on Vice President Arthur.

ATTACK AND ARREST: This scene depicts the ladies' room of the Baltimore and Ohio Railroad depot the day Garfield was shot. Many Americans pointed to the fight between Garfield and the Stalwarts as the cause of the attempt on the president's life.

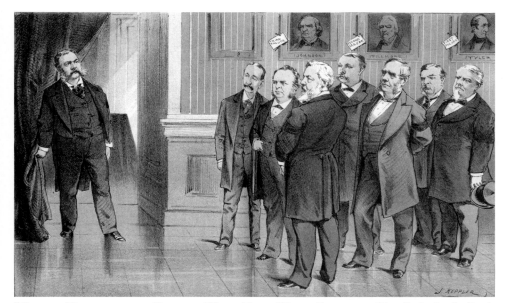

"On the Threshold of Office—What Have We to Expect of Him?": Arthur's digni-fied behavior during the summer of 1881 had softened the public's attitude toward him, but many regarded his ascension with dread.

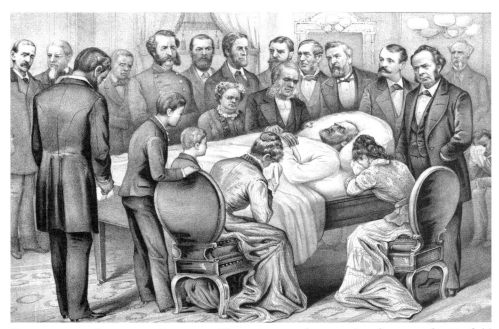

The death of President Garfield: The end came after months of agony—for Garfield and for the country.

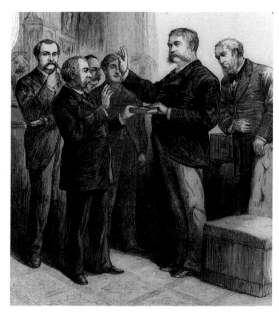

ARTHUR TAKES THE OATH OF OFFICE AT HIS RESIDENCE IN NEW YORK ON SEPTEMBER 20, 1881: Judge John R. Brady of the New York Supreme Court, who had been fetched out of bed, administered the oath of office at 2:15 a.m.

ARTHUR'S AWKWARD "WHITE ELEPHANT": Many were convinced that Conkling, not Arthur, would be running the country.

"The Living President's Tribute to the Dead President": Ohio Republicans, still mourning their murdered hero Garfield, were especially appalled by Arthur's decision to nominate Conkling for the Supreme Court.

William E. Chandler: The navy secretary became President Arthur's closest adviser.

"Shutting the Stable-Door after the Horse Is Stolen": Arthur's machine buddies considered him a traitor, but reformers never believed he was committed to their cause.

PRESIDENT ARTHUR ON BELLEVUE AVENUE IN NEWPORT: Arthur fit in well among the elites who vacationed at the upper-class resort.

PRESIDENT CHESTER A. ARTHUR: Arthur's social appeal went beyond his appreciation for first-rate food and drink and his fashionable attire.

ELLEN HERNDON ARTHUR: President Arthur took pains to protect his children—especially young "Miss Nellie"—from the prying eyes of the public.

MARY ARTHUR McELROY: With Nell gone, Arthur's sister assumed the duties of First Lady.

JULIA SAND: "If there is a spark of true nobility in you, now is the occasion to let it shine," she wrote to the beleaguered vice president.

PRESIDENT ARTHUR IN YELLOWSTONE NATIONAL PARK: Arthur said his 1883 sojourn in the park was "better than anything I ever tried before." He failed to win the Republican presidential nomination in 1884 and left the office in 1885. He died a year and a half later.

test the gun's accuracy, and O'Meara recommended that he go down to the Potomac River to practice. He followed that advice, firing the weapon at a sapling on the shore, and into the water.

When he felt confident enough, he began watching the president's movements. In the middle of June he began to spend time in Lafayette Park, opposite the Executive Mansion.

On June 18, he trailed Garfield to the railway station, but was held back by the presence of Mrs. Garfield, who was frail and clung tenderly to the arm of her husband. The shock might have killed her, and he felt sorry for her.

On his bed at the Riggs House, the preacher recalled his latest chance, just a few hours before. Sitting in Lafayette Park early in the evening, he had seen President Garfield exit the White House alone. He trembled with delight—surely fate or something else was working in his favor. Walking on the opposite side of the street, he followed the president as he walked down Pennsylvania Avenue toward 15th Street. But there were too many people in the road to take a clear shot, and then Garfield disappeared into Blaine's house. The preacher waited around the corner on H Street, slipping into an alley when people began to take notice of him. While he waited patiently for the president to reappear, he examined his pistol. Finally Garfield emerged, accompanied by Blaine. The preacher followed the two men back to the White House. Once or twice he thought he had his man, but at the last moment somebody got in the way.

Now the preacher cursed his cowardice. The president had come right to him to be shot, and he had let his heart get in the way of his head and his hand. It was time to stiffen up, to show some backbone. He swore he would not let the next opportunity slip by.

• ◆ •

Weary of Washington, Garfield awoke on the morning of July 2 eager to start his summer vacation in New Jersey (where he would meet his wife and daughter), New York, and New England. He was so giddy at the prospect of leaving the capital he turned handsprings over the bed of his 17-year-old son Harry, then he wrestled with the boy and his 15-year-old brother James while singing "I mixed those children up" from "A Many Years Ago," a popular song from Gilbert and Sullivan's new comic opera, *H.M.S. Pinafore*. At 9 a.m., he shook hands with members of the White House staff who had lined up to bid him farewell and climbed into a carriage with Blaine, who would accompany him to the Baltimore and Potomac Railroad depot at the corner of 6th and B Streets. Harry and James followed in a second carriage.

They arrived at the brick-and-stone depot at about 9:20 a.m. A policeman named Patrick Kearney strode forward to open the carriage door. "How much time have we, officer?" Garfield asked. "About 10 minutes, sir," Kearney replied.

Inside, the preacher was waiting. He had gotten his shoes shined, and now he was pacing the floor. He wore a ragged dark suit, and his gray eyes flashed under his black slouch hat. In his coat pocket, he carried an ivory-handled British Bulldog revolver.

As Garfield and Blaine crossed the ladies' waiting room, arm in arm, the preacher crept up behind the pair, drew his pistol, and fired a shot at the president from about five feet away. "My God, what is that?" Garfield cried out, flinging up his arms. The bullet passed through the president's right coat sleeve, grazing his shoulder. The preacher squeezed the trigger once more, firing a bullet into Garfield's back. When this bullet struck him, Garfield turned sharply to the right and then collapsed, hitting a chair as he tumbled to the floor. Blood spurted from his wound. "Rockwell! Rockwell! Where is Rockwell?" Blaine shouted, looking for Garfield's personal assistant and longtime friend, Colonel Almon Rockwell. Sarah White, the railroad employee in charge of the ladies' waiting room, rushed to Garfield's side and called for water. When it was brought, White gently raised Garfield's head onto her lap and bathed his face. The president was silent, but when Harry came running from an outer platform and knelt by his father's side, weeping, Garfield opened his eyes and murmured something to him. The first physician to arrive on the scene was Dr. Smith Townsend, who tried to locate the bullet by probing the president's wound with his finger.

Within minutes the depot was packed with people, desperate for a glimpse of the wounded president. The crowd pressed in closer, sucking the oxygen out of the stifling room. A mattress appeared, and several men took Garfield in their arms and gingerly placed him on it. Then they lifted the mattress and carried the president, his light gray trousers soaked with blood, up to the railroad offices on the second floor. Upstairs, Secretary of the Treasury William Windom bent over Garfield and asked him where he was wounded. "Go and telegraph my wife that I am hurt and ask her, if she feels able, to come on to Washington at once," Garfield mumbled.

Another cabinet officer on the scene was Secretary of War Robert Todd Lincoln, whose father had been assassinated 16 years before. Lincoln ordered several police officers to summon Dr. D. Willard Bliss, who had treated President Lincoln when he was shot. The officers mounted their horses and raced off. When they brought back Bliss, Townsend pulled him aside and whispered his assessment of the president's condition. Bliss examined Garfield himself and concluded it would be too dangerous to probe again for the bullet. "This is an ugly wound," he said.

About an hour after the shooting, Townsend and Bliss agreed that Garfield should be moved to the White House, and they called for a police ambulance. When it arrived, a pathway was cleared and the president was carried downstairs. As Garfield was lifted into the ambulance, witnesses noticed that he was ghostly pale. His eyes were half closed, and his lips were slightly parted. A huge throng followed the ambulance, which was accompanied by a detachment of mounted police, as it rumbled toward the White House. Most of the streets between the depot and the White House were smoothly paved, but as the ambulance rolled down 15th Street it hit a rough patch of road and Garfield moaned in agony. The crowd followed the ambulance as it drove into the broad carriageway on the White House grounds, even as police officers tried to push them back. As men carefully lifted the mattress out of the vehicle, Garfield glanced up at the windows of the mansion and spied some familiar faces. He smiled wanly, raised his right hand, and saluted.

Garfield was carried up to a bedroom in the southwest corner of the White House. He was feverish and his pulse was rapid. The surgeons were concerned when he complained of a twitching in his feet—evidence, they feared, of spinal injury—and did not dare probe his wound. But the president's head remained clear.

"Blaine, what motive do you think that man could have had in trying to assassinate me?" he asked the secretary, who sat at his bedside.

"I do not know, Mr. President. He says he had no motive. He must be insane."

But the would-be assassin had expressed a motive—one that cast suspicion on Vice President Arthur.

After shooting Garfield, the preacher calmly put his pistol back in his pocket and turned to leave the station. He did not intend to flee. Instead, he planned to ride to jail in a cab waiting outside. But as he made his way down the steps, the police officer who had greeted Garfield just moments before grabbed him. "I must arrest you," Kearney said. "Alright," replied the preacher, whose name was Charles Julius Guiteau. "I did it and I will go to jail for it. I am a Stalwart, and Arthur will be president."

●◆●

Guiteau's attack on Garfield at the Baltimore and Potomac depot was the violent climax of a tortured life.

Born in Freeport, Illinois, in 1841, Guiteau's mother died when he was seven. His father, Luther, was an officer at the local bank who also served two terms as a court clerk and founded Freeport's first Sunday school. Luther was an ardent opponent of slavery, a Republican who revered Horace Greeley and Henry Ward Beecher. When Charles was a child, Luther became interested in the "Bible communism" of John Humphrey Noyes, founder of the Oneida Community, a religious commune in New York State that practiced free love. Noyes and his followers, called "Perfectionists," rejected traditional moral standards. It was possible to be free of sin, Noyes preached, because the perfection God demanded was based not on external deeds but on one's internal attitude. Luther sought to inculcate Charles with Noyes's beliefs.

In 1859, Charles told his father he wanted to go to college, and Luther reluctantly agreed. Charles's intention was to spend two years at the University of Michigan studying for a career in the law. But in June 1860, encouraged by his father, Charles quit college and joined Noyes's Oneida Community. "I pray that God may open your mind and heart to the great and glorious truths of 'Bible communism,'" Charles wrote to his sister Frances in 1861, about a year after he joined the commune.

But Guiteau left the Oneida Community in April 1865. Years later, he described Noyes as harsh and cruel, and complained that women in the commune treated him poorly. But in a letter he wrote to his father around the time he left, he said he remained faithful to Noyes's beliefs but wanted to promote them by founding a daily newspaper, to be called the *Daily Theocrat*. He moved to Hoboken, New Jersey, to chase his dream, but his attempt to launch a newspaper failed, and in November 1865 he rejoined the commune. He quit again a year later.

For the next decade, Guiteau moved between New York and Chicago, floundering in a series of jobs in law offices and at newspapers. In 1869 he married a librarian named Annie Bunn, whom he had met at the local YMCA. But Guiteau abused her, reportedly locking her in a closet at night, and in 1874 she divorced him. Over the next couple of years, after failing to obtain the collateral for another newspaper venture, Guiteau lived off and on with his sister Frances and her husband. His behavior became stranger: he threatened Frances with an axe and dropped the family's puppy over a bannister, breaking its leg. When guests visited, Guiteau preached from a religious tract he had written and violently denounced anyone who dared to question it. "I wanted him taken to Chicago and tried by a jury, and found insane, as I had no doubt he would be, and put in an insane asylum," Frances recalled.

After disappearing for a time, Guiteau reemerged as a regular participant in evangelist Dwight Moody's revivalist meetings. For the next several years, he became a traveling preacher himself. In 1880, he turned his attention to politics.

"I knew that my brother had been for years insane to a certain degree," John Guiteau said after his younger brother's political obsession exploded into violence. What lit the fuse? John Guiteau believed that Charles "committed the act in a moment of mad frenzy under the hallucination excited by the failure of his crazy attempt to get an office and the interest he had taken in the Senatorial fight at Albany."

•◆•

In the issue of *Harper's Weekly* published the day Arthur and Conkling left Albany, cartoonist Thomas Nast drew the vice president of the United States as a bootblack in an apron, polishing the shoes of New York's ex-senators. "Out-'shining' everybody in humiliation at Albany," the caption read. Arthur's employer in the cartoon—a woman symbolizing the American people—says, "I did not engage you, Vice-President Arthur, to do this kind of work." It was a demeaning image, and it wounded Arthur all the more deeply because he knew it was accurate. Lounging in the saloon of the *St. John*, listening to his longtime boss plot his next moves, Arthur was ashamed of what his loyalty had cost him.

Looking outside, Arthur saw black-smudged sky ahead—they were close to the northern tip of Manhattan. Within minutes, swirling ferry traffic enveloped the *St. John*. The shrieking of the gulls mingled with the shouts of stevedores and the slapping of the waves against the hulls of ships in their berths. At about 10:30 a.m., from the Canal Street pier, there was a shout directed at the *St. John*: President Garfield has been assassinated!

Standing on the *St. John*, Steward Burdett heard the message, but he could hardly believe it. He rushed into the saloon to tell Arthur and Conkling. "It can't be true," Arthur gasped. "This must be some stock speculation." When he read the telegram confirming the news, he crumpled into his chair, overcome with grief and fear. In the feud between Conkling and Garfield, he had cast his lot with the New York boss. The vice presidency was a higher office than he had ever dreamed of attaining; he could not conceive of being president. Would his countrymen accept him as Garfield's replacement? Would they blame him for the president's murder?

The shocking news of Garfield's shooting momentarily paralyzed Arthur and Conkling, but they soon sprang into action. Ordering their baggage to be sent after them, they flew off the ship and hailed a two-wheeled hansom cab. They clambered in and Conkling opened the trap door in the roof to bark out their destination: the Fifth Avenue Hotel. The driver snapped the reins and headed east on Canal Street. At the corner of Canal and Broadway, he turned uptown, navigating through coupes and cabs, four-wheeled growlers and omnibuses.

At Astor Place, Arthur and Conkling glimpsed the Cooper Union, the Italianate brownstone sanctified by Lincoln's famous speech two decades before, and the elevated railway rising beyond it. They rode past the great publishing houses and A. T. Stewart's six-story "Iron Palace," fronted by long rows of private carriages. Grace Church, with its white marble rectory, was just above Stewart's. A few blocks farther uptown, the cab passed Tiffany & Company, the country's largest jewelry store, and Brentano's News Depot.

By this time, there was scarcely a man, woman, or child in Manhattan who hadn't heard the horrifying news. The newspapers had received the first dispatch from the capital at around 10 a.m., just when the downtown streets were starting to fill up with merchants and businessmen. That initial report included few details, but it left the impression that Garfield had been killed. New York's leading newspapers were all clustered in Printing House Square, across Park Row from City Hall Park, and they immediately posted bulletins outside their buildings.

"My God! President Garfield has been shot!" exclaimed one man who was strolling by the *Tribune* building and was one of the first to see the plain white piece of paper posted on the granite wall.

"It can't be true. It must be a canard," another replied.

"If it is true," a third said solemnly, "this will be a sad day for the country."

People converged around the grand buildings housing the *Tribune*, the *Times*, the *Herald,* and the *Sun.* The police dispatched half a dozen officers to each newspaper building to clear the sidewalks, but the throngs quickly bubbled over into the street. One white-haired old man forced his way through the crowd outside the *Tribune.* "What is the country coming to!" he declared, raising his hand in a despairing gesture. "I'm glad of it," growled a rough-looking man at the edge of the crowd. "It's just what Garfield deserved!" Shouts of "Let me at that man!" and "Kill him!" and "Shoot the scoundrel!" rang out. The crowd scuffled and swayed, and several men detached themselves from the mass to confront the speaker, but he fled down Nassau Street and was swallowed up by the shade of its somber houses.

The telegraph spread the word to all the principal hotels. In Wall Street offices, it appeared on the tape that delivered stock quotes, and it was posted on bulletin boards outside drug stores. Soon the news had radiated to every corner of the island, from the mansions on Fifth Avenue to the tenements on the Lower East Side. Scores of men rushed to the Western Union Telegraph office hoping to debunk it, only to have their worst fears confirmed.

Suddenly the flags on the post office and on City Hall were lowered to half-staff, and a shudder went through the crowd in Printing House Square.

●—◆—●

When they arrived at the Fifth Avenue Hotel, Conkling and Arthur stepped into the marble-tiled and frescoed reception hall and were engulfed by friends who supposed they had the latest information. But Arthur told them he had just returned from Albany, and was desperate for news himself. "What is the latest news from Washington? Have you anything further?" he inquired frantically. He was trying to remain calm. As always, his hair was carefully combed, but his normally ruddy cheeks were ashen, and his blue eyes were glassy. A reporter asked him whether he wanted to make any public statement regarding the shooting of the president. Arthur paused. He did not know any particulars, he said haltingly, and was not certain about the danger the president might be in. Yes, of course, he was horrified at the crime and extremely sorry for the president and his family. He was shocked—so shocked he did not feel capable of expressing his feelings. Begging to be excused, he left to join Conkling in room 38, where the boss always stayed when he was in the city. A stream of visitors' cards followed them, but the two men declined to see anybody.

●—◆—●

At 11 a.m., the flags on City Hall and the post office were suddenly raised again, prompting cheers from the crowd broiling in the sun: the latest bulletins suggested that Garfield's physicians did not think his wounds were fatal. The same news reached the Fifth Avenue Hotel via telegraph, and shortly after 11 Arthur emerged from Conkling's room and left the hotel to return to his home on Lexington Avenue. At about 11:15, the vice president alighted from his carriage in front of his brownstone and was met by his neighbor, New York City Comptroller Allan Campbell.

"What is your latest information?" Campbell asked.

"From all I can learn I do not believe the president's wounds are mortal," Arthur replied. Then he hurriedly bade Campbell good morning and went inside.

At noon the newspaper extras appeared, and the newsboys and newsgirls pushed their way into the throngs around the bulletin boards and flew uptown as fast as the elevated trains could carry them. The demand for papers was intense, and their bundles disappeared quickly. Many buyers were so eager to devour their papers they didn't bother the peddlers for their change. Nearly all the passengers riding the horse-drawn streetcars, which ran on rails along the major avenues, held newspapers in their hands. Over the next several hours, the dispatches from Washington grew more optimistic: the president had been moved to the White House, he was conscious, and the doctors thought he might survive his wounds.

Early in the afternoon, an encouraging telegram arrived at Arthur's home. It was from Blaine, who was at Garfield's bedside at the White House: "At this hour, 1 o'clock, P.M., the President's symptoms are not regarded as unfavorable, but no definite assurance can be given until after the probing of the wound at 3 o'clock," Blaine wrote. "There is strong ground for hope, and at the same time the greatest anxiety as to the final results."

Meanwhile, additional details trickled out of Washington. Word spread that the shooter was named Guiteau, that he was a Stalwart who wanted Arthur to be president. A letter the police found in Guiteau's pocket shed additional light on his motives. "The President's tragic death was a sad necessity, but it will unite the Republican Party and save the Republic," the letter stated. "I had no ill-will toward the President. His death was a political necessity."

This intelligence created a stir in Printing House Square.

"Is a man of so pure and noble a character as President Garfield to be shot because his ideas do not happen to suit a certain lot of politicians?" one man exclaimed when the *Tribune* posted a bulletin detailing Guiteau's motives.

Another man objected. "But you don't know that the assassin was prompted by anyone," he said. "He is probably some lunatic."

The first man scoffed at that suggestion. "So was the assassin Booth a lunatic. There is altogether too much method about this kind of madness, however."

At the Fifth Avenue Hotel, former secretary of the navy Richard W. Thompson rejected comparisons to the assassination of Lincoln 16 years before. "Lincoln was assassinated when the bitterness and strife of war was all over the land. President Garfield is struck down in a time of peace. Assassination in a time of peace is worse than assassination in a time of war," Thompson said, as men around him nodded in agreement. "The country has seldom been in a better condition than now, and, with the exception of a local faction contest in this state, harmony prevails everywhere."

At around 3 p.m. the bulletins began to take on a darker cast: Garfield was hemorrhaging, they reported, and fading fast. The Fifth Avenue Hotel even received one dispatch that claimed, falsely, that the President had died. This news was quickly determined to be untrue, but the crowds in Printing House Square grew silent, mournfully anticipating the bulletin that would announce Garfield's demise. Common laborers stood in the sun side-by-side with wealthy merchants, speaking, when they spoke at all, in subdued tones. Grizzled men in ragged clothes, who under normal circumstances would have attracted police attention if seen loitering near more respectable citizens, stood with tears in their eyes, utterly harmless. There was some pushing and edging forward to get a better view of the bulletins, but it was done gently and quietly.

On Lexington Avenue, Arthur received another telegram from Blaine. "At this hour, 3:30, the symptoms of the President are not favorable," it stated. "Anxiety deepens." This prompted the vice president to return to the Fifth Avenue Hotel to consult with Conkling and other Stalwarts. After meeting with them for a couple of hours, he drove back to his home to sit in his doorway and await further dispatches. A reporter found him there. "I am utterly broken down," Arthur murmured. He had tears in his eyes, and his voice faltered. Several times, he had to turn away to compose himself. "I have nothing to say. What can I say? The news is terrible."

Park Row was now "a solid, throbbing mass" of men, women, and children. Hundreds of newsboys ran through the crowd shouting "Extra!" Streetcar drivers had to slow their horses to a walk, and they shouted themselves hoarse urging people to clear the way. Their passengers recklessly stuck their heads out of the car windows, trying to read the bulletins as they passed by. At the corner of Park Row and Beekman Street, a crowd clustered around a newsstand that had numerous portraits of President Garfield on display.

Still the crowds grew larger, spilling south onto Broadway. In front of St. Paul's Church, five hundred people stood in the middle of the street, seemingly indifferent to the danger of being trampled by passing vehicles. Outside the 10-story brick-and-stone headquarters of the *Evening Post* on the corner of Broadway and Fulton Street, about six hundred people waited impatiently for the next bulletin. Finally, at 4 p.m., a copyist began writing the latest news on the board in front of the building. "President Garfield's symptoms are very . . ." Here he paused to begin a new line. "Oh, I hope they are good," somebody said softly. But the copyist's next word was "unfavorable." Several people melted away from the board when the depressing news was posted, but others quickly filled their places.

Sitting in his doorway on Lexington Avenue, Arthur received another telegram from Blaine: "At this hour, 6 o'clock, the condition of the President is very alarming. He is losing his strength, and the worst may be apprehended." Once again Arthur returned to the Fifth Avenue Hotel, where he received yet another message from Blaine. "Mrs. Garfield has just arrived, at 6:45 o'clock. The President was able to recognize and converse with her, but, in the judgment of his physicians, he is rapidly sinking."

On a normal evening, the Fifth Avenue Hotel was a mecca for merchants, stockbrokers, and the idle rich—clusters of well-dressed men bathed in honey-colored gaslight. The second-floor parlors, which overlooked the fountains and statues of Madison Square, hummed with conversation. Glasses clinked in the bar, barbers worked on customers in the shaving saloon, and porters carrying huge trunks pushed their way through the crowd in the lobby. The office bell rang constantly, summoning servants to execute the orders of the guests. Tonight, an anxious, surging crowd made it almost impossible to get from one end of the main hall to the other. The densest crush was around the telegraph in the reading room, and around the stock indicator in the bar. Occasionally, someone would forget himself for a moment, and puncture the gloom by laughing in conversation with a friend. When that happened, every man within hearing turned and frowned at the offender.

Arthur made his way through the crowd surrounding the telegraph and dictated a response to Blaine: "Your 6:45 telegram is very distressing. I still hope for more favorable tidings, and ask you to keep me advised. Please do not fail to express to Mrs. Garfield my deepest sympathy." Asked whether he intended to go to Washington, Arthur insisted he would not go until officially notified of Garfield's death. He did not want to seem overly eager to assume the presidency—especially in light of Guiteau's stated wish for his succession. Arthur ordered a coupe and returned to Lexington Avenue, this time in the company of New York City Police Commissioner Stephen B. French, a close friend and political confidant. At 10:30 p.m., he received another telegram there, this one from the current secretary of the navy, William H. Hunt, and Postmaster General Thomas L. James. "Sincere thanks for your expressions of sympathy," the cabinet officers wrote. "The President is no better, and we fear is sinking." Once again, Arthur rode to the Fifth Avenue Hotel to consult with Conkling.

On most nights, Broadway pulsed with life, ablaze in electric light shining on people pouring in and out of theaters, restaurants, and cafés. Respectable families jostled for scarce sidewalk space with swaggering toughs and flashily dressed prostitutes trolling for customers. Lit up by lanterns, the omnibuses and carriages skittered on the roadway like fireflies. Tonight, at the corner of Broadway and 23rd Street, New Yorkers were waiting for their president to die. A large crowd stood in Madison Square, where a stereopticon projected the latest bulletins on a wall. At 10:30 p.m., there was a ray of hope: a bulletin announced that when Garfield's physicians had told him he had a "slight chance" for recovery, the president had replied, "I'll take that chance." A hearty cheer rent the air at this evidence of Garfield's fighting spirit. But gloom settled on the square again as the hours passed without any news of improvement in the president's condition.

To Arthur and Conkling, it now seemed certain that Garfield would die, and soon. After conferring with other members of the New York machine, they decided that Arthur should go to Washington after all. Shortly after 11 p.m., Arthur, Conkling, French, and Senator John P. Jones of Nevada climbed into a coach that was waiting in front of the Fifth Avenue Hotel's marble porch. Frank Cosgrove, a police detective, had orders to drive the party to the Desbrosses Street pier, where they planned to catch the last ferry to the Pennsylvania Railroad depot in Jersey City. Vice President Arthur would ride on the midnight train to the capital.

At the depot the entire party boarded the sleeping car, but Conkling, still focused on the struggle in Albany for his old Senate seat, would not be traveling with his protégé. Before the train left he stepped out and bade Arthur goodbye on the platform. The two men shook hands. "Goodbye. God bless you. I'll meet you on Thursday," Conkling said. The ex-senator stood on the platform until the train departed. A reporter asked him why Arthur had changed his mind. If Garfield was going to die, Conkling explained, it would be best for the vice president to be there when it happened. And if he survived, it was an act of courtesy for Arthur to be present. "I am not going to Washington myself now," he added. "I cannot say about the future."

At 41 Park Row, the five-story stone headquarters of the *Times*, an editorial writer was putting the finishing touches on his piece for the next day's newspaper.

"When James A. Garfield was yesterday reported as lying at the point of death new bitterness was added to the poignancy of public grief by the thought that Chester A. Arthur would be his successor," it read. "Gen. Arthur is about the last man who would be considered eligible to that position, did the choice depend on the voice either of a majority of his own party or of a majority of the people of the United States."

From midnight until 7 a.m., the immense Hoe presses in the basement would be running constantly to print the daily edition. By the time readers held it in their hands, President Garfield almost surely would be dead.

CHAPTER FIFTEEN

A Mysterious Correspondent

MOST AMERICANS DREADED the prospect of an Arthur presidency. The *Chicago Tribune* called it "a pending calamity of the utmost magnitude," while the *Nation* noted the widespread fear that "a very obnoxious person named Conkling will 'run' the government as he has long run the 'machine.'" Some newspapers, pointing out that Arthur and Conkling were the main beneficiaries of the crime, accused the Stalwarts of inspiring Guiteau—and perhaps directing him. "What the country will not forget is that the deed is done in their name, and that they and their followers will derive place and power from the President's death," the *Charleston News and Courier* declared.

The *Louisville Courier-Journal* compared Arthur and Conkling to Mary Surratt, the Washington boardinghouse owner executed for aiding the assassination of President Lincoln. "Mrs. Surratt was hanged on less circumstantial evidence than occurs to the mind as to Roscoe Conkling and Chester A. Arthur," the newspaper seethed.

Reformers were disappointed with Garfield, but they were appalled at the idea of a President Arthur. Former president Hayes wrote in his diary that Garfield's death "would be a national calamity whose consequences we can not now confidently conjecture. Arthur for President! Conkling the power behind the throne, superior to the throne!" Andrew Dickson White, a New York state senator who became president of Cornell University and a diplomat, recalled that when news of the shooting reached him in Europe, his first reaction was not "horror at the death of Garfield, but stupefaction at the elevation of Arthur." According to White, "it was a common saying of that time among those who knew him best, '"Chet" Arthur President of the United States! Good God!'"

Arthur was afraid to appear in public. He received death threats, and was deeply shaken by the widespread belief that he was complicit in the crime. "No one deplores the calamity more than Senator Conkling and myself. These reports are so base and unfounded that I cannot believe they will be credited," he protested to one reporter. "Good God! If such a thing were possible then liberty is impossible. Such a calamity as this should be treated as national, not only by every citizen but by the entire press of the country. Party and faction should be forgotten in the general grief."

• ◆ •

Arthur arrived in Washington early on Sunday morning and went directly to the home of Senator John Jones, who had accompanied him to the capital. For most of the day, the vice president remained secluded inside Jones's large granite house. In the afternoon, Arthur sent the Nevada senator to the White House with a request to visit the wounded president, but Garfield's doctors said their patient needed absolute quiet, and forbade any visitors except the First Lady. Even outside the mansion, where businessmen and fashionably dressed ladies clung to the iron railings with hatless and coatless laborers, an eerie quiet prevailed, broken only by the occasional shouts of newsboys.

The next morning Arthur and Jones showed up at the White House at 10 a.m. The pair's sudden appearance in the vestibule surprised the gaggle of reporters there, who pressed forward shouting questions. Arthur and Jones ignored them and bounded upstairs, where they were ushered into the darkened cabinet room, next to Garfield's sick chamber. The sound of water splashing in a fountain tiptoed through the open window, and a gentle breeze from the Potomac tickled the draperies. Secretary of the Treasury William Windom, Attorney General Wayne MacVeagh, and Postmaster General Thomas James slumped in their chairs or paced the floor, anxiously awaiting the next scrap of news from Garfield's doctors.

Soon Blaine joined them. The other cabinet members watched with trepidation as Conkling's greatest enemy strode across the room toward Conkling's greatest friend. "General, I am glad that you have arrived," Blaine said. He extended his hand toward the sitting Arthur, who seized it eagerly. "And Mr. Secretary, I am glad to be here, but cannot too fully regret the great trouble that has fallen upon us," Arthur replied, his voice breaking. Arthur asked to see Mrs. Garfield and was taken into her private parlor. Smiling bravely at the sight of the vice president, Lucretia inquired about his health and apologized for the sudden summons to Washington. With God's help, she said, her husband would be spared. Arthur had tears in his eyes as he clasped both of her hands in his and lamented the tragedy that had befallen her and the nation. After 20 minutes, Arthur returned to the cabinet room. "I pray to God that the president will recover," he told the men assembled there. "God knows I do not want the place I was never elected to."

Returning to Jones's house, Arthur retreated to a first-floor parlor where furniture was being stored for the summer. A reporter found him sitting on a covered sofa with his head bowed, staring out an open window. Hearing somebody enter the room, Arthur looked up: his eyes were bloodshot and moist, and there were traces of tears on his ruddy cheeks. When the reporter addressed him, the vice president replied softly in just a few words, afraid that if he said too much his emotions would overcome him. His friends said he was as distraught as when Nell died. The reporter described him as "still in a kind of stupor. He sees, of course, what is going on, and he has not lost possession of his faculties, but he is overwhelmed by the magnitude of the calamity and of the task which he may be called upon to perform."

In the following days, members of the cabinet visited Arthur with regular updates. Gradually, their reports grew sunnier. A week after the shooting, Garfield's doctors still could not locate the bullet in his back, but they knew they didn't have to remove it to save him—after all, hundreds of Civil War veterans were thriving with lead balls inside them. "With the lapse of every 24 hours the condition of the President has seemed to improve," the *Times* reported one week after the shooting. "His doctors feel that the grand crisis has passed, and that unless something which is now totally unexpected occurs there is no danger whatever of his life being taken by the bullet of the assassin." With Garfield increasingly cheerful and confident, the doctors turned their attention to his comfort: As temperatures climbed into the 90s, navy engineers were rigging up a primitive air conditioner using a compressor from a Nevada silver mine and 10 tons of ice they carted into the White House basement. In the meantime, Almon Rockwell fanned his friend with an Indian *punkah*. With only good news coming out of the White House, the crowds that had been glued to the gates outside melted away.

On July 13, 1881, Garfield's temperature was normal and his pulse was 90—the lowest since the shooting. The doctors continued to drain his wound using a flexible bone pipe, but they no longer feared sepsis or abdominal inflammation. Garfield had been subsisting on chicken broth and milk with rum. Now his doctors felt he was ready for breast of woodcock, which he chewed but did not swallow. Arthur felt so confident in the president's recovery he returned to Manhattan.

In Albany, meanwhile, Conkling fought on to regain his Senate seat. Like Arthur, he read the newspaper editorials that blamed him for the shooting, but unlike the vice president, he didn't let the charges shake his confidence. The attacks would all "in due time rebound upon the assassins who fulminate them," he assured a friend. His critics, he said, "have seized a dark and dangerous hour for what you call their 'devilish' machinations; but in the end reason and judgment will prevail."

But Guiteau's bloody act had fatally wounded the Stalwart chieftain. For nearly three weeks, Conkling and his supporters managed to prevent anybody else from securing a majority in the Senate contest. On July 22, on the 56th ballot, the Lordly Roscoe's magnificent edifice finally crumbled: Republicans chose Congressman Elbridge Lapham, who had defected from the Conkling ranks, to replace the boss in the Senate.

Conkling received the news in his suite at the Fifth Avenue Hotel. He walked outside and wandered the streets of the neighborhood, "alone and apparently in deep thought." When he returned, he sent a telegram to one of his legislative supporters. "The heroic constancy of the spartan [sic] band which so long has stood for principle and truth has my deepest gratitude and admiration. . . . The near future will vindicate their wisdom and crown them with approval." And what of Conkling's future? One of his followers suggested he might run for New York's open House seat (Congressman Warner Miller had taken Platt's place in the Senate), and bid to become Speaker of the House. But Conkling refused to talk about the defeat or what he might do next.

That evening a handful of reporters came to call on the once mighty boss, "and they were, as usual, denied the pleasure of conversing with him." Many expected Arthur to come to the Fifth Avenue Hotel to comfort his longtime patron, but the vice president never showed up.

Lying in his White House sickbed, the recovering Garfield was magnanimous. "I am glad it is over. I am sorry for Conkling. He has made a great mistake [in resigning], in my judgment," Garfield said. "I will offer him any favor he may ask, or any appointment he may desire."

•◆•

With the exception of a brief relapse the day after Conkling's defeat in Albany, Garfield's condition steadily improved for the next several weeks. By early August, he was doing so well his convalescence dropped off the front pages. New York newspapers turned their attention to the summer season in Saratoga, which was in full swing. The resort suffered when vacationing businessmen packed up their families and abruptly returned to New York after the shooting, "fearing the unsettled state of things that must follow the sudden death of the President." Now the crowds were coming back, and hotel managers were predicting a prosperous season.

With Garfield recovering and the Albany drama finished, Arthur slipped back into the shadows. He left Manhattan to spend a few days in Newport, but people no longer paid much attention to his comings and goings. The main thing on New Yorkers' minds was the heat, which quivered over the pavement, turning the city into a steaming saucepan. Drivers leaned back under the hoods of their vehicles to find a sliver of shade, and flakes of foam fell from the mouths of overheated horses. Only the saloonkeepers were happy: they hustled all day to supply the thirsty masses with iced drinks and beer, too busy to mop their glistening faces. The night offered scant relief, especially for the city's tenement dwellers. They lingered on the stoops under a blood-red moon, dreading the slog up to their airless bedrooms. Some slept in chairs tipped against houses, or in wagons. In barroom doorways, men and women gulped three-cent schooners of beer and bellowed songs into the panting dark.

Several times a day, Garfield's doctors posted bulletins on a large tree near the east gate of the White House. On August 15, the 8:30 a.m. bulletin roused the nation from its summer torpor: the president's fever and pulse had reached frightening heights, and he was vomiting. His vital signs had spiked before, but now they were staying at elevated levels. Doctors were even more concerned about his inability to retain any nourishment, even water. "The great trouble now is that the stomach refuses to assist us by performing its legitimate functions," said Dr. Bliss, still playing the chief physician's role he claimed on the day of the shooting. Once again, the concerned and the curious gathered outside the White House gates.

There were minor improvements in Garfield's condition over the next 10 days, but they were always followed by setbacks. The newspapers dutifully documented every twist and turn, but gradually the full picture was coming into focus, and it was grim. Arthur's old patron, former governor Edwin Morgan, felt compelled to write a reassuring letter to his former protégé. "I have said elsewhere, and very often, that you will make a good President—I have never doubted it, I do not doubt it now," Morgan wrote. "It is a great and unlooked for responsibility thrown upon you, but with this responsibility there is a great opportunity . . . only exercise your own good judgment in meeting this responsibility, and all will be well. You have talent and qualifications equal to it."

By August 25, members of the cabinet had nearly given up hope, and Garfield's doctors were telling the First Lady it was highly unlikely her husband would recover. "I have not lost hope, but I feel very anxious now. The case is very critical," Bliss said. "The outlook is less promising than ever before."

For the first time in weeks, New Yorkers converged on the Fifth Avenue Hotel seeking the latest bulletins from Washington. Politicians and merchants, lawyers and men of leisure clustered in the vestibule, on the sidewalk and under the portico, exchanging opinions on the president's prospects. The consensus was that the end was fast approaching. Hidden in his Lexington Avenue brownstone behind drawn curtains, Arthur waited for the latest news and prepared to leave for Washington at a moment's notice. Conkling and other machine boys came to advise him on strategy. Surrounded by decanters and cigar smoke, they tried to disentangle the thorny problem vexing the vice president: How could Arthur fulfill his constitutional responsibilities and exhibit the appropriate level of concern for the president, without appearing too eager to assume the presidency?

On August 26, Lucretia Garfield sent a telegram to her brother, who was taking care of the youngest Garfield sons at the Mentor homestead, urging him to come to Washington at once. The cabinet met to discuss whether it was time to summon Arthur, too. They called in Garfield's surgeons for an assessment of his condition, and they were alarmed by what they heard. Nevertheless, they "decided that they would not subject Gen. Arthur to the embarrassment of a criticism that he had come to Washington to wait for a dead man's shoes."

Outside, the August sun baked the broad, dusty streets and parched parks of the sleepy capital. A single soldier in a white helmet stood sentry on Pennsylvania Avenue with his saber drawn, while a policeman posted behind him twirled his club, chatting with bystanders. On the White House steps, clusters of reporters quietly debated how long Garfield might last. When a carriage rumbled away from the mansion, people craned their necks to peek inside. It was Blaine. "He looks downhearted, don't he?" one man commented. The crowd of reporters on the steps thickened when it was almost time for the next bulletin. Some waited inside the White House vestibule, where a full-length portrait of the murdered Lincoln seemed to deepen the gloom.

In New York, the *Sun* could not post updates fast enough to satisfy the public's voracious appetite for information. Crowds blocked the sidewalks outside 170 Nassau Street, and many drivers drew rein in front of the *Sun* building to read the large, plain lettering on the boards. At the corner of Park Row and Broadway, two hundred people gathered to read the latest news projected by electric light. An army of shrill-voiced newsboys mingled with the crowd, peddling extra editions of the evening newspapers. Pickpockets also circulated, collecting about $6,000 from distracted spectators.

On August 27, Postmaster General James sneaked into New York for several hours to meet secretly with Arthur, who was still secluded in his home with Conkling and Jones. The cabinet had sent James as an envoy to communicate the seriousness of Garfield's condition. Spotted by a reporter on the midnight train back to Washington, a nervous and exhausted James refused to divulge his mission, admitting only that he had been in New York "on private business." The next day, Arthur didn't emerge from his home until 8:30 in the evening, when he took a solitary ride through Central Park in an open barouche.

•◆•

On East 74th Street, a 31-year-old woman read the dire accounts in the newspapers and sat down to write a seven-page letter to the vice president.

Julia I. Sand was the unmarried eighth daughter of Christian Henry Sand, a German immigrant who rose to become president of the Metropolitan Gas Light Company of New York. When Christian Sand died in 1867, his family left Brooklyn for Pleasant Valley, New Jersey. In 1880, the Sands settled at 46 East 74th Street, which was owned by Julia's brother, Theodore V. Sand, a banker. As the pampered daughter of a wealthy father, Julia read French, enjoyed poetry, and vacationed in Saratoga and Newport. But by the time she wrote Arthur she was an invalid, plagued by spinal pain and other ailments that kept her at home. As a woman, Julia was excluded from public life, but she followed politics closely through the newspapers, and she had an especially keen interest in Chester Arthur.

The vice president had never met Sand, or even heard of her. They were complete strangers. But her words penetrated the husk that had grown around the son of Elder Arthur. "The hours of Garfield's life are numbered—before this meets your eye, you may be President," the letter began. "The people are bowed in grief; but—do you realize it?—not so much because he is dying, as because _you_ are his successor."

> What president ever entered office under circumstances so sad! The day he was shot, the thought rose in a thousand minds that you might be the instigator of the foul act. Is not that a humiliation which cuts deeper than

any bullet can pierce? Your best friends said: "Arthur must resign—he cannot accept office, with such a suspicion resting upon him." And now your kindest opponents say: "Arthur will try to do right"—adding gloomily, "He won't succeed, though—making a man President cannot change him."

Julia Sand did not share that pessimistic view. "But making a man President can change him!" she declared. "Great emergencies awaken generous traits which have lain dormant half a life. If there is a spark of true nobility in you, now is the occasion to let it shine."

Faith in your better nature forces me to write to you—but not to beg you to resign. Do what is more difficult & more brave. Reform! It is not the proof of highest goodness never to have done wrong—but it is a proof of it, sometime in one's career, to pause & ponder, to recognize the evil, to turn resolutely against it & devote the remainder of one's life to that only which is pure & exalted. Such resolutions of the soul are not common. No step towards them is easy. In the humdrum drift of daily life, they are impossible. But once in a while there comes a crisis which renders miracles feasible. The great tidal wave of sorrow which has rolled over the country has swept you loose from your old moorings and set you on a mountain top, alone.

As president—especially one who had not been elected—Arthur could sever his unsavory political associations and make a clean start, Sand argued. "You are free—free to be as able & as honorable as any man who ever filled the presidential chair." She continued with words that could have come from the pen of Elder Arthur:

Your past—you know best what it has been. You have lived for worldly things. Fairly or unfairly, you have won them. You are rich, powerful—tomorrow, perhaps, you will be President. And what is it all worth? Are you peaceful—are you happy? What if a few days hence the hand of the next unsatisfied ruffian should lay you low & you should drag through months of weary suffering in the White House, knowing that all over the land not a prayer was uttered in your behalf, not a tear shed, that the great American people was glad to be rid of you—would not worldly honors seem rather empty then?

It was still possible, she contended, for Arthur to chart a different course. "Rise to the emergency. Disappoint our fears. Force the nation to have faith in you. Show from the first that you have none but the purest aims," she wrote. "It may be difficult at once to inspire confidence, but persevere. In time—when you have given reason for it—the country will love & trust you.

"Your name is now on the annals of history," she concluded. "You cannot slink back into obscurity, if you would. A hundred years hence, school boys will recite your name in the list of Presidents and tell of your administration. And what shall posterity say? It is for you to choose whether your record shall be written in black or in gold."

Arthur was intrigued—who was this mysterious woman who dared to challenge him so boldly? She signed the letter, "Yours Respectfully, Julia I. Sand," but she included no other personal information. Eager to learn more about her, Arthur checked the return address. On a card embossed with "The Union League Club" at the top, he jotted down what he discovered: "Theodore V. Sand, Banker, 54 Wall St (Sand, Hamilton & Co.) lives at No. 46 East 74 St." Then he folded Julia Sand's letter and filed it away in a safe place.

•◆•

On a breathless gray morning a week later, an Adams Express wagon and four carriages were arrayed in front of the North Portico of the White House. At about 5:40 a.m., the large crowd pressed against the gates watched as President Garfield was carried out of the mansion on a stretcher. He lay under a white wool blanket with red borders, and his forehead was wrapped in a white cloth. Gently, several attendants lifted the stretcher into the wagon and placed it on a low walnut bed. Once the patient was safely situated, some of Garfield's doctors and family members climbed into the carriages and sped off, but Colonel Rockwell, Dr. Bliss, and several other doctors and attendants joined the president in the wagon. Rockwell and Bliss fanned him vigorously, Bliss using his straw hat. Two stout bay horses were hitched to the vehicle. Its springs had been carefully oiled, and the most experienced driver in Washington held the reins.

The doctors had decided the swampy Washington weather was impeding Garfield's recovery, and that breathing the fresh sea air of Long Branch, New Jersey, might revive him. The journey was risky, but after two months of Garfield's making little progress, they were ready to try a change of scenery. As the wagon left the White House grounds, the public got its first look at the wounded president, and they were encouraged by what they saw: his face was pale with a yellowish tint, but it was fuller than recent bulletins had led them to expect.

Some of the onlookers walked alongside the procession as it made its way down Pennsylvania Avenue. At the Department of the Treasury, a group of men standing on a platform used to receive bullion doffed their hats as the wagon passed by. To avoid jostling the president, the horses proceeded at a slow walk, and sawdust had been piled on the streetcar tracks at some intersections to cushion the wagon wheels. A stray dog howled, but a bystander promptly grabbed it and shook it into silence. At 11th Street, the president opened his eyes and turned his head to look at the citizens lined up along the route, some them weeping. "How good it is to see the people," he murmured before dozing off again.

About 20 minutes after leaving the White House, the wagon arrived at 6th Street and Pennsylvania Avenue, where the presidential train waited on temporary tracks that had been laid on the street. The horses were detached from the wagon and a squad of soldiers wearing cork helmets surrounded it and gently maneuvered it against the door of the railroad car. It took them three tries to get it lined up perfectly. "God save the president!" one onlooker cried, but otherwise the large crowd watched silently. Attendants grasped the handles of Garfield's stretcher and lifted him, feet first, into the car. When one of the handles banged into the doorway, the president winced in pain.

The journey north was uneventful and about seven hours after leaving the White House Garfield was resting comfortably in a seaside room in Francklyn Cottage, behind the Elberon Hotel. During the next two weeks, no detail was overlooked in the desperate attempt to restore the president's health. His attendants used only well-seasoned hardwood to fuel the fire in his room, and the Red Gate Farm in nearby Newton sent the pick of its herd of Alderney cows to provide the highest-quality milk for the president. Installed in the Elberon stables, two-year-old "Repartee" received thrice-daily meals of 10 quarts of cottonseed meal, linseed, and corn meal, mixed with six quarts of bran.

For about a week, Garfield seemed to be gaining strength. But on September 16, 1881, he suffered another serious relapse. The president's agony appeared to be nearing its end; Arthur feared his was just beginning. The vice president, speaking "with a depth of feeling that no man could ever forget," told Chauncey Depew he was terrified Garfield would die. "The most frightful responsibility which ever devolved upon any one would be the casting of the Presidency upon me under the conditions which you and all my friends so well understand," he said.

Shortly before 11 a.m. on September 19, Arthur received a telegram from Attorney General MacVeagh, who was with Garfield in New Jersey. "It is impossible to conceal from ourselves that the President is rapidly growing worse," MacVeagh wrote. "The two chills occurring within fourteen hours warn us to be prepared for any sorrow with which God in His mercy may afflict us." For the next 11 hours, Arthur remained shut inside his house. At around 10 p.m., his personal secretary, John Reed, arrived with New York District Attorney Daniel Rollins and prominent Republican lawyer Elihu Root. After greeting them, Arthur grabbed his cane and announced he was stepping out for a walk. He wanted to be alone, but asked them to wait for his return.

Arthur walked to 28th Street, then east to Third Avenue. He was wearing a dark sack suit that matched his mood. Making his way uptown, he crossed Third Avenue in front of the streetcar depot and paused to read some posters, but the words hardly registered in his brain. Only three years before, he had been sacked as Custom House collector, his political career apparently finished. Now he would be president—incredible! Despite the presence of his political friends—did he have any other kind?—he felt utterly alone. Nell was gone. Many of his countrymen believed him to be a party hack— or worse. The rigid moralism of Elder Arthur and the hopeful idealism of his youth could not buttress him now, for he had tossed away both long before. For years he had been a machine politician. Certainly, he was skilled at greasing the wheels with jobs and clever conversation, supplemented by liquor, cigars, and girls. But did that qualify him to be president?

When Arthur walked up the steps of his brownstone, it was nearly 10:30 p.m. For the next hour, the only sound outside was the occasional clatter of a passing milk wagon or butcher's cart.

At 11:30, a *Sun* reporter knocked on the door. Had the vice president received the news? Arthur's doorkeeper and valet, a black man named Aleck Powell, said his employer had received nothing since the regular evening bulletin issued by Garfield's doctors. "The president is dead," the reporter said. At that moment, Arthur appeared in the hall. "The president is dead," the reporter repeated.

Arthur blanched. "Oh, no! It cannot be true. It cannot be. I have heard nothing."

"The dispatch has just been received at the *Sun* office."

"I hope—my God, I do hope it is a mistake!" Arthur's voice broke, and his eyes welled up. He rushed into the back room where Root and Rollins were waiting. "They say he is dead," Arthur murmured. "A dispatch has been received at the *Sun* office." Nobody said a word.

The official telegram from the Cabinet arrived a few moments later. Arthur broke it open slowly, read its contents, and buried his head in his hands. He remained in that position as the men passed it around.

"It becomes our painful duty to inform you of the death of President Garfield, and to advise you to take the oath of office as President of the United States without delay," the telegram said. "If it concur with your judgment, we will be very glad if you will come here on the earliest train tomorrow morning."

A reporter from the *Times* arrived on Arthur's doorstep several minutes later. He asked Powell whether the next president of the United States would like to make a statement regarding his future plans. "I daren't ask him," Powell replied. "He is sitting alone in his room sobbing like a child, with his head on his desk and his face buried in his hands. I dare not disturb him."

CHAPTER SIXTEEN

"He Is Our President"

IN THE FIRST-FLOOR parlor, Rollins, Root, Reed, and Police Commissioner Stephen French watched Powell rearrange the green curtains and light the chandelier. Chester Alan Arthur II, a student at the College of New Jersey (later called Princeton), stood with them, having raced his coupe to Lexington Avenue when he heard that Garfield's death was imminent.

Alan had arrived just in time to see his father become the 21st president of the United States.

Judge John R. Brady of the New York Supreme Court, who had been fetched out of bed, administered the oath of office at 2:15 a.m. Arthur recited the words solemnly, kissed his son, and accepted the congratulations of his friends. There were several carriages and a handful of reporters outside Arthur's brownstone, and French had ordered two police officers to patrol the sidewalk in front. Otherwise, there was nothing to indicate that history had been made behind the closed blinds of 123 Lexington Avenue. Too nervous and excited to sleep, President Arthur retired to the second-floor library to chat and smoke with Reed. It was nearly 5 a.m. when he turned down the gaslight and went to bed.

Two hours later, the neighborhood servants stepped outside to scour the steps and sidewalks with their brushes and brooms. Arthur was still sleeping, and Powell had to turn away a steady stream of messengers and visitors as the sun rose higher. By late morning, knots of curious New Yorkers were gathering on the sidewalk in front of Arthur's brownstone, their interest heightened by the appearance of a coach drawn by a pair of spirited bays. This was the carriage that would take Arthur to the ferry of the Central New Jersey Railroad. He was going to Long Branch for the afternoon, to view Garfield's body and comfort his widow.

Dressed in black, with red and swollen eyes, President Arthur finally emerged shortly after 11 o'clock, looking a decade older than Vice President Arthur had the day before. Accompanied by his son, he tipped his hat and climbed into the waiting carriage as Powell mounted the box. The driver snapped the reins and the horses galloped down Lexington Avenue.

That afternoon, Arthur leaned on Blaine for support as he stood on the lawn behind the Elberon Hotel, staring at the Francklyn Cottage. The doors and windows facing him were closed, and soldiers in fatigues were busy packing away all of the medical appliances that had been brought from Washington. Fearing he might weep again, Arthur turned his face toward the sea.

The next day Arthur went back to Long Branch to board the funeral train that would carry Garfield's remains to Washington. He left Manhattan early, with a hatbox and two leather trunks marked "C.A.A." He was wearing a Prince Albert coat, buttoned up tight, and a black silk tie. On the train ride to the shore, he held his crape-banded hat on his lap and stared out the window, sunk in solitude. Former president Grant, who rode the same train, didn't dare disturb him.

At the Elberon railway station, Arthur and Grant transferred to the funeral train. The engine was the same one that had borne the injured Garfield to Long Branch, but now the dark red woodwork on the outside of each car was draped in black cloth. Arthur and Grant settled into a first-class passenger car, joining members of the cabinet and other dignitaries. Mrs. Garfield and her household were in a special drawing-room car usually reserved for the president of the railroad. It had a library, and was equipped with "electric knobs for the summoning of a waiter." In the car that carried Garfield's coffin all the seats had been removed, and the casket sat on a draped dais, guarded at each corner by a sitting soldier. A tall cross of yellow and white rosebuds, carnations, tuberoses, and smilax was tipped against it. At 10 a.m., the wheels grated on the rusty temporary tracks and the train began its sad journey south.

Thousands stood alongside the tracks to watch the train pass by. Flags fluttered at half-staff, and the roofs of houses and factories were festooned in black. In sparsely settled country, farm families paused in their fields, while at Princeton Junction, three hundred college students tossed flowers. Just beyond Trenton, nuns wearing black gowns and white coifs stood with their pupils. At the suburban stations outside Philadelphia, onlookers were so still and solemn the policemen deployed to maintain order had little to do.

At 4:30 p.m., the funeral train clattered into the Baltimore and Potomac Railroad depot—the station where Guiteau had fired his fatal shots almost three months before. Hissing steam hushed the waiting crowd. Mrs. Garfield disembarked first, wearing a long veil that nearly touched the ground. The widow was taking her family straight to the home of Attorney General MacVeagh, where they would stay until the ceremonies in the capital were over. She did not want to step foot in the White House ever again.

Eight US Army artillerymen hoisted Garfield's coffin onto their shoulders and carried it slowly toward the street, halting at the gate as a band played "Nearer, My God, to Thee." When the last note had died away, the soldiers placed the coffin in a hearse hitched to six gray horses, each led by a groom. Arthur and members of the cabinet climbed into carriages in front of the hearse. On either side of the vehicle, and streaming far behind it, were two hundred army and navy officers in full-dress uniform.

Police officers, on horseback and on foot, guarded both sides of Pennsylvania Avenue to prevent people from impeding the funeral procession as it traveled the three-quarter-mile route from the depot to the Capitol. The sidewalks were packed with spectators, and hundreds more watched from windows and roofs. The dipped colors and drum rolls of Garfield's inauguration had been inverted—now the flags were draped and the drums were muffled, a black-and-white negative of that faraway day.

At the Capitol, the artillerymen carried the coffin inside the rotunda and set it on a catafalque covered in heavy black velvet, the same one that had supported Lincoln's casket in 1865. The lid of the coffin was lifted, and Arthur and Blaine shuffled around to take a last look at the slain president. Garfield's face was pinched and shrunken—nearly unrecognizable. Earlier in the day, during a public viewing at the Francklyn Cottage, some had cried out in surprise and pain at the sight, but Arthur and Blaine betrayed no emotion. After a few moments, they headed for the east door and their waiting carriages.

The next day, as tens of thousands of Americans filed past Garfield's body, Arthur repeated the oath of office before US Supreme Court Chief Justice Morrison Waite. About 40 people witnessed the event in the Vice President's Room in the Capitol, including former presidents Hayes and Grant, associate justices John Harlan and Stanley Matthews, members of Garfield's cabinet, seven senators, and six House members.

Standing ramrod straight, Arthur pulled a piece of paper from his pocket and began to read the three paragraphs he had written. "For the fourth time in the history of the Republic its Chief Magistrate has been removed by death," he began. "All hearts are filled with grief and horror at the hideous crime which has darkened our land, and the memory of the murdered President, his protracted sufferings, his unyielding fortitude, the example and achievements of his life, and the pathos of his death will forever illumine the pages of our history.

"Men may die, but the fabrics of our free institutions remain unshaken," he said, his voice trembling. He looked up from his text and gazed directly at the audience.

> All the noble aspirations of my lamented predecessor which found ex-
> pression in his life, the measures devised and suggested during his brief
> Administration to correct abuses, to enforce economy, to advance prosper-
> ity, and to promote the general welfare, to ensure domestic security and
> maintain friendly and honorable relations with the nations of the earth,
> will be garnered in the hearts of the people; and it will be my earnest en-
> deavor to profit, and to see that the nation shall profit, by his example and
> experience.

• ◆ •

The speech was well received, but Arthur "entered the White House as President with either the hostility or the distrust or the coldness of nine-tenths of the American people," according to Chauncey Depew. His political position was weak: Garfield's cabinet members were expected to resign, and Blaine, John Sherman, and other leading Republicans were already plotting to seize the GOP nomination from him in 1884. The likelihood that this accidental president would serve a single term diminished his leverage on Capitol Hill.

Julia Sand acknowledged the peculiarity of Arthur's position in a second letter to him, which she wrote a week after he took the oath of office in the Capitol. The whole country was in mourning, but she understood that nobody was suffering quite like him—not even Garfield's family.

> And so Garfield is really dead and you are President. For a time it seemed
> as if we all were mistaken—as if he meant to disappoint our fears. Then I
> felt I owed you an apology for what I had written. Perhaps I owe you one
> now, for writing at all. My only excuse for this letter is the deep sympathy
> I feel for you in your sorrow. All through these sad, dreary days, I have fol-
> lowed your name in the newspapers with the feeling that you were the chief
> mourner. Even contemplating the wife, the mother, the children of the de-
> parted, has not changed your position. Great as their suffering is, it is what
> hundreds, in the obscurity of private life, have suffered before them—what

thousands suffered in the old war times—& they have the consolations which come to all who mourn for the brave and the true. But your affliction is different. The very thoughts which assuage their grief but add a pang to yours. What we all endured during the terrible months of anxiety just past, you too endured, intensified a thousand fold by the reflection that you were the one human being to benefit by his death, that you had been opposed to him, that some believed you capable of having plotted for his cruel end. You were alone in your sorrow—perfectly isolated.

Sand was intimately familiar with the grief so many American families had endured in "the old war times." In September 1862, her beloved older brother Henry Sand, a captain in the 103rd New York Volunteers, had been mortally wounded during the Battle of Antietam. When the color bearer of the regiment was shot down, Captain Sand seized the flag and ran along the line exhorting his men. But a rebel sharpshooter shot him in the thigh. He died from his wounds at a hospital in Sharpsburg, Maryland, six weeks later.

But after expressing sympathy for Arthur's political predicament and mental state, Julia Sand sought to pump up his confidence. "You are a better & a nobler man than you were a very short time ago," she assured him. "Nothing could be more beautiful than the manner in which you have borne yourself through this long, hard ordeal. The people feel it so.

"You have disarmed the majority of your opponents," she continued. "It is true some regard your whole course as a matter of policy, your conduct as a fine piece of acting—perhaps they have an appreciation of what is fine in nature—& they expect that soon you will change. It is sad to endure, when your motives all are good. But it is what you will have to bear—the natural consequence of your past career. However, in time, you can prove to them that they are mistaken."

Sand was right: Arthur's dignified behavior during the torturous summer of 1881 had softened the public's attitude toward him. "His conduct during the trying period of President Garfield's struggle with death has been such as to command the respect of those most disposed to find fault with him," the *Times* observed. "He has effaced himself after a fashion as manly as it was statesmanlike. . . . He has never visibly lost sight of the fact that he was merely the Vice-President of the United States, watching like the rest of his fellow-citizens over a life which he and they were alike sincerely anxious should be spared."

Even the reform-minded *Tribune* was willing to give him the benefit of the doubt. "It is not the time to recall past mistakes or to insist upon any harsh interpretation of acts which may be open to question," it argued. "He is our President, made such by an awful calamity which has chastened the hearts of all good citizens."

But even those who praised Arthur were uneasy about the men he had huddled with as Garfield succumbed to his wounds. They were the men he had always leaned on: Roscoe Conkling and the Stalwarts, and in the wake of Garfield's death their motives and methods inspired greater distaste than ever before. The *Times* acknowledged that Arthur's loyalty to his friends was understandable, and had carried him far. But it warned that qualities praiseworthy in a private citizen or local pol could destroy a presidency. "If he is to prove equal to the great position he occupies he must know principles rather than individuals, he must subordinate personal preference as well as acquired prejudice to the accomplishment of certain well-defined public ends." The *Tribune* suggested that Arthur could earn "the loyal and powerful allegiance of those true hearts now mourning for the death of Garfield," but only "on one simple condition—that he be President of the Nation and not the chief of a faction."

The editorial writers urged Arthur to leave Conkling and his cronies behind—and to go further, by actively pursuing civil service reform. "He can disarm the public distrust which his elevation excites by leaving undone anything that is obviously superfluous, and by walking steadily in the path of reform which was marked out for his predecessor," the *Times* wrote. "He can earn for himself everlasting odium and for his party disunion and defeat by repeating as President blunders which he has already made in a lower sphere."

In the days following the inauguration, there were ominous signs. Arthur wanted the White House to be thoroughly cleaned and redecorated before he moved in. In the meantime, he took up residence at the Capitol Hill home of Senator Jones. When Jones traveled to Utica to meet with Conkling the week after Arthur moved in, many took it as evidence that New York's ex-senator would be the real power in the new administration. Conkling's advice for Arthur, delivered to Jones, was to keep Garfield's cabinet in place until Congress reconvened in December. By that time, he predicted, public excitement over the momentous events of the past months would have faded, and Arthur would be free to make whatever changes he wished without much criticism. Conkling was clearly energized by what Jones told him about President Arthur's plans. Bidding the Nevada senator farewell at the Utica station, Conkling had "that air of one whose defeat has been changed into victory." He bowed and shook hands with anybody who approached him, and he looked much healthier than he had when his Senate seat slipped away from him in Albany.

When Arthur became president, John Hay, who had been personal secretary to President Lincoln, was filling in for Whitelaw Reid as editor of the *Tribune* while Reid was on an extended trip to Europe. Like many Republican reformers, Hay feared the worst. "Everything is at sea about Arthur," he wrote to Reid in London. "Perhaps the cable will tell you in a day or two what he is up to. But at present the Cabinet knows nothing whatever of his intentions. The facts are: 1. He is living with Jones. 2. Jones has gone to Utica to confer with Conkling. 3. The Grant crowd seems happy."

Arthur's return to Manhattan at the end of September added fuel to such fears. He claimed he had come home to turn over his law business and arrange for some of his personal possessions to be transferred to Washington, but newspapers noted the stream of Stalwarts coming in and out of the Lexington Avenue brownstone. Senator Jones came directly from his Utica meeting with Conkling who, it was said, wanted to replace his hated rival Blaine as secretary of state. Some suspected Arthur was in town to work his old magic in the upcoming New York elections. Republican leaders in Garfield's home state of Ohio warned that Conkling's influence on Arthur might dampen GOP turnout there, perhaps handing the governor's office, the legislature, and Ohio's congressional delegation to the Democrats. "Let President Arthur show a disposition to be advised or led by ex-Senator Conkling and there will be no voice raised for him in Ohio and no hand held out to help his Administration," a *Times* correspondent warned. "The feeling toward Mr. Conkling throughout this state is one of anger, distrust, and disgust; and law-abiding as are the people of Northern and Central Ohio, the late senior Senator from New-York could hardly travel about here in safety from open insult, if not from bodily harm."

Even Arthur's biggest fan, Julia Sand, was concerned. "Well, you have gone. So much the better. But they say you are coming back again, very soon. Please don't!!!" she wrote to him in a letter dated October 5. "New York is the one spot on the continent where you positively ought not to be this fall. If your private affairs require attention, show your patriotism in letting them suffer. It will take months for you to live down the injury you have done yourself in being here for just a few days. And it is not for the good of the country that it should lose confidence in you now."

Taken at large, one branch of the Republican party is about as good as the other—"that man from Maine" [Blaine] does not lead a band of angels, any more than that man from the other place—but in the state of New York it is different. Here an absolute right & wrong are in conflict. Unfortunately, you have been connected with the side which represents the wrong—"the machine"—the thing which I politely request you to smash. Perhaps it was expecting too much of human nature that you should take pride in doing that. But no effort on your part is necessary. Only be passive. Stay in Washington, absorbed in national affairs, not showing by the movement of an eyelash that you take an interest in what is going on here. And when the electioneering excitement is over, you have merely to bow gracefully to that great law of nature, the survival of the fittest. Depend on it, the fittest will not be your old machine. If there is a soul in the Republican party, it is on the other side.

Then, for the first time, Sand revealed a little more about her own life and reasons for writing him.

And now you are thinking that I am insanely conceited for giving you such an avalanche of ideas? Probably. I admit I have let facts speak loudly against me. Yet I am not prompted by egotism. I know that my opinion, as mine, can have no weight with you. If it has any value, it is because we are strangers, because our paths have never crossed & are not likely ever to meet, because while taking an intense interest in politics, I have no political ties. . . . But I will not trouble you much oftener—possibly this is the last time. There are reasons why it is difficult for me to write to you. I am not fond of talking, when it is to no purpose. Soon you will show what you intend to do. Half measures have no place in your programme—they would make too flat a failure. If you choose one course, you will have all the praise you want, without mine. If you choose the other, I shall know that if my first appeal to you was in vain, nothing that I could say to you now would avail. But I will not admit that "if"—I intend to go on having faith in you.

Sand held on to the letter for a few days before mailing it. On October 8, she added a postscript. "By the way, do you take any care of your health?" she asked the president. "Perhaps naturally it is good; but, there are limits to human strength. You have been under a great nerve strain for months past. And now we read constantly of your being 'hard at work,' or 'receiving callers,' but rarely of your going anywhere. You ought to be out every day and early in the day too—not when the sunset chill is in the atmosphere & malaria is prowling around in search of its victims."

Nothing supplies the place of fresh air and sunshine. By force of will we can accomplish a great deal, &, under the excitement of it, fancy that we are thriving, but if the health is neglected, the break down is certain to come—& when it comes, it is not easily mended. If one thing more than another would make the duties of your position intolerable to you, it would be to have to meet them with a perpetual headache. Therefore ward it off—do not sit still all day & let the blood go crowding to your brain. If you are not too heavy—your pictures vary about 100 lbs in weight—and it would be cruelty to animals to have a depressing effect upon them—why not ride on horseback all through the bright, bracing autumn weather? Of all things in the world, that is the exercise which most quickly sets the blood in motion & brings refreshment alike to body & mind.

She offered one more bit of political advice—that Arthur should keep the popular postmaster general Thomas James—before concluding with words of encouragement. "You have a great responsibility resting on you, but you will prove equal to it. With the best hopes & wishes for your future, farewell. Sincerely, your friend, J.I.S."

•◆•

At noon on October 8, Conkling sat down with President Arthur for the first time. The two old friends met in Jones's grand granite house, in the second-floor room Arthur was using as an office. Arthur's private secretary and the clerical staff he inherited from Garfield occupied almost the entire first floor. Each day messengers scurried back and forth from the White House, carrying mail and documents to be examined and signed. Reporters assumed Arthur and Conkling were discussing the new cabinet and Conkling's place in it. Reformers held their breath, sure that Roscoe Conkling's puppet was about to bring the worst features of New York machine politics into the White House.

In fact, much of the discussion revolved around a single, familiar issue: the New York Custom House. Conkling needed control of Custom House patronage to revive his sagging political fortunes and rebuild his Empire State machine. Conkling had lost his Senate seat fighting Garfield over the appointment of William Robertson as collector. Now Garfield was dead, and the new president was a Stalwart. To Conkling, Arthur's obligation to his friends was clear: he must fire Robertson and put a Stalwart in his place.

Conkling's request—or was it an order?—surprised the president. Conkling was frozen in one of his withering stares. Eyes flashing, jaw clenched, the New York boss might have been back on the Senate floor, eviscerating another impudent opponent. Arthur felt the heat rising in his cheeks, and suddenly his collar seemed to tighten around his neck. He had always been loyal to Conkling and the machine. Even as vice president he had gone to Albany to help the boss, and had endured vicious criticism because of it. He knew that if he had not been Conkling's man, Republicans would not have put him on the ticket with Garfield.

But watching Garfield's long ordeal, and the suffering of the dying man's family, had greatly affected Chester Arthur. Secluded in his Lexington Avenue brownstone as the summer dragged on, he had contemplated his own history, and the place he might occupy in the history of his country. He had been a machine politician for decades, but before that he had been something else: the son of a backwoods preacher; the young lawyer who helped integrate New York City's streetcars; the Union Army quartermaster who served his country honorably while so many others fed from the public trough.

Arthur did not want to be disloyal. He valued Conkling's support and friendship, and told him so. Nevertheless, he said, he was "morally bound to continue the policy of the former president." No—he would not remove Robertson from the Custom House.

Conkling's eyes grew wide. Pounding his fist on the table, he bellowed that Arthur was not bound "morally nor politically nor any other way." Again, he argued that Robertson's presence at the Custom House was an affront to the Stalwarts. But Arthur stood firm. He knew the American people would never have chosen him to be president. Now he was determined to show he was worthy of the job.

Upon his return to New York, Conkling disparaged Arthur as a traitor and a coward, and most of Arthur's old cronies from the machine agreed. But at least one Stalwart understood what Arthur had done. "The president is right," John O'Brien told a reporter. "He isn't 'Chet' Arthur anymore—he's the president and must demonstrate that he's nobody's servant."

Arthur did not want to banish Conkling from his circle of advisers, but when it came to Collector Robertson, he would not budge. "For the vice presidency I was indebted to Mr. Conkling," he said. "But for the presidency of the United States, my debt is to the Almighty."

CHAPTER SEVENTEEN

"A Splendid Henry V"

D URING THE FALL of 1881, a poster memorializing America's murdered president hung in every post office in the country. "In memory of James Abram Garfield," it said, "a martyr to the fierceness of factional politics and the victim of that accursed greed for spoils of office which was the bane of his brief conscious existence as President, and is the gravest peril that threatens the future of his country."

Guiteau was deranged—few Americans doubted that—but most saw his bloody act as the inevitable consequence of an evil system. Before the assassination, the *Times* observed, there was a general sense "that patronage had corrupted and perverted politics." Something had to change—but people had only a vague notion of what that something should be. Garfield's agonizing death brought the remedy into focus. "It is now very clearly seen that the change must be in the abolition of patronage, and that it can only be accomplished by making appointments depend on merit tested by competition open to all who enter the service," the *Times* concluded. In the weeks following Garfield's death, civil service reform groups sprang up from Massachusetts to California.

Reformers had momentum. What they didn't have, apparently, was a friend in the White House. Arthur had rejected Conkling's request to remove Robertson from the Custom House and had pledged to continue Garfield's policies. But few knew he had rebuffed Conkling, and his promises to follow his predecessor's path were vague. He had built his political career on patronage. How could he disavow the spoils system now—much less lead the charge for reform? The shuffling of cabinet positions during his first months in office didn't inspire much hope. Arthur asked Garfield's advisers to stay on, but several who were friendly to reform soon departed or announced their intention to do so. Postmaster General James, who had introduced competitive exams at the postal service; Secretary of the Treasury Windom, who vigorously enforced reform principles at the Custom House; and Attorney General MacVeagh, a longtime reform advocate—all left, replaced by men less dedicated to the cause. When Blaine resigned in mid-December, Arthur refused to give his job to Conkling, as several of his New York cronies urged him to do. He did, however, fill the crucial post with a Stalwart recommended by Grant: Frederick Frelinghuysen, a former senator from New Jersey.

In 1880, the historian and intellectual Henry Adams published, anonymously, a best-selling book about Washington. In *Democracy: An American Novel*, Adams portrayed a corrupt capital where everybody was for sale, and politicians sacrificed their principles on the altar of ambition. "Where did the public good enter into all this maze of personal intrigue, this wilderness of stunted natures where no straight road is to be found, but only the tortuous and aimless travels of beasts and things that crawl?" the heroine of the novel muses.

Adams, the grandson and great-grandson of presidents, observed the beginning of the Arthur administration from his home in Lafayette Square, across from the White House. What he saw depressed him. "Our friend MacVeagh, after an heroic and desperate as well as prolonged struggle to drag President Arthur into the assertion of reform principles, has utterly and hopelessly failed," he wrote to his friend Henry Cabot Lodge in mid-November 1881. "The new administration will be the centre for every element of corruption, south and north. The outlook is very discouraging." A week later, Adams invited Lodge to "come and see how things are. You certainly will not find many reformers; all that swarm have vanished like smoke, and even I have ceased to lisp the word. . . . My mouth is shut on reform politics for at least two years to come; I have not the physical strength to cry like St. John in the wilderness."

•◆•

The widespread skepticism did not infect Julia Sand, who reaffirmed her faith in Arthur in three more letters she sent to him in the fall of 1881. "What a splendid Henry V you are making!" she wrote on October 27, while admitting that "as yet I have not met anybody who believes in you as I do." She complimented him on his recent speech marking the hundredth anniversary of the British surrender at Yorktown.

Persons not inclined to admire you are ready to admit that you have excellent taste and tact. Just what that means cannot be easily measured. Taste and tact may be merely the polish of which any hard surface is capable. But I do not like to think of men as blocks of marble, things that may be cut down in the finishing, but cannot be made to expand. I prefer to think of them as things with infinite powers of growth. And to me tact and taste are the sweet-scented flowers which spring from the root of true sentiment and deep feeling.

In the same letter, Sand designated herself as Arthur's "little dwarf"—the one person in a royal court allowed to speak the truth to the king. In that role, she reserved the right to "say all the unpleasant things I choose." She started by urging Arthur to be wary of former president Grant. "Do not let the people believe that he is to influence your administration. He will never give you an idea that is new, or deep, or even bright," she advised. "To him, politics means, which man is to get a place—& very little else. As to real statesmanship, he has no more conception of it than has a wild elephant."

By the fall of 1881, Sand had been an invalid for five years. Sometimes she languished on the parlor sofa, eyes shut tight, for a week or more, and she couldn't muster the strength to leave the house to visit anybody. And yet, when she read in the newspapers that Arthur might be attending a ball in New York, she burned with the idea of meeting him there. She said it was because she "had an idea, if I could see your face & hear the sound of your voice, I should know whether I were right or wrong in believing what I believe of you." But beneath her banter there was a gnawing loneliness—and perhaps a deeper desire.

I thought of the pleasure of my mother at seeing her little girl in a ball dress again, of the approbation of my saucy nephews, who frequently say to me, "Aunt Julia, if you only would put on a little more style!"—of my own delight at catching such a concentrated glimpse of the world, after having lived in the moon so long—& I did want to go to that ball with an earnestness unknown to my early days. Then I thought of the trouble it would be to my brother—that is, if he would take it—to find tickets, for the regular sale had closed—of the flurry of procuring a dress—my last ball was at Annapolis in '74, & though a costume from Queen Anne's time might be fashionable, one of King Grant's reign would be obsolete—& I thought of five years of unbroken suffering, of the desperate efforts to build up the little health I have, of the absolute necessity of adding to my strength and not wasting it—& then I shut the ball out of my thoughts altogether.

Having given up on the idea of attending the ball, Sand made an even bolder suggestion: that the president of the United States should come to 46 East 74th Street to visit *her*. She noted, coquettishly, that if Arthur came between 11 in the morning and noon he almost certainly would find her alone. At any time, she assured him, it was unlikely that he'd run into anybody he knew. Then, having dipped her toe into deeper waters, she quickly pulled it out. "I am quite aware that I have not the shadow of a claim upon you. I merely feel that, if you should want to know who it is that has written to you, you have a perfect right to that knowledge. If not, it is of no consequence."

·—◆—·

In early December, President Arthur submitted his first "Annual Message" (now known as the State of the Union address) to Congress. The president began with a detailed review of the country's foreign relations, and proposed to repeal all internal revenue taxes, save those on tobacco and distilled and fermented liquors. He called for an army of 30,000 men, largely to protect settlers and their property against Indians, while at the same time asking for legislation to prevent settlers from encroaching on land that had been set aside for the Indians. He also suggested that Congress use money from the sale of public lands to help pay for the education of freed slaves.

Then, to everybody's surprise, the erstwhile party hack proclaimed his support for civil service reform.

Arthur, quoting from the statement he issued upon his nomination as Garfield's running mate, asserted that "no man should be the incumbent of an office the duties of which he is for any cause unfit to perform; who is lacking in the ability, fidelity, or integrity which a proper administration of such office demands." These basic principles, he wrote, "are doubtless shared by all intelligent and patriotic citizens, however divergent in their opinions as to the best methods of putting them into practical operation."

This broad endorsement didn't mean much without specifics, but Arthur went further. He admitted he was wary of relying too heavily on tests, lest college graduates monopolize appointments at the expense of applicants with less book learning but difficult-to-measure attributes such as "probity, industry, good sense, good habits, good temper, patience, order, courtesy, tact, self-reliance, manly deference to superior officers, and manly consideration for inferiors." Instead, he proposed the creation of a central examining board that would review the candidates for certain offices, "without the resort to a competitive test."

However, noting the "grave importance" of the issue, Arthur assured lawmakers and the public that he wasn't making these observations in a "spirit of opposition." He promised that "if Congress should deem it advisable at the present session to establish competitive tests for admission to the service, no doubts such as have been suggested shall deter me from giving the measure my earnest support." If Congress did not pass a bill, Arthur said, he hoped it would at least spend $25,000 to reactivate the moribund Civil Service Commission.

Reformers were shocked—and thrilled—by Arthur's pronouncement. E. L. Godkin of the *Nation* latched on to Arthur's favorable reference to the British civil service system. "Hitherto the Stalwarts have never been able to refer to it with straight faces, and the fact that their spokesman has stopped laughing at it, and made an explicit announcement that it must be treated as a serious political question, is an encouraging sign of the times."

On the day Arthur delivered his Annual Message to Congress, Senator George Hunt Pendleton, an Ohio Democrat known as "Gentleman George," reintroduced a civil service reform bill he had put forward a year earlier. Pendleton was an unlikely champion: in 1864, he had been General George B. McClellan's running mate on the Democratic ticket, when virtually all reformers supported Lincoln and the war. As president of the Kentucky Central Railroad during the Grant administration, Pendleton capitalized on his friendship with the wife of the corrupt secretary of war to collect a $148,000 claim against the government, personally pocketing half of it.

But Pendleton's desire for reform was sincere. In 1880, he asked Arthur's old college friend and Custom House adversary Silas Burt—whose reform credentials were unsurpassed—to review his bill. Pendleton assured Burt it was "framed after much consideration, and a thorough examination of the civil service in Great Britain and the methods already tried in our own country, and whilst I am not wedded to it, as it stands, I desire extremely to see the ideas embodied in it carried out."

Pendleton's idea was to require applicants for certain positions to take competitive examinations, and to give jobs only to those with the highest scores. He wanted to base promotions on merit and competition. And he would ban the "voluntary" assessments that Arthur had used to such great effect in New York: party operatives could not force employees to contribute either time or money to political campaigns. "The fact is patent that [Guiteau] wanted an office and did not get it, and he believed the president was responsible for his failure," Pendleton said on the Senate floor. "We must supplant this system; we must chase it out with hue and cry. In its place we must put the other and better system founded on the idea that public offices are public trusts to be administered solely for the public good."

Civil service reform groups from around the country rallied behind Pendleton's proposal, bombarding Congress with more than 50 petitions in favor of it. Ten thousand Bostonians signed one petition, and reformers from New York City, Chicago, Philadelphia, Baltimore, and Cincinnati submitted their own. Supportive congressmen pointed to the distinguished Americans backing the effort: one petition included the signatures of Harvard president Charles W. Eliot, poet Henry Wadsworth Longfellow, and philosopher William James.

Sand believed that Arthur's actions—or failure to act—on civil service reform would define his presidency. "The vital question before the country today is Civil Service Reform," Sand wrote to Arthur in January. "The vital question before you is how you will meet it."

> Evasion in any form will be a proof of weakness. Yet if you fight the rampant evil—though more than half the country will back you—you will do it at your own risk. Are you a coward? Do you fear to face the same danger that Garfield faced? It is for you to choose. Are you content to sit, like a snake charmer, & let loathsome serpents coil about you, priding yourself on it that not one of them dares sting you? I would rather think of you, like St. George, in shining armor, striking death to the heart of the dragon.

Sand began that January letter by extending holiday greetings to the president. Her own Christmas, she told him, had been gloomy. Confined to her room by her illness, her celebration had been limited to listening to her nieces and nephews cavorting in the parlor downstairs. Finally, somebody closed the parlor door and the sounds of laughter and music grew fainter. Then the front door bell rang sharply, and she heard somebody climbing the stairs. It was her sister, carrying a horseshoe of flowers: pink rosebuds and carnations and velvety pansies, surrounded by sweet-smelling mignonette. "This is for you," her sister said, placing the flowers beside Julia, "but we can not make out who sent it." She held out a card with a monogram printed in purple ink. Julia could not believe her eyes: the flowers were from President Arthur! She lingered over the gift "with the rapt devotion of a child of nature—the serene vanity of a society woman—the morbid tenderness of an invalid." Then something startled her out of her reverie. She looked up and her sister, the flowers, and the card were gone—only a glass of water and a bottle of camphor remained.

She had been dreaming.

"How could I help what I saw—far less what other people chose to do—when my eyes were shut?" she wrote. "Still, for a mid winter day dream, don't you think it was rather poetic?"

•━•

At the beginning of 1882 Roscoe Conkling was in a desperate state, still reeling from Arthur's refusal to fire Robertson from the Custom House. "Perhaps only you and I know how ill-judged and unfortunate Mr. C's last visit to Washington was," Kate Chase Sprague wrote to Arthur. She admitted it was on her advice that Conkling had gone to the president and "laid bare his heart." Now she was filled with regret. "When I saw him after-wards, & saw how he was suffering, I urged his quitting Washington without delay. Friends who have seen him within a day or two report him as very ill." In the same letter, she urged the president to appoint her longtime lover as secretary of the treasury—a request Arthur ignored. Instead, he chose his—and Conkling's—longtime friend Charles J. Folger, who was chief justice of the New York Supreme Court.

In late January, a New York newspaper editor gave Arthur a similar assessment of Conkling's condition: the once omnipotent boss had lost his Senate seat, his machine, and his friends, and he was deeply depressed. Even as Arthur tried to transcend his past, he felt honor-bound to help his old patron. He had passed over Conkling for the major cabinet posts, but he did have one plum to offer: a place on the US Supreme Court. Conkling had rejected President Grant's offer of a court seat, and it was unclear whether he wanted one now. Arthur nominated Conkling anyway, and in early March senators confirmed their former colleague 39–12.

Many reformers criticized Arthur's choice. Ohio Republicans, still mourning their murdered hero Garfield, were especially appalled. "Better for Conkling, that he pass at least a decent probation in the seclusion of private life, and better for Arthur not to force under the nostrils of the American people an unsavory smelling object," the Youngstown *News Register* said. In the end, Conkling rejected Arthur's gesture, and opted to remain in exile.

As the year wore on, Conkling and other machine politicians could take heart from one development: Pendleton's civil service reform bill was going nowhere.

Reform activity was strongest in major cities, and urban congressmen were under tremendous pressure to back the Pendleton proposal. But Congress as a whole remained resistant. In the House, Speaker Joseph Warren Keifer of Ohio populated the Select Committee on Civil Service Reform with members who were adamantly opposed to the idea. "If Jonah was one of these modern civil-service reformers my sympathies are all with the whale," panel member Roswell G. Horr of Michigan proclaimed, sparking laughter and applause on the House floor. After six months of work, the committee produced "a bill to enlarge the powers and duties of the Department of Agriculture." Congress also rejected Arthur's call for $25,000 to restart the Civil Service Commission.

•—◆—•

Arthur mourned his predecessor for the first six months of his presidency. During that time he dressed in black, used writing paper with a broad black border, and declined all invitations to theatrical performances. As a sign of respect, he delayed holding an official reception until the second day of 1882, about a month after moving into the redecorated White House. It was a stripped down affair: instead of elaborate decorations of flags, plants, and flowers, there were only a few ferns and palms set up in the corridor, along with smilax wrapped around the chandeliers and mirrors of the parlors. The Marine Band played in the vestibule while Arthur, wearing a Prince Albert coat, a dark blue satin necktie, and pearl-tinted gloves, greeted guests for three hours.

Fortunately, the refurbished Executive Mansion no longer needed the dressing up it had required during its shabbier days. As part of the renovation, 24 wagonloads of furniture, carpets, and drapes, some dating back to the John Adams administration, had been hauled away and sold at public auction. Louis C. Tiffany of New York, son of the famous jeweler and one of the nation's foremost decorators, sent designers to work on the project, and Arthur took a keen interest in it. While living at the Jones house, the president had strolled over to the White House almost every evening to check in and make suggestions.

Many parts of the mansion had been transformed. In the main corridor, the walls were now tinted a pale olive and the large niches covered with squares of gold leaf. The ceiling was decorated in gold and silver, broken by traceries in colors spelling out "U.S.A." In the Red Room, a cherry mantel-piece, a jeweled glass screen, and panels of Japanese leather surrounded the open fireplace. Tiffany made a 50-foot jeweled glass screen, fitted with imitation marble columns, to replace the old glass doors that formerly separated the main corridor from the north vestibule.

Arthur paid special attention to the redecoration of the president's private dining room on the first floor. He had the walls covered with heavy gold paper in large designs, and pomegranate plush hangings were draped over the windows and mantelpiece. It was his idea to have an open fireplace with crimson glass sidelights. Even James Blaine's wife, Harriet, who was quick to criticize Arthur, was impressed by the changes. "I dined at the President's Wednesday," she wrote to her daughter on March 13, 1882. "The dinner was extremely elegant, hardly a trace of the old White House taint being perceptible anywhere, the flowers, the damask, the silver, the attendants, all showing the latest style and an abandon in expense and taste."

As a widower, Arthur had to find somebody to perform the social duties of the First Lady, and he tapped his youngest sister for the role. Forty-year-old Mary Arthur McElroy was petite, with dark hair and eyes. She lived with her husband, insurance man John E. McElroy, and their four children in Albany, but the president convinced her to live in Washington four months a year to serve as "Mistress of the White House." A graduate of Emma Willard's Troy Female Seminary in Troy, New York, the president's graceful sister was immediately popular, charming the capital's socialites by inviting them to receive with her at receptions. During events she usually kept her daughter, May, and her 10-year-old niece, Nell, close at hand, "and the gay girls always soon did away with any stiffness there might have been."

But it was the president himself who made the biggest splash on the social scene. Arthur was a sophisticated New Yorker, well versed in the pleasures and demands of upper-class society. "He wanted the best of everything, and wanted it served in the best manner," recalled Colonel William Crook, the White House doorkeeper who served presidents from Lincoln to Wilson. Arthur treated himself and his guests to the best food, liquors, and cigars.

The new president also took great pride in wearing the finest clothes, made by a well-known—and high-priced—New York tailor. One day, it was said, he tried on 20 pairs of trousers made to his measurements before finally choosing the pair he wanted. During business hours he wore the choicest tweeds. In the afternoons, he put on a black frock coat, a white or gray waistcoat, gray trousers, and a silk hat. For dinner, he dressed in a tuxedo.

Crook, who had served five presidents by the time Arthur took office, said the New Yorker was the first one to have a personal valet (the Lexington Avenue doorkeeper, Aleck Powell, served in the role) and described Arthur as "always well groomed; almost faultless in his dress."

Arthur's social appeal went beyond his appreciation for first-rate food and drink and his fashionable attire. It was how he carried himself, and how he treated others, that earned him acclaim. In an age when manners mattered, his were impeccable. "It is not that he is handsome and agreeable—for he was both long ago," one admirer wrote, "but it is his ease, polish and perfect manner that makes him the greatest society lion we have had in many years." Arthur could "open a door, restore a handkerchief, or hand a chair to a lady without exhibiting a colossal amount of clumsy dignity as did the eminent Rutherford B. Hayes; nor, on the other hand, does he effervesce with the effusive gallantry of men of distinction from the South." But Arthur was no snob: when walking or riding through the streets of Washington, he always raised his hat and bowed to the citizens he met, even the lowest laborers.

Arthur hosted his first formal White House event, a dinner in honor of General and Mrs. Grant, in late March 1882. He had large azalea trees placed along the walls and in the niches of the state dining room, and the table was decorated with branches of wax lights along with crimson and gold roses, red and white azaleas, and pink carnations. Each of the 36 place settings included six wine glasses, a goblet, and a heavy, gilt-edge card embossed with the national coat of arms and the guest's name. Each lady received a large corsage tied with blue satin ribbon, and each gentleman got a boutonniere. At 8 o'clock, President Arthur escorted Mrs. Grant, who was wearing crimson velvet that set off her diamonds and pearls, to the table and sat her on his right. For two and a half hours, the guests, mostly cabinet members, senators, and representatives, enjoyed 18 courses and six kinds of wine as the Marine Band played, illuminated by calcium lights projected through colored glass.

The president's son Alan was in college at Princeton, but he visited often and "did much to add to the gayety of the White House," Crook remembered. Tall and handsome with alabaster skin and piercing black eyes, Alan spent money freely and was an inveterate partygoer and lady-chaser. Whenever he was weary of Princeton, Alan stepped on a train and came to Washington, sometimes arriving late at night. No matter what time it was, the first thing he did was order his team of horses from the White House stable so he could whirl off to visit a young lady or some chums who lived in town. More than once, the president was surprised when Alan appeared at the White House breakfast table when he was supposed to be in New Jersey, immersed in his studies. Sometimes, Alan did his entertaining at the Executive Mansion. After one White House performance by the Princeton Glee Club, Alan and his friends enjoyed two suppers—one served at midnight, and another at 3:30 a.m. The wine and champagne flowed prodigiously, and "at a late hour there was a regular romp including a display of leaping by one of the young men who was quite an athlete in the east room." On another occasion, Alan and the crown prince of Siam got drunk and were arrested for swimming nude in a White House fountain.

But dark undercurrents flowed beneath the frothy surface of Arthur's White House. Nell's death, Garfield's months of agony, the savage attacks in the press—all had wounded Arthur deeply. He had not sought the presidency, and the burdens of the office weighed heavily on him. "When you go into his office in the morning, there you see a man oppressed with either duties or the inversion of his natural hours, or staggering under a sense of responsibility which he does not like," one member of the administration said. As collector, Arthur had concentrated on machine politics and left the day-to-day drudgery to his subordinates. "But in the Presidency, he cannot delegate much, and the successive shocks of conflict over every office, and his desire not to offend either public opinion or the large personal influences which make up his party, keep him in a measure stunned, uncertain, and in any event moody, possibly unhappy." Arthur often felt depressed and exhausted, and suffered bouts of nausea. Dr. Brodie Herndon, invited by Arthur to stay at the White House for several months in 1882, recorded his concerns in his diary, describing the president as "sick in body and soul."

Unaware of his ailments, hostile newspapers accused Arthur of not working hard enough. He usually rose at about 9:30 a.m. and ate a roll and drank a cup of coffee while getting dressed. He began the workday by reading private letters and dictating replies to official communications. Then he spent an hour or so receiving members of Congress and people seeking federal jobs. Especially aggressive office-seekers sometimes broke past the presidential secretaries in their desperation to reach the president.

At noon Arthur ate a light meal—usually fish, fruit, and oatmeal—before returning to his office until around 4 p.m. In the late afternoon he enjoyed taking a ride around the city, either on horseback or in a carriage, usually joined by his daughter or other guests. At around 6 p.m., he ate dinner with his family. His favorite meal was a mutton chop with a glass of Bass ale, or a slice of rare roast beef with a glass of claret, a baked potato, and fruit. After dinner he returned to his office to read documents and letters submitted to him by heads of departments. On nights when he had no social obligation, Arthur might continue working until the early morning hours.

Arthur dreaded days when he had to receive general callers in the White House library. For three hours or more, he had to shake hands and make small talk with anybody who wanted to meet the president, sometimes as many as three thousand people. Gentlemen deposited their coats in the president's private dining room, while ladies piled their wraps in the state dining room. To keep the crowd moving along, White House workers had to reconfigure one of the large lower windows as a second exit. With his sister standing gamely by his side, Arthur greeted each person in line, shifting back and forth on his feet when he wanted to cut short an especially unpleasant encounter.

It was dispiriting, Arthur told a reporter, that unlike a New York businessman he could not disconnect from his workday worries and find rest and recreation in a domestic sanctuary; the president had to work and live in the same place. He deeply resented his lack of privacy, and took pains to protect his children—especially young "Miss Nellie"—from the prying eyes of the public. Since Andrew Jackson's time, presidents' families had been put on display, their children treated as if they were the nation's offspring. The Arthurs departed from that tradition. "Madam, I may be president of the United States, but my private life is nobody's damned business," he snapped at one visitor.

As skilled as he was at hosting large events, Arthur much preferred to be in the company of close friends. He was at his best at small dinner parties, chatting over cigars. He especially enjoyed walking the deserted streets of Washington after midnight, accompanied by one or two of his old New York cronies. He was a man who did not like to be alone. "I have sat up with him until midnight, and then, when I excused myself, he would say, 'Oh, General, don't go; stay and let us have a good time,'" the Civil War hero General William T. Sherman recalled.

Washington wondered whether the widower was seeking female companionship. Henry Adams's wife Marian described one gathering in early 1882. "Our good king Arthur was there, all the pretty girls taken up to him and presented—it was more like royalty than anything I have ever seen—not being a pretty girl I did not compete in the ceremony."

Julia Sand teased the president about his frequent visits to New York, suggesting that perhaps he had a secret lover, or even a fiancée, in the city. "Do you remember any other President as restless as yourself—who was rushing home every few weeks? If, as Washington gossip hints, you are engaged—& wish to see the lady without having her name dragged before the public—of course the end justified the means." Some of the rumors swirled around one of the daughters of Secretary of State Frelinghuysen.

The press pounced when word leaked out of the White House that President Arthur ordered fresh flowers every day and arranged them around the photograph of a woman, which he kept in his bedroom.

But the disclosure of the mystery lady's identity silenced the wagging tongues: the woman in the photograph was the president's beloved wife, Nell.

CHAPTER EIGHTEEN

A Surprise Visit

F OR JULIA SAND, clutching the smooth leather felt like seizing a second chance. She loosened the reins and "Frank" trotted east on Union Avenue, away from Congress Park. The stiff April breeze carried the scent of fir and pine, and the Green Mountains glowed bluish in the sunlight. Julia felt steadier: a few months before, she had suffered through a sleigh ride with a young man, torn between her impulse to cling to his arm and her determination not to. Setting out today, she feared she would clip the wheel of a passing wagon or topple her own, but she had done neither, and she swelled with confidence and pride as she piloted Frank past the resort town's famous racetrack.

Sand was in Saratoga Springs, New York, in the spring of 1882 to regain her health. There were a hundred mineral springs in the crescent-shaped valley between Ballston Spa and Quaker Springs. Saratoga, nestled in the center of the valley, was a mecca for visitors seeking the therapeutic benefits of drinking or bathing in the waters. It was a place with "greater advantages for the recovery of health than any other place in America, if not in the world," and Julia was making the most of it.

By 1882, Saratoga's races and regattas had become summer attractions for the social elite, and the village boasted several first-class hotels. Musicians played every morning in the piazzas of the Grand Union Hotel, supposedly the world's largest. The Grand Union could accommodate 1,500 guests; 1,200 of them could eat at one time in the hotel dining room, which extended the length of a city block. The Grand Union ballroom featured Frenchman Adolphe Yvon's allegorical painting, *The Genius of America*, which measured 2,400 square feet and had a frame that weighed three thousand pounds. The north veranda of the nearby United States Hotel was an

attraction in its own right: tourists used opera glasses to observe the railroad barons rocking on what became known as "The Millionaires' Piazza."
One popular pastime was promenading on elm-shaded Broadway, Saratoga's
main thoroughfare. The famous actress Lillian Russell liked to stroll with
her Japanese Spaniel, "Mooksie," who sported a $2,000 diamond-encrusted
collar. Sometimes the buxom actress pedaled down Broadway on her gold-
plated bicycle, which had handlebars decorated with her initials in diamonds
and emeralds. The collar and the bike were gifts from her boyfriend, the railroad magnate Diamond Jim Brady.

Sand was in high spirits on the day of her wagon ride, and not just because her health was improving. She was encouraged by the performance of
her president—especially his courageous veto of a bill she considered "a step
back into barbarism."

A month earlier, Congress had overwhelmingly approved the first significant restriction on free immigration in US history. The Chinese Exclusion
Act barred Chinese laborers from entering the country for 20 years, and denied citizenship to the Chinese already here. Those who wished to leave but
planned to return had to register at the US Custom House. And even those
Chinese citizens who were allowed to come to the United States could not
do so unless they procured a passport, written in English and countersigned
by an American consular representative in China, describing the holder and
his intentions. Labor unions had objected to the Chinese workers' willing-
ness to toil for low wages on railroads and in mines. But the measure also
was rooted in racism and revulsion at the newcomers' unfamiliar customs.
"A congress of ignorant school boys could not devise more idiotic legislation," Sand wrote to Arthur shortly after Congress approved the bill. "It is
not only behind the age, but behind several ages—not only opposed to the
spirit of American institutions but opposed to the spirit of civilization all the
world over." She implored him to "please give it a most emphatic veto."

Arthur did. On April 4, he sent a long and forceful veto message to
Capitol Hill. The president acknowledged that an 1880 treaty with China
allowed the United States to "regulate, limit or suspend" the immigration
of Chinese laborers if the influx seemed to threaten public order, but he
argued that barring immigration for 20 years, "nearly a generation," went
far beyond the treaty and would be "a breach of our national faith." He
described the registration and passport requirements as "undemocratic and
hostile to the spirit of our institutions." He also noted that the Chinese laborers had made significant contributions to the development of the West,
and warned that the draconian bill "must have a direct tendency to repel

Oriental nations from us and to drive their trade and commerce into more friendly hands."

The *Times* hailed Arthur for his "firmness and wisdom," and Sand was thrilled. "I must tell you that your veto of the Chinese Bill delighted me," she wrote from Saratoga. "And, what is more to the point, a great many other people also were pleased—pleased and surprised. Don't you feel flattered how awfully surprised they are, whenever you do anything good? Well, go on surprising them. But I am never surprised, because I expected it of you."

Arthur had taken a courageous stand—but it was short-lived. After a failed attempt to override the veto, Congress approved a revised version of the Chinese Exclusion Act. It cut the restriction period to 10 years but included all of the other provisions Arthur had denounced so eloquently just a few weeks before. Nevertheless, Arthur signed it. Sand was crestfallen. "What is there to admire in mediocrity?" she chastised him.

> Why do you take such comfort in half measures? Does it never strike you that there must be back of them only half a mind—a certain half heartedness—in fact, only half a man? Why do you not do what you do with your whole soul?—or have you only half of one? When you vetoed the Chinese Bill, the better class of people throughout the country were delighted. Now you sign it. And what is the difference, as it now stands? In quantity less, but in quality just as idiotic & unnecessary as the first. Unnecessary legislation is a positive evil, in any case, but this is worse, for it is contrary to the spirit of our institutions & the civilization of the age. The Czar of Russia might well respond to your remonstrance against the persecution of the Jews, with an expostulation against your persecution of the Chinese.

"Are you going to let your Administration be a failure?" she concluded. "What you do now, if you do right, will wash out all the harm you ever did in our life—but nothing you can do after will obliterate your Presidential record." Sand resolved never to write to Arthur again.

Arthur got another chance to prove his mettle a few months later, when Congress sent him the latest "River and Harbor" bill. In 1822, the first such measure contained federal money for the upkeep and replacement of lighthouses, buoys, and other navigation tools. But over time, this mechanism to repair and replace essential infrastructure became larded with pork-barrel projects. Congressmen used River and Harbor bills to funnel federal money to their districts, boosting their reelection prospects—and often lining their own pockets—in the process. Between 1870 and 1881 the cost of the package grew from under $4 million to $11.5 million.

The version that landed on President Arthur's desk in July 1882 totaled nearly $19 million, and it sparked public outrage. "This Congress is voting millions into the air and into the pockets of rapscallions, and the President is called upon to sign away the money," the *Sun* wrote. "What an opportunity for a shrewd and brave man! What an opportunity for CHESTER A. ARTHUR!" The *Times* also urged a veto, calling the bill "a monstrous swindle" and "a scandalous misappropriation of public money for the advancement of local jobbery." The president "has an excellent opportunity to place himself on the side of economy and public decency by vetoing it."

Sand, who returned to Manhattan at the end of July, closely followed the debate in Washington. Every morning and evening she checked the newspapers for word of Arthur's decision. She knew the political pressure on him was intense—nearly every member of Congress had a financial stake in the bill. Finally, on August 2, her brother Theodore peered over the top of his newspaper and cheerfully announced the verdict: "It's vetoed." Julia turned her head to hide the tears that were welling up in her eyes, fearing her family would laugh at her. As it was, her siblings treated her, the youngest, as if she were a child. "For a woman to weep over the veto of her own little bills is quite rational, I suppose, but to get excited about a bill down in Washington, with which she had nothing to do, is inexcusable," she wrote to Arthur. "Still I was deeply moved by your action concerning this one, for I realized what a struggle you had passed through—how you had been worried, perplexed, tormented—what an opposition you had to stand up against in coming to your final decision." Though Congress quickly overrode Arthur's veto, Sand reassured him that he had "rendered the country a real service & the country will not forget it."

Sand wrote Arthur twice more in the next two and a half weeks. But with Congress adjourned for the summer, her focus shifted away from politics and policy. She knew the president was coming to New York and she wanted him to visit her. "Well, have you not five minutes to spare for me—when I have spared so many hours for you, in this long, sad, exciting year?" she wrote on August 15. "When I was an invalid & hardly ever went anywhere or saw anyone, it seemed quite natural that I should not see you—you were as far from me in New York as in Washington—but now it is different. . . . I would not on any account have you run the smallest risk, or subject yourself to the slightest annoyance for my sake, but if it is possible, I do want to see you."

In her next letter, written less than a week later, Sand wondered whether Arthur was snubbing her because of "the few harsh things" she had written to him.

> Are you offended with me—really—seriously? Do the few harsh things that I have said to you outweigh all else—the fact that for a whole year I have thought of & felt with you in your cares & perplexities—that last summer, when you were bowed down in gloom & seemed almost broken in spirit, I did my best to arouse your manhood & your courage—that I had faith in you, when hardly anyone who had the welfare of the country at heart, hoped anything good of you? I did not ask you to answer my letters, for I knew you could not speak to me on the subjects I chose to discuss—but it never crossed my mind, till now, that you distrusted me.

•◆•

At 8 p.m. on August 20, 1882, two men in claret livery drove a short rig down East 74th Street. The carriage halted outside no. 46, and a large man wearing a black frock coat, a white waistcoat, and gray trousers stepped out. He put on his silk hat and strode up to the brownstone owned by the banker Theodore Sand.

Inside the house, Julia was sprawled on the lounge, sunk in a sour mood. Her family had dined on roast beef and peach pie, but she was too depressed to eat. She had been writing Chester Arthur for a year, holding up a torch to guide him through the gloom, sending a spark to rekindle the idealism of his youth—for his sake, and for the sake of the country. She knew him only through the newspapers, but somehow she sensed he was better than the press portrayed him. She was just a young woman, made doubly powerless by her illness, but was it unreasonable to expect some acknowledgment of her efforts? He hadn't deigned to scribble a line or two on a card, much less pay her the visit she craved. She swore she would not write again to that horrid man—not a single word.

The sound of the doorbell roused Julia from her musings. She heard an unfamiliar voice in the parlor: a stranger who spoke gently, like an Episcopal minister. She held her breath and strained to listen. The few scraps of conversation that floated in piqued her curiosity. Could it be? She jumped off the lounge and flew through the house to see for herself.

Yes—it *was* the president of the United States standing in the parlor.

Theodore introduced his sister and Julia, chest heaving, stammered a greeting. Her pen had disgorged a torrent of words in the past year; now she couldn't seem to utter a single one. Her brother later joked that she was like the man in the Arabian Nights who finally coaxed the genie out of the bottle, then became so frightened he immediately wanted to stuff him back into it. Amused by Julia's reaction, the president said she ought to have known he was coming. It was left to Theodore to invite their guest to sit down on the sofa, and Julia settled into an armchair next to it.

It would have been different without her mother, sisters, brothers, and nephews there. Of all the days Arthur had been in town, of all the hours in the day he could have appeared on her doorstep, there was not another time when the house would have been so full of Sands. Their presence made Julia's conversation with the president uncomfortably stiff. At first, they avoided talking about politics. She gave him an opening to scold her for her impertinence, but he refused to seize it. She resorted to small talk, inquiring whether he was fond of music. "Reasonably," Arthur replied. What an unreasonable answer, she thought. If he had been a bit more enthusiastic, perhaps she would have persuaded her sister and brothers to sing a long trio from German or Italian opera. That would have lightened the mood!

As her siblings peppered the president with mundane questions, Julia concentrated on Arthur's voice, his manner, and his facial expressions. She hardly heard what he said. She was elated when he looked at her, but her excitement was laced with melancholy—he seemed weary and worn out. What a disgrace to the country that the White House should be so unhealthy! Julia wanted to do something for him, to insist that he lie down on the sofa and rest for an hour, to have some dinner. But that natural reaction would be quite unnatural in the case of a president, wouldn't it? Surely he would think her demented!

After the Sands' flustered butler served Arthur claret in a sherry glass, Julia gently turned the conversation toward more substantial topics, slowly putting on the persona she had adopted in her letters. Why, she asked, had he recently pardoned a notorious embezzler?

Arthur paused. Well, he replied evenly, the attorney general recommended the pardon.

Julia objected. It might be the attorney general's place to investigate cases, she said, and to give the president the chief points and to express his opinion. But was it the attorney general's job to be the keeper of the president's conscience?

Arthur smiled. She did him an injustice, he said. In this and many other instances, she shouldn't believe everything she read in the newspapers. If she knew the truth, she would judge him differently.

Somehow an hour had passed, and Arthur rose to leave. Your sister believes I should be an angel, the president joked to his hosts, and she condemns me when I fall short of that high standard. Julia cringed at the accusation. How false! She had never for a moment been under any such hallucination. She believed moral progress was possible, that there was no such thing as standing still and remaining the same. Sometimes men progressed slowly, sometimes rapidly, and much depended on circumstances. But it was possible to become a better person—that much she knew.

As Arthur put on his hat, Julia asked him whether he had forgiven her for some of the harsh things she had written in her letters. "No," he said with a wry smile. His tone and his stiff handshake made her wonder whether he was kidding.

Sand was still stewing over Arthur's parting words when she wrote him again a few days after his visit. "The Presidency puts a man terribly to the test," she wrote. "If he has fine qualities, they will shine with double brilliancy. If he is commonplace, it kills him."

What has Grant been good for since—except to eat dinners? Will Hayes ever be heard of again—unless at a Sunday School festival? It has not killed you yet—& will not, unless you, at some important turning-point, deliberately choose the wrong path. Setting aside all cant about sudden conversion—I hope you do not understand me as believing in that—& thinking simply of what it is to meet a great emergency, to rise to it, or to fail, are you not wiser & better than you were? Look back on the past year—did you ever in your life work harder?—& has not almost all of that work been for others? Even in your pleasures, have you not considered more what you could give, than receive? Have you had larger thoughts in your mind? When Vice-President, you had no dignity to keep or to lose— forgive me for saying anything so hateful, but it is true. As President—so far as the world knows—you have never lost your dignity once. Opponents have been forced to admire you. You have done better than friend or foe expected. And it is to your honor that it is so. You should not deny it & be ashamed.

•—◆—•

Julia thought the president's visit would begin a new chapter in their relationship. In mid-September, she chastised him for failing to write, and she fully expected him to stop by her house again when he returned to New York. "I have made one little visit out of town, since I saw you, & expect to make two more before going to Saratoga, but will not run away just now, if there is any probability of my seeing you," she wrote. Sometimes she sat in the same armchair she had occupied during Arthur's visit and stared sadly at the empty sofa. One day, when she came downstairs to greet a girlfriend, she thought she spied a familiar figure in the parlor. "I ran down stairs, looking like an angel, in dotted white muslin. (I hope you know that the angels always wear that—probably because there are so many of them, that they have to be economical—& it is pretty, considering.) Through the half-open door, I caught a glimpse of some grayish hair & a fine, large figure—not at all like my friend's—& I thought!—what do you think I thought?" This time, Julia was disappointed. As she was introduced to a "Dr. Van Buren," her face glowed with a "seraphic look of surprise and delight" meant for somebody else.

In a subsequent letter, Julia tried to entice Arthur by offering to paint his portrait. As the fall dragged on without a presidential visit, she expressed growing concern about what exactly Arthur *was* doing when he came to Manhattan—especially with critical state elections looming.

Many were paying close attention to the 1882 governor's race in New York. Republicans and Democrats were evenly divided in the Empire State, and the state GOP remained riven by factional warfare between Stalwarts, Half-Breeds, and reformers. Out of office, Conkling was "just as rampant as he ever was, and you can spend the most disagreeable hour and a half with him if you happen to be his friend that you ever have in your life," one Stalwart said. The former boss felt betrayed by his former protégé's refusal to remove Robertson from the Custom House, but he hadn't given up hope of regaining his machine. "He upbraids everyone, assails the course of events, regards himself as defrauded, duped and sold out." The battle in the country's most populous state—between Republicans and Democrats and within the GOP—would be a barometer of the Republicans' prospects for retaining the White House in 1884.

Half-Breeds and independents backed the incumbent governor, Republican Alonzo Cornell, believing him to be honest and efficient. But Stalwarts bitterly recalled Cornell's half-hearted support for Conkling's bid to rejoin the Senate, and felt he had been stingy with state patronage. Conkling referred to Cornell as "that lizard on the hill."

The Stalwarts supported Treasury Secretary Charles Folger—despite their mixed feelings about him. They thought Folger would be more useful in Albany than in Washington, where he had been less than energetic in handing out federal jobs to Stalwarts. "The old machine that Arthur brought up by hand is determined to have Folger out of the Treasury Department, and there is no way to get him out but to nominate him for Governor," the *Cincinnati Enquirer* explained.

President Arthur insisted he did not want to get involved in a factional fight, and swore he was staying out of the New York race. Nobody believed him.

As the September state convention approached, newspapers reported that "Administration men" were plotting against Cornell, and the governor claimed he was a marked man. Arthur left for Washington shortly before New York Republicans convened in Saratoga, eager to show he did not intend to influence events there.

But when Folger won the GOP nomination, many saw Arthur's fingerprints all over Cornell's defeat. George William Curtis wrote that Folger's nomination "was procured by the combined power of fraud and patronage, and to support it at the polls would be to acquiesce in fraud and patronage as legitimate forces in a nominating convention." Even Sand assumed the worst, speculating that Arthur had not come to see her in September because he was ashamed of what he was up to in New York.

> I felt that you were doing things which made you feel that you could not, with comfort, look me in the face. Invalid as I am, for more than a year I have poured out my best strength in one continuous appeal to your finer nature—& what has it availed? The dew might as well fall on polished marble in the hope of producing a flower. You have had an opportunity for good such as does not come to one man in a million. And what have you done with it? Look at your friends. To lie, to cheat, to steal, to forge, to bribe & be bribed—those are what they consider the avenues to your favor. Do you realize what the reflection is upon yourself?

"You know I do not wish to do you injustice—that it pains me beyond measure to think ill of you," she concluded. "But I love my country too much to call myself your friend, while I believe you are doing it an injury. Am I wrong in believing that? If I am, come & tell me so yourself."

Democrats were well positioned to take advantage of the perceived crookedness of the GOP, having nominated Grover Cleveland, the

45-year-old reform mayor of Buffalo, as their gubernatorial candidate. President Arthur fulfilled his pledge to stay out of the race. He might have raised money, sent speakers and strategists, or made a personal appeal for Republican unity. He did none of those things, in marked contrast to his use of the vice presidency to aid Conkling's reelection bid just a year before. Nevertheless, Cleveland made "presidential interference" a major theme of his campaign, and the charge stuck: the Democrat crushed Folger by more than 190,000 votes—the largest margin of victory in any state election up to that point. To make matters worse, the Democrats claimed a large majority in the US House of Representatives and scored state victories in Ohio, Pennsylvania, Indiana, Connecticut, New Jersey, and Massachusetts. The shattering defeat prompted many Republicans to call for new leadership. "The Republican Party's message to President Arthur reads something like this: 'Mind your own business, which is not that of interfering in the local politics of your own or any other state. Cease trying to be a ward politician and the Executive of the Nation at the same time,'" the *Times* editorialized.

Sand shared the prevailing view. "Had you remained at your post of duty in Washington, or at least kept out of the state of New-York, for the last six weeks, you would not be in the deplorable position you are now," she wrote on the same day the *Times* pointed its finger at the president. "If there was anything deeply humiliating in your defeat, it consisted in not what your opponents prepared for you, but in what you prepared for yourself. You have been your own worst enemy."

• ◆ •

Politicians in both parties believed that voters had trumpeted their support for civil service reform. The consensus was that Cleveland's enthusiastic endorsement of reform had helped propel him to victory, and that the issue tipped the scales toward the Democratic gubernatorial candidate in Pennsylvania, too. Many Republican voters supposedly stayed home to protest GOP infighting and corruption, and there was widespread outrage at reports that the Republican Congressional Committee had leaned hard on government employees to contribute to the party's coffers. "Never has the popular feeling against the demoralizing abuses of the spoils system been as definite, sincere and strong as it is now," E. L. Godkin wrote in the *Nation*. "Never has the demand for the abolition of that system, and for a thorough reform of the civil service, been as loud and as general as it is to-day."

In Arthur's second Annual Message, delivered to the lame-duck Congress in December 1882, he capitalized on the public mood. "The people of the country, apparently without distinction of party, have in various ways and upon frequent occasions given expression to their earnest wish for prompt and definite action," Arthur declared. For the first time, he acknowledged that party leaders often coerced public employees into making political contributions—the "assessments" he had enthusiastically collected at the Custom House. He called on Congress to ban assessments, and urged passage of the Pendleton bill, even though it required the competitive examinations he had long opposed. "It may safely be said that the Message has taken many persons by surprise," the *Times* observed. "One hears it said on the streets and in the hotels that the President has heard the verdict of the people and been guided by it."

Congressmen heard "the verdict of the people" loud and clear. Less than a month after Arthur's endorsement, the Pendleton bill sailed through the Senate, 38–5. The House debated for only half an hour before approving the measure, 155–47. Chester Arthur, who had mastered machine politics in the service of Roscoe Conkling and the Stalwarts, signed the nation's first civil service reform into law on January 16, 1883.

The law Arthur signed was limited: it applied only to federal departments in Washington and to custom houses and post offices with more than 50 employees, about 10 percent of all federal jobs. The law did not apply to the nation's 47,000 postmasters, veterans, "mere workmen," or presidential appointees confirmed by the Senate. Most important, its success or failure depended heavily on the goodwill of the president. He might or might not appoint a three-man bipartisan commission to craft the required regulations, and he could stall, or decline to extend, the rules it produced. Members of Congress were unlikely to object to such tactics, since for most of them support for civil service reform was purely politics. "We are not legislating on this subject in response to our own judgment . . . but in response to some sort of judgment which has been expressed outside," one senator had groused during the debate.

Julia Sand wanted to believe that Arthur was dedicated to civil service reform, but she feared there was "something tricky in [his] nature," something that made it difficult for him to "put all double-dealing out of [his] life."

"Do you know how the people regard your Message? They don't regard it at all. You gave a splendid one last year—but you did not live up to it," Sand wrote. "People have a great aversion to being made fools of—especially for the second time. Words will never serve you again—actions only will count."

Would Chester Arthur faithfully execute the new law? Julia and many other Americans doubted it.

CHAPTER NINETEEN

An Attack in Savannah

I N DECEMBER 1882, the lame-duck Congress overhauled the country's civil service. Three months later, it finished its work by laying the keel of the modern American navy.

Many Americans didn't see the point. The European powers were an ocean away and America had no overseas colonies to defend. Since the War of 1812, the US Navy's principal mission had been to protect American harbors, and nobody expected it to venture too far from shore. But the navy had deteriorated dramatically in the 15 years since the Civil War, making it inferior not only to European navies but to those of some Latin American countries as well. When Arthur took office, it had only 52 ramshackle ships, down from almost seven hundred vessels during the war. Moreover, at a time when other nations were rapidly constructing steel navies, nearly every American ship was made of wood.

The men in the navy weren't much better than the ships. There were 1,817 officers in the US Navy, one for every five seamen. Many high-ranking officers were political appointees, and more than a few were incompetent drunkards. Some had been treating the ships under their command as private yachts. "Never was there such a hopeless, broken-down, tattered, forlorn apology for a navy," one British journal asserted.

From the time he took office, Arthur pushed for improvements in both the navy and the merchant marine. He recognized that European powers had designs on Latin America, and that the United States would need overseas markets for its booming productive capacity. "We must be ready to defend our harbors against aggression," he declared in his first Annual Message to Congress, "to protect, by the distribution of our ships of war over the highways of commerce, the varied interests of our foreign trade and the persons and property of our citizens abroad; to maintain everywhere the honor of our flag and the distinguished position which we may rightfully claim among the nations of the world."

In Secretary of the Navy William E. Chandler, President Arthur had just the right man to wring the required money out of a reluctant Congress.

Born in 1835, in Concord, New Hampshire, Chandler studied law at Harvard and served in the state legislature. In 1864, the navy department employed him to prosecute fraud in the Philadelphia Navy Yard. President Lincoln later appointed him to be the navy department's solicitor and judge advocate. During the Grant administration, Chandler was the principal lobbyist for John Roach, a prominent shipbuilder and the secretary of the Republican National Committee.

The morning after the 1876 election between Samuel Tilden and Rutherford B. Hayes, Chandler had arrived in New York to learn that his party had, it appeared, lost the White House. But then he ran into the managing editor of the *Times*, who told him that Tilden's margin of victory was razor thin, and that the final result would depend on the count in South Carolina, Florida, and Louisiana. On his own initiative, Chandler immediately wired Republicans in those states, instructing them to concede nothing. He soon set out for Florida to represent the Republican National Committee's interests, and played a leading role in turning the election in favor of Hayes and the Republicans.

When the navy secretary began pushing for more ships, Capitol Hill skeptics snickered at Chandler's connection to Roach the shipbuilder, but Arthur and Chandler were undaunted. Not long before Chandler's appointment, the House Committee on Naval Affairs had studied the issue and called for the appointment of a Naval Advisory Board. Chandler chose the members, and in December 1882 the panel recommended the construction of three steel cruisers and a dispatch boat. At Chandler's request, the resulting legislation included a provision barring the repair of any vessel if the expense exceeded 20 percent of its original cost. The clause guaranteed the retirement of many aging and obsolete ships—and enraged congressmen eager to hand work to their local navy yards. Nevertheless, Congress approved the bill and Arthur signed it into law in March 1883. "I think that I did my best work in destroying the old Navy, although I did build four new ships," Chandler later quipped.

The ships that were built were not large or powerful by European standards—some nations had ships that displaced 15,000 tons, while the largest of the new American ships displaced only 4,500. But Arthur and Chandler set the United States on course to become a world naval power. During the next four years, Congress authorized 30 additional vessels with an aggregate displacement of 100,000 tons.

By the time Arthur signed the navy bill, he was mentally and physically exhausted. "I have been so ill since the adjournment [of Congress] that I have hardly been able to dispose of the accumulation of business still before me," the President confided to his son in a letter dated March 11, 1883, a week after the 47th Congress completed its work and left town.

The 48th Congress would not convene until December 1883, giving Arthur the opportunity to take a real vacation. In April, he decided, he would travel to a newly popular destination for wealthy Americans: Florida. The Sunshine State had a salubrious climate, and it was a hunting and fishing paradise. President Arthur, a first-class angler, was eager to experience it.

On April 5, 1883, the presidential carriage halted outside the Baltimore and Potomac station. As usual, pedestrians gawked at Arthur's elegant equipage: his landau was painted a mellow green with red trim, and the harness was heavily mounted with plain silver. The horses were a perfectly matched pair of mahogany bays with black points, without a white spot anywhere. The animals, half-brothers, had been raised by the same man and were always driven together. The president climbed out looking healthier and more cheerful than he had in a long time. He would be traveling to Florida with a tight group of aides and personal friends: Chandler, who was fast becoming his most trusted adviser; Charles E. Miller, a close friend from New York; his private secretary, Fred Phillips; Aleck Powell, his trusted valet and doorkeeper; and the White House chef, "Monsieur Cuppinger," who sported an apron, a baker's cap, and a waxed moustache. Four reporters also were allowed to tag along.

As the other travelers boarded the fast mail train that would carry them south, the rotund French cook scurried around the platform searching for a hamper of provisions sent to the White House by mistake. He was still looking when a gong sounded and the conductor shouted, "All aboard!" As the train rolled out of the station, Arthur exchanged his high silk hat for a broad-brimmed, light-colored felt one. By the time the grass-grown streets of Alexandria, Virginia, came into view, he began to feel, finally, that he was out of harness.

But the next two days of train travel were hardly an idyllic escape. Between Petersburg, Virginia, and Weldon, North Carolina, a punctilious conductor, unaware that Arthur was aboard, ordered the commander in chief to hand over the fare. Arthur was reaching for his wallet when a porter prevailed on the conductor to stand down. Outside Wilmington, North Carolina, the train was stalled for more than an hour while workmen changed the tracks to a wider gauge. Unable to sleep, Arthur sat astride a camp stool on the rear platform of his car. He was wrapped in a thick coat, and wore the felt hat he had put on when his journey began. In the glare of an engine's headlight, he puffed a cigar as a damp breeze blew in from the Cape Fear River, laden with the aromas of turpentine and resin. A group of black men, who had come to the station with lanterns and torches to see the president, stood in a silent semicircle, watching him smoke.

During a short stop in tiny Folkston, Georgia, the president emerged from the train smirched with dust and soot from the wood-burning locomotive. Chandler's face was darkened with layers of Georgia dirt, and rivulets of perspiration traced bright lines of mud across the chef's broad face. "I have poot on tree shirt dees tay," Monsieur Cuppinger grumbled to reporters, one of whom took a stab at recreating the chef's French accent for his readers. "Ven I poot on vun, in fife minute it look like I sweep de shimney."

So far, only the people of Goldsboro, North Carolina, had come out en masse to greet the president. That changed in Jacksonville, Florida, where Arthur and his companions gladly left the rails to board the steamboat that would take them up the St. Johns River. Several military companies and city leaders wearing swallow-tail coats with posies in their buttonholes greeted Arthur and led him through cheering crowds to a carriage drawn by six gray horses. A cannon belched a salute and brass music blared. The cacophony startled the horses, but the driver deftly guided the prancing animals through the city to the wharf, where Arthur and his companions boarded the steamboat *Frederick De Bary*.

Arthur lit a cigar and stood on deck chatting with Chandler as the *De Bary* steamed upriver, leaving the twinkling lights of Jacksonville behind to explore the darkness ahead. Magnolia, Green Cove Spring, and other riverside towns burned bonfires and lit up the sky with fireworks as the president passed by. The party turned in early—though at six feet two inches tall, Arthur struggled to sleep in a berth that was only five feet eight inches long. Following the narrow windings of the river, the *De Bary* crept past cypress trees draped with gray moss and blue and white herons stalking in pools along shore. Water hens, curlews, and long-billed sandhill cranes flew overhead, uttering strange cries as they fluttered away.

At noon the next day, the *De Bary* reached breeze-ruffled Lake Monroe. The steamboat headed for the north shore and the town of Enterprise, where a crowd waited on the wharf. As the boat approached, soldiers fired a 21-gun salute and more people, many of them black, streamed out of a nearby hotel to greet the president. When the *De Bary* reached the pier, a young African American man named Jackson rushed on board and met Arthur in the forward saloon. Jackson, dressed patriotically in a red shirt, a white necktie, and a blue coat with a badge on it, had traveled 35 miles with a gift from the black community: a young bald eagle. Arthur expressed his appreciation, but said he was obliged to decline the bird, since he could not take it with him.

The next stop for the president and his party was Sanford, on the south shore of the lake. They visited an orange grove—Chandler threw off his coat and climbed a tree to pick three juicy samples—and spent the evening at a hotel called the Sanford House. At dusk, in a wide hall where guests gathered to chat and play cards, a black musician strummed a banjo accompanied by a half dozen singing and dancing comrades. "*Oh! Where is my beauty gone? Meet me by moonlight alone,*" the troupe sang. Arthur and his party enjoyed the entertainment until close to midnight, when the performers passed a hat for coins and bowed to the president before departing.

Arthur spent the next week in the interior of Florida, enjoying the strange scenery, the fragrance of the pinewoods and the magnolias, and the fishing on the Kissimmee River, where he caught bass, trout, and catfish from a dugout canoe, and where Fred Phillips shot an alligator. One evening, the presidential party visited Fort Gardiner, where they met Tom Tigertail, a Seminole chief who was accompanied by two of his wives, his baby, and his mother. The chief wore "a gay bandana handkerchief" wrapped around his head like a turban, with several feathers stuck in its folds. The flaps of his calico shirt floated in the breeze, and his legs were bare. He shook hands with the president and replied to his questions in a solemn monotone. The Seminole's stern features spread into a smile, however, when Arthur drew a cigar from his pocket and offered it to him. The chief grabbed the cigar, bit off the end, and snatched the cigar from Arthur's mouth to light his own.

By the end of the week, the president's cheeks were "burned to blisters" from the sun—a condition he treated by bathing them with hazel extract—and he had been mauled by mosquitoes. He was ready to return to the coast and begin the long trek home. Traveling by steamboat and wagon, the presidential party reached the port of St. Augustine on April 15. At dawn three days later, the *Tallapoosa* weighed anchor and steamed north with the presidential party on board. It was bound for Savannah, where Arthur and his companions would board a train for the trip home.

Within half an hour, the *Tallapoosa* was rolling in heavy seas. Waves dashed over the starboard bow, exploding in clouds of spray. Arthur had risen early, and was standing on the quarterdeck with Chandler, Phillips, and two ladies who had joined the party for the trip to Savannah. After 15 minutes, the navy secretary muttered an apology through ashy lips and fled to his stateroom, followed shortly by the two female passengers. Arthur endured the corkscrew motion of the ship a bit longer before he too grew pale and lurched to his room. The next morning, he was the only one who showed up to breakfast.

Cheered by the return to solid ground, the queasy passengers were in high spirits when they arrived in Savannah on April 19. Once again, African Americans were especially excited to greet a president from the party of Lincoln: nearly two hundred black residents clustered on the wharf when Arthur arrived. The president shook hands with all of them—some more than once. Despite the scorching sun, he toured Savannah in an open carriage and attended a rifle-shooting contest in a park on the outskirts of the city. The organizers of the event served him a sumptuous lunch, highlighted by deviled crab and the local delicacy, "Savannah shrimp salad." True to form, Arthur "partook of this agreeable dish very liberally." Afterward, he rode back into town to attend an official reception at the City Exchange building.

Arthur returned to the *Tallapoosa*, anchored just off the city docks, shortly before midnight. The water was calm, and the ship lay like a log on a sand bank. Chandler and Phillips thought the president was in an unusually cheerful mood—the vacation had done him good. He smoked a final cigar and went to bed.

At about 2 a.m., Arthur bolted awake. A sharp pain ripped into his abdomen, he was trembling, and his brow was beaded with clammy sweat. He tried to call out, but the only sound that escaped his lips was a raspy whisper. Finally he managed to cry weakly, "Aleck . . . Aleck!" The valet rushed into the president's stateroom and was shocked at what he saw: Arthur was as pale as his pillow. Powell immediately summoned the ship's physician, Dr. Black. "I saw instantly that he was grievously ill," the doctor recalled. "I knew that speedy and heroic treatment was necessary." He called for pails of hot water, dunked towels in them, and applied them to the president's body. He tried mustard poultices and sedatives, but after two hours he had not relieved Arthur's agony. Chandler, who had joined the others at Arthur's bedside, said he would telegraph Washington at 6 a.m. if his condition remained dire. The ship's surgeon frequently checked the president's pulse, and he grew increasingly alarmed as the time ticked by without any improvement. He feared the country was about to lose another president—and on his watch. After hours of fruitless treatment, Dr. Black administered an enema, which seemed to give Arthur some relief. The president dozed off, and the crisis passed. Chandler returned to his stateroom.

Arthur, still under the influence of the sedatives, drowsed throughout the morning. He refused nourishment until 11 a.m., when he requested ginger ale and swallowed it with relish. Late in the afternoon, he crawled out on the upper deck to get some fresh air, but he was pale and feeble, and soon returned to his bed.

Dr. Black told Chandler and Phillips that Arthur had suffered an acute attack of indigestion, caused by overeating, overexposure to the sun, and the "malarious" night air he had breathed on Florida's rivers. Had he been as seasick as the other passengers between St. Augustine and Savannah, the doctor speculated, he might have avoided the episode. Instead, he was "stirred up by the heavy seas." Chandler briefed reporters, and the president's illness was front-page news.

Arthur remained weak and dreaded the prospect of another dusty train trip, but he was eager to get back to Washington. Late on the afternoon of April 21, 1883, the presidential party rode to the Savannah train station to begin the journey home. While waiting for his private car to be attached to the fast mail train, an angry Arthur learned that his illness had become public knowledge, and that Phillips had failed to mention that hundreds of telegrams had poured in, anxiously inquiring about his condition. When the train left Savannah, Arthur sat moodily in the corner of his car, alone. For supper he drank a cupful of chicken broth, but turned away other food. Soon afterward he ordered his bed made up and retired, complaining of a pain in his side.

When the train reached Washington at 9:30 p.m. on April 22, Arthur's son, the attorney general, a handful of friends, and a mob of newspaper reporters were waiting on the platform. The president stepped out into a hail of questions. What had caused his attack in Savannah? Was he fully recovered? Was it likely to happen again? Arthur downplayed the significance of the incident, claiming he had never felt better in his life. Standing in the glare of the lights on the platform, he appeared to be fine. A friend made his way forward and shook the president's hand. "How are you feeling? I came down here because I feared from the reports that you might be seriously ill."

Arthur smiled. "I am feeling perfectly well—as well as ever, in fact. I have not been sick at all."

Buttonholed by a *Tribune* reporter, Chandler backtracked from what he had told the correspondents traveling with the presidential party. "The president's slight indisposition at Savannah I attribute to a long ride in the hot sun, but it lasted only a few hours," he said. "The statement telegraphed by some of the correspondents giving him 'malaria' and 'chills' are purely sensational. He had had neither at any time. On the other hand, he has been greatly benefited by his excursion, and has visibly gained in health and vigor."

The reporters "recorded many incidents which actually occurred," Chandler said, "but are all blessed with lively imaginations and great rhetorical gifts."

• ◆ •

After returning from Florida, President Arthur surprised civil service reformers—and Julia Sand—by proving that his conversion to the cause was sincere.

After he had signed the civil service bill in January 1883, Arthur took his time choosing people to serve on the new Civil Service Commission, causing some reformers to wonder whether he intended to make the appointments at all. But in February he had named three members who were qualified and dedicated to reform. Then, when the commission issued its rules in May 1883, reformers feared Arthur would gut them. Instead, he accepted them with only minor modifications. "The reports, republished from time to time since [the rules] were submitted to the effect that they were being badly cut up and changed were very wide of the mark," the *Times* acknowledged.

As the months went by, it became clear that the president was implementing the regulations with vigor. Addressing the Civil Service Reform League in August 1883, Conkling's bête noire, George William Curtis, complimented Arthur for "his desire to give the reform system fair play" and noted that his attitude was surprising, given his history. "The president's previous course, and his faith in the spoils system as essential to effective party organization, had excited great apprehension that he would use his vast patronage in a manner to confirm and aggravate the evils of that system," Curtis said. "But this apprehension has not been justified."

Then Curtis went further, praising the president for rejecting his New York cronies' demands for jobs and favors—and for confounding his critics.

The president's steady refusal to satisfy the faction of his party which de-mands that the public patronage shall be prostituted to a factional inter-est is most honorable to the magistrate; and, whatever exception may be taken to many acts of the administration in regard to appointments and removals, it will not be denied by fair men of every party that a president whose accession by means of a most tragical event was generally regarded as a serious misfortune, if not calamity, has not only allayed all apprehen-sion of a gross misuse of the patronage of the government, but by his pa-cific and temperate administration has gained the approval of the country.

For once, the Stalwarts agreed with Curtis. The president served his ma-chine buddies the finest food and wine when he hosted them at late-night dinners in the Executive Mansion. But he withheld the political plums they assumed would be theirs once their good friend "Chet" was in the White House. "We regard Arthur as our leader," said one, "and when he became president, knowing as he did the thankless tasks we have to do here, we ex-pected that we would be appreciated—not to say rewarded. We thought he would throw in our direction enough patronage to make our work less oner-ous. On the contrary, he has done less for us than Garfield, or even Hayes." For many members of Conkling's old machine, Arthur's refusal to help Tom Murphy, who had fallen on hard times, was especially egregious. "I tell you it is pretty hard to see Murphy, who made Arthur, going around without a cent in his pocket, and Arthur running the whole United States, and too timorous to reward Tom Murphy with any position whatever."

John Smyth, who had been one of Conkling's top lieutenants, grumbled that "no one who had ever arisen to great power in this country ever caused so many wrecks to be scattered on the shore."

By the early 1880s, Yellowstone National Park, which had been established in 1872, was under increasing pressure from mining companies, loggers, and hunters who wanted to overturn the federal prohibitions against re-source development. So far, the park's remote location had limited the num-ber of visitors, but the extension of the Northern Pacific Railroad to nearby Livingston, Montana, promised to open America's first national park to the world—and many were interested in profiting from the anticipated influx. In December 1882, General Philip H. Sheridan, whose military jurisdiction included the park, produced a much-publicized report in which he warned against leasing the park to private corporations, which were already deploying swarms of lobbyists on Capitol Hill.

Arthur was sympathetic to Sheridan's view. In his second Annual Message to Congress, he called for legislation to preserve forests in the public domain. "The condition of the forests of the country and the wasteful manner in which their destruction is taking place give cause for serious apprehension," he declared. "Their action in protecting the earth's surface, in modifying the extremes of climate, and in regulating and sustaining the flow of springs and streams is now well understood, and their importance in relation to the growth and prosperity of the country can not be safely disregarded."

Sheridan believed Arthur would be an even stronger ally if he could experience the wonders of the park for himself, and in January 1883 he and Senator George G. Vest, a Missouri Democrat, began planning a presidential tour. Some months later, Arthur formally accepted the offer. He had heard there was spectacular fishing in the West, and he was desperate to escape Washington. Furthermore, his health remained fragile, and he hoped that another vacation would reinvigorate him. Sheridan drew up plans designed to give him plenty of rest and relaxation.

Arthur departed Washington on the morning of July 30, 1883. Two days later, in Louisville, he participated in ceremonies opening the Southern Cotton Exposition and was cheered by boisterous crowds. "I have often heard, of course, of the hospitality of the Southern people, but it has never been my privilege before to see it so exemplified," Arthur told a reporter. "Did your impressions sustain Louisville's reputation for beautiful ladies?" the correspondent asked. "I had heard much of that, too, and am thoroughly converted on that score," the president replied. "I had chance to see two things on which Kentucky plumes herself—her horses and her beautiful women—and now I am a thorough believer in both of them."

Arthur's locomotive was decorated with American flags, and his portrait was mounted over the headlight, above a wreath of evergreens and an elaborate arrangement of flowers. Crossing into Indiana, the train curled under bluffs, past fields of rustling corn tassels and meadows filled with nodding flowers. During a stop in Lafayette, a policeman with a tin star on his lapel struggled to control a thousand people by wielding a wagon spoke as a club. Arthur, wearing a blue flannel suit and a Scotch silk cap, delighted the crowd with his prediction that Indiana would soon be one of the greatest states in the Union. After his speech, a young African American boy gave him a "ship of state" made of flowers and a plaque thanking him for his devotion to "justice to an oppressed people."

To welcome Arthur to Chicago, the Chicago *Daily News* published 15 columns of letters from distinguished Americans assessing the president's performance. "I can hardly imagine how he could have done better, in the very trying circumstances which surrounded his administration," the famous clergyman Henry Ward Beecher wrote. Mark Twain cautioned that he was only one man among 55 million Americans, but that in his view "it would be hard indeed to better President Arthur's administration." Chicago reporters thought Arthur had changed in appearance—mostly for the better—since he had been in town for the dramatic 1880 convention. His hair and muttonchops were streaked with gray, giving him a more distinguished look, and he now had "far less of the flabby—some might say beefy—appearance which then somewhat forcibly struck the average beholder."

Arthur was taken aback by the aggressiveness of the Chicago press—especially reporters' use of a new journalistic technique called "interviewing." When one reporter observed, "your administration is meeting with considerable popular favor," Arthur's ears pricked up, but he suspected a trap. "Yes? Well, I am glad to hear it," he replied suspiciously. The reporter tried to ask a follow-up question, but Arthur shut him down. "You really must excuse me. I make it a habit not to talk politics with you gentlemen of the press. . . . By the way, I hope you are not interviewing me—I believe that is the word—or intending to quote what I have been saying."

Arthur wanted to "have a good time and get away from official cares," and during his three weeks in Yellowstone, he did just that. He and his companions rose at 5 a.m., and by 6 they were in the saddle. They rode until the afternoon and then camped beside a stream so they could spend the afternoon hunting, fishing, and hiking. They crossed the Continental Divide three times, and at one point camped at a point nine thousand feet above sea level. One day toward the end of the trip, Arthur and Senator Vest caught 105 pounds of fish. The president said his sojourn in the park was "better than anything I ever tried before," and by the time it was over he felt "strong and rested."

On September 4, 1883, he returned to Chicago on his way back to Washington, looking fit and tanned from the days he had spent outdoors. The throngs of politicians and party officials in the Grand Pacific Hotel, where Arthur was staying, seemed to herald the beginning of the 1884 campaign. "Whether it was the intention of the managers or not the Arthur boom was pushed for all it was worth," the *Times* observed. The enthusiasm for Arthur contrasted sharply with the scene in the same hotel three years earlier, when Republicans could hardly hide their distaste for the man chosen to be Garfield's running mate. "The feeling expressed was that if Arthur was only an accident, he is a pretty fair one, and deserved to be rewarded for the trials which came to his lot out of the great calamity," one reporter wrote.

Arthur's handlers and local supporters thought a public reception would highlight the president's strong political standing and win him additional friends. The following night from 8 o'clock until 10, Arthur stood in the same Grand Pacific parlor where he had accepted the vice-presidential nomination in 1880 and "submitted to the pump-handle operation," affably greeting the nearly ten thousand people who wanted to meet him. When the parlor doors were shut and it was finally over, local leaders looked forward to a few hours of more intimate socializing with the president. But Arthur quickly donned an overcoat and escaped. "I know you will excuse me for not talking to you at any great length tonight, as I am somewhat exhausted after the reception," he said. "I thank you for the reception and for your sweet music. Leaving you my very best wishes, I bid you good night."

Arthur arrived in Washington on September 7, 1883. Publicly, he said he was in excellent health, and that the trip had done him good. Privately, he sent an urgent summons to his personal physician: his arms and legs were swollen, he told the doctor, and he was in excruciating pain.

CHAPTER TWENTY

"Between Two Stools"

A WEEK AFTER ARTHUR returned to Washington, he received another letter from Julia Sand, addressed to "My very bad friend (Who does not deserve that I should care where he goes, or what becomes of him!)." Reeling from her own infirmities, still pining over her magical meeting with the president, she succumbed to self-pity. "It seems a very long time since I saw you last summer. I feel about ten years older—I have had so much care & sorrow," she wrote. "I thought then that I had suffered all I could suffer— but I was mistaken. Now I believe we do not reach that point until we are dead. I came near reaching it, though—in the spring I was very, very ill. But somehow I pulled through & at present I am stronger than I have been for years. Yet I don't feel it—because so many sad things happen in my life & wear me out."

Sand was in Newport, Rhode Island, staying at the Ives Cottage on placid Brinley Street. She told the president she had seen his son at the Newport Casino, a popular entertainment spot where visitors couldn't gamble but could enjoy concerts, dancing, archery, billiards, bowling, and other diversions. She joked that young Alan "did not seem silly & dudefied at all—in spite of what you & some other men say about him," though he was "talking to the ladies in front of me for quite a while." Julia eavesdropped on their conversation, but she didn't hear Alan mention his father's travel plans. She couldn't help wondering: Would the president be coming to Newport?

Sometimes—does this strike you as very comical?—when I feel exceedingly gloomy, I have an idea I would like you to come & talk to me. It is absurd, I know—but I can't help it. I like the sound of your voice—even if you are such an awful old sinner!—and I would like you to tell me

about your trip out West. I enjoy hearing about places I have never visited
& interesting things I expect never to see. Will you come? Of course, if
you are an old bundle of worldliness & have no heart at all, you needn't.
But you know best whether you are that, or not. If you can remember a
time when you were very unhappy, & I tried to say things to comfort you,
& you did care for my sympathy, then do come. It is very hard for me to
take hold of life again—& I am very grateful to those who help me at all
to be cheerful.

It was the 23rd letter Julia Sand wrote to the president—and the last
one that scholars would discover in the special envelope Arthur used to preserve them. Either Julia stopped writing to the president or her later letters
have been lost to history.

• ◆ •

Even if she didn't put pen to paper, the president's "little dwarf" likely had
strong opinions about Arthur's response to a monumental US Supreme
Court decision in October 1883.

The Civil Rights Act of 1875 barred the owners of inns, restaurants, and
railroads and other public facilities from discriminating against blacks. But
in an 8–1 decision on October 15, 1883, the high court ruled that Congress
did not have the power to safeguard black citizens against the actions of
private individuals. The decision severely restricted the power of the federal
government to guarantee equal status under the law, laying the groundwork
for the Jim Crow laws that would oppress blacks for almost a century.

At the time the decision was enormously popular, even among Republicans who favored equal rights for black citizens. Many viewed it as logical
and unsurprising; the *Times,* the *Sun,* and the *Tribune* didn't even run the
story on the front page. "In the temper which the people have now reached
in dealing with questions that formerly had a sectional significance and that
pertain to the relations of the races in this country it seems as though nothing were necessary but a careful reading of the [14th] amendment to show
that it did not authorize such legislation as the Civil Rights act," the *Times*
editorialized. The 14th Amendment, it noted, prohibits "the making and
enforcing of laws by the States which shall abridge the privileges and immu-
nities of citizens." Even if equal accommodations in public transportation
and places of entertainment were among the protected privileges, the newspaper argued, Congress could only counteract *state laws* that violated them;
it could not control the actions of private individuals.

Even a progressive bastion like the *Nation* shrugged. The civil rights law "was really rather an admonition, or statement of moral obligation, than a legal command," it argued. "Probably nine-tenths of those who voted for it knew very well that whenever it came before the Supreme Court it would be torn to pieces."

According to the *Times*, most observers believed that the demise of the law "would not entail any hardship upon the colored people or deprive them of any privileges which they have enjoyed since the war."

Black leaders knew better. Frederick Douglass peered into the future when he spoke at a gathering of civil rights leaders in Washington's Lincoln Hall a week after the ruling. "The cause which has brought us here to-night is neither common nor trivial. Few events in our national history have surpassed it in magnitude, importance and significance. It has swept over the land like a moral cyclone, leaving moral desolation in its track," Douglass declared. The 1875 law "meant to protect the newly enfranchised citizen from injustice and wrong, not merely from a State, but from the individual members of a State. It meant to give him the protection to which his citizenship, his loyalty, his allegiance, and his services entitled him, and this meaning, and this purpose, and this intention, is now declared unconstitutional and void, by the Supreme Court of the United States."

As a young lawyer, Arthur had defended Elizabeth Jennings's right to be treated with dignity on a New York streetcar, and his victory in that case helped desegregate public transportation in the city. He knew the bigotry of private citizens could do great harm, whether or not it was state sanctioned. Given the tenor of the times, Arthur held enlightened views on race. The abolitionist's son pushed for federal money for African American schools, contributed privately to a black church, and personally awarded diplomas to black high school graduates. He invited the choir from historically black Fisk University to sing at the White House—and was moved to tears by its performance. He also appointed African Americans to important government positions, such as surveyor of the port of New Orleans. Aleck Powell, his black valet, was his friend and confidant.

Encouraged by Chandler, Arthur also forged a political alliance with Virginia's Readjuster Party. The Readjusters demanded relief of Virginia's Civil War debt, but they also united white and black Virginians with their calls for more school spending, honest elections, and the abolition of the poll tax, dueling, and the whipping post. By the end of 1881, the Readjusters had captured both houses of the Virginia legislature and elected a governor and two US senators. To be sure, Arthur and Chandler were motivated by their desire to break the Democrats' political stranglehold on the South, but they also believed the alliance with the Readjusters would help curb violence against blacks and advance the causes of "free speech, free education, free suffrage, and an honest counting of ballots," according to Chandler. The administration tried to forge coalitions between Republicans and independents in other parts of the South, too. Black leaders such as Douglass and leading African American newspapers heartily endorsed Arthur's Southern strategy.

Less than two months after the Supreme Court ruling, Arthur wove another thread into the pattern. In his third Annual Message, he forcefully called on Congress to approve a new civil rights law that would withstand judicial scrutiny. "Any legislation whereby Congress may lawfully supplement the guaranties which the Constitution affords for the equal enjoyment by all the citizens of the United States by every right, privilege and immunity of citizenship will receive my unhesitating approval," he proclaimed.

But that was it—the president didn't send Chandler or anybody else to Capitol Hill to lobby for such a law. Given popular prejudices and his shaky health, Arthur's chances of success would have been slim. But as Julia Sand might have told him, there would have been honor in trying.

•◆•

Americans had turned out in droves to cheer Arthur on his way to and from Yellowstone. The public reception he had received in Chicago—the site of the 1884 Republican National Convention—suggested that ordinary people were happy with their president. He had defied the dire predictions: Roscoe Conkling was in political exile, not in the White House. Arthur had not re-created the New York machine on a national scale. By reforming the civil service, he had restored Americans' trust in their government, laying the groundwork for the progressive presidents to come.

But as the 1884 election drew near, Arthur's claim on the GOP nomination was tenuous at best. One problem was that he had few allies on Capitol Hill. Many of the leading Republicans in Congress had been fervent supporters of the River and Harbor bill, and they were still seething over Arthur's veto. The president "knew perfectly well when he took up his pen to write the veto message that he was about to write his own sentence of doom," according to the *Sun*. "There is no doubt now that the veto did make personal enemies of men who otherwise would have been friendly to his nomination." Many GOP lawmakers also feared a repeat of the party's landslide defeat of 1882, for which they blamed Arthur.

Arthur wasn't the top choice of any of the party's rival factions. Stalwarts considered him to be a traitor, a zealous convert to "snivel service reform" who denied them jobs and favors. Former president Grant described the Arthur administration as "ad interim," and claimed it had "fewer positively hearty friends than any except Hayes possibly."

At the same time, Arthur's diligent implementation of civil service reform didn't convince suspicious reformers, who continued to sniff each presidential appointee for the taint of machine politics. The president "has sought to conciliate the bosses and reformers by turns, and has fallen between two stools," E. L. Godkin observed in the *Nation*.

Meanwhile, the Half-Breed faction of the party believed that James Blaine's turn had finally come. Rather than returning to Maine, the former secretary of state took up residence in a luxurious home in northwest Washington, where he often entertained. Blaine wasn't shy about telling Congress and the press what he thought of Arthur's performance—and frequently his reviews were critical. The former senator liked to plant stories in the *Tribune* denouncing Arthur, who declined to respond.

Publicly, Blaine and Arthur remained cordial, tipping their hats and smiling at each other at parties and receptions. Blaine and his wife Harriet invited the president to their home, and Arthur reciprocated. Privately, however, the couple sneered at the lightweight in the White House. "All his ambition seems to center in the social aspect of the situation," Harriet wrote to her daughter after she and her husband ran into Arthur on the streets of Washington. "Flowers and wine and food, and slow pacing with a lady on his arm, and a quotation from Thackeray or Dickens, or an old [joke] told with an uninterfered with particularity, for who would interrupt or refuse to laugh at a President's joke, make up his book of life, whose leaves are certainly not for the healing of the nation."

Another prominent member of the Garfield cabinet, former attorney general Wayne MacVeagh, didn't bother to disguise his disdain. Two weeks before the Republican convention, the *Times* published a scathing letter from MacVeagh on its front page. "Nobody has forgotten the pregnant fact that Guiteau was the original Arthur man; that he killed President Garfield expressly to make Mr. Arthur President, and that he did make him President by the act for nearly four years," it said.

"Now, in view of this awful tragedy and its results, it has always seemed to a good many people—outside of Wall-street, of course—that a proper sense of decency and of the fitness of things would have led President Arthur and his friends to see that his true course was to be satisfied with the one term thus secured to him, and not to challenge his countrymen to review his political career and to express their opinion of it."

With biting sarcasm, MacVeagh went through a litany of Arthur's sins. Among them: building the New York City machine; defying President Hayes by refusing to give up his Custom House job; using dirty tricks in Indiana in 1880 (and then boasting about them at Delmonico's); supporting Conkling and Platt in their efforts to win back their Senate seats; and inserting himself into the New York gubernatorial race in 1882. Only the last charge was untrue.

As MacVeagh had noted, Arthur did inspire enthusiasm among New York businessmen. On the same day his letter was published, the city's foremost merchants, bankers, and professional men rallied at the Cooper Union to give a boost to the president. A hundred of them would travel to Chicago to bolster his candidacy. Despite Arthur's disadvantages, political veterans said it was foolish to underestimate him. Surely, they said, the old machine pol had a few tricks up his sleeve. Former Conkling crony Stephen Dorsey boasted that Arthur would have the New York delegation all sewn up before the balloting began in Chicago. "One thing is certain, that there will be nothing left undone on the part of himself and friends to secure a solid delegation, and those who underrate his power and his active management will be left behind in the race."

Chandler, who would chair the New Hampshire delegation to the convention and marshal the Arthur forces in Chicago, began preparing a battle plan. He expected his mission to be difficult but not impossible—as long as the president was willing to wield the powers of his office to sway delegates.

•—◆—•

Shortly before the convention, Arthur asked Chandler to remain behind after a cabinet meeting in the White House. The men settled into their chairs, and then the president delivered an order so shocking Chandler thought he must have misunderstood it: Arthur did not want the navy secretary to go to Chicago.

Chandler was aghast. "Why, Mr. President," he protested, "if you don't let me go as a delegate to the convention you will not have any one there with practical leadership in national politics to direct the delegates who have been elected to support you. You know enough about politics to know what that would mean." Blaine would have "some very foxy politicians" in his corner, Chandler reminded Arthur, and so would the other leading candidates. Why wasn't Arthur willing to match them?

"I know," Arthur replied, "but I do not want to be nominated as the result of any political manipulation. I want a nomination that will reflect the desire of the party, or none at all. I don't believe it is dignified or proper for a cabinet officer to appear at a national convention and there work for the nomination of his chief." After an hour-long discussion, Chandler staggered out of the White House feeling "mentally sick."

Arthur didn't want to resort to the machine methods that had convinced so many of his countrymen that he was unfit for the presidency—that much was true. But he withheld from Chandler the main reason he was forfeiting his office: he was dying.

Nearly two years before, Arthur had been diagnosed with what was then known as "Bright's disease," a chronic inflammation of the blood vessels in his kidneys. At the time, the disease was almost always fatal. The Associated Press had reported the news, but the White House strongly denied the story, and Americans largely dismissed it as unfounded.

It is likely that Bright's disease caused the nausea, depression, and lethargy that plagued Arthur throughout his presidency. But he was determined to keep his failing health a secret, and he confided in just a handful of close friends and family members. The president also disclosed his illness to the ship's surgeon on the *Tallapoosa*, who blamed the disease for Arthur's nighttime attack. But at Arthur's request, the surgeon did not reveal what he knew.

Arthur subscribed to the Victorian belief that it was undignified and unmanly to suffer in public. "He could not bear to have his friends or the public know that the strong man whom they knew in health was slowly fading away, and even after the first reports of his serious illness had been published there were many who failed to realize its solemn import, so difficult was it to get any confirmation of the sad news," the *Times* later wrote.

Bowing out of the race would look weak. So Arthur carried on, though he would not take the steps necessary to secure the nomination.

A few days before the convention opened, he refused to trade the postmaster general's portfolio for 18 delegates. And when Edward Stokes, part owner of the Hoffman House, a popular Manhattan hotel, showed up in Chicago with $100,000 in cash for the Arthur campaign, the president telegraphed an order to reject it. For the duration of the convention, the businessmen backing Arthur scarcely had enough money to pay their hotel bills, even as "the delegates hung around their headquarters like so many cormorants, supposing they had millions of dollars."

The convention opened on June 3, 1884, in the same Interstate Exposition Building where Garfield and Arthur had been nominated four years before. The cavernous hall was draped in flags and bunting, and a brass band played as the delegates filed in. Swallows swooped in and out of the open windows, adding their chatter to the urgent clicking of the telegraphs.

On that first day, "a slight, almost boyish" New York state assemblyman delivered a memorable speech urging the delegates to choose a black man, John Lynch of Mississippi, as temporary chairman. The light-haired, gray-eyed speaker threw off his straw hat and "scrambled to his perch in the chair with juvenile activity." With his hand on his hip, 25-year-old Theodore Roosevelt Jr. reminded the delegates that nearly 25 years before, the party had nominated Abraham Lincoln, "who broke the fetters of the slave and rent them asunder forever." It would be fitting, Roosevelt said, "for us to choose to preside over this convention one of that race whose right to sit within these walls is due to the blood and the treasure so lavishly spent by the founders of the Republican Party." Roosevelt's speech hit the mark, and Lynch was elected chairman.

During the next two days, the delegates tussled over rules and procedures on the floor, while the jockeying and coalition building that was the real work of the convention went on behind closed doors. Arthur's supporters should have had a built-in advantage: many wavering delegates wanted government jobs for themselves or their relatives in exchange for their votes. But the president refused to use his patronage power to win the nomination. "This is no time to discuss such matters," was his reply to one Pennsylvania delegate who wanted a position for his son.

At 7:35 p.m. on June 5, the delegates reconvened to nominate presidential candidates. Every square foot of the hall was crammed with people. Many ladies with tickets arrived to find no seats and scarce standing room, forcing them to congregate in the side aisles, until a few gallant Pennsylvania delegates relinquished their seats. Thousands of fans flittered in the sultry air.

The secretary began the roll call of the states. Alabama, Arkansas, and California passed. Connecticut's delegation was the first to speak up, and it nominated Senator Joseph R. Hawley, a newspaper editor and former governor who had been a general during the Civil War. Illinois put forward Senator John Logan. When the roll call reached Maine, Blaine's home state, the hall erupted. For a full 10 minutes, Blaine's supporters shook their hats, handkerchiefs, and fans and stamped their feet, creating a roar like distant thunder. The pandemonium continued as Judge William H. West, the famous "Blind Orator" of Ohio, was led to the platform. "Through all the conflicts of its progress, from the baptism of blood on the plains of Kansas to the fall of the immortal Garfield, whenever humanity needed succor, or freedom needed protection, or country a champion, whenever blows fell thickest and fastest, there in the forefront of the battle, was seen to wave the white plume of James G. Blaine, our Henry of Navarre," West declared. West was alluding to Blaine's well-known nickname, "The Plumed Knight," which Civil War veteran Colonel Robert Ingersoll had bestowed upon him during the 1876 convention.

After Blaine's name was placed in nomination, somebody paid tribute to him by placing a garlanded helmet with a white plume on a flagpole and hoisting it into the air. The frenzied crowd ripped the decorative flags from the galleries and waved them in celebration. One man in the balcony accidentally dropped his flagpole, which tumbled onto the head of a delegate on the floor below. The delegate was knocked unconscious and was carried out of the hall as the cheering continued.

Finally the roll call reached New York. Without Chandler there to supervise, the Arthur camp had failed to designate a principal convention speaker until the proceedings were already under way. An elderly district attorney from Troy, Martin I. Townsend, ended up filling the role. He performed it poorly, and he later admitted that his speech was "extemporaneous from necessity." Townsend rambled on about the virtues of the Bible and argued that Arthur should not be "struck down and cast into oblivion." At least twice, people hissed loudly, and at one point conversations in the hall grew so loud the convention chairman had to bang his gavel to restore order.

The balloting began the next day. On the first ballot Arthur got 278 votes, second to Blaine's 334. When he received the tally by wire, the president frowned; he had expected a higher total. Even as he refused to work for the nomination, he desperately craved the approval of his party. His tally shrunk with each ballot—from 278 to 276, to 274, to 207—but Arthur "preserved an even temper and yielded to the inevitable with better grace than many persons had expected." Blaine clinched the nomination on the fourth ballot, with 541 votes. Arthur immediately sent a telegram to the nominee expressing his "earnest and cordial support." Then he ordered his carriage and disappeared into the streets of Washington.

Chandler believed that if Arthur had let him go to Chicago, things might have turned out differently. "I know now many of the inside details of that meeting and I can say to you that there was one moment during the preliminary work of the convention when, had I been there, I am certain I could have brought about an agreement among certain groups of delegates which would have led to the nomination of Arthur instead of Blaine," he told a reporter. "The golden moment passed with no one to take advantage of it, for, as I feared the day the president forbade my attending the convention, the skilled politicians opposing him were more than a match for the practically leaderless delegates who had been sent to Chicago to support him."

A month later, the Democrats convened in the Interstate Exposition Building to choose their candidate. They nominated New York governor Grover Cleveland, a symbol of clean government who, they hoped, could win the Empire State and the votes of reform-minded independents. The Democrats, losers of six straight presidential elections, were desperate to regain the White House.

On a beautiful summer afternoon shortly after Cleveland's nomination, Arthur went for a solitary stroll on Connecticut Avenue in Washington. Congress had adjourned and the president was about to leave the deserted capital for his own summer vacation. He spied a friend who had been at both parties' Chicago conventions, and invited the man to walk with him. Arthur, always interested in political gossip, was hungry for information about the Democratic nominee.

"Mr. Hewitt, I see, speaks of Mr. Cleveland as the man of destiny, yet I have lived long enough to learn that it is not until a man's career is ended that it is safe to say much about his destiny. But Governor Cleveland, from the little I know of him, has impressed me favorably," Arthur remarked.

His companion replied that perhaps the president didn't realize how many people regretted that it was Blaine, rather than Arthur, who would be taking on Cleveland that fall.

The president was silent for a few moments. "I think I do know of the regret you speak of," he said slowly. "I have met with it, and it has occurred to me many times lately to think how much truth there is in the saying of someone, that the consolations of failure are sweeter sometimes than the joy of success." He paused again before continuing. "There was nothing of surprise, nothing of personal disappointment to me in the action of the Republican Convention," he said. "I long ago determined to do what was at hand as well as I might, and let each day be complete for itself. Then I am prepared for whatever happens. Such a course may not bring many of the joys of anticipation, but it certainly entails none of the sorrows of disappointment."

Arthur was ready to retire from the arena. Despite his promise to support Blaine, he stayed out of the 1884 campaign.

CHAPTER TWENTY-ONE

"Fame Is a Bubble"

MANY STALWARTS FOLLOWED the president's lead. In New York, where they would have been most helpful, they made only half-hearted efforts on behalf of the national ticket. Conkling was especially uninterested in helping his old nemesis—in fact he did what he could to help Cleveland. When Republicans asked him to help the Blaine campaign, he snarled, "No thank you, I don't engage in criminal practice."

As it turned out, assistance from the White House might have made a difference: The popular election was one of the closest in the nation's history. With almost 10 million ballots cast, Cleveland triumphed by a mere 57,500 votes. Cleveland won 219 electoral votes to Blaine's 182, so the Democrat's victory in New York, which was worth 36 electoral votes, was decisive. The margin in the Empire State was just 1,047 votes out of 1.7 million.

Arthur's illness worsened in the months following the election. He could have remained secluded in the White House for the remainder of his presidency, but he did not want to reveal his weakness to the country, so he continued to attend the public receptions and banquets that were expected of him. At the same time, he began looking forward to his life after he left office—however long it might last. In January 1885, he announced that he planned to resume practicing law in New York. While in the White House he had spent most of his $50,000 annual salary on personal and official expenses, and there was no pension for a former chief executive. But he had valuable stock and real estate holdings and could command a healthy income as a lawyer. He wasn't worried about money.

Arthur hosted his last public reception on February 21, 1885, after participating in the dedication of the newly completed Washington Monument, which had taken 36 years to construct. Fireworks were still exploding over the monument at 9 p.m. when the president descended from his private quarters and nearly three thousand citizens began filing in. A company of the President's Guards from Philadelphia was first, showily attired in white doeskin breeches and high boots. As the crush increased and people poured into the Blue Room three and four at a time, the visitors were asked to introduce themselves to the president, rather than whisper their names to an attendant, in order to speed things along. Arthur was flanked by two of his sisters, one wearing a cream-white silk gown with a red velvet collar, the other dressed in black velvet, with a pink satin vest and petticoat. After two hours, it was over.

On March 4, 1885, President Arthur, President-Elect Cleveland, and other dignitaries filed onto a platform erected on the East Front of the Capitol. The day of Cleveland's inauguration was warm and sunny, with a gentle breeze that barely budged the lacy clouds brushing the blue sky. The current and soon-to-be presidents both wore black broadcloth suits. Cleveland was stouter than Arthur, and his head reached only to the taller man's eyes. Arthur's white whiskers and lined face made him look ten years older than he had during Garfield's inauguration, but his complexion was clear and his eyes sparkled. Squinting in the brightness, Arthur studied the scene in front of him—the vast crowd, numbering 50,000 or more; the fringes of humanity on nearby roofs; the schoolboys hanging like fruit from the trees. He smiled and bowed at familiar faces before sitting down.

Cleveland smoothed his thinning hair and delivered his inaugural address in a voice that penetrated far into the crowd. His pledges to promote national unity, the rights of Southern blacks, and civil service reform were well received. After he was sworn in, Cleveland and Arthur returned to the White House, where the ex-president hosted a luncheon for his successor.

At about 6 o'clock, the outgoing chief executive bade an emotional farewell to the White House staff. The Arthurs' possessions had already been packed into crates for the move back to Manhattan, and the stable looked deserted after Arthur's stud of 11 horses had been removed. Nellie scooped up her Skye terrier, "Taddie," and held him high above her head in the porte-cochere. "Say goodbye to everybody, Taddie!" she exclaimed. As the Arthurs climbed into the waiting carriage, somebody shouted, "Three cheers for the most patient, conservative, and best president the White House has ever seen!" As the last echoes died away, the driver whipped up his horses and the carriage rumbled off.

•—◆—•

After handing the nation's reins to Cleveland, Arthur moved back to New York. His health continued to deteriorate: in the spring of 1885, physicians made frequent visits to 123 Lexington Avenue. The ex-president received daily massage treatments, and he rarely made it to his law office. But as the burdens of the presidency slipped from his shoulders, he recovered some of his strength. In June, he went to Princeton for Alan's college graduation, and 10 days later he took his son to Canada to go salmon fishing in the Restigouche River, near Montreal.

On July 23, 1885, Ulysses S. Grant succumbed to throat cancer. By the time Grant died, most Americans had forgotten about the Whiskey Ring and the other stains on his presidential record. Instead, they venerated the Union's commanding general as the hero of Appomattox. Within hours of Grant's death, New York mayor William Russell Grace sent a telegram to his wife and children proposing a burial spot in one of the city's public parks, which the Grants accepted. The mayor subsequently sent a letter suggesting Riverside Park, on Manhattan's Upper West Side.

As soon as the Grants approved the selection, Grace ordered the parks department to begin constructing a temporary vault for the general's remains, just steps away from a giant oak tree that had been struck by lightning around the same time Grant had died. Meanwhile, Grace turned his attention to the construction of a permanent monument. On July 24, he sent a letter to dozens of New York's most distinguished citizens, inviting them to serve on a committee to oversee the project. Eighty-five of them, including ex-president Arthur, answered the call. The primary task facing the Grant Monument Committee was to raise enough money for a suitable memorial, a sum estimated to be $1 million. Arthur, the legendary fundraiser for the New York machine, was chosen as chairman.

On August 8, 1885, well over a million spectators lined Broadway and Fifth Avenue to watch Grant's catafalque, which was drawn by 24 black horses, each one attended by an African American groom, make its way from City Hall to Riverside Park. The columns of sixty thousand soldiers accompanying the fallen hero stretched three miles long, and it took five hours to pass by. Grant's death had united Americans in their grief—even former Confederates paid tribute to the savior of the Union. Union generals William Tecumseh Sherman and Philip Sheridan were pallbearers, but so were Confederate generals Simon Bolivar Buckner and Joseph Johnston. Union officers and Confederate officers rode together in the same carriages. Sharing the spirit of reconciliation, Arthur and the man who had fired him from the Custom House, former president Rutherford B. Hayes, also traveled together.

Grateful Americans were eager to help pay for a Grant monument, and as early as July 30, newspapers began publishing the names of contributors. On that date, the *Times* noted on its front page that the Western Union Telegraph Company had pitched in $5,000 (about $120,000 in today's dollars). A few days later, bankers Drexel, Morgan, and Company topped the list with a gift of $2,500. Many of the contributions published in the *Times* were more personal: "Two Yankee Women" gave 20 cents, "A German Who Gives Up His Beer" donated 15 cents, and "A Poor Soldier's Orphan" gave five cents.

Despite the fast start, controversy over the burial site put a damper on fundraising. Many Americans objected to the choice of New York City, even though the Grants had requested it. They thought Grant should be buried in Washington, DC, or at West Point. Some suggested that cagey New York businessmen had engineered the choice to raise the value of their real estate holdings near Riverside Park.

Two weeks after Grant was laid to rest in his temporary tomb, Arthur took a break from his fundraising duties to sample the late summer social scene in Newport. He took rooms at the Ocean House, a hotel on a bluff overlooking the ocean, and on August 22 he attended a reception hosted by Caroline Astor, wife of William Backhouse Astor Jr., at the couple's palatial estate on Bellevue Avenue. The New York caterer who prepared the food "had carte blanche for the occasion, and he prepared what was modestly termed a lunch," the *Times* noted. About 350 guests were on hand to enjoy the feast. Five days later, Arthur dined at the home of William Waldorf Astor, who hosted a dinner party in the ex-president's honor.

Arthur rarely appeared in public after returning to New York in the autumn of 1885. On November 3, however, newspapers noted his presence at a little cigar store at 402 Third Avenue. It was Election Day, and the store was a polling place. At 3:55 p.m., five minutes before the polls were scheduled to close, the ex-president swept into the store, his face ruddy from walking briskly.

"Straight Republican, Mr. Arthur?" asked a poll worker, handing the old machine politician a handful of ballots.

"Well," responded the ex-president, "I'll look at them and see."

The inspectors glanced nervously at the clock as Arthur examined the choices. At 3:58, Arthur called for another bunch of Republican ballots, compared them to the ones he already had, and then dropped the second batch into the boxes.

"He votes them all!" the inspector shouted. Arthur smiled, wished everybody a good afternoon, and walked home.

As 1885 drew to a close, Arthur appeared at a dinner to raise money for the pedestal for the new Statue of Liberty; was the honorary guest of the New York Farmers at their annual dinner at the Hotel Brunswick; and presided over the retirement ceremony of the chief justice of the New York Court of Common Pleas.

He would never appear in public again.

•—◆—•

In April 1886, the *Times* reported that Arthur was afflicted with Bright's disease, and that despite the efforts of his family and friends to conceal the seriousness of his illness, it was evident that he was "in so desperate a condition as to leave no room for doubt that his days are numbered and that within a very short time the country will be called upon to follow the remains of another of its Chief Magistrates to the grave." The ex-president was subsisting on "milk punches" because his stomach could not handle anything else, and he was experiencing heart trouble, a condition associated with Bright's disease. His son and two of his sisters had moved in to help care for him.

In June 1886, Arthur rallied slightly, and his family took him to stay at a cottage near the Pequot House in New London, Connecticut, hopeful that the sea air would do him good. Despite his dire condition, Arthur maintained a positive attitude for his visitors and correspondents. In August, he wrote a sunny letter to former postmaster general Walter Q. Gresham, assuring him that "my progress in recovering my health is slow and tedious, but I have strong hope that ere the summer is past I shall be as good as new." In New London the ex-president had time to reflect on his life and career, telling one visitor that he regretted much of what he had done in politics before reaching the White House. He advised Alan not to follow the same path, telling him the price of power was far too high.

When Arthur returned to Manhattan on October 1, 1886, he felt like he might be able to hold on for several years. But he lived the life of an invalid. He woke up late, had the newspapers read to him, received callers and tended to minor business matters with the help of his former private secretary, John Reed. But he passed most of his time in a reclining chair in his bedroom on the second floor, looking out on Lexington Avenue.

Increasingly ashamed of his machine past, Arthur decided to destroy the evidence. He asked Alan to summon an old Custom House crony named Jimmy Smith to do the job. While Alan watched, Smith filled three large garbage cans with bundles of Arthur's personal and official papers and lit them on fire. When the flames died down he added more fuel, filling and re-filling the barrels until nearly every record of Arthur's political career before the White House was reduced to ashes.

On Tuesday, November 16, 1886, Arthur awoke in good spirits. He entertained several visitors, signed some legal documents, and dictated a few letters to Reed. His personal physician, Dr. George Peters, came to examine him and departed at around 9 o'clock in the evening. Shortly after mid-night, the ex-president bade a cheerful good night to his nurse and went to bed. At 8 o'clock the next morning, the housemaid went into Arthur's bedroom to prepare it for the day. She had seen him move and thought he was awake, but when she inquired about his comfort she received no answer. Alarmed by Arthur's silence and the strange look on his face, she summoned the rest of the household and the doctors. When Peters and his assistant arrived, they found that a blood vessel had ruptured in the left side of Arthur's brain, leaving him partially paralyzed and unable to speak. He was conscious, however, and able to recognize the people around him. Peters took his hand. "Chester, if you know me, press my hand." He felt a feeble pressure. Arthur was able to swallow liquids and stick out his tongue, but that was all.

That afternoon, the 57-year-old patient lost consciousness. His breath-ing was labored, and sometimes it paused, prompting those around his bed-side to fear the end had come. As the night dragged on, Arthur's children retired to their rooms while his sisters and his nephew stood vigil with Dr. William Valentine, Dr. Peters's assistant. The gaslights were turned low, and the bedcoverings were drawn up to Arthur's neck. One of his arms lay across this chest, the other at his side. Valentine held the patient's hand and fanned him periodically. As the morning approached, Arthur's breath became shorter. At around 5 o'clock, Valentine bent low over the former president to listen for his breathing, since his chest did not appear to be moving. Alan and Nellie were summoned, and when they arrived Valentine shook his head sadly and said it was all over. Nellie broke down in sobs, and Arthur's sisters led her away.

When dawn broke, the 21st president of the United States was lying alone in the room where his wife had died nine years before. He had a sweet smile on his lips, as if in pleasant dreams. "I believe that he knew he was dying, and I think he was glad the time had come," Peters said.

On Monday, the day of the funeral, the shutters at 123 Lexington Av-enue were closed and crape hung from the door. Arthur's body had been placed in a cloth-covered oak coffin, and once members of his family said their farewells, the lid was closed and covered with a wreath of roses, a bunch of palm leaves, and a pillow of violets. At 8 a.m., President Cleveland and his cabinet arrived to pay their respects to the bereaved family, and a half hour later the hearse, drawn by two black horses, pulled up in front of the brownstone. The police kept the block between 28th and 29th Streets clear, but the other sidewalks and stoops were filled with people looking on in respectful silence.

Thirty policemen preceded the hearse as it made its way to the Church of the Heavenly Rest, on Fifth Avenue just north of 45th Street. Citizens lined the sidewalks along the route, and they removed their hats as the hearse passed. A thousand policemen, wearing white gloves and batons in their belts, controlled the throngs that had gathered near the church—an "infinitesimal" crowd, it was noted, compared to the one that had come out for Grant's funeral in July of 1885. Six companies of US artillery, with rifles but without cannon, 150 marines, and one hundred sailors stood at attention on the west side of the avenue in front of the church. The porch and pillars of the church entrance were draped with crape. A line of soldiers stood on one side, a line of sailors on the other.

When the hearse arrived at 8:55, most of the pews were already filled. The invitation-only crowd included President Cleveland, members of the cabinet, Supreme Court justices, US senators, US representatives, and top state and city officials. Hayes and Blaine were there, as was former senator Conkling, his famous Hyperion curl turned snow white. Arthur's coffin was placed lengthwise in the aisle on a low catafalque. Soft light poured in from the large stained-glass windows. The service was simple and brief, as Arthur had requested. An hour later, the funeral train was on its way to Albany, with the ex-president's coffin inside Cornelius Vanderbilt's private railcar.

It took a little more than three hours for the train to reach Albany's Rural Cemetery, which spreads across three ridges three miles north of the capital. The Arthur family plot is on the most westerly one, facing the setting sun. There the former president was laid to rest close to his parents, his beloved wife, the toddler son he buried during the Civil War, and his mother-in-law. Nearby, a small granite cenotaph memorialized Arthur's father-in-law, William Herndon, the heroic captain who had gone down with the steamer *Central America* in 1857.

In the days following Arthur's death, newspapers were filled with praise for the ex-president. "The conspicuous public office which Chester A. Arthur attained was due rather to accident than to any previous achievement in statesmanship, and yet he met its requirements in a manner that gives him an honorable place in the roll of American Presidents," the *Times* observed, before referring delicately to the fears Americans had when he took office. "His memory will have the benefit of a record as President which raised him steadily in the esteem and respect of the Nation and left him a distinction which at the age of 50 he had no ground for expecting and which no one could have predicted for him."

The *Sun*, a Democratic paper, went even further. "It is not too much to say that he was one of the most successful and meritorious in our whole list of Presidents."

But Arthur had no illusions about where he was likely to stand in the annals of American history. The week after the funeral, the *Sun* published a New York state senator's recollection of a conversation he had had with President Arthur regarding the senator's lack of interest in pursuing a seat in Congress. The senator told Arthur that he had little political ambition, "and did not think the honors were worth the struggle, even if successful."

The president sat up straight in his chair. "So you would not wish, then, to be a member of Congress?"

"No, sir; nor even president of the United States."

Arthur guffawed, incredulous. The senator hastened to add that he did not mean to show disrespect to Arthur or to the office he held. He knew, he said, that whether Arthur's administration was successful or not, "his name would be nailed to the record, and he would become a historic man." Nevertheless, the senator said, he recognized that "the highest political fame was but a mere bubble, no matter how iridescent its hues," and "when it broke it would be but a spot of suds upon the floor."

A cloud of sadness passed over Arthur's face. He rose from his chair, displaying his "magnificent physique," and straightened his arms at his sides, his hands clenched into fists.

"I feel that I am as strong as any man alive, and yet, yesterday, when the duties of the day were over, I held here a levee, standing to satisfy the curiosity of a crowd who wished simply to look upon the Chief Magistrate of the republic, shaking each man and woman of the 500 that came by the hand until all the electricity was taken out of me, and I went to bed like a crushed rag.

"Very true," Arthur mused. "Fame is a bubble, and broken is but suds."

Epilogue

THE STORM OF the century sneaked into the city on a Sunday, disguised as steady rain. On Monday, March 12, 1888, New Yorkers woke to find their metropolis clamped in the jaws of a blizzard. A howling wind corkscrewed through the streets, toppling signs, horse cars, and telegraph wires, and piling sticky snow into huge drifts. The city looked like a battlefield, with only a few scattered wagons and feeble pedestrians rambling through the wreckage. Travel was treacherous—50 trainloads of passengers were stuck on the main lines. One elevated train, on its way from Harlem to Wall Street with a contingent of stockbrokers, had to be abandoned at 23rd Street, having taken nearly four hours to make it that far. The marooned passengers sheltered in nearby restaurants and hotels, where the bars and billiard rooms were packed for the rest of the day. Of the 500 brokers who usually toiled on the floor of the New York Stock Exchange, only 21 made it in.

Roscoe Conkling, now an attorney in private practice, was due in court that morning to defend the will of the widow of A. T. Stewart, the department store magnate. Undaunted by the weather, he managed to travel from his lodgings at the Hoffman House, on Broadway between 24th and 25th Streets, to the courthouse downtown, only to receive word that the judge was snowbound and had postponed the hearing. Conkling went to his office on the corner of Broadway and Wall Street to work for a few hours.

Late in the afternoon, with the blizzard still raging, the lawyer decided he'd better head back to the Hoffman House, roughly two and a half miles away. The few horse car drivers who were operating in the snow were demanding $50 for a ride uptown—more than $1,200 in today's dollars. Indignant, Conkling set out on foot. "It was dark, and it was useless to try to pick out a path, so I went magnificently along, shouldering through drifts, and headed for the north," he recalled. By the time he reached Union Square, at 14th Street, Conkling was exhausted. Somewhere in the middle of the park, he got stuck in a drift up to his arms. Blinded by the windblown snow, it occurred to him for the first time that the blizzards described by Russian novelists were not pure fiction. For a few mournful moments, the indefatigable ex-senator "came as near giving right up and sinking down there to die as a man can and not do it." Finally, on the verge of being buried alive, Conkling summoned the strength to go on.

Three hours after leaving his office, Conkling stumbled into the New York Club on 25th Street. He was caked in snow and ice, but he was safe. Hearing Conkling recount his adventure, the men at the club had a hard time believing he had come all the way from Wall Street.

At first, the only consequence of Conkling's harrowing experience was a slight cold. He ignored his doctor's recommendation to rest, and carried on with his work. But his condition worsened, and two weeks after the blizzard, he couldn't get out of bed. About a week later, he slipped into a coma from which he never woke. He died on April 18, 1888, at the age of 59. An editorial in the *Times* predicted that "the name of Roscoe Conkling is one that will live in this State. No more striking personality ever appeared in the arena of New-York politics."

It concluded charitably: "Beneath a cold, proud and pompous exterior Mr. Conkling carried a warm heart."

•—◆—•

Eleven years later, many of the surviving members of Conkling's Republican machine gathered in the northeast corner of Madison Square to honor Chester Arthur, the man who had kept the machine running. A group of Arthur's friends had raised $25,000 to erect a statue of the late president, and on June 13, 1899, several hundred people waited in the afternoon sun for the unveiling of the bronze figure, which was concealed by an American flag. The featured speaker was Elihu Root, Arthur's personal lawyer, whom the president had tapped to be US attorney for the Southern District of New York. (Root would go on to serve as secretary of war in the McKinley and Roosevelt administrations, and was later elected to the US Senate.)

Root began by recalling the summer of 1881—President Garfield lingering on his deathbed, the strife within the Republican Party, the horror and rage many Americans felt when an assassin's bullet put one of the leading Stalwarts on the threshold of the presidency. "Dark suspicions and angry threatenings filled the public mind, and for the moment there was doubt—grave doubt—and imminent peril that the orderly succession of power under the Constitution might not take its peaceful course," Root said.

> Surely no more lonely and pathetic figure was ever seen assuming the powers of Government. [Arthur] had no people behind him, for Garfield, not he, was the people's choice; he had no party behind him, for the dominant faction of his party hated his name, were enraged by his advancement, and distrusted his motives. He had not even his own faction behind him, for he already knew that the just discharge of his duties would not accord with the ardent desires of their partisanship and that disappointment and estrangement lay before him there. . . . He was alone. He was bowed down by the weight of fearful responsibility and crushed to the earth by the feeling, exaggerated but not unfounded, that he took up his heavy burden surrounded by dislike, suspicion, distrust, and condemnation as an enemy of the martyred Garfield and the beneficiary of his murder. Deep and settled melancholy possessed him; almost despair overwhelmed him. He went to power walking through the valley of the shadow of death, and ascended the steps of a throne as one who is accused goes to his trial.

But in Chester Arthur, Root continued, "our ever fortunate Republic had again found the man for the hour." Arthur earned the people's trust by respecting the memory and goals of his fallen predecessor, Root said, and "the dignified courtesy of his manners and the considerate sincerity of his speech conciliated the friendship even of his enemies." Arthur recognized that the moment Garfield died, Arthur was "no longer a leader of a faction, but the president of the whole people, conscious of all his obligations and determined to execute the people's will."

Root finished speaking at 3:30 p.m., and then Arthur's sister, Mary Arthur McElroy, who had served her widowed brother as First Lady, pulled a cord to reveal the statue. The nine-foot figure portrayed Arthur having just risen from a chair, standing perfectly and confidently straight. The spectators cheered.

As the crowd dispersed, those heading downtown likely noticed another statue, slightly smaller, that stood in the southeast corner of Madison Square: a bronze figure of Roscoe Conkling. The boss glared across the square, seemingly still perturbed at the unexpected president who quit the machine to serve his country.

•◆•

When President Arthur's son Alan died in 1937, his son—Chester Arthur III—inherited 1,800 documents by and about his grandfather. For almost four decades, the papers had been locked away in a Colorado Springs bank vault, hidden from historians. When the president's grandson read them, he was most intrigued by the 23 letters from Julia Sand.

Eager to learn more about his grandfather's mysterious correspondent, Arthur placed an advertisement in the *New York Herald Tribune* on February 10, 1938, seeking information from Sand's surviving relatives, if there were any. The *Herald Tribune* and other papers turned the query into a story, and Arthur soon heard from one of Sand's nephews. Paul B. Rossire, a retired businessman living in Miami Beach, told Arthur about his aunt and the political discussions that roiled mealtimes at 46 East 74th Street. "Every one, especially Aunt Julia, was interested in politics," he told Arthur. "It was all civil service. The Tariff—do you ever hear anything about that now? I was brought up on it."

Rossire vividly recalled the magical evening in August 1882 when the president of the United States paid a surprise visit to his Aunt Julia. "A wonderful short rig drove up with two men on the box in claret livery," he remembered. The members of the Sand household were astonished when the president was announced "but managed nevertheless to remain in the room during the entire visit of the president with his young lady adviser."

Following the death of their mother, Julia and her two sisters moved to a small apartment in Brooklyn. "A talented woman, something of a blue-stocking," according to her nephew, Julia wrote occasionally for magazines but gradually withdrew from the world. She died in 1933 at age 83, having never disclosed that as a young woman, she had been the conscience of a president.

Acknowledgments

RESEARCHING AND WRITING this book took nearly four years, and you wouldn't be holding it in your hands if I hadn't received a lot of help and support along the way.

My agent, Victoria Skurnick, helped me keep my chin up when I began to doubt that I'd sell this book (or any other). I printed out her encouraging emails and carried them around with me for months. I feel lucky and grateful to have her in my corner.

I also owe a debt of gratitude to Robert Pigeon at Da Capo Press, a true history lover and a talented editor who believed in the book and improved it immensely. His enthusiasm for the manuscript gave me a much-needed boost when all the late nights began taking a toll.

I want to thank the librarians at Schaffer Library at Union College, the Manuscripts Division of the Library of Congress, and the Manuscripts and Archives Division at the New York Public Library, who helped me scour their holdings for material related to Chester Arthur. I owe special thanks to Michelle A. Krowl of the Library of Congress, who showed me the original Julia Sand letters, and was an enthusiastic fellow guest on a *Washington Post* presidential podcast. I thank Lillian Cunningham and David Fahrenthold of the *Post* for inviting me to participate in the podcast, and for being such interested and well-informed hosts.

I also should express my gratitude to Thomas C. Reeves, whose seminal biography, *Gentleman Boss*, remains the gold standard in Arthur scholarship. *Gentleman Boss* provided an invaluable roadmap for me as I embarked on my own telling of Arthur's story. And by donating his own papers to the Library of Congress, Reeves unselfishly provided a tremendous resource to other historians.

Though they are long gone, I feel compelled to tip my hat to the "ink-stained wretches" of the late nineteenth century, especially reporters from the *New York Times*, the *New York Sun*, the *New York Tribune*, and the *New*

York Herald. Their wonderfully vivid descriptions of people, places, and events painted pictures for their readers and made it possible for a twenty-first-century reader to immerse himself in a bygone era.

Closer to home, I want to acknowledge my mother, Phyllis Greenberger, who urged me to dream big, and taught a houseful of boys to respect and appreciate the power of women. I want to thank my father, Robert Greenberger, who had the courage to fulfill his journalism dream and inspired me to pursue mine. He showed me that you should love what you do, that words are precious, and that there really is a blind spot.

My daughter Sydney and my son Eli embraced this project with love and good humor, and served as constant reminders of what is most important in my life. I am thankful for them every day.

Most important, I want to thank my wife, Michele. She is a skilled writer and editor, a steadfast partner, and the love of my life. She makes this, and all things, possible.

Notes

Prologue

1   The *St. John* sliced through the last wisps: "The Vice-President's Movements," *New York Tribune,* July 3, 1881.

1   an advertisement for Drake's Plantation Bitters: *Harper's Weekly* cartoon published October 28, 1865, accessed at http://www.harpweek.com/09Cartoon /BrowseByDateCartoon.asp?Month=October&Date=28.

1   On the shore: McCabe, *New York by Sunlight and Gaslight,* 88–89.

1   The engine thrumming in the belly: Ibid., 362; and Ewen, *Steamboats on the Hudson River,* 19.

2   The boss of New York's vaunted Republican machine: "The Lordly Roscoe," *New York Commercial Gazette,* June 18, 1883, quoted in Reeves, *Gentleman Boss: The Life of Chester Alan Arthur,* 42.

2   His loyal lieutenant was an inch shorter: This description of Arthur's appearance comes from "President Arthur—Life in the White House," *New York Tribune,* April 16, 1882; Lang (ed.), *The Autobiography of Thomas Collier Platt,* 182; and Silas Burt's unpublished manuscript about Chester Arthur (hereafter cited as *Chester Arthur Biography*), which is included in the Silas W. Burt Papers at the New York Public Library.

2   extraordinary powers of digestion: Burt, *Chester Arthur Biography,* 17.

3   "We have to deal with a widespread evil": Quoted in Hoogenboom, *Outlawing the Spoils: A History of the Civil Service Reform Movement 1865–1883,* 1.

3   Near the Canal Street pier: McCabe, *New York by Sunlight and Gaslight,* 366.

3   the *St. John* finally came within hailing distance: "Vice President Arthur," *New York Sun,* July 3, 1881; "The Vice-President's Movements," *New York Tribune,* July 3, 1881.

3   At first they didn't believe him: Ibid.

Chapter One: Elder Arthur

5   "Open the way!": Morrison, "Gentlemen of Proper Understanding: A Closer Look at Utica's Anti-Abolitionist Mob," *New York History,* vol. 62, no. 1 (January 1981), 61–82.

5   The steeple of the Second Presbyterian Church: Seward, "The Bleecker Street Church, Utica," *Transactions of the Oneida Historical Society at Utica 1887–1889*, vol. 4, 145.

5   "wicked or deluded men": Sevitch, "Well-Planned Riot," 255.

6   "The disgrace of having an abolition convention": Sevitch, "The Well-Planned Riot of October 21, 1835: Utica's Answer to Abolitionism," *New York History*, vol. 50, no. 3 (April 1969), 256.

6   The shutters softened the sunlight: Seward, "Bleecker Street Church," 145.

6   "If you are driven from this sacred temple dedicated to God": Sevitch, "Well-Planned Riot," 255–259.

7   "Sects and creeds, doctrines and disquisitions": Dewey, *Letters of an English Traveller to His Friend in England on the "Revivals of Religion" in America*, 2.

7   It was a revival meeting in Burlington: Howe, *Chester A. Arthur: A Quarter-Century of Machine Politics*, 4; Reeves, "The Diaries of Malvina Arthur: Windows into the Past of Our 21st President," *Vermont History*, vol. 38, no. 3 (Summer 1970), 79.

8   Women and girls sat on planks and blocks of wood: Coffin, *The Life of James A. Garfield with a Sketch of the Life of Chester A. Arthur*, 365.

8   "became so weary and excited": Quoted in Hinman, *How a British Subject Became President of the United States*, 52.

8   At one Baptist convention: Howe, *Chester A. Arthur*, 6.

8   "Instead of my attending school": Quoted in Hinman, *How a British Subject Became President of the United States*, 51–52.

9   Unable to contain his happiness: Howe, *Chester A. Arthur*, 5.

9   "who formed his opinions without much reference to the views of others": Quoted in Reeves, *Gentleman Boss*, 6.

9   When the church doors banged open: Ibid., 258–261; and "Defensor" (William Thomas), *The Enemies of the Constitution Discovered, or, An Inquiry into the Origin and Tendency of Popular Violence*, 82–92.

11   Even before Elder Arthur arrived: Howe, *Chester A. Arthur*, 7.

11   "Disgraceful punishments are not inflicted": *Union College Catalogue*, Union College.

12   the three hundred students were required to attend morning prayers: Somers (ed.), *Encyclopedia of Union College History*, 148.

12   Each day started at 6:30 a.m.: Ibid., 134.

12   The unpopular bells were a frequent target of student mischief: Ibid., 95.

12   He once threw the West College bell into the Erie Canal: Bronner, "Arthur, His College Years," in *Chester Alan Arthur Class of 1848*, 9.

12   "a perpetual contest of our wits against his": Somers, *Encyclopedia of Union College History*, 426.

13   Slender and sociable, with fashionably long hair: Burt, *Chester Arthur Biography*, 4; Howe, *Chester A. Arthur*, 9; Bronner, "Arthur, His College Years," 8.

13   Arthur's graduation ceremony: Bronner, "Arthur, His College Years," 10.

13   "sitting up like owls till two or three in the morning": Chester Arthur to Campbell Allen, December 6, 1853, Chester Alan Arthur Papers, Library of Congress.

13 On his first morning in class: Reeves, *Gentleman Boss*, 11–12; Howe, *Chester A. Arthur*, 11.

14 Malvina described a typical night's entertainment: Diary of Malvina Arthur, January 19, 1853, Arthur Family Papers, Library of Congress.

14 "Had a miserable time": Ibid., February 29, 1853.

15 "I do wonder that I can sit unmoved": Ibid., October 23, 1853.

Chapter Two: "This Is the Place"

17 "I feel often sad and lonely": Chester Arthur to Campbell Allen, December 11, 1853, Chester Alan Arthur Papers, Library of Congress.

17 "How innumerable are the thoughts": Chester Arthur to Campbell Allen, January 1, 1854, Chester Alan Arthur Papers, Library of Congress.

17 they also were filled with apologies: Chester Arthur to Campbell Allen, February 15, 1854, Chester Alan Arthur Papers, Library of Congress.

18 "more like the palaces of kings": Quoted in Still, *Mirror for Gotham: New York as Seen by Contemporaries from Dutch Days to the Present*, 125–126.

18 "the sound of Niagara . . . but sharper and harsher": Quoted in Spann, *The New Metropolis: New York City 1840–1857*, 95.

18 Gentlemen gallantly jumped out: Still, *Mirror for Gotham*, 143.

18 To reach the safety of the sidewalk: Ibid., 154.

18 cashmere shawls could be had: Spann, *New Metropolis*, 223.

18 The frescoed floor and ceilings: Ibid., 97–98.

18 warm air was blown in from below: Ibid., 97–98.

18 In the hotel's mirrored dining room: Still, *Mirror for Gotham*, 139.

18 "There are southerners sighing for their sunny homes": Quoted in ibid., 155–156.

19 Taylor's had a marble floor: Norton, *Norton's Hand Book of New York City*, 8.

19 "redolent with the perfume of orange blossoms": Quoted in Still, *Mirror for Gotham*, 139.

19 large reservoirs that shined like polished silver: Ibid., 157.

19 "'Tis here that mothers suffer young daughters": Robinson, *Hot Corn: Life Scenes in New York Illustrated*, 221.

19 "they are frequently visited by gentlemen": Quoted in Spann, *New Metropolis*, 99.

19 "at once determined to secure his services": Barnum, *Struggles and Triumphs, or Forty Years' Recollections of P. T. Barnum*, 163.

19 the businessmen who swaggered down Broadway: Spann, *New Metropolis*, 96.

20 "the most magnificent street on this continent": Quoted in Still, *Mirror for Gotham*, 126–127.

20 "gorgeously fitted up with satin and velvet draperies": Quoted in ibid., 142–143.

20 "in a state of constant fluctuation": Quoted in ibid., 133.

20 Men such as John Jacob Astor: Spann, *New Metropolis*, 205–206.

20 old hats without crowns: Still, *Mirror for Gotham*, 148.

20 "Hot corn! Here's your nice hot corn": Robinson, *Hot Corn*, 14.

21   "No one can walk the length of Broadway": Quoted in Spann, *New Metropolis*, 262–263.

21   "Debauchery has made the very houses prematurely old," Dickens, *American Notes*, 667–668.

21   "atmospheric poison": Quoted in Spann, *New Metropolis*, 134.

21   Poor sanitation contributed: Ibid., 135.

22   A young schoolteacher who refused to tolerate: Sterling (ed.), *Speak Out in Thunder Tones: Letters and Other Writings by Black Northerners 1787–1865*, 141–142.

24   "Railroads, steamboats, omnibuses, and ferry boats": "City Items," *New York Tribune*, February 23, 1855.

24   "I have been quite well": Chester Arthur to (sister) Annie Arthur, March 11, 1855, Chester Alan Arthur Papers, Library of Congress.

25   "I have not been to a place of amusement three times during the winter": Chester Arthur to (mother) Malvina Arthur, April 3, 1855, Chester Alan Arthur Papers, Library of Congress.

25   a wispy beard and stylishly long hair: Reeves, *Gentleman Boss*, 14.

25   "I am yet heart-whole and bid fair," Chester Arthur to Annie Arthur, March 11, 1855, Chester Alan Arthur Papers, Library of Congress.

25   They wore the finest and costliest embroidered muslin: Still, *Mirror for Gotham*, 142–143.

25   "Surely Solomon in all his glory": Quoted in ibid., 134.

25   Ellen Herndon's dark brown hair: Burt, *Chester Arthur Biography*, 13–14; Reeves, *Gentleman Boss*, 20.

26   "one of the best specimens of the Southern woman": "Gath," *Cincinnati Enquirer*, September 2, 1883.

26   "soft moonlight nights of June": Chester Arthur to Ellen Herndon, August 30, 1857, Chester Alan Arthur Papers, Library of Congress.

26   "I know you are thinking of me now": Chester Arthur to Ellen Herndon, August 30, 1857, Chester Alan Arthur Papers, Library of Congress.

Chapter Three: Bleeding Kansas

27   Heavy snow was so rare: Walter, "History of Kanzas," 16–17.

28   Marching under a South Carolina flag: Reynolds, *John Brown, Abolitionist: The Man Who Killed Slavery, Sparked the Civil War, and Seeded Civil Rights*, 156.

28   "I determined to make the fanatics bow before me": Quoted in ibid., 156–157.

28   They were armed with revolvers: Carton, *Patriotic Treason: John Brown and the Soul of America*, 168.

29   Brown and his followers didn't find anybody: Cutler, *History of the State of Kansas* (Franklin County, Part 3).

29   "In traveling through slave States": Walter, "History of Kanzas," 16.

30   "It is a great waste of time to travel on the river": Chester Arthur to Ellen Herndon, August 30, 1857, Chester Alan Arthur Papers, Library of Congress.

30   In a region where some hotels posted signs: Diary of Cyrus K. Holliday, November–December 1854, Kansas Memory, Kansas Historical Society.

30   its light and airy bedrooms: Moore, *Early History of Leavenworth City and County*, 165.

31   "including earnest young lawyers from the South": "Arthur's Visit to Kansas," *New York Times*, August 1, 1883.

31   The solid-oak coach: Pratt, "Ten Cents a Mile and a Fence Rail," *Annals of Iowa*, vol. 39, no. 8 (Spring 1969), 598–600.

31   Arthur spoke to Lane and Walker: "Arthur's Visit to Kansas," *New York Times*, August 1, 1883.

32   Suddenly, several horsemen approached: Ibid.

32   "If this principle should be defeated here": Inaugural Address of R. T. Walker, Governor of Kansas Territory, delivered in Lecompton, Kansas Territory, May 27, 1857, Territorial Kansas Online, Kansas State Historical Society.

33   the *Central America* was sleek and black: Kinder, *Ship of Gold in the Deep Blue Sea*, 20, 31.

33   "We were jubilant": Quoted in ibid., 20.

33   Long after the nightly card games: Ibid., 20–24.

33   His red beard ran along the fringe of his jaw: Ibid., 22.

34   a troublesome meal of monkey meat and monkey soup: Herndon, *Exploration of the Valley of the Amazon, 1851–1852*, 151–152.

34   "I'll never survive my ship": Lincoln, *The Story of Our Wedding Journey*, 16.

34   "changed our feelings and drove the waves": Quoted in Kinder, *Ship of Gold*, 26.

34   "there was a raging storm": Ibid., 26.

34   "the crying of children": "Statement of B. M. Lee," *New York Herald*, September 21, 1857.

34   "Let it blow": "The Central America (Mr. Badger's Narrative)," *New York Times*, September 23, 1857.

35   Ashby was less confident than he let on: Kinder, *Ship of Gold*, 30.

35   the rising water had popped out the floor plates: Ibid., 34.

35   frightened passengers huddled in the dining saloon: Ibid., 35.

35   two little girls giggled at the dishes smashing: "Statement of Mrs. Almira Kittredge," *New York Herald*, September 27, 1857.

35   "All hands down below to pass buckets": Quoted in Kinder, *Ship of Gold*, 38.

35   "burst into lamentations": Ibid., 38.

35   "All men prepare for bailing the ship": Lincoln, *The Story of Our Wedding Journey*, 17.

35   "You must take off your broadcloth": Quoted in Kinder, *Ship of Gold*, 38.

35   "Work on, m'boys": "Statement of Mr. Robert Hutchinson," *New York Times*, September 22, 1857.

35   the men sang songs: "The Fearful Shipwreck," *New York Herald*, September 21, 1857.

36   "shrieking, crying, weeping": "Statement of Mrs. William McNeil," *New York Herald*, September 21, 1857.

36   The *Central America* left Havana with six lifeboats: Kinder, *Ship of Gold*, 54.

36   Captain Herndon didn't know how many people he could save: "Statement of George E. Ashby, Chief Engineer," *Sacramento Daily Union*, October 24, 1857.

36   they were given life preservers: "Statement of R. T. Brown," *Sacramento Daily Union*, October 24, 1857.

36   "The captain tied a rope around me": "Mrs. Harris' Story," *New York Tribune*, September 21, 1857.

37   "If you are saved": "Statement of Theodore Payne, of San Francisco," *Sacramento Daily Union*, October 24, 1857.

37   "The prayers of the pious and the penitent": "Statement of Mr. Chase, of Michigan," *Sacramento Daily Union*, October 24, 1857.

37   Captain Herndon retired to his quarters: Maury, "Loss of the Steamer Central America," *The Nautical Magazine and Naval Chronicle for 1858*, 44.

38   "Devotion to duty, Christian conduct and genuine heroism": "Tribute to the Memory of Capt. Herndon," *New York Times*, September 20, 1858.

Chapter Four: Playing the Game

39   "In Wall Street every man carries Pressure, Anxiety, Loss": Quoted in Still, *Mirror for Gotham*, 137.

39   Shipbuilding ceased and foundries fired hundreds: Burrows and Wallace, *Gotham: A History of New York City to 1898*, 842–849.

39   many young women who had worked as milliners: Gilfoyle, *City of Eros: New York City, Prostitution and the Commercialization of Sex 1790–1920*, 59–60.

39   "Every human being has a RIGHT to live": Quoted in Burrows and Wallace, *Gotham*, 849.

40   "Ladies throng Broadway every day": Quoted in ibid., 849.

40   Weed entertained legislators of both parties: Brummer, "Political History of New York State during the Period of the Civil War," 21–22.

40   He was tall and powerfully built: Van Deusen, *Thurlow Weed: Wizard of the Lobby*, 213–214.

40   He often came to the rescue: Ibid., 215.

41   an America that was poor and sparsely populated: Ibid., 212–213.

41   "Obnoxious as the admission is to a just sense of right": Quoted in Brummer, "Political History of New York State," 23.

41   He believed that industrial growth was good for the country: Van Deusen, *Thurlow Weed*, 226.

41   "There have been legislative measures": Quoted in Brummer, "Political History of New York State," 22–23.

42   positions for policemen, health wardens, tax assessors: Spann, *New Metropolis*, 351.

42   "I am shakey": Quoted in Van Deusen, *Thurlow Weed*, 215.

43   "scarcely been a session of the Legislature": Quoted in Brummer, "Political History of New York State," 22.

43   "I do not dislike Mr. Barnard": Quoted in Van Deusen, *Thurlow Weed*, 216.

44   Chester Arthur embraced Weed's approach to politics: Burt, *Chester Arthur Biography*, 16.

44   "There is but one subject of thought and conversation": Smith, "The Diary of Dr. Brodie S. Herndon, 1853–1860," *Fredericksburg History & Biography* (2008), 31.

44   "The NY Herald said": Ibid.

44   the row of silver maples: Ibid., 9.

44   There was a "slave house" in the back: Ibid., 8.

45   "He is a fine looking man": Quoted in Reeves, *Gentleman Boss*, 21.

45   "Lewis Herndon Arthur aged 4 ½ hours": Chester Arthur to family, December 10, 1860, Chester Alan Arthur Papers, Library of Congress.

46   "Mr. Weed had won over a large majority of the delegates": Depew, *My Memories of Eighty Years*, 20.

46   Weed told Morgan he had a perfect candidate: Howe, *Chester A. Arthur*, 18–19; Reeves, *Gentleman Boss*, 19.

Chapter Five: Barracks and Blankets

47   No soldiers snapped to attention: Lincoln's arrival at the Hudson River Railroad depot is described in "Mr. Lincoln in New York," *New York Illustrated News*, March 2, 1861, which appears in *Civil War Extra: A Newspaper History of the Civil War from Nat Turner to 1863*, vol. 1, 43.

47   "moved forward on the white bosom of a huge linen billow": Ibid.

48   "escort of mounted policemen": Nevins and Thomas (eds.), *The Diary of George Templeton Strong: The Civil War 1860–1865*, 101.

48   He was dressed entirely in black: Whitman, "Death of Abraham Lincoln," *Complete Prose Works*, 307–309.

49   "Oh, indeed, is that so?": Quoted in Burrows and Wallace, *Gotham*, 867.

49   "one thousand opera glasses": Holzer, *Lincoln President-Elect: Abraham Lincoln and the Great Secession Winter 1860–1861*, 365–366.

49   the poet was walking down Broadway: Whitman's account of the night he heard about the attack on Fort Sumter is in *Specimen Days*, published in Whitman, *Complete Prose Works*, 21.

50   It seemed that the Stars and Stripes hung from every window: Still, *Mirror for Gotham*, 168.

50   "The battle cry was sounded from almost every pulpit": Russell, *My Diary North and South*, 370.

50   From his second-floor office: Burt, *Chester Arthur Biography*, 12–13.

50   State regulations prescribed the uniform of the New York militiaman: Burt, *My Memories of the Military History of New York State during the War for the Union, 1861–65*, 20.

51   The New York Assembly ended up hauling the Brooks brothers: *Documents of the Assembly of the State of New York*, Eighty-Fifth Session—1862, vol. 7.

51   a dog-fighting and rat-baiting house: Burrows and Wallace, *Gotham*, 871–872.

51   Colonel Wilson formally mustered his men at Tammany Hall: Kirkland, *The Pictorial Book of Anecdotes of the Rebellion*, 184–185.

52   Wilson strutted into Arthur's Walker Street office: Reeves, *Gentleman Boss*, 24–25.

52   charging restaurant meals to Jefferson Davis: Burrows and Wallace, *Gotham*, 872.

52   One day the men refused to obey: Reeves, *Gentleman Boss*, 25.

53   "my chief reliance": Quoted in ibid., 30.

53   "Mr. Arthur is an officer in Lincoln's army": Quoted in ibid., 32.

53   "We can hear nothing from our army": Barile and Willis (eds.), *A Woman in a War-Torn Town: The Journal of Jane Howison Beale, Fredericksburg, Virginia, 1850–1862*, 73–74.

53   Arthur "was very affectionate & kind": Quoted in Reeves, *Gentleman Boss*, 32.

54   "little rebel wife": Ibid.

54   "but she certainly suppressed them": Burt, *Chester Arthur Biography*, 21.

54   "now beginning cautiously to tamper with": Quoted in Still, *Mirror for Gotham*, 169.

55   Though Arthur could have volunteered to fight: Reeves, *Gentleman Boss*, 33.

55   "Slavery has nothing whatever to do with the tremendous issues": "The Issue at the North," *New York Times*, April 6, 1861.

55   "great interest in matters of dress": Burt, *Chester Arthur Biography*, 17.

Chapter Six: The Shoddy Aristocracy

57   they put on velvet coats and convened around the curved mahogany bar: Burrows and Wallace, *Gotham,* 877–879.

57   lips slickened by beer foam and roasted meat: Ibid., 879.

57   could support a soldier and his family for a year: Ibid.

57   the madams of the finest houses: Gilfoyle, *City of Eros*, 163.

57   Their wives, cocooned in mink and sable: Burrows and Wallace, *Gotham*, 879.

57   Mme. Demorest's Imperial "dress-elevator": Ibid.

57   The demand for such shawls was "monstrous": Still, *Mirror for Gotham*, 170.

57   Nearly every city industry was being stoked by war contracts: Burrows and Wallace, *Gotham*, 875–879.

58   "Things here at the North are in a great state of prosperity": Quoted in ibid., 877.

58   "this boasted insensibility to the havoc of war": "The Fortunes of War," *Harper's New Monthly Magazine*, vol. 29 (June–November 1864), 227.

58   "celebrated for the speed": "Gath," *Cincinnati Enquirer*, September 5, 1881.

58   five stories high, with cast iron railings: Reeves, *Gentleman Boss*, 34.

59   "how long will you live in rebellion against God": Malvina Arthur to William Arthur Jr., January 26, 1863, Arthur Family Papers, Library of Congress.

59   "a partially secret and ignominious retreat": "Our Special Army Correspondence," *New York Times,* July 8, 1863.

59   "the crowning sheaf in the full harvest of Independence Day Victories": "Vicksburg," *New York Times,* July 8, 1863.

59   "We have lost our darling boy": Chester Arthur to William Arthur Jr., July 9, 1863, Arthur Family Papers, Library of Congress.

60   the Arthurs indulged him lavishly: Reeves, *Gentleman Boss,* 35.

60   Barouches with wounded officers rolled by: Alcott, *Hospital Sketches,* 77.

60   "loaded with pretty children": Ibid.

60   "hit in the face, the ball entering the right side of the cheek": Quoted in Reeves, *Gentleman Boss,* 35–36, from Chester A. Arthur to Mary McElroy, August 30, 1864, Vernon Boyce Hampton Papers, Library of Congress.

61   "almost a copperhead": Quoted in Reeves, *Gentleman Boss,* 33.

61   Arthur took on a new lobbying client: Burt, *Chester Arthur Biography,* 26–27.

62   Morgan played an important role: Reeves, *Gentleman Boss,* 38.

62   George Templeton Strong's recollection of the fall of Richmond is in Nevins and Thomas, *Diary of George Templeton Strong,* 574–575.

62   "O, fatal day": The Diary of Horatio Nelson Taft, 1861–1865, vol. 3, January 1, 1864–May 30, 1865 (April 14, 1865), Library of Congress.

62   "hardly a building on Wall Street": Nevins and Thomas, *Diary of George Templeton Strong,* 587.

63   "Never, I think, has sorrow for a leader": Ibid., 588.

63   many New Yorkers who had expressed pity: Ibid., 582–584.

63   Some of the men wore "wide-awake" military caps: Still, *Mirror for Gotham,* 195.

63   knapsacks, bronzed faces, and loud talk: Ibid., 194.

63   "the well-known ring and footstep": Crowley, *Echoes from Niagara: Historical, Political, Personal,* 150.

64   Arthur made valuable connections at Murphy's house: Reeves, *Gentleman Boss,* 41.

64   "expressed less interest in the principles then agitating parties": Burt, *Chester Arthur Biography,* 35.

Chapter Seven: The Lordly Roscoe

65   He cringed when somebody laid a hand on his shoulder: Chidsey, *The Gentleman from New York: A Life of Roscoe Conkling,* 4.

65   He always folded a bill into quarters: Ibid., 5.

65   He did not borrow or lend books: Ibid.

65   Conkling's political education began early: Conkling, *The Life and Letters of Roscoe Conkling,* 12–13.

65   a horse kicked him and broke his jaw: Ibid., 9–10.

65   "very athletic, vigorous in his movements, and easily superior": Quoted in ibid., 13.

66   They pored over a textbook: Ibid., 12.

66 "like a tall, blond young lady": Jordan, *Roscoe Conkling of New York: Voice in the Senate*, 6.

66 He tried his first case in Utica before a familiar judge: Chidsey, *Gentleman from New York*, 9.

66 he always wrapped his legal books in paper: Conkling, *Life and Letters of Roscoe Conkling*, 44.

66 "Are you going to sum up *this* case?": Ibid., 47.

66 "his arrows were never entangled in the quiver": Quoted in ibid., 21.

66 "I shall send Mr. Conkling": Ibid., 16.

66 Conkling's seemingly effortless oratory: Chidsey, *Gentleman from New York*, 132; Conkling, *Life and Letters of Roscoe Conkling*, 371.

67 he tended to concentrate his gaze on two or three listeners: Conkling, *Life and Letters of Roscoe Conkling*, 366.

67 Occasionally he referred to notes: Chidsey, *Gentleman from New York*, 39.

67 he clashed repeatedly with his cocksure brother-in-law: Jordan, *Roscoe Conkling*, 14.

67 with broad shoulders and "an erect carriage": This description of Conkling's personal appearance comes from Barry, *Forty Years in Washington*, 70–71; and Poore, *Perley's Reminiscences of Sixty Years in the National Metropolis*, vol. 2, 206.

67 the handwriting of "an ultra-fashionable schoolgirl": Barry, *Forty Years in Washington*, 71.

68 "He did not dress, or talk, or walk, or play, as other men did, and do": Ibid., 70.

68 "He is irresistible": Hudson, *Random Recollections of an Old Political Reporter*, 128.

68 "as jealous of each other as two women rivals in love": Barry, *Forty Years in Washington*, 69.

68 "if the member from Maine had the least idea": The incident between Conkling and Blaine on the House floor is recounted in ibid., 71.

69 "Tall, well proportioned, with his vest opening down to the waist": Poore, *Perley's Reminiscences*, vol. 2, 326.

69 Conkling clapped his hands above his head: Barry, *Forty Years in Washington*, 71.

69 "no new senator has ever made in so short a time such rapid strides": Quoted in Alexander, *A Political History of the State of New York*, vol. 3, *1861–1882*, 172.

69 The ladies' gallery was always packed: Jordan, *Roscoe Conkling*, 144.

69 "Do you intend to print this article?": This story is recounted in ibid., 145.

70 in the front row of the ladies' gallery: Ross, *Proud Kate: Portrait of an Ambitious Woman*, 219.

70 The March levee was Mary Lincoln's introduction: Willets, *Inside History of the White House*, 311–312.

70 She wore a bright rose-colored moiré antique dress: Ross, *Proud Kate*, 64.

70 her guests kept turning to watch the stately Kate: Ibid.

70   "with the graceful lightness of a bird": Schurz, *The Reminiscences of Carl Schurz*, vol. 2, *1852–1863*, 169.

70   The wedding ceremony was held in Secretary Chase's Washington home: "The Nuptials of Miss Kate Chase and Ex-Gov. Sprague," *New York Times* (from the *Washington Chronicle*), November 15, 1863.

71   "I know your bright mind will solve this": Ross, *Proud Kate*, 231.

72   "as much sentiment over political relations": Young (ed.), *Men and Memories: Personal Reminiscences of John Russell Young*, vol. 1, 215.

72   "can go around in his stockings": Ibid.

72   Fenton took the Senate floor: "Confirmations by the Senate," (Washington) *Evening Star*, July 12, 1870.

72   Conkling confided in his friend and ally: This account of the struggle between Fenton and Conkling over the Murphy nomination comes from Brown (ed.), *Reminiscences of Senator William M. Stewart of Nevada*, 256–257.

73   "If you had spoken of me in that way": Conkling, *Life and Letters of Roscoe Conkling*, 374.

73   "holding high carnival over their victory": "Washington," *New York Tribune*, July 12, 1870.

Chapter Eight: The Collector

75   liked to wear a green frock coat: Burt, *Chester Arthur Biography*, 5.

75   "had grown stout": Ibid., 6.

75   Burt noticed a change in his friend: Reeves, "Silas Burt and Chester Arthur: A Reformer's View of the Twenty-First President," *New-York Historical Society Quarterly*, vol. 54, no. 4 (October 1970), 323–324.

76   ample opportunities for graft: Callow, *The Tweed Ring*, 81.

76   fortunes in printing and advertising: Ibid., 174–175.

76   city jobs, bowls of soup, and beds: Ibid., 62.

76   Murphy also sat on a three-member commission: Ibid., 180.

76   Arthur certainly was in a position to provide favors: Reeves, *Gentleman Boss*, 49–50.

76   "greedy adventurers": "The Week," *Nation*, September 28, 1871.

77   "jubilantly sarcastic concerning the fate of Fenton": Burt, *Chester Arthur Biography*, 42.

77   Arthur proceeded to explain: Ibid., 42.

77   "the whole party machinery could be consolidated": Ibid., 43.

77   "a fair exposition of Arthur's political creed": Ibid., 44.

77   Murphy devoted almost all of his time to politics: Reeves, *Gentleman Boss*, 58.

77   "found more profit in running the Custom-House": "Estimation in Which the New Collector Is Held in Washington," *New York Tribune*, November 21, 1871.

77   Their swindle was simple: "Collector Murphy's Maladministration," *New York Tribune*, November 21, 1871.

78 Together they sold $10,000 worth of whiskey: Broxmeyer, "Politics as a Sphere of Wealth Accumulation: Cases of Gilded Age New York, 1855–1888" (2014), CUNY Academic Works, 149.

78 "taking the extra precaution of delegating a person": "Collector Murphy's Maladministration," *New York Tribune*, November 21, 1871.

78 Murphy ingratiated himself with the Grant administration: Reeves, *Gentleman Boss*, 58–59.

78 "a record as rotten as his hats": "Marshal Murray Comes to the Front," *New York Tribune*, September 25, 1871.

78 "began to cry and sob like a child": "The Shoddy Collector," *New York Tribune*, September 25, 1871.

79 "We mean to make his standing so plain": "Marshal Murray Comes to the Front," *New York Tribune*, September 25, 1871.

79 "he intended only nominally to relinquish the Collectorship": "Collector Murphy Resigns," *New York Tribune*, November 21, 1871.

79 "Tom Murphy under another name": Ibid.

79 "he can 'run the machine' of party politics": "Our New Collector," *New York Tribune*, November 22, 1871.

79 On the night he got the job: "Collector Murphy Resigns," *New York Tribune*, November 21, 1871.

79 The ground was frozen: "The First Fun on Skates," *New York Sun*, December 2, 1871; "The Cold Weather," *New York Times*, December 2, 1871.

79 "one of the handsomest structures in the city": McCabe, *Lights and Shadows of New York Life*, 843–847.

80 Arthur secured a seat: Broxmeyer, "Politics as a Sphere of Wealth Accumulation," 156–158.

80 Arthur was a dandy: Reeves, *Gentleman Boss*, 85–86.

80 "upon a pile of bank-books": McCabe, *Lights and Shadows of New York Life*, 135.

80 the hosts rolled out a carpet: Ibid., 163.

80 French servants wearing black swallowtail coats: Ibid., 164.

80 "as active as a set of monkeys": Ibid.

80 "Mrs. Arthur was a very ambitious woman": Quoted in Reeves, *Gentleman Boss*, 84.

81 "the Mikes, Jakes and Barneys of politics": "Government," *Nation*, vol. 68, no. 1769 (May 25, 1899), 389.

81 the collector didn't show up at the Custom House until 1 p.m.: Burt, *Chester Arthur Biography*, 63.

81 "Arthur was always the last man to go to bed": "Gath," *Cincinnati Enquirer*, March 28, 1882.

81 "could drink a great deal": Burt, *Chester Arthur Biography*, 67–68.

81 "the many nefarious places visited": Charles N. Brackett to James B. Butler, June 30, 1883, James B. Butler Papers, New York Public Library.

81 "waiter-girls" wearing low bodices: Burrows and Wallace, *Gotham*, 957.

81 "respectable, though by no means stilted": Quoted in ibid.

81 A favorite haunt . . . was Harry Hill's: Crapsey, *The Nether Side of New York*, 161; Smith, *Sunshine and Shadow in New York*, 435–437; Gilfoyle, *City of Eros*, 227.

82 "as if upper New York, in their best outfit": Smith, *Sunshine and Shadow in New York*, 439.

82 "most of them have just begun their life of shame": Ibid., 438.

82 "An hour cannot be spent more pleasantly": *The Gentleman's Directory 1870*, 13.

82 Nell resented Chester's frequent absences: Chester Alan Arthur III to Carey McWilliams, October 22, 1946, Arthur Family Papers, Library of Congress.

82 he started wearing a corset: Burt, *Chester Arthur Biography*, 61.

83 cases of champagne for Grant: Reeves, *Gentleman Boss*, 72.

83 "treated with a jocular indulgence": Burt, *Chester Arthur Biography*, 52.

83 "gave outward respect to the law": Ibid.

83 "wholly without my knowledge or communication": Quoted in Reeves, *Gentleman Boss*, 78.

84 he called his old friend into his office: This encounter is described in Burt, *Chester Arthur Biography*, 54–55.

84 Arthur made sure they were a farce: Ibid., 74–80.

85 "You are one of these goody-goody fellows": Ibid., 71.

85 Burt was amazed at Arthur's "double life": Ibid., 65–66.

85 "The whole civil service of the country": Bancroft (ed.), *Speeches, Correspondence and Political Papers of Carl Schurz*, vol. 2, 405–406.

85 Arthur made sure that Custom House employees did their part: Burt, *Chester Arthur Biography*, 54.

86 in a temporary wooden structure: Grant's disastrous second inaugural ball is described in Chidsey, *Gentleman from New York*, 174–175.

Chapter Nine: From Grant to Hayes

87 "the President did not consider it possible": Gerry (ed.), *Through Five Administrations: Reminiscences of Colonel William H. Crook, Bodyguard to President Lincoln*, 165.

87 "the all-time low point in statesmanship": Woodward, "The Lowest Ebb," *American Heritage*, vol. 8, no. 3 (April 1957).

87 A devoted family man: Details of Grant's family life in the White House are in Gerry, *Through Five Administrations*, 179–180.

88 "One of my superstitions": Grant, *Memoirs of U. S. Grant*, vol. 1, 35.

88 "Selfish men and ambitious men": Hoar, *Autobiography of Seventy Years*, vol. 1, 197.

90 "fished for gold in every stinking cesspool": Hesseltine, *Ulysses S. Grant, Politician*, 381.

90 cigar boxes filled with thousand dollar bills: Ibid.

90 strong-armed the respected importing firm: These details of the Phelps, Dodge and Company case can be found in Reeves, *Gentleman Boss*, 83; Wells, *Congress and Phelps, Dodge & Co.: An Extraordinary History*, 116; "The

Moieties Question," *New York Times*, March 20, 1874; "The Moiety System," *New York Times*, March 21, 1874.

91   the widowed Elder Arthur remained: Reeves, *Gentleman Boss*, 86, from an interview with Chester Arthur III on December 29, 1970.

91   "Chester is here": The scene at Elder Arthur's deathbed is detailed in a letter from Regina Caw (one of Chester Arthur's sisters) to William and Alice Arthur, November 2, 1875, Arthur Family Papers, Library of Congress.

92   "silver-haired and priestly": McCullough, *Mornings on Horseback: The Story of an Extraordinary Family, a Vanished Way of Life, and the Unique Child Who Became Theodore Roosevelt*, 150–151.

92   "The time has come": Norton (ed.), *Orations and Addresses of George William Curtis*, vol. 2, 27–28.

93   a train packed with about 150 Conkling supporters: "Arrival of the Republican Club at Its Destination," *New York Times*, June 10, 1876.

93   "almost as if they had captured the city": "The Conkling Game of Bluff," *New York Times,* June 12, 1876.

93   "During the day they have their band": "The National Campaign," *New York Times*, June 11, 1876.

93   "The machine is in the very best working order": "The Conkling Game of Bluff," *New York Times*, June 12, 1876.

94   "All these things are designed to affect the outside crowd": "The National Convention," *New York Times*, June 13, 1876.

94   from one steamy hotel room to another: McCullough, *Mornings on Horseback*, 155.

94   "altogether like a scene": Theodore Roosevelt to Bamie Roosevelt, June 13, 1876, quoted in ibid., 156–157.

94   Arthur and other Republican dignitaries: This description of the convention hall comes from "The Republican Campaign," *New York Times*, June 10, 1876.

95   "Federal office-holders have here usurped the organization": *Proceedings of the Republican National Convention Held at Cincinnati, Ohio, on Wednesday, Thursday and Friday, June 14, 15 and 16, 1876*, 17.

95   "How is New York?": Arthur's immediate reaction to the Hayes nomination is recounted in "Response of the Country," *New York Times*, June 17, 1876.

96   "never for a moment sullied": Howells, *Sketch of the Life and Character of Rutherford B. Hayes*, 110.

96   "This system destroys the independence": Letter from Rutherford B. Hayes accepting the Republican nomination, July 8, 1876, the Rutherford B. Hayes and Hayes Family Papers, Rutherford B. Hayes Presidential Libraries and Museums.

96   Arthur did his duty: Burt, *Chester Arthur Biography*, 86–88.

97   "The more meetings you can address": Rutherford B. Hayes to Roscoe Conkling, August 15, 1876, quoted in Conkling, *Life and Letters of Roscoe Conkling*, 509.

97   "It seems, in some quarters, to be regarded": Quoted in ibid., 510.

97   "this whole assessment business": Rutherford B. Hayes to Carl Schurz, September 15, 1876, in Bancroft, *Political Papers of Carl Schurz*, vol. 3, 339.

97   "Gen. Arthur's activity": Chandler, "Chester A. Arthur," in Wilson, *The Presidents of the United States, 1789–1894*, 448.

98   "one grand ovation": "From White House to Capitol," *New York Times*, March 6, 1877.

98   "I ask the attention of the public": "President Hayes' Inaugural," *New York Times*, March 6, 1877.

Chapter Ten: His Fraudulency the President

99   Conkling "was under my professional care": Quoted in Conkling, *Life and Letters of Roscoe Conkling*, 511.

99   "never spoke of [Hayes] in public or private": Hoar, *Autobiography of Seventy Years*, vol. 1, 382–383.

99   "forcibly and with much feeling": Williams, *The Life of Rutherford Birchard Hayes, Nineteenth President of the United States*, vol. 1, 514–515.

99   the dour Ohioan in the plain frock coat: Hayes and his wife are described in Barry, *Forty Years in Washington*, 25–26.

99   They entertained their Sunday guests: Chidsey, *Gentleman from New York*, 236.

100   a box made from the frozen skin of an orange: Hoar, *Autobiography of Seventy Years*, vol. 2, 15.

100   "The water flowed like champagne": Ibid.

100   he was bitter about Conkling's failure: Reeves, *Gentleman Boss*, 112.

100   Hayes attended a Chamber of Commerce dinner: The account of the dinner, including Schurz's speech, comes from "A Merchant's Banquet," *New York Times*, May 15, 1877.

101   "at the request of politicians and political associations": *Commissions to Examine Certain Custom-Houses of the United States*, House Executive Document No. 8, 45th Congress, 1st Session, 1877–1878, 15.

101   "unsound in principle, dangerous in practice": Ibid.

101   "the evils wrought by mismanagement and corruption": Ibid., 16.

101   "Party leaders should have no more influence": Quoted in Jay, "Civil-Service Reform," *North American Review*, vol. 127 (September–October 1878), 275.

102   "ignorance and incapacity on the part of the employees": Quoted in Shores, "The Hayes-Conkling Controversy 1877–1879," *Smith College Studies in History*, vol. 4, no. 4 (July 1919), 232–233.

102   "gaily decked with bunting": "Mr. Conkling's Welcome," *New York Sun*, August 11, 1877.

102   "Mr. Conkling seems the picture of health": "Conkling's Return," *New York Tribune*, August 11, 1877.

103   "no statesman returning to his native land": "Mr. Conkling's Welcome," *New York Sun*, August 11, 1877.

103   "a number of fashionably attired ladies": "Conkling's Return," *New York Tribune*, August 11, 1877.

103   "listened rather impatiently": Ibid.

103   Conkling finally emerged: Ibid.

103   He spoke briefly from his car: Shores, "Hayes-Conkling Controversy," 223.

103   Sherman wrote in a confidential letter: Reeves, *Gentleman Boss*, 123; Sherman, *Recollections of Forty Years in the House, Senate and Cabinet: An Autobiography*, vol. 2, 679–681; "New York Custom-House," *New York Times*, September 7, 1877.

103   "informing me officially of facts which had already come to my knowledge": Quoted in Reeves, *Gentleman Boss*, 123.

104   Sherman was relieved: Ibid., 125.

104   "the lawful title of Rutherford B. Hayes to the Presidency": Conkling, *Life and Letters of Roscoe Conkling*, 537.

104   The Conkling delegates buzzed: "The State Convention," *New York Tribune*, September 28, 1877.

104   "Who are these men": Conkling's speech was reprinted in "Republican Convention," *New York Herald*, September 27, 1877.

104   The Conkling delegates exploded with laughter: Jordan, *Roscoe Conkling*, 279.

104   Curtis was staggered by Conkling's vitriol: Depew, *My Memories of Eighty Years*, 79–80; Lang, *Autobiography of Thomas Collier Platt*, 85; "Republican Convention," *New York Herald*, September 27, 1877.

105   "every resource of sarcasm": Depew, *My Memories of Eighty Years*, 80.

105   "bristling with good points": Quoted in Jordan, *Roscoe Conkling*, 280.

105   "The Great Senator of New-York": "The State Convention," *New York Tribune*, September 28, 1877.

105   "It was the saddest sight I ever knew": Quoted in Cary, *George William Curtis*, 258.

106   "The treatment of the whole matter": Quoted in Reeves, *Gentleman Boss*, 126.

106   one cup of coffee at breakfast: Chidsey, *Gentleman from New York*, 235.

106   "I am clear that I am right": Quoted in Williams, *Life of Rutherford Birchard Hayes*, vol. 2, 83.

Chapter Eleven: "The One I Loved Dearest"

107   on many Sundays he attended not one service but two: McCullough, *Mornings on Horseback*, 23.

107   "To see him put on her wraps and escort her": Quoted in Riis, *Theodore Roosevelt the Citizen*, 11.

107   Roosevelt had no great love for music and art: McCullough, *Mornings on Horseback*, 23.

107   "My personal impression": Ibid.

107   "the sunshine of his affection": Quoted in ibid., 31.

107   he had little interest in the work: Ibid., 27–28.

108   "Whatever he had to do": Quoted in ibid., 28.

ॉ-ーॉチக ಠääöäääöö

108 "maniacal benevolence": Ibid., 28.

108 "as much as I enjoy loafing": Ibid., 28.

108 his "troublesome conscience": Ibid., 29.

108 "the image and figure of the citizen": Ibid., 151.

108 "I will take the office": Ibid., 177.

108 "the great fundamental evil of the system": "Bad State of Public Charities," *New York Times*, October 31, 1877.

109 "There are about 300 persons here": "Roscoe Conkling," *New York Herald*, November 9, 1877.

109 Conkling sent President Hayes a detailed request: Reeves, *Gentleman Boss*, 127; and "New York and Chicago Officials," *New York Times*, November 16, 1877.

110 "sought out all that could be said": Quoted in Shores, "Hayes-Conkling Controversy," 236.

110 "I am now in a contest": Quoted in Williams, *Life of Rutherford Birchard Hayes*, vol. 2, 87.

110 "The triumph of Senator Conkling": "Conkling's Great Victory," *New York Sun*, December 13, 1877.

111 "I cannot tell you how gratified I am": Chester Arthur to Roscoe Conkling, December 13, 1877, quoted in Reeves, *Gentleman Boss*, 131.

111 "In the language of the press": Quoted in Williams, *Life of Rutherford Birchard Hayes*, vol. 2, 87.

111 "The machine politicians have shown their colors": Theodore Roosevelt Sr. to Theodore Roosevelt Jr., December 16, 1877, quoted in McCullough, *Mornings on Horseback*, 180.

111 "The friends of reform": Editorial in *New York Times*, January 5, 1878.

111 Roosevelt's stomach pains: McCullough, *Mornings on Horseback*, 182–183.

112 the patient opened his eyes: Ibid., 184.

112 "the one I loved dearest on earth": Quoted in ibid., 190.

113 Roscoe Conkling's long affair with Kate Sprague: This account of the confrontation between Conkling and Sprague comes from "The Encounter with Mr. Conkling," *New York Sun*, August 17, 1879.

114 "The Conkling scandal is the newspaper sensation of the time": Quoted in Williams, *Diary and Letters of Rutherford Birchard Hayes*, vol. 3, 570.

114 Arthur was helping Sharpe: Reeves, *Gentleman Boss*, 158.

114 The only way Arthur could get back: "Dangerous Illness of Mrs. Gen. Arthur," *New York Times*, January 13, 1880.

114 Arthur could see ice floes: "The Ice in the Hudson Moving," *New York Times*, January 12, 1880.

114 "a precious sacred trust": Chester Arthur to Ellen Herndon, August 30, 1857, Chester Alan Arthur Papers, Library of Congress.

114 "the shock and nervous tension caused by her bereavement": "Dangerous Illness of Mrs. Gen. Arthur," *New York Times*, January 13, 1880.

115 By the time Arthur finally reached his Lexington Avenue brownstone: Ibid.; Reeves, *Gentleman Boss*, 158.

115   Arthur was surrounded: "Mrs. Arthur's Funeral," *New York Times*, January 16, 1880.

115   Arthur was "completely unnerved and prostrated": Reeves, *Gentleman Boss*, 158–159.

115   Arthur kept Murphy walking: "Bee," *Cincinnati Enquirer*, November 22, 1883.

Chapter Twelve: Dark Horse

117   The sun rose in a cloudless sky: "The National Convention," *New York Times*, June 3, 1880.

117   "Here's your Blaine lemonade!": Ibid.

118   Whenever Conkling appeared: Ibid.; "The Convention and Its Work," *New York Times*, June 3, 1880.

118   Striding arm-in-arm: "The Convention and Its Work," *New York Times*, June 3, 1880.

118   As the Lordly Roscoe passed down the aisle: "The Struggle at Chicago," *New York Times*, June 4, 1880.

118   Queen Victoria's youngest son, Prince Leopold: Prince Leopold's appearance is described in "The Fight against Grant," *New York Times*, June 5, 1880; and "Grant's Strength Tested," *New York Sun*, June 5, 1880.

118   On Thursday night at the Grand Pacific Hotel: "Incidents of the Struggle," *New York Times*, June 4, 1880.

119   wearing a light blue tie: "A Ballot Not Yet Reached," *New York Sun*, June 6, 1880.

119   The clerk called the roll of the states: *Proceedings of the Republican National Convention Held at Chicago, Illinois (1880)*, 179–180.

119   Conkling paused: Conkling's nomination speech is described in "Grant's Name Presented," *New York Sun*, June 6, 1880; and Chidsey, *Gentleman from New York*, 286.

120   "By speaking very deliberately": Conkling, *Life and Letters of Roscoe Conkling*, 601.

120   "this assemblage seemed to me a human ocean": *Proceedings of the Republican National Convention Held at Chicago, Illinois (1880)*, 184.

120   "The sickly manner in which Garfield presented your name": J. H. Geiger to John Sherman, June 6, 1880, John Sherman Papers, Library of Congress.

120   a stiff gale from the north and sheets of rain: "Ominous Storm in Chicago," *New York Sun*, June 7, 1880.

121   The pious Massachusetts delegates: Ibid.

121   Corks popped: Ibid.

121   with frowsy beards and unoiled hair: Ibid.

121   the roses arranged around a painting of Grant: Ibid.

121   Conkling and Grant backers visited the Southern delegations: "The Day's Doings," *Chicago Tribune*, June 7, 1880.

121   the band played selections: "The Candidate Not Named," *New York Sun*, June 8, 1880.

121 ladies fluttered their handkerchiefs: Ibid.

121 His wife Julia, fearing a deadlock: Ackerman, *Dark Horse: The Surprise Election and Political Murder of President James A. Garfield*, 87.

121 16 of the 20 Wisconsin delegates: Garfield's dramatic nomination is detailed in "Garfield and Arthur," *New York Sun*, June 9, 1880; "The Story of the Balloting," *New York Times*, June 9, 1880; and *Proceedings of the Republican National Convention Held at Chicago, Illinois (1880)*, 267–277.

123 Arthur found Conkling in a room: The encounter between Arthur and Conkling is described in Hudson, *Random Recollections of an Old Political Reporter*, 96–99. Hudson happened to be in the room when the confrontation occurred.

124 "In behalf of a large number of the New York delegation": Arthur's nomination as vice president is described in *Proceedings of the Republican National Convention Held at Chicago, Illinois (1880)*, 287–296.

124 swelled Arthur's right hand: "Gen. Arthur at Home," *New York Times*, June 12, 1880.

124 "The nomination of Arthur is a ridiculous burlesque": Quoted in Burton, *John Sherman*, 296–297.

125 "there is no place in which [Arthur's] powers of mischief": Quoted in Reeves, *Gentleman Boss*, 183.

125 The first shouts rang out: Arthur's return to New York after the convention is described in "Gen. Arthur at Home," *New York Times*, June 12, 1880.

125 Nell presented her father with a bouquet: Regina Caw to Alice (Mrs. William) Arthur, June 11, 1880, Arthur Family Papers.

126 a Connecticut-bound steamship: This account of the collision between the *Narragansett* and the *Stonington* comes from "How the Disaster Occurred," *New York Times*, June 13, 1880; and "Heroic Women and Cowardly Men," *New York Times*, June 13, 1880.

127 "I drifted alongside of a mattress": "Heroic Women and Cowardly Men," *New York Times*, June 13, 1880.

127 "I saw and heard the wailing": *Report of the Proceedings in the Case of the United States v. Charles J. Guiteau, Tried in the Supreme Court of the District of Columbia, Holding a Criminal Term, and Beginning November 14, 1881*, Part 1 (hereafter referred to as *United States v. Charles J. Guiteau*), 584.

127 the preacher believed God had spared him: Ibid., 598.

Chapter Thirteen: "A Great Deal of Soap"

129 Republicans drew inspiration: This information on Garfield's early life comes from Rutkow, *James A. Garfield*, 4–12.

129 "glory in defending unpopular truth against popular error": Ibid., 6.

130 "I do not see any way": Quoted in Balch, *Life of James A. Garfield: Late President of the United States*, 121.

131 "He was a man who gained friends": Barry, *Forty Years in Washington*, 80.

131 "He was a large, well developed, handsome man": Sherman, *Recollections of Forty Years*, vol. 2, 807.

132   Garfield declined to endorse: Smalley, *The Republican Manual,* 297–298.

132   "positive abandonment of ground taken": Bancroft, *Political Papers of Carl Schurz,* vol. 4, 1.

132   "appointments should be based upon ascertained fitness": "Gen. Arthur's Acceptance," *New York Times,* July 19, 1880.

132   "Arthur's letter is very amusing": George William Curtis to Silas Burt, July 22, 1880, quoted in Reeves, *Gentleman Boss,* 189.

132   he and his protégé traveled to Canada: "Notes of the Campaign," *New York Times,* July 16, 1880.

132   "Every day and everything was enjoyable": Roscoe Conkling to Levi Morton, August 1, 1880, quoted in Reeves, *Gentleman Boss,* 191.

132   a booming artillery salute at Harlem: Garfield's arrival in New York City is described in "The Greeting in This City," *New York Times,* August 5, 1880.

133   "chagrin, mortification and indignation": Lang, *Autobiography of Thomas Collier Platt,* 127.

133   "Telegrams were sent to various points": Ibid., 128.

133   The men exchanged greetings: This account of the meeting at the Fifth Avenue Hotel comes from ibid., 129–132.

134   "no obstacles stood in the way": "Leaders in Consultation," *New York Times,* August 6, 1880.

134   "No trades, no shackles": Diary of James A. Garfield, August 9, 1880, in James A. Garfield Papers, Library of Congress.

134   From his headquarters at the Fifth Avenue Hotel: Arthur's role in the 1880 campaign is described in Reeves, *Gentleman Boss,* 198–201.

135   Hancock went to his grave convinced: Clancy, *The Presidential Election of 1880,* 243.

135   Arthur basked in the victory: "Gen. Arthur Congratulated," *New York Times,* November 4, 1880.

135   "Thank you for your congratulations": Chester Arthur to Mary Dun, November 10, 1880, Shapell Manuscript Foundation.

136   "I will not tolerate nor act upon any understanding": Quoted in Reeves, *Gentleman Boss,* 206.

136   "all the desperate bad men of the party": James Blaine to James Garfield, December 16, 1880, quoted in Reeves, *Gentleman Boss,* 211.

136   "The Senator, your friend, never passes the table": Kate Chase Sprague to Chester Arthur, "Strictly Confidential," January 18, 1881, Chester Alan Arthur Papers, Library of Congress.

136   The dinner was in honor of Stephen Dorsey: Arthur's speech at Delmonico's is recounted in "Indiana's October Vote," *New York Times,* February 12, 1881.

137   "The cynicism of this": "The Week," *Nation,* vol. 32, February 24, 1881, 122.

137   The weather on Inauguration Day: Poore, *Perley's Reminiscences,* vol. 2, 388–391; "A New Chief Magistrate," *New York Times,* March 5, 1881.

138   Out-of-town visitors had taken every room: Poore, *Perley's Reminiscences,* vol. 2, 388.

138 Their spirits lifted: "A New Chief Magistrate," *New York Times*, March 5, 1881.

138 In the Senate Chamber: The scene in the chamber is described in "The Cere- monies in the Senate," *New York Times*, March 5, 1881; "Scenes in the Senate Chamber," *New York Times*, March 5, 1881; and "In the Senate Chamber," *New York Tribune*, March 5, 1881.

139 "strong, keen-eyed, and handsome": "The Crowd Outside the Capitol," *New York Times*, March 5, 1881.

139 When Arthur saw the name at the top: Poore, *Perley's Reminiscences*, vol. 2, 402–403; "Robertson for Collector," *New York Sun*, March 24, 1881.

139 "The nomination of Senator Robertson was a complete surprise": "Robertson for Collector," *New York Sun*, March 24, 1881.

139 "This brings on the contest at once": Quoted in Reeves, *Gentleman Boss*, 224.

139 "reprehensible and disgusting": Ibid., 226.

140 Connery wasn't sure: Connery recounts this episode in Connery, "Secret History of the Garfield-Conkling Tragedy," *Cosmopolitan Magazine*, vol. 23 (June 1897), 146–150.

141 Republican senators discussed the Robertson nomination: "Mr. Conkling's Grievances," *New York Times*, May 10, 1881.

141 some grumbled that it was impolitic: "The Republican Caucus," *New York Times*, May 11, 1881.

141 The reservations had spread: "The Robertson Contest," *New York Times*, May 14, 1881.

141 But Senator Platt had an idea: Lang, *Autobiography of Thomas Collier Platt*, 150–151.

141 Arthur entered the Senate Chamber: The resignation announcement and sen- ators' reaction to it are described in "A Sensation in Politics," *New York Times*, May 17, 1881.

142 "The sensation created to-day": Ibid.

142 cracks in the scheme appeared: "The Protesting Senators," *New York Times*, May 18, 1881.

142 "There are two men in the country": "Comments of the Press," *New York Times*, May 18, 1881.

143 "Senators Conkling and Platt have not resigned out of pique": Ibid.

143 most New Yorkers felt "impatience and disgust": Editorial, *New York Times*, May 17, 1881.

143 "It is to be hoped that the risk and humiliation": "The Cost of the Spoils Sys- tem," *New York Times*, May 18, 1881.

143 Arthur sneaked into the side entrance: "The New-York Senators," *New York Times*, May 23, 1881.

143 Conkling was ebullient: "Beginning the Contest," *New York Times*, May 25, 1881.

143 "put up with even the most tiresome men": "Consulting with His Friends," *New York Times*, May 25, 1881.

143 cooling his flushed face with a large fan: "The Senatorial Contest," *New York Tribune*, May 26, 1881.

143   "It is not enough to say": "A Public Scandal," *New York Tribune*, May 26, 1881.

144   Democrats challenged Stalwarts to a baseball game: "Legislators at the Bat," *New York Times*, June 25, 1881.

144   "an alleged escapade last night": "The Wearisome Deadlock," *New York Sun*, July 1, 1881.

144   "of social rather than political character": "A Surprise at Albany," *New York Times*, July 2, 1881.

144   The *Chicago Tribune* had no such compunctions: "Extraordinary Scandal," *Chicago Tribune*, July 1, 1881.

Chapter Fourteen: "An Ugly Wound"

147   he had accepted Garfield's nomination: Guiteau's state of mind and his actions in the weeks leading up to the shooting are detailed in the testimony he provided at his trial, which may be found in *United States v. Charles J. Guiteau*, 584–594, 616–621, 637–643. See also Charles Guiteau, "Address to the American People," June 16, 1881, Charles J. Guiteau Collection, Booth Family Center for Special Collections, Georgetown University Libraries; and *Guiteau's Confession*, 12.

149   He was so giddy at the prospect: Peskin, *Garfield: A Biography*, 595.

150   They arrived at the brick-and-stone depot: The events at the Baltimore and Potomac Railroad depot are detailed in "A Great Nation in Grief," *New York Times*, July 3, 1881; "The President Shot," *New York Sun*, July 3, 1881; and *United States v. Charles J. Guiteau*, 140–163, 168–172.

152   Guiteau's mother died: These details of Guiteau's life come from *A Complete History of the Life and Trial of Charles Julius Guiteau, Assassin of President Garfield*, 22–26.

152   "I pray that God may open your mind": Charles Guiteau to Frances (Guiteau) Scoville, August 9, 1861, quoted in *United States v. Charles J. Guiteau*, 531.

152   he described Noyes as harsh and cruel: *Complete History of the Life and Trial of Charles Julius Guiteau*, 25–26.

152   he remained faithful to Noyes's beliefs: Charles Guiteau to Luther Guiteau, April 10, 1865, quoted in *United States v. Charles J. Guiteau*, 536.

152   Guiteau lived occasionally with his sister: Ibid., 469–480.

153   "I knew that my brother had been for years insane": "The Guiteau Family," *New York Times*, July 12, 1881.

153   Thomas Nast drew the vice president: Paine, *Thomas Nast: His Period and His Pictures*, 449.

153   it wounded Arthur all the more deeply: Ibid., 486–487.

153   "It can't be true": "Vice President Arthur," *New York Sun*, July 3, 1881.

154   At Astor Place, Arthur and Conkling glimpsed the Cooper Union: The buildings Arthur and Conkling would have seen on their route to the Fifth Avenue Hotel are described in McCabe, *New York by Sunlight and Gaslight*, 146–149.

154   it left the impression that Garfield had been killed: "The News in This City," *New York Times*, July 3, 1881.

154 "President Garfield has been shot!": "Sorrow in the City," *New York Tribune*, July 3, 1881.

155 a shudder went through the crowd: Ibid.

155 "What is the latest news from Washington?": "Vice-President Arthur," *New York Sun*, July 3, 1881.

155 he was horrified at the crime: "The Vice-President's Movements," *New York Tribune*, July 3, 1881.

155 A stream of visitors' cards followed them: "Vice-President Arthur," *New York Sun*, July 3, 1881; "Gen. Arthur's Movements," *New York Times*, July 3, 1881.

155 prompting cheers from the crowd broiling in the sun: "Sorrow in the City," *New York Tribune*, July 3, 1881.

156 "What is your latest information": "Vice-President Arthur," *New York Sun*, July 3, 1881.

156 At noon the newspaper extras appeared: "The News in This City," *New York Times*, July 3, 1881.

156 "the President's symptoms are not regarded as unfavorable": "Gen. Arthur's Movements," *New York Times*, July 3, 1881.

156 A letter the police found in Guiteau's pocket shed additional light on his motives: *United States v. Charles J. Guiteau*, 215–216.

156 "Is a man of so pure and noble a character": "Sorrow in the City," *New York Tribune*, July 3, 1881.

157 "Lincoln was assassinated": "At the Fifth Avenue Hotel," *New York Times*, July 3, 1881.

157 the crowds in Printing House Square grew silent: "The News in This City," *New York Times*, July 3, 1881.

157 "the symptoms of the President are not favorable": "Gen. Arthur's Movements," *New York Times*, July 3, 1881.

157 "I am utterly broken down": "Vice-President Arthur," *New York Sun*, July 3, 1881.

157 "a solid, throbbing mass": "Sorrow in the City," *New York Tribune*, July 3, 1881.

158 a copyist began writing the latest news: Ibid.

158 Arthur received another telegram from Blaine: "Gen. Arthur's Movements," *New York Times*, July 3, 1881; "Vice-President Arthur," *New York Sun*, July 3, 1881.

158 the Fifth Avenue Hotel was a mecca: McCabe, *Lights and Shadows of New York Life*, 308–312.

158 The densest crush was around the telegraph: "At the Fifth Avenue Hotel," *New York Times*, July 3, 1881.

158 "Your 6:45 telegram is very distressing": "Gen. Arthur's Movements," *New York Times*, July 3, 1881.

159 "Sincere thanks for your expressions of sympathy": Ibid.

159 a stereopticon projected the latest bulletins: "At the Fifth Avenue Hotel," *New York Times*, July 3, 1881.

159 bade Arthur goodbye on the platform: "Gen. Arthur's Movements," *New York Times*, July 3, 1881; "Vice-President Arthur," *New York Sun*, July 3, 1881.

160 "When James A. Garfield was yesterday reported": Editorial, *New York Times*, July 3, 1881.

160 the immense Hoe presses in the basement: McCabe, *New York by Sunlight and Gaslight*, 596.

Chapter Fifteen: A Mysterious Correspondent

161 "a pending calamity of the utmost magnitude": Editorial, *Chicago Tribune*, July 3, 1881.

161 "a very obnoxious person named Conkling": "The Week," *Nation*, vol. 33, July 7, 1881, 1.

161 "What the country will not forget": "The Opinions of the Press," *New York Times*, July 3, 1881.

161 "Mrs. Surratt was hanged on less circumstantial evidence": Ibid.

161 "would be a national calamity": Williams, *Diary and Letters of Rutherford Birchard Hayes*, vol. 4, 23.

161 "horror at the death of Garfield": White, *Autobiography of Andrew Dickson White*, vol. 1, 193.

162 "No one deplores the calamity more": "Mr. Arthur's Movements," *New York Sun*, July 5, 1881.

162 businessmen and fashionably dressed ladies: "The Popular Sympathy," (Washington) *Evening Star*, July 3, 1881.

162 The pair's sudden appearance: "Vice-President Arthur at the White House," (Washington) *Evening Critic*, July 4, 1881.

162 The sound of water splashing in a fountain: "Watching and Waiting," *New York Sun*, July 5, 1881.

162 a gentle breeze from the Potomac: Ibid.

162 "General, I am glad that you have arrived": "Vice-President Arthur at the White House," (Washington) *Evening Critic*, July 4, 1881.

162 Lucretia inquired about his health: "Vice President Arthur Calls and Is Received by Mrs. Garfield," (Washington) *Evening Star*, July 4, 1881.

163 "I pray to God that the president will recover": Ibid.

163 A reporter found him sitting on a covered sofa: "Vice President Arthur," *New York Times*, July 5, 1881.

163 "the condition of the President has seemed to improve": "The Patient's Hopeful Condition," *New York Times*, July 10, 1881.

163 navy engineers were rigging up a primitive air conditioner: "Almost Out of Danger," *New York Times*, July 11, 1881.

163 Almon Rockwell fanned his friend: "The Patient's Hopeful Condition," *New York Times*, July 10, 1881.

163 The doctors continued to drain his wound: "The Danger Line Passed," *New York Times*, July 14, 1881.

164 "in due time rebound": Roscoe Conkling to Alexander T. Brown, July 9, 1881, quoted in Reeves, *Gentleman Boss*, 243.

164 "alone and apparently in deep thought": "Conkling to His Followers," *New York Times*, July 23, 1881.

164 Garfield was magnanimous: Bliss, "The Story of President Garfield's Illness, Told by the Physician in Charge," *Century Illustrated Monthly Magazine,* vol. 23 (November 1881–April 1882), 299–305.

165 "fearing the unsettled state of things": "The Season at Saratoga," *New York Times*, August 2, 1881.

165 The main thing on New Yorkers' minds: "Trying Summer Weather," *New York Sun*, August 5, 1881.

165 The night offered scant relief: "Still Up in the Nineties," *New York Sun*, August 7, 1881.

165 The president's fever and pulse: "Alarm for the President," *New York Sun*, August 16, 1881; "The President Very Low," *New York Times*, August 16, 1881; "A Very Serious Crisis," *New York Tribune*, August 16, 1881.

165 "I have said elsewhere": Edwin D. Morgan to Chester Arthur, August 22, 1881, Chester Alan Arthur Papers, Library of Congress.

166 "I have not lost hope": "Anxiety Dispelling Hope," *New York Times*, August 26, 1881.

166 New Yorkers converged on the Fifth Avenue Hotel: Ibid.

166 Hidden in his Lexington Avenue brownstone: Wise, *Recollections of Thirteen Presidents,* 150; "Renewed Forebodings in This City," *New York Tribune*, August 26, 1881; "Vice President Arthur," *New York Sun*, August 26, 1881.

166 Surrounded by decanters and cigar smoke: Wise, *Recollections of Thirteen Presidents,* 150.

166 Lucretia Garfield sent a telegram to her brother: "Still Clinging to Life," *New York Sun*, August 27, 1881.

166 "decided that they would not subject Gen. Arthur": Ibid.

166 Outside, the August sun: The scene outside the White House is described in "One Thought Absorbing All Others," *New York Tribune*, August 27, 1881.

166 a full-length portrait of the murdered Lincoln: Ibid.

166 the *Sun* could not post updates fast enough: "The News in the City," *New York Sun*, August 27, 1881.

167 An army of shrill-voiced newsboys: "Anxiety of the People," *New York Times*, August 27, 1881.

167 Pickpockets also circulated: "The News in the City," *New York Sun*, August 27, 1881.

167 Postmaster General James sneaked into New York: "Postmaster-General James's Visit," *New York Times*, August 28, 1881; "The Vice-President," *New York Sun*, August 28, 1881.

167 he took a solitary ride: "Vice-President Arthur," *New York Times*, August 29, 1881.

167 Julia I. Sand was the unmarried eighth daughter: This biographical information on Julia Sand comes from Reeves, "The President's Dwarf: The Letters of Julia Sand to Chester A. Arthur," *New York History,* vol. 52 (January 1971), 73–83.

167 "The hours of Garfield's life are numbered": Julia Sand to Chester Arthur, August 27, 1881, Chester Alan Arthur Papers, Library of Congress.

169   On a card embossed with "The Union League Club": This card is in the Chester Alan Arthur Papers, Library of Congress.

169   On a breathless gray morning: Garfield's departure from the White House is described in "Taken from Washington," *New York Times*, September 7, 1881.

170   Some of the onlookers walked alongside: Ibid.

170   "God save the president!": Ibid.

170   only well-seasoned hardwood: "Steps Toward Recovery," *New York Times*, September 11, 1881.

170   the Red Gate Farm: Ibid.

170   "a depth of feeling that no man could ever forget": "Giving Voice to Sorrow," *New York Times*, November 21, 1886.

170   "The most frightful responsibility": Ibid.

171   "It is impossible to conceal from ourselves": "The News Borne to Gen. Arthur," *New York Sun*, September 20, 1881.

171   Arthur grabbed his cane: Ibid.

171   Arthur walked to 28th Street: Ibid.

171   the occasional clatter of a passing milk wagon: Ibid.

171   a *Sun* reporter knocked on the door: Ibid.

172   "I daren't ask him": "The Oath Administered," *New York Times*, September 20, 1881.

Chapter Sixteen: "He Is Our President"

173   In the first-floor parlor: "The Oath Administered," *New York Times*, September 20, 1881; "The New Chief Executive," *New York Times*, September 21, 1881.

173   the neighborhood servants stepped outside: "The New Chief Executive," *New York Times*, September 21, 1881.

173   knots of curious New Yorkers: Ibid.

174   Dressed in black, with red and swollen eyes: Ibid.

174   Arthur leaned on Blaine for support: "The Arrival at Long Branch," *New York Sun*, September 21, 1881.

174   a hatbox and two leather trunks: "President Arthur's Journey," *New York Times*, September 22, 1881.

174   he held his crape-banded hat on his lap: Ibid.

174   the dark red woodwork on the outside of each car: "The Nation's Dead Chief," *New York Times*, September 22, 1881.

174   "electric knobs for the summoning of a waiter": "The Body Lying in State," *New York Sun*, September 22, 1881.

174   the casket sat on a draped dais: "The Nation's Dead Chief," *New York Times*, September 22, 1881.

174   Thousands stood alongside the tracks: These details of the funeral train's journey to Washington come from "The Journey to the Capitol," *New York Times*, September 22, 1881; and "The Funeral Train," *New York Sun*, September 22, 1881.

175 a long veil that nearly touched the ground: These details of the arrival of Gar-
field's body in Washington and the scene in the Capitol rotunda come from
"The Body Lying in State," *New York Sun*, September 22, 1881; and "The
Journey to the Capitol," *New York Times*, September 22, 1881.

175 Arthur repeated the oath of office: "The New Administration," *New York
Times*, September 23, 1881.

175 "For the fourth time in the history of the Republic": Ibid.

176 "either the hostility or the distrust or the coldness": "Giving Voice to Sorrow,"
New York Times, November 21, 1886.

176 "And so Garfield is really dead": Julia Sand to Chester Arthur, September 28,
1881, Chester Alan Arthur Papers, Library of Congress.

177 Captain Sand seized the flag: Sand and McLaughlin (eds.), *Crossing Antietam:
The Civil War Letters of Captain Henry Augustus Sand, Company A, 103rd
New York Volunteers*, 136.

177 "You are a better & a nobler man": Julia Sand to Chester Arthur, September
28, 1881, Chester Alan Arthur Papers, Library of Congress.

177 "His conduct during the trying period": "President Arthur," *New York Times*,
September 21, 1881.

177 "It is not the time to recall past mistakes": Ibid.

178 "If he is to prove equal to the great position he occupies": Ibid.

178 "the loyal and powerful allegiance": "President Arthur," *New York Tribune*,
September 20, 1881.

178 "He can disarm the public distrust": "President Arthur," *New York Times*,
September 21, 1881.

178 "that air of one whose defeat has been changed": "The Conference at Utica,"
New York Times, October 1, 1881.

179 "Everything is at sea about Arthur": Cortissoz, *Life of Whitelaw Reid*, vol. 2, 76.

179 newspapers noted the stream of Stalwarts: "The President's Plans," *New York
Times*, October 1, 1881.

179 wanted to replace his hated rival Blaine: Crowley, *Echoes from Niagara*, 227.

179 "Let President Arthur show a disposition": "The President Warned," *New York
Times*, October 1, 1881.

179 "Well, you have gone": Julia Sand to Chester Arthur, October 5, 1881, Chester Alan Arthur Papers, Library of Congress.

181 Conkling sat down with President Arthur: "The President and Ex-Senator
Conkling," (Washington) *Evening Critic*, October 8, 1881; "Is Gen. Arthur
President?" *New York Sun*, October 10, 1881.

181 To Conkling, Arthur's obligation: Neither Arthur nor Conkling wrote about
their confrontation, so there is no firsthand account of their meeting. However, their respective attitudes are detailed in Crowley, *Echoes from Niagara*,
231; Hudson, *Random Recollections of an Old Political Reporter*, 125–127;
Lang, *Autobiography of Thomas Collier Platt*, 180; and White, *Autobiography
of Andrew Dickson White*, vol. 1, 193–194.

182 "morally bound to continue the policy": Lang, *Autobiography of Thomas Collier Platt*, 180.

182   "morally nor politically nor any other way": Ibid.
182   "The president is right": Hudson, *Random Recollections of an Old Political Reporter,* 126.
182   "For the vice presidency I was indebted": White, *Autobiography of Andrew Dickson White,* vol. 1, 194.

Chapter Seventeen: "A Splendid Henry V"

183   a poster memorializing America's murdered president: Hoogenboom, *Outlawing the Spoils,* 213.
183   "patronage had corrupted": "Public Opinion and Reform," *New York Times,* September 29, 1881.
183   civil service reform groups sprang up: Editorial, *New York Times,* October 26, 1881.
183   The shuffling of cabinet positions: "Public Opinion and Reform," *New York Times,* September 29, 1881.
184   "Where did the public good enter": Adams, *Democracy: An American Novel,* 131.
184   "Our friend MacVeagh": Henry Adams to Henry Cabot Lodge, November 15, 1881, in Ford (ed.), *Letters of Henry Adams 1858–1891,* 331.
184   "come and see how things are": Ibid., 332.
184   "What a splendid Henry V": Julia Sand to Chester Arthur, October 27, 1881, Chester Alan Arthur Papers, Library of Congress.
185   "say all the unpleasant things I choose": Ibid.
185   "Do not let the people believe": Ibid.
185   Sometimes she languished: Julia Sand to Chester Arthur, November 8, 1881, Chester Alan Arthur Papers, Library of Congress.
185   she burned with the idea: Ibid.
185   "had an idea, if I could see your face": Ibid.
185   "I thought of the pleasure of my mother": Ibid.
186   "I am quite aware": Ibid.
186   "no man should be the incumbent of an office": Richardson (ed.), *A Compilation of the Messages and Papers of the Presidents, 1789–1902,* vol. 8, 60–63.
187   "Hitherto the Stalwarts": "The Week," *Nation,* vol. 33, December 8, 1881, 441.
187   Pendleton was an unlikely champion: Hoogenboom, *Outlawing the Spoils,* 200.
187   "framed after much consideration": George Hunt Pendleton to Silas Burt, December 22, 1880, quoted in ibid., 200.
188   "The fact is patent": "Both Houses in Session," *New York Times,* December 14, 1881.
188   Civil service reform groups from around the country: Hoogenboom, *Outlawing the Spoils,* 223.
188   "The vital question before the country": Julia Sand to Chester Arthur, January 7, 1882, Chester Alan Arthur Papers, Library of Congress.
188   "Evasion in any form": Ibid.

188 Her own Christmas: Ibid. In the same letter, Sand goes on to describe her daydream in minute detail.

189 "Perhaps only you and I know": Kate Chase Sprague to Chester Arthur, October 21, 1881, Chester Alan Arthur Papers, Library of Congress.

189 "Better for Conkling": Quoted in "The Nomination of Conkling," *New York Times*, March 4, 1882.

190 But Congress as a whole: Hoogenboom, *Outlawing the Spoils,* 223–224.

190 Arthur mourned his predecessor: Poore, *Perley's Reminiscences,* vol. 2, 452.

190 It was a stripped down affair: "A White House Reception," *New York Times*, January 3, 1882.

190 24 wagonloads of furniture: Singleton, *The Story of the White House,* vol. 2, 179–180.

190 Arthur took a keen interest in it: Rood (ed.), *Memories of the White House: The Home Life of Our Presidents from Lincoln to Roosevelt, Being Personal Recollections of Col. W. H. Crook,* 159–160; Gerry, *Through Five Administrations,* 275.

190 Many parts of the mansion: "New White House Decorations," *New York Times*, December 20, 1882; "The White House," *New York Herald*, October 2, 1883; Smalley, "The White House," *Century Magazine*, vol. 27 (April 1884), 806–815.

191 Even James Blaine's wife: "A Banquet at the White House, *New York Times*, March 9, 1882; Beale (ed.), *Letters of Mrs. James G. Blaine,* vol. 2, 4–5.

191 petite, with dark hair and eyes: Reeves, *Gentleman Boss,* 269.

191 "and the gay girls": Quoted in ibid.

191 "He wanted the best of everything": Rood, *Memories of the White House,* 163.

191 took great pride in wearing the finest clothes: Reeves, *Gentleman Boss,* 271; Rood, *Memories of the White House,* 163.

192 "It is not that he is handsome": Reeves, *Gentleman Boss,* 272.

192 Arthur hosted his first formal White House event: "Festivities at the White House," *New York Times*, March 23, 1882; Poore, *Perley's Reminiscences,* vol. 2, 459–462.

192 "did much to add to the gayety": Rood, *Memories of the White House,* 161–162.

193 "at a late hour there was a regular romp": Austin Snead to Rutherford B. Hayes, May 11, 1883, quoted in Reeves, *Gentleman Boss,* 275–276.

193 Alan and the crown prince of Siam got drunk: Reeves interview with Chester A. Arthur III, July 26, 1969, cited in Reeves, *Gentleman Boss,* 475.

193 "When you go into his office in the morning": Quoted in Reeves, *Gentleman Boss,* 273–274.

193 "sick in body and soul": Quoted in ibid., 274.

193 He usually rose at about 9:30 a.m.: These details of Arthur's daily life in the White House come from Poore, *Perley's Reminiscences,* vol. 2, 453; and Rood, *Memories of the White House,* 162–164.

193 Especially aggressive office-seekers: Reeves, *Gentleman Boss,* 274.

194 he had to shake hands: "Reception at the White House," *New York Times,* January 31, 1883; "The President's Public Levee, *New York Times*, February 6, 1884.

194 he could not disconnect from his workday worries: Reeves, *Gentleman Boss,* 274.

194   "I have sat up with him until midnight": "Giving Voice to Sorrow," *New York Times*, November 21, 1886.

194   "Our good king Arthur was there": Thoron, *First of Hearts: Selected Letters of Mrs. Henry Adams*, 128.

194   "Do you remember any other President": Julia Sand to Chester Arthur, January 7, 1882, Chester Alan Arthur Papers, Library of Congress.

195   the disclosure of the mystery lady's identity: Gerry, *Through Five Administrations*, 275–276.

Chapter Eighteen: A Surprise Visit

197   clutching the smooth leather: Julia Sand to Chester Arthur, April (*no day*), 1882, Chester Alan Arthur Papers, Library of Congress.

197   a hundred mineral springs: Dearborn, *Saratoga and How to See It*, 47.

197   Saratoga's races and regattas: Saratoga and its characters during this period are described in Sterngass, *First Resorts: Pursuing Pleasure at Saratoga Springs, Newport & Coney Island,* 157–159, 180–181; Gollner, *Gollner's Pocket Guide of Saratoga Springs,* 16–17, 42–43; Fields, *Lillian Russell: A Biography of "America's Beauty,"* 107; and Holmes and Stonequist, *Saratoga Springs: A Historical Portrait,* 107.

198   "a step back into barbarism": Julia Sand to Chester Arthur, March (*no day*) 1882, Chester Alan Arthur Papers, Library of Congress.

198   "A congress of ignorant school boys": Ibid.

198   he sent a long and forceful veto message: Richardson, *Messages and Papers of the Presidents*, vol. 8, 112–118; "The President's Veto," *New York Times*, April 5, 1882.

199   "firmness and wisdom": "The President's Veto," *New York Times*, April 5, 1882.

199   "I must tell you that your veto": Julia Sand to Chester Arthur, April (*no day*) 1882, Chester Alan Arthur Papers, Library of Congress.

199   "What is there to admire in mediocrity?": Julia Sand to Chester Arthur, May (*no day*) 1882, Chester Alan Arthur Papers, Library of Congress.

200   "This Congress is voting millions into the air": "Use the Veto," *New York Sun*, July 14, 1882.

200   "a monstrous swindle": "The River and Harbor Job," *New York Times*, July 27, 1882.

200   Every morning and evening she checked: Julia Sand to Chester Arthur, August 2, 1882, Chester Alan Arthur Papers, Library of Congress.

200   her brother Theodore: Ibid.

200   "For a woman to weep over the veto": Ibid.

200   "Well, have you not five minutes": Julia Sand to Chester Arthur, August 15, 1882, Chester Alan Arthur Papers, Library of Congress.

201   "the few harsh things": Julia Sand to Chester Arthur, August 19, 1882, Chester Alan Arthur Papers, Library of Congress.

201   two men in claret livery: Reeves, "President's Dwarf," 83.

201   Julia was sprawled on the lounge: Julia Sand recalls Arthur's visit in great detail in letters she wrote to him on August 24, 1882; August 28, 1882; October

9, 1882; and December 29, 1882. All are included in the Chester Alan Arthur Papers at the Library of Congress.

203 "The Presidency puts a man terribly to the test": Julia Sand to Chester Arthur, August 24, 1882, Chester Alan Arthur Papers, Library of Congress.

204 "I have made one little visit out of town": Julia Sand to Chester Arthur, September 13, 1882, Chester Alan Arthur Papers, Library of Congress.

204 Sometimes she sat in the same armchair: Julia Sand to Chester Arthur, August 28, 1882, Chester Alan Arthur Papers, Library of Congress.

204 she thought she spied a familiar figure: Julia Sand to Chester Arthur, September 13, 1882, Chester Alan Arthur Papers, Library of Congress.

204 "just as rampant as he ever was": Quoted in Reeves, *Gentleman Boss*, 313–314.

204 "that lizard on the hill": "Folger's Ardent Friends," *New York Times*, April 3, 1882.

205 "The old machine that Arthur brought up by hand": "Dry Rot," *Cincinnati Enquirer*, June 1, 1882.

205 "Administration men" were plotting: "The New-York Governorship," *New York Times*, June 15, 1882; "The Coming Governor," *New York Times*, July 19, 1882; "Governor Cornell and His Traducers," *New York Times*, August 26, 1882.

205 "was procured by the combined power": "Mr. Curtis's Emphatic Protest," *New York Times*, October 4, 1882.

205 "I felt that you were doing things": Julia Sand to Chester Arthur, October 9, 1882, Chester Alan Arthur Papers, Library of Congress.

205 "You know I do not wish to do you injustice": Ibid.

206 "The Republican Party's message": Editorial, *New York Times*, November 8, 1882.

206 "Had you remained at your post of duty": Julia Sand to Chester Arthur, November 8, 1882, Chester Alan Arthur Papers, Library of Congress.

206 "Never has the popular feeling": "The November Elections," *Nation,* vol. 35, November 16, 1882, 416.

206 "The people of the country": Richardson, *Messages and Papers of the Presidents*, vol. 8, 145–147.

207 "It may safely be said": "The Message and Documents," *New York Times*, December 5, 1882.

207 "We are not legislating on this subject": Quoted in Hoogenboom, *Outlawing the Spoils*, 251.

207 "something tricky in [his] nature": Julia Sand to Chester Arthur, December 29, 1882, Chester Alan Arthur Papers, Library of Congress.

207 "Do you know how the people regard your Message?": Ibid.

Chapter Nineteen: An Attack in Savannah

209 only 52 ramshackle ships: This description of the state of the US Navy when Arthur took office, including the quotation from the British journal, comes from Reeves, *Gentleman Boss*, 337–339.

209 "We must be ready to defend our harbors": Richardson, *Messages and Papers of the Presidents*, vol. 8, 51–52.

210   The morning after the 1876 election: "Of Politics and William Chandler," *New York Times*, January 26, 1941; "Wm. E. Chandler, Ex-Senator, Dead," *New York Times*, December 1, 1917.

210   "I think that I did my best work": Quoted in Reeves, *Gentleman Boss*, 342.

211   "I have been so ill since the adjournment": Chester Arthur to Alan Arthur, March 11, 1883, Chester Alan Arthur Papers, Library of Congress.

211   his landau was painted a mellow green: "The President's Carriage," *New York Times*, December 20, 1881.

211   The president climbed out looking healthier: "The President's Journey," *New York Times*, April 6, 1883.

211   the rotund French cook: Ibid.

211   Arthur exchanged his high silk hat: Ibid.

211   a punctilious conductor: "The President Off for Florida," *New York Tribune*, April 6, 1883.

212   Arthur sat astride a camp stool: This episode is described in "The President in Florida," *New York Times*, April 7, 1883; and "The President's Jaunt," *New York Sun*, April 13, 1883.

212   the president emerged from the train: "The President in Florida," *New York Times*, April 13, 1883.

212   Chandler's face was darkened: Ibid.

212   "I have poot on tree shirt": Ibid.

212   Several military companies: Ibid.; "The President's Jaunt," *New York Sun*, April 13, 1883.

212   Arthur lit a cigar and stood on deck: "The President's Jaunt," *New York Sun*, April 13, 1883.

212   cypress trees draped with gray moss: "The President in Florida," *New York Times*, April 13, 1883.

213   a young African American man named Jackson: Ibid.

213   Chandler threw off his coat and climbed a tree: Ibid.

213   a black musician strummed a banjo: Ibid.

213   Fred Phillips shot an alligator: "The President's Vacation," *New York Times*, April 11, 1883.

213   met Tom Tigertail, a Seminole chief: "An Incident of the Trip," *New York Sun*, April 22, 1883.

214   the president's cheeks were "burned to blisters": "Great Sport in Florida," *New York Sun*, April 14, 1883.

214   the *Tallapoosa* was rolling in heavy seas: "President Arthur at Sea," *New York Times*, April 20, 1883.

214   the queasy passengers were in high spirits: Ibid.

214   he toured Savannah in an open carriage: "The President Taken Ill," *New York Times*, April 21, 1883.

214   Arthur bolted awake: This account of Arthur's illness on board the *Tallapoosa* comes from ibid.; "Sick in the Tallapoosa," *New York Sun*, April 21, 1883; and "Story of a Presidential Tragedy That the Nation Narrowly Escaped," *Pittsburgh Gazette-Times*, January 12, 1911.

215 his illness had become public knowledge: "The President's Illness," *New York Times*, April 22, 1883.

215 Arthur sat moodily: "The President Still Sick," *New York Tribune*, April 22, 1883.

215 The president stepped out: "The President at Home," *New York Times*, April 23, 1883.

215 "How are you feeling?": "The President in Washington," *New York Tribune*, April 23, 1883.

216 "The president's slight indisposition": Ibid.

216 he accepted them with only minor modifications: "The Civil Service Rules," *New York Times*, May 8, 1883.

216 "his desire to give the reform system fair play": Norton, *Orations and Addresses of George William Curtis*, vol. 2, 236.

217 "The president's steady refusal": Ibid., 237.

217 "We regard Arthur as our leader": "Bee," *Cincinnati Enquirer*, November 22, 1883.

217 "I tell you it is pretty hard": "Gath," *Cincinnati Enquirer*, September 2, 1883.

217 "no one who had ever arisen to great power": Crowley, *Echoes from Niagara*, 227.

218 "The condition of the forests of the country": Richardson, *Messages and Papers of the Presidents*, vol. 8, 144–145.

218 Sheridan believed Arthur would be an even stronger ally: Reeves, "President Arthur in Yellowstone National Park," *Montana, the Magazine of Western History*, vol. 9 (Summer 1969), 18–19.

218 "the hospitality of the Southern people": "The President," *Chicago Tribune*, August 3, 1883.

218 Arthur's locomotive was decorated: Ibid.

218 a policeman with a tin star: Ibid.

218 a young African American boy: Ibid.

219 "I can hardly imagine": Quoted in Reeves, *Gentleman Boss*, 369.

219 Arthur was taken aback: "The President," *Chicago Tribune*, August 3, 1883.

219 "have a good time and get away": "The Passing of Arthur," (Chicago) *Daily Inter Ocean*, September 5, 1883.

219 He and his companions rose at 5 a.m.: These details of Arthur's Yellowstone trip come from Reeves, *Gentleman Boss*, 366–367.

219 "better than anything I ever tried before": "The Passing of Arthur," (Chicago) *Daily Inter Ocean*, September 5, 1883.

219 "Whether it was the intention of the managers or not": "Arthur and Logan for '84," *New York Times*, September 6, 1883.

220 Arthur's handlers and local supporters: "Booming Arthur in Chicago," *New York Times*, September 4, 1883.

220 "submitted to the pump-handle operation": "Arthur and Logan for '84," *New York Times*, September 6, 1883.

220 "I know you will excuse me for not talking to you": "A Popular President," (Chicago) *Daily Inter Ocean*, September 6, 1883.

220 he sent an urgent summons to his personal physician: "Twice Critically Ill," *New York Times*, December 13, 1886.

Chapter Twenty: "Between Two Stools"

221 "My very bad friend": Julia Sand to Chester Arthur, September 15, 1883, Chester Alan Arthur Papers, Library of Congress.

222 "In the temper which the people have now reached": "Civil Rights Cases Decided," *New York Times*, October 16, 1884.

223 Even a progressive bastion like the *Nation*: "The End of the Civil Rights Bill," *Nation,* vol. 37, October 18, 1883, 326.

223 "would not entail any hardship upon the colored people": "The Civil Rights Decision," *New York Times*, October 16, 1883.

223 "The cause which has brought us here to-night": Proceedings of the Civil Rights Mass-Meeting Held at Lincoln Hall, October 22, 1883, Frederick Douglass Papers, Library of Congress.

224 "free speech, free education, free suffrage": Quoted in Reeves, *Gentleman Boss*, 311.

224 he forcefully called on Congress: Richardson, *Messages and Papers of the Presidents*, vol. 8, 188.

224 "knew perfectly well when he took up his pen": "Anecdotes of Mr. Arthur," *New York Sun*, November 28, 1886.

225 "fewer positively hearty friends": Ulysses S. Grant to Adam Badeau, April 8, 1884, quoted in Badeau, *Grant in Peace: From Appomattox to Mount McGregor*, 559.

225 "has sought to conciliate the bosses": "The Boom Candidates," *Nation,* vol. 38, April 17, 1884, 334–335.

225 Blaine and Arthur remained cordial: Reeves, *Gentleman Boss*, 369.

225 "All his ambition seems to center in the social aspect": Beale, *Letters of Mrs. James G. Blaine*, vol. 2, 8.

225 "Nobody has forgotten the pregnant fact": "Wayne MacVeagh Speaks," *New York Times*, May 20, 1884.

226 "One thing is certain": "Dorsey Discourses," *Rocky Mountain News*, January 20, 1884, quoted in Reeves, *Gentleman Boss*, 370.

226 Arthur asked Chandler to remain behind: This account comes from "Anecdotes of Mr. Arthur," *New York Sun*, November 28, 1886; and "How Arthur Helped to Defeat Himself at the Republican National Convention," *Pittsburgh Post-Gazette*, May 25, 1910.

227 Nearly two years before: "President Arthur's Health," *New York Herald*, October 21, 1882; "Dead Among His Kindred," *New York Times*, November 19, 1886; "Chester Arthur Dead," *New York Sun*, November 19, 1886; "Twice Critically Ill," *New York Times*, December 13, 1886; "Story of a Presidential Tragedy That the Nation Narrowly Escaped," *Pittsburgh Gazette-Times*, January 12, 1911.

227 The president also disclosed his illness: "Story of a Presidential Tragedy That the Nation Narrowly Escaped," *Pittsburgh Gazette-Times*, January 12, 1911.

227 "He could not bear to have his friends or the public know": "Dead Among His Kindred," *New York Times*, November 19, 1886.

227 he refused to trade the postmaster general's portfolio: "Anecdotes of Mr. Arthur," *New York Sun*, November 28, 1886.

227 "the delegates hung around their headquarters": Ibid.

228 "a slight, almost boyish" New York state assemblyman: Roosevelt's speech at the convention is described in "The Convention's First Work," *New York Times*, June 4, 1884.

228 "This is no time to discuss such matters": "Anecdotes of Mr. Arthur," *New York Sun*, November 28, 1886.

228 Every square foot of the hall was crammed: The scene in the hall and the roll call of the states is described in "The Presentation Speeches," *New York Times*, June 6, 1884.

229 "extemporaneous from necessity": Martin Townsend to Chester Arthur, June 13, 1884, Chester Alan Arthur Papers, Library of Congress.

229 rambled on about the virtues of the Bible: "The Presentation Speeches," *New York Times*, June 6, 1884.

229 "preserved an even temper and yielded to the inevitable": "The News in Washington," *New York Times*, June 7, 1884.

229 he ordered his carriage and disappeared: Ibid.

229 "I know now many of the inside details": "How Arthur Helped to Defeat Himself at the Republican National Convention," *Pittsburgh Post-Gazette*, May 25, 1910.

230 On a beautiful summer afternoon: This encounter is described in "Anecdotes of Mr. Arthur," *New York Sun*, November 28, 1886.

Chapter Twenty-One: "Fame Is a Bubble"

231 "I don't engage in criminal practice": Quoted in Reeves, *Gentleman Boss*, 388.

231 Arthur hosted his last public reception: "The President's Guests," *New York Times*, February 22, 1885.

232 both wore black broadcloth suits: "Cleveland Sworn In," *New York Sun*, March 5, 1885.

232 Squinting in the brightness: Ibid.

232 Cleveland smoothed his thinning hair: "The Inaugural Address," *New York Times*, March 5, 1885.

232 Nellie scooped up her Skye terrier: "The Events of President Arthur's Last Day at the White House," *New York Sun*, March 5, 1885.

233 His health continued to deteriorate: Reeves, *Gentleman Boss*, 416–417.

233 he went to Princeton: "Mr. Brewster's Tribute," *New York Times*, November 19, 1886.

233 he took his son to Canada: "Gen. Arthur Gone Fishing," *New York Times*, June 26, 1885.

233 Grace sent a telegram: "The Dead General," *New York Tribune*, July 25, 1885.

233 a giant oak tree that had been struck by lightning: "Grave of General Grant," *New York Times*, February 21, 1897.

233 dozens of New York's most distinguished citizens: "A Monument for the Dead Hero," *New York Tribune*, July 25, 1885.

233 24 black horses: Kahn, "General Grant National Memorial Historical Resource Study," January 1980, 25.

233 five hours to pass by: "Pictures in the Line of March," *New York Times*, August 9, 1885.

233 Grant's death had united Americans in their grief: "The Hero's Pallbearers," *New York Times*, July 31, 1885; "The Universal Tribute," *New York Times*, August 8, 1885; "A Nation at a Tomb," *New York Times*, August 9, 1885; "The Hero Laid to Rest," *New York Sun*, August 9, 1885.

234 the Western Union Telegraph Company had pitched in: "Monument Subscriptions," *New York Times*, July 30, 1885.

234 Drexel, Morgan and Company topped the list: "Money Coming in Faster," *New York Times*, August 4, 1885.

234 "Two Yankee Women": "Subscriptions Coming In," *New York Times*, August 2, 1885; Kahn, "General Grant National Memorial," 30.

234 "A German Who Gives Up His Beer": Kahn, "General Grant National Memorial," 30.

234 "A Poor Soldier's Orphan": Ibid.

234 Many Americans objected: Ibid., 33–35.

234 he attended a reception hosted by Caroline Astor: "Newport at Its Best," *New York Times*, August 23, 1885.

234 "had carte blanche for the occasion": Ibid.

234 Arthur dined at the home of William Waldorf Astor: "Social Pleasures at Newport," *New York Times*, August 28, 1885.

234 newspapers noted his presence at a little cigar store: "Their Ballots Rejected," *New York Times*, November 4, 1885.

235 a dinner to raise money for the pedestal: "What Met Bartholdi's Gaze," *New York Times*, November 22, 1885.

235 the honorary guest of the New York Farmers: "The New-York Farmers," *New York Times*, December 20, 1885.

235 the retirement ceremony of the chief justice: "Justice Daly Honored," *New York Times*, December 31, 1885.

235 "in so desperate a condition": "Mr. Arthur's Condition," *New York Times*, April 24, 1886.

235 "my progress in recovering my health": Chester Arthur to Walter Q. Gresham, August (*no day*) 1886, Walter Quintin Gresham Papers, Library of Congress.

235 In New London the ex-president had time to reflect: Reeves, *Gentleman Boss*, 418.

235 He advised Alan not to follow the same path: Chester A. Arthur III to Carey McWilliams, October 22, 1946, Arthur Family Papers, Library of Congress.

235 he lived the life of an invalid: "Chester A. Arthur Dead," *New York Sun*, November 19, 1886.

235 Arthur decided to destroy the evidence: Reeves, *Gentleman Boss*, 417–418; Library of Congress, *Index to the Chester A. Arthur Papers* (Washington, 1961);

Chester Alan Arthur III to Thomas C. Reeves, January 17, 1970, Thomas C. Reeves Papers, Library of Congress; Charles Pinkerton to Thomas C. Reeves, April 14, 1970, Thomas C. Reeves Papers, Library of Congress.

236 Arthur awoke in good spirits: These details of Arthur's last hours come from "Chester A. Arthur Dead," *New York Sun*, November 19, 1886; "Dead among His Kindred," *New York Times*, November 19, 1886; and "Ex-President Arthur Dead," *New York Tribune*, November 19, 1886.

236 the shutters at 123 Lexington Avenue were closed: The scene at Arthur's home on the day of his funeral is described in "Buried Near His Wife," *New York Sun*, November 23, 1886.

237 Thirty policemen preceded the hearse: These details of the funeral procession and the service in the Church of the Heavenly Rest come from "Buried Near His Wife," *New York Sun*, November 23, 1886; and "Arthur's Funeral," *The Two Hundred and Forty Ninth Annual Record of the Ancient and Honorable Artillery Co. Massachusetts 1886–87*, 23–29.

237 an "infinitesimal" crowd: "Arthur's Funeral," *The Two Hundred and Forty Ninth Annual Record of the Ancient and Honorable Artillery Co. Massachusetts 1886–87*, 23.

237 It took a little more than three hours: Ibid., 31–34.

237 "The conspicuous public office which Chester A. Arthur attained": "Chester A. Arthur," *New York Times*, November 19, 1886.

238 "It is not too much to say": Editorial, *New York Sun*, November 19, 1886.

238 But Arthur had no illusions: This encounter is described in "Anecdotes of Mr. Arthur," *New York Sun*, November 28, 1886.

Epilogue

239 The storm of the century: These details of the historic storm come from "Blizzard Was King," *New York Sun*, March 13, 1888.

239 Undaunted by the weather: Jordan, *Roscoe Conkling*, 427.

239 "It was dark, and it was useless": Conkling's account of his adventure appeared in "Roscoe Conkling Nearly Dead," *New York Sun*, March 14, 1888.

240 He ignored his doctor's recommendation: "Roscoe Conkling Dead," *New York Times*, April 18, 1888.

240 "the name of Roscoe Conkling is one": "Mr. Conkling's Career," *New York Times*, April 18, 1888.

240 several hundred people waited: The unveiling of the Arthur statue, and Elihu Root's remarks at the event, are detailed in "Arthur Statue Unveiled," *New York Times*, June 14, 1899; "Arthur Statue Unveiled," *New York Sun*, June 14, 1899; and "Arthur Statue Unveiled," *New York Tribune*, June 14, 1899.

242 When President Arthur's son Alan died: The story of how Julia Sand's letters came to light is recounted in Reeves, "President's Dwarf," 82–83.

Bibliography

Manuscript Sources

Arthur Family Papers, Library of Congress, Manuscript Division

Charles J. Guiteau Collection, Booth Family Center for Special Collections, Georgetown University Libraries

Chester Alan Arthur Papers, Library of Congress, Manuscript Division

The Diary of Horatio Nelson Taft, 1861–1865, Library of Congress, Manuscript Division

Frederick Douglass Papers, Library of Congress, Manuscript Division

James A. Garfield Papers, Library of Congress, Manuscript Division

James B. Butler Papers, New York Public Library, Manuscripts and Archives Division

John Sherman Papers, Library of Congress, Manuscript Division

Kansas Memory, Kansas Historical Society

The Rutherford B. Hayes and Hayes Family Papers, Rutherford B. Hayes Presidential Libraries and Museums

Shapell Manuscript Foundation

Silas A. Burt Papers, New York Public Library, Manuscripts and Archives Division

Territorial Kansas Online, Kansas Historical Society

Thomas C. Reeves Papers, Library of Congress, Manuscript Division

Walter Quintin Gresham Papers, Library of Congress, Manuscript Division

White House Historical Association

Select Bibliography

Ackerman, Kenneth D. *Dark Horse: The Surprise Election and Political Murder of President James A. Garfield*. Falls Church, VA: Viral History Press, 2011.

Adams, Henry. *Democracy: An American Novel*. London: Macmillan and Company, 1882.

Alcott, Louisa May. *Hospital Sketches*. Boston: James Redpath, 1863.

Alexander, DeAlva Stanwood. *A Political History of the State of New York,* Vol. 3, *1861–1882*. New York: Henry Holt and Company, 1909.

Anthony, Carl Sferrazza. *First Ladies: The Saga of the Presidents' Wives and Their Power, 1789–1961*. New York: William Morrow and Company, Inc., 1990.

Badeau, Adam. *Grant in Peace: From Appomattox to Mount McGregor*. Hartford, CT: S. S. Scranton & Co., 1887.

Balch, William Ralston. *Life of James A. Garfield: Late President of the United States*. Philadelphia: J. C. McCurdy and Co., 1881.

Bancroft, Frederic, ed. *Speeches, Correspondence and Political Papers of Carl Schurz*. 6 vols. New York: G. P. Putnam's Sons, 1913.

Barile, Kerri S., and Barbara P. Willis, eds. *A Woman in a War-Torn Town: The Journal of Jane Howison Beale, Fredericksburg, Virginia, 1850–1862*. Virginia Beach, VA: The Donning Company Publishers, 1979.

Barnum, P. T. *Struggles and Triumphs, or Forty Years' Recollections of P. T. Barnum*. Buffalo: Warren, Johnson & Co., 1872.

Barry, David S. *Forty Years in Washington*. Boston: Little, Brown and Company, 1924.

Beale, Harriet S. Blaine, ed. *Letters of Mrs. James G. Blaine,* 2 vols. New York: Duffield and Company, 1908.

Bliss, D. W. "The Story of President Garfield's Illness, Told by the Physician in Charge." *Century Illustrated Monthly Magazine*, vol. 23 (November 1881–April 1882): 299–305.

Bronner, Frederick Lidell. "Arthur, His College Years." *Chester Alan Arthur Class of 1848*. Schenectady, NY: Union College Press, 1948.

Brown, George Rothwell, ed. *Reminiscences of Senator William M. Stewart of Nevada*. New York: The Neale Publishing Company, 1908.

Broxmeyer, Jeffrey D. "Politics as a Sphere of Wealth Accumulation: Cases of Gilded Age New York, 1855–1888." CUNY Academic Works, 2014.

Brummer, Sidney D. "Political History of New York State during the Period of the Civil War." PhD diss., Columbia University, 1911.

Bumgarner, John R. *The Health of the Presidents: The 41 United States Presidents through 1993 from a Physician's Point of View*. Jefferson, NC: McFarland & Company, Inc., Publishers, 1994.

Burrows, Edwin G., and Mike Wallace. *Gotham: A History of New York City to 1898*. New York: Oxford University Press, 1999.

Burt, Silas W. *My Memories of the Military History of New York State during the War for the Union, 1861–65*. Albany, NY: J. B. Lyon Company, 1902.

Burton, Theodore E. *John Sherman*. Boston: Houghton Mifflin Company, 1906.

Callow, Alexander B., Jr. *The Tweed Ring*. London: Oxford University Press, 1965.

Carton, Evan. *Patriotic Treason: John Brown and the Soul of America*. New York: Simon and Schuster, 2006.

Cary, Edward. *George William Curtis*. Boston: Houghton, Mifflin and Company, 1895.

Chidsey, Donald Barr. *The Gentleman from New York: A Life of Roscoe Conkling*. New Haven, CT: Yale University Press, 1935.

Civil War Extra, Vol. 1, *A Newspaper History of the Civil War from Nat Turner to 1863*. Edison, NJ: Castle Books, 1999.

Clancy, Herbert J. *The Presidential Election of 1880*. Chicago: S. J. Loyola University Press, 1958.

Coffin, Charles Carleton. *The Life of James A. Garfield with a Sketch of the Life of Chester A. Arthur*. Boston: James A. Earle, 1880.

Colman, Edna M. *White House Gossip, from Andrew Johnson to Calvin Coolidge*. Garden City, NY: Doubleday, Page & Co., 1927.

Commissions to Examine Certain Custom-Houses of the United States. House Executive Document No. 8, 45th Congress, 1st Session, 1877–1878.

A Complete History of the Life and Trial of Charles Julius Guiteau, Assassin of President Garfield. Philadelphia: Hubbard Brothers, 1882.

Conkling, Alfred R. *The Life and Letters of Roscoe Conkling*. New York: Charles L. Webster & Co., 1889.

Connery, T. B. "Secret History of the Garfield-Conkling Tragedy." *Cosmopolitan Magazine*, vol. 23 (June 1897): 145–162.

Cortissoz, Royal. *The Life of Whitelaw Reid*, Vol. 2, *Politics—Diplomacy*. London: Thornton Butterworth Limited, 1921.

Crapsey, Edward. *The Nether Side of New York*. New York: Sheldon & Company, 1872.

Crowley, Julia. *Echoes from Niagara: Historical, Political, Personal*. Buffalo, NY: Charles Wells Moulton, 1890.

Cutler, William G. *History of the State of Kansas* (Franklin County, Part 3). Chicago: A. T. Andreas, 1883.

Dearborn, R. F. *Saratoga and How to See It*. Saratoga, NY: R. F. Dearborn, 1871.

Depew, Chauncey M. *My Memories of Eighty Years*. New York: Charles Scribner's Sons, 1921.

Dewey, Orville. *Letters of an English Traveller to His Friend in England on the "Revivals of Religion" in America*. Boston: Bowles and Dearborn, 1828.

Dickens, Charles. *American Notes*. New York: John W. Lovell Company, 1883.

Documents of the Assembly of the State of New York. Eighty-Fifth Session, 1862, Vol. 7. Albany: Charles Van Benthuysen, 1862.

Dreiser, Theodore. *Sister Carrie*. New York: Doubleday, Page, 1900.

Ewen, William H., Jr. *Steamboats on the Hudson River*. Charleston, SC: Arcadia Publishing, 2011.

Faust, Drew Gilpin. *This Republic of Suffering: Death and the American Civil War*. New York: Random House, 2008.

Fields, Armond. *Lillian Russell: A Biography of "America's Beauty."* Jefferson, NC: McFarland & Company, Inc., 1999.

Ford, Worthington Chauncey, ed. *Letters of Henry Adams 1858–1891*. Cambridge: Riverside Press, 1930.

The Gentleman's Directory 1870, n.p., copy held by the New-York Historical Society.

Gerry, Margarita Spalding, ed. *Through Five Administrations: Reminiscences of Colonel William H. Crook, Bodyguard to President Lincoln*. New York: Harper & Brothers Publishers, 1910.

Gilfoyle, Timothy J. *City of Eros: New York City, Prostitution and the Commercialization of Sex 1790–1920*. New York: W. W. Norton and Company, 1992.

Gollner, E. G. *Gollner's Pocket Guide of Saratoga Springs*. Trenton: W. S. Sharp, 1881.

Grant, Ulysses S. *Memoirs of U. S. Grant*, Vol. 1. Charles Webster and Co., 1894.

Guiteau's Confession. Philadelphia: The Old Franklin Publishing House, 1881.

Herndon, William Lewis. *Exploration of the Valley of the Amazon, 1851–1852*, Part 1. Washington, DC: Robert Armstrong, Public Printer, 1853.

Hesseltine, William B. *Ulysses S. Grant, Politician*. New York: Dodd, Mead and Co., 1935.

Hinman, Arthur P. *How a British Subject Became President of the United States*. New York: n.p., 1884.

Hoar, George F. *Autobiography of Seventy Years*, 2 vols. New York: Charles Scribner's Sons, 1906.

Holmes, Timothy A., and Martha Stonequist. *Saratoga Springs: A Historical Portrait*. Charleston, SC: Arcadia Publishing, 2000.

Holzer, Harold. *Lincoln President-Elect: Abraham Lincoln and the Great Secession Winter 1860–1861*. New York: Simon and Schuster, 2008.

Hoogenboom, Ari. *Outlawing the Spoils: A History of the Civil Service Reform Movement, 1865–1883*. Urbana: University of Illinois Press, 1968.

Howe, George F. *Chester A. Arthur: A Quarter-Century of Machine Politics*. New York: Dodd, Meade and Company, 1934.

Howells, William Dean. *A Hazard of New Fortunes*. New York: Harper and Bros., 1890.

———. *Sketch of the Life and Character of Rutherford B. Hayes*. New York: Hurd and Houghton, 1876.

Hudson, William C. *Random Recollections of an Old Political Reporter*. New York: Cupples & Leon, 1911.

Jay, John. "Civil-Service Reform." *North American Review*, vol. 127 (1878): 273–287.

Jordan, David M. *Roscoe Conkling of New York: Voice in the Senate*. Ithaca: Cornell University Press, 1971.

Kahn, David M. "General Grant National Memorial Historical Resource Study." January 1980.

Kinder, Gary. *Ship of Gold in the Deep Blue Sea*. New York: Grove Press, 1998.

Kirkland, Frazar. *The Pictorial Book of Anecdotes of the Rebellion*. Hillsdale, MI: W. E. Allen & Co., 1887.

Lang, Louis J., ed. *The Autobiography of Thomas Collier Platt*. New York: B. W. Dodge and Co., 1910.

Lears, Jackson. *Rebirth of a Nation: The Making of Modern America, 1877–1920*. New York: HarperCollins Publishers, 2009.

Lincoln, Nellie Olmstead. *The Story of Our Wedding Journey*. San Francisco: privately published, 1911.

Maury, Matthew F. "Loss of the Steamer Central America." *The Nautical Magazine and Naval Chronicle for 1858*: 39–45.

McCabe, James D., Jr. *Lights and Shadows of New York Life*. Philadelphia: National Publishing Company, 1872.

————. *New York by Sunlight and Gaslight*. Philadelphia: Douglass Brothers, 1882.

McCullough, David. *Mornings on Horseback: The Story of an Extraordinary Family, a Vanished Way of Life, and the Unique Child Who Became Theodore Roosevelt*. New York: Simon and Schuster, 1981.

Millard, Candice. *Destiny of the Republic: A Tale of Madness, Medicine, and the Murder of a President*. New York: Random House, 2011.

Moore, Henry Miles. *Early History of Leavenworth City and County*. Leavenworth, KS: Samuel Dodsworth Book Company, 1906.

Morrison, Howard Alexander. "Gentlemen of Proper Understanding: A Closer Look at Utica's Anti-Abolitionist Mob." *New York History*, vol. 62 (January 1981): 61–82.

Nevins, Allan, and Milton Halsey Thomas, eds. *The Diary of George Templeton Strong: The Civil War 1860–1865*. New York: The Macmillan Company, 1952.

Norton, Alfred. *Norton's Hand Book of New York City*. New York: Alfred Norton, 1859.

Norton, Charles Eliot, ed. *Orations and Addresses of George William Curtis*, Vol. 2, *Addresses and Reports on the Reform of the Civil Service of the United States*. New York: Harper and Brothers, 1894.

Official Proceedings of the Republican National Convention Held at Chicago, June 3, 4, 5, and 6, 1884. Minneapolis, MN: Charles W. Johnson, 1903.

Paine, Albert B. *Thomas Nast: His Period and His Pictures*. New York: The Macmillan Company, 1904.

Peskin, Allan. *Garfield: A Biography*. Kent, OH: Kent State University Press, 1978.

Poore, Ben Perley. *Perley's Reminiscences of Sixty Years in the National Metropolis*, Vol. 2. Philadelphia: Hubbard Brothers, 1886.

Pratt, LeRoy. "Ten Cents a Mile and a Fence Rail." *The Annals of Iowa*, vol. 39 (Spring 1969): 597–603.

Proceedings of the Republican National Convention Held at Chicago, Illinois, Wednesday, Thursday, Friday, Saturday, Monday and Tuesday, June 2d, 3d, 4th, 5th, 7th and 8th, 1880. Chicago: Jno. Jeffery Printing and Publishing House, 1881.

Proceedings of the Republican National Convention Held at Cincinnati, Ohio, on Wednesday, Thursday and Friday, June 14, 15 and 16, 1876. Concord, NH: Republican Press Association, 1876.

Rawley, James A. *Edwin D. Morgan, 1811–1883, Merchant in Politics*. New York: Columbia University Press, 1955.

Reeves, Thomas C. "Chester A. Arthur and the Campaign of 1880." *Political Science Quarterly*, vol. 84 (December 1969): 628–637.

————. "The Diaries of Malvina Arthur: Windows into the Past of Our 21st President." *Vermont History*, vol. 38 (Summer 1970): 177–188.

————. *Gentleman Boss: The Life of Chester Alan Arthur*. New York: Alfred A. Knopf, 1975.

————. "President Arthur in Yellowstone National Park." *Montana, the Magazine of Western History*, vol. 9 (Summer 1969): 18–29.

————. "The President's Dwarf: The Letters of Julia Sand to Chester A. Arthur." *New York History*, vol. 52 (January 1971): 73–83.

————. "Silas Burt and Chester Arthur: A Reformer's View of the Twenty-First President." *The New-York Historical Society Quarterly*, vol. 54 (October 1970): 319–333.

Report of the Committee on Investigation and Retrenchment, on Alleged Abuses in the New York Custom-House, Vol. 1. Washington: Government Printing Office, 1872.

Report of the Proceedings in the Case of the United States v. Charles J. Guiteau, Tried in the Supreme Court of the District of Columbia, Holding a Criminal Term, and Beginning November 14, 1881, Part 1. Washington, DC: Government Printing Office, 1882.

Reynolds, David S. *John Brown, Abolitionist: The Man Who Killed Slavery, Sparked the Civil War, and Seeded Civil Rights*. New York: Random House, 2005.

Richardson, James D., ed. *A Compilation of the Messages and Papers of the Presidents, 1789–1902*, Vol. 8. New York: Bureau of National Literature and Art, 1903.

Riis, Jacob A. *How the Other Half Lives*. New York: Charles Scribner's Sons, 1890.

————. *Theodore Roosevelt the Citizen*. New York: The Macmillan Company, 1912.

Robinson, Solon. *Hot Corn: Life Scenes in New York Illustrated*. New York: De Witt and Davenport, 1854.

Rood, Henry, ed. *Memories of the White House: The Home Life of Our Presidents from Lincoln to Roosevelt, Being Personal Recollections of Col. W. H. Crook*. Boston: Little, Brown and Company, 1911.

Ross, Ishbel. *Proud Kate: Portrait of an Ambitious Woman*. New York: Harper Brothers Publishers, 1953.

Russell, William Howard. *My Diary North and South*. Boston: T.O.H.P. Burnham, 1863.

Rutkow, Ira. *James A. Garfield*. New York: Henry Holt and Company, 2006.

Sand, Peter H., and John F. McLaughlin, eds. *Crossing Antietam: The Civil War Letters of Captain Henry Augustus Sand, Company A, 103rd New York Volunteers*. Jefferson, NC: McFarland and Company, Inc., 2016.

Schurz, Carl. *The Reminiscences of Carl Schurz*, Vol. 2, *1852–1863*. New York: Doubleday, Page & Company, 1913.

Sevitch, Benjamin. "The Well-Planned Riot of October 21, 1835: Utica's Answer to Abolitionism." *New York History*, vol. 50, no. 3 (April 1969): 251–263.

Seward, Thomas W. "The Bleecker Street Church, Utica." *Transactions of the Oneida Historical Society at Utica, 1887–1889*, vol. 4, 143–158. Utica, NY: Ellis H. Roberts and Co., 1889.

Sherman, John. *Recollections of Forty Years in the House, Senate and Cabinet: An Autobiography*, Vol. 2. Chicago: The Werner Company, 1895.

Shores, Venila Lovina. "The Hayes-Conkling Controversy 1877–1879." *Smith College Studies in History*, vol. 4 (July 1919): 215–277.

Singleton, Esther. *The Story of the White House*. New York: The McClure Company, 1907.

Smalley, E. V. *The Republican Manual*. New York: American Book Exchange, 1880.

————. "The White House." *Century Magazine*, vol. 27 (April 1884): 806–815.

Smith, Matthew Hale. *Sunshine and Shadow in New York*. Hartford, CT: J. B. Brown and Company, 1868.

Smith, Russell P. "The Diary of Dr. Brodie S. Herndon, 1853–1860." *Fredericksburg History & Biography* (2008).

Somers, Wayne, ed. *Encyclopedia of Union College History*. Schenectady, NY: Union College Press, 2003.

Spann, Edward K. *The New Metropolis: New York City 1840–1857*. New York: Columbia University Press, 1981.

Sterling, Dorothy, ed. *Speak Out in Thunder Tones: Letters and Other Writings by Black Northerners, 1787–1865*. Boston: Da Capo Press, 1998.

Sterngass, John. *First Resorts: Pursuing Pleasure at Saratoga Springs, Newport & Coney Island*. Baltimore: Johns Hopkins University Press, 2001.

Still, Bayrd. *Mirror for Gotham: New York as Seen by Contemporaries from Dutch Days to the Present*. New York: New York University Press, 1956.

Teachout, Zephyr. *Corruption in America: From Benjamin Franklin's Snuff Box to Citizens United*. Cambridge, MA: Harvard University Press, 2014.

Thomas, William [Defensor, pseud.]. *The Enemies of the Constitution Discovered, or An Inquiry into the Origin and Tendency of Popular Violence*. New York: Leavitt, Lord & Company, 1835.

Thoron, Ward. *First of Hearts: Selected Letters of Mrs. Henry Adams*. Boston: Atlantic Monthly Press, 1936.

Trachtenberg, Alan. *The Incorporation of America: Culture and Society in the Gilded Age*. New York: Farrar, Straus and Giroux, 1982.

Twain, Mark, and Charles Dudley Warner. *The Gilded Age: A Tale of Today*. Hartford, CT: American Publishing Company, 1873.

The Two Hundred and Forty Ninth Annual Record of the Ancient and Honorable Artillery Co. Massachusetts, 1886–87. Boston: Alfred Mudge & Son, 1887.

Union College Catalogue, Schaffer Library, Union College.

Van Deusen, Glyndon G. *Thurlow Weed: Wizard of the Lobby*. Boston: Little, Brown and Company, 1947.

Vidal, Gore. *1876: A Novel*. New York: Random House, 1976.

Walter, George. "History of Kanzas." New York: New York Kanzas League, 1855.

Wells, David Ames. *Congress and Phelps, Dodge & Co.: An Extraordinary History*. New York, 1875.

Wharton, Edith. *The Age of Innocence*. New York: D. Appleton and Company, 1920.

White, Andrew Dickson. *Autobiography of Andrew Dickson White*, Vol. 1. New York: The Century Company, 1906.

Whitman, Walt. *Complete Prose Works*. Philadelphia: David McKay, 1892.

Wiebe, Robert H. *The Search for Order 1877–1920*. New York: Farrar, Straus and Giroux, 1967.

Willets, Gilson. *Inside History of the White House*. New York: The Christian Herald, 1908.

Williams, Charles Richard, ed. *Diary and Letters of Rutherford Birchard Hayes, Nineteenth President of the United States*, 4 vols. Columbus: Ohio State Archaeological and Historical Society, 1922–1925.

————. *The Life of Rutherford Birchard Hayes, Nineteenth President of the United States*, 2 vols. Boston: Houghton Mifflin Company, 1914.

Wilson, James Grant, ed. *The Presidents of the United States, 1789–1894*. New York: D. Appleton and Company, 1894.

Wise, John S. *Recollections of Thirteen Presidents*. New York: Doubleday, Page and Company, 1906.

Woodward, C. Vann. "The Lowest Ebb." *American Heritage*, vol. 8, no. 3 (April 1957): 53–108.

Young, May D. Russell, ed. *Men and Memories: Personal Reminiscences of John Russell Young*, Vol. 1. New York: F. Tennyson Neely, 1901.

Index

Abell, Dr. Chester, 9
abolition
    anti-abolitionists, 5–6, 9–10
    New York's gradual abolition law
      of 1799, 22
abolitionists
    in Kansas, 27–30
    Utica meeting October 21, 1835,
      5–6, 9–10
Adams, Henry, 184
Adams, John Quincy, 65
Adams, Marian, 194
Adams, Sarah, 22–23
African Americans, in New York City,
    22–24
African Free School, 22
Allen, Campbell, 13, 14
American Museum, 19, 22
American Museum of Natural History,
    108
American Revolution, 7
Amistad, 9
anti-abolitionists, 5–6, 9–10
Anti-Moiety Act, 91
Appomattox Court House, 62, 90,
    119
aristocracy, shoddy, 58
Arthur, Almeda (sister of Chester), 7,
    13–15
Arthur, Ann Eliza (sister of Chester), 7,
    24–25
Arthur, Chester A.
    Annual Message to Congress
      (1881), 186–187, 209–210

Annual Message to Congress
    (1882), 206–207, 218
Annual Message to Congress
    (1883), 224
antislavery sentiments, 44–45
assumption of the presidency,
    173–181
birth, 8–9
birth of Chester II (son), 60
Blaine and, 140, 156–158, 162,
    174, 225–226, 230
Chinese Exclusion Act, 198–199
at Cincinnati convention (1876),
    93, 95
civil service reform, 84, 132, 178,
    183–184, 186–188, 190,
    206–207, 216, 225
Civil War commissions, 50–55
at Cleveland inauguration, 232
Conkling and, 74, 110–111, 123–
    124, 132, 134, 139, 143–145,
    153, 157, 159, 161–162, 167,
    178–179, 181–182
Conkling friendship, 74, 136, 178,
    181–182, 189
connections, quest for, 45–46
correspondence with Nell, 30, 38
counsel for tax commission, 76
Custom House, removal from,
    102–103, 114, 123, 171, 233
as Custom House collector, 79–84,
    91, 96, 100–104, 109–112, 226
death of William Lewis Herndon
    Arthur (son), 59–60